MEMOIRS
ON THE
HISTORY, FOLK-LORE AND DISTRIBUTION
OF THE
RACES
OF THE
NORTH WESTERN PROVINCES OF INDIA

MEMOIRS
ON THE
HISTORY, FOLK-LORE AND DISTRIBUTION
OF THE
RACES
OF THE
NORTH WESTERN PROVINCES OF INDIA

BEING AN AMPLIFIED EDITION OF THE ORIGINAL

SUPPLEMENTAL GLOSSARY OF INDIAN TERMS

HENRY M. ELLIOT

EDITED, REVISED AND RE-ARRANGED BY

JOHN BEAMES

IN TWO VOLUMES
VOL. II

GYAN

Published by

GYAN

Gyan Publishing House
5, Ansari Road
Daryaganj, New Delhi-110002
Phone: 011-47034999, 9811692060
E-mail: books@gyanbooks.com

Distribution Network
gyanbooks.com
India, USA, Canada, UK, Australia, France

ISBN : 978-81-212-3776-5 (Set)
ISBN : 978-81-212-5000-9 (HB)
First Published, London, 1869

2nd Impression 2020

Printed at: Gyan Press, Delhi.

The book at your disposal is the edition of an old book originally published long back. The Text quality of this book may not be at par as compared to our other books but many readers approached us to reprint this important book so that it could satiate their hunger. We request all the readers of this book to help us to improve its quality by providing the necessary text of those pages which are not properly visible. Your valuable support in this case will be highly appreciated and acknowledged and our future readers will be benefitted immensely.

MEMOIRS

ON THE

HISTORY, FOLK-LORE, AND DISTRIBUTION

OF THE

RACES

OF THE

NORTH WESTERN PROVINCES OF INDIA;

BEING AN AMPLIFIED EDITION OF THE ORIGINAL

SUPPLEMENTAL GLOSSARY OF INDIAN TERMS,

BY THE LATE

SIR HENRY M. ELLIOT, K.C.B.,

OF THE HON. EAST INDIA COMPANY'S BENGAL CIVIL SERVICE.

EDITED, REVISED, AND RE-ARRANGED

BY

JOHN BEAMES, M.R.A.S.,

BENGAL CIVIL SERVICE;

MEMBER OF THE GERMAN ORIENTAL SOCIETY, OF THE ASIATIC SOCIETIES OF PARIS AND BENGAL, AND OF THE PHILOLOGICAL SOCIETY OF LONDON.

IN TWO VOLUMES.

VOL. II.

LONDON:

TRÜBNER & CO., 8 AND 60, PATERNOSTER ROW.

MDCCCLXIX.

STEPHEN AUSTIN,

PRINTER, HERTFORD.

SUPPLEMENTAL GLOSSARY

OF TERMS USED IN THE

NORTH WESTERN PROVINCES.

PART III.

REVENUE AND OFFICIAL TERMS.

[Under this head are included—1. All words in use in the revenue offices both of the past and present governments; 2. Words descriptive of tenures, divisions of crops, fiscal accounts, and the like; 3. Some articles relating to ancient territorial divisions, whether obsolete or still existing, with one or two geographical notices, which fall more appropriately under this head than any other.—B.]

Ábkár, آبکار आबकार

A distiller, a vendor of spirituous liquors. Ábkárí, or the tax on spirituous liquors, is noticed in the Glossary.

With the initial *a* unaccented, Abkar means agriculture.

Adábandí, ادابندي अदाबंदी

The fixing a period for the performance of a contract or payment of instalments. From ادا performance, and بستن (root بَند) to bind.

Ádhbaṭái, آدهبٹائي आधबटाई

Division of produce in equal shares; from आधा half, and बटाई division.

Adhelá, ادهيله अधेला

Half a pice, comprising 12½ dams, or 4 damrís, *q.v.* [Also an eight-ana piece, or half a rupee.]

Adhelí, ادهيلي अधेली

Half a Chauthia, *q.v.* A measure used for corn.—Saugor.
Small fractional divisions of land.—Gaṛhwál.
Also an eight-ana piece, or half a rupee.

Adheliyá, ادهيليا अधेलिया

Adhelia, or Ádhia, signifies a proprietor of a half share.

Adhiyár, ادهيار अधियार

A man who passes half his time in one village, and half in another, is said to be adhiyár karná; called adhbar in Rohilkhand. Adhiyár differs from páhíkásht, inasmuch as adhiyár implies that there are two establishments, one in each of the two villages which are visited, [whereas páhíkásht is a man who lives in one village and cultivates land in another].

Adhiyárí, ادهياري अधियारी

A half share. The word आधा half, enters into the composition of all these words.

Adhkachchá, ادهکچا अधकच्चा

A soil lying between the land named Pahára and the Taráí, in the district of Sahéranpúr.

Adhkarí, ادهكري अधकरी

An instalment of eight anas in the rupee, or half of the Government Jama.

Aghaní, اگهني अगहनी

The produce of part of the Kharíf season, or of the month of Aghan, اگهن (November-December).

*** In Behar there are two rice crops, one in Bhádon, the other in Aghan; the produce of the former is less valuable than that of the latter, and is only eaten by the lower classes, and by animals.—B.

Agaur, اگور अगौर

An advance of rent paid by Asámís to Zamíndárs in the months of Jeth and Asarh.—E. Oudh. The word is derived from *áge* آگي, before, beyond.

'Ahd, عهد अ़हद

An agreement or contract. Ahdnáma عهدنامه is the written document containing an agreement.

'Ahddár, عهددار अ़हददार

Literally, holder of a contract. An officer of the Mughal Government, who, for a commission of 2 or 3 per cent., engaged for the revenue of a district, and made himself responsible for the balance.

Ajaurí, اجوري अजौरी

Advances, particularly to agricultural labourers.—Eastern Oudh. Agraurihí is used in a similar sense in Baiswara. Both words are, perhaps, derived from *áge,* before, in advance.

Álí, آلي आली

A land measure equivalent to four Bisís. Nine Alí go to a

Júlá.—Gaṛhwál and Kamáon. See further under the articles Bísí and Júlá.

Algí, الگي अलगी

A separate cess levied by Zamíndárs in part of Behar over and above the regular Jama. They generally do this when short of funds.—W.

Áltamghá,* آلتمغا आलतमग़ा

A royal grant, which the British Government have declared to convey a title to a rent-free tenure in perpetuity.

Altamghá is derived from two Turkish words, Al and Tamghá: both of which signify the royal signet. Al in Persian implies also a scarlet colour, سرخ نيم رنگ را گويند, and therefore it has been supposed to mean the Emperor's *red* signet (Gladwin says, "a red patent," and Harington, in his "Analysis," I., 4, "a red seal—from which its name is derived"): but it may be doubted if the Altamghá seal is necessarily a *red* one; and the "Burḥán-i Ḳáti'," the "Farhang-i Jahángírí," and the "Haft Ḳulzam," while they give the meaning of scarlet to Al in Persian, and at the same time mention the Hindí Al, noticed in a separate article, also add that, in Turkish, "it is the seal and ring of the king," without any special mention of its being a *red* seal, or a *red* ring. It would appear, however, from the extract from the "Farhang-i Rashídí," given below, that Altamghá originally meant a *red* seal, and that Al, by itself, was never taken in the sense of signet, except by reason of its having been coupled with Tamghá, to imply that the Tamghá was *red*.

و بترکي مهر بادشاهان که آنرا التمغا گويند اي مهر سرخ و گاهي بجهت تخفيف تمغا انداخته تنها آل گويند

* The word is generally written التمغا *altamghá*, not *áltamghá*, in Persian.—B.

"And in Turkish it signifies the seal of the Padshah, which they call Altamghá, *i.e.*, 'red seal,' and sometimes they call it Ál, for short, rejecting Tamghá."

The assertion therefore rests upon which is the best authority —the Burḥán-i Ḳáti', coupled with the Jahángírí, or the Rashídí. The Haft Ḳulzam is a mere copy, and of no weight in such controversies.

It is difficult to say when Altamghá began first to be used in the revenue language of India in the sense either of a seal or grant. In Persia and Central Asia we have notices of its use at an early period. Towards the close of the 13th century the illustrious Ghazan Khan caused the Altamghá, or the imperial seal of state, to be altered from a quadrangular to an oval shape, considered the most auspicious as well as most elegant of all forms, and on this he at the same time directed to be engraved the Mahomedan profession of faith.—Price's "Retrospect of Mahomedan History," Vol. II., p. 612.

Again, Timúr bestows upon the son of Bajazet the Government of Anatolia, under a patent containing the impression of his hand in *red* ink (Ibid. Vol. III., p. 423; and "Sherefeddin," Lib. v., Cap. 60); but it is not stated whether the title of this patent was Altamghá. In the Institutes of this tyrant, we find no mention of anything but Tamghá, and that with a different meaning.

But, with respect to India, the term certainly does not appear to have been in common and practical use in the fiscal language of the country in Akbar's time; though, as we have seen from the extract just quoted, that it is mentioned in the "Farhang-i Jahángírí," which was compiled at his dictation and dedicated to his son; but then it is to be considered that the authority of certain poets is given for its use;—which would of itself seem to imply that the word was a foreign importation, and up to that time had merely found admission into dictionaries and literary compositions. It is not once mentioned in the passage on Sayúrghal, in his Institutes; the perusal of which chapter, by the way, would afford an instructive lesson to those who assert that the Mughal Government never resumed rent-free tenures, for in it we have the very founder of the system enjoining resumption, and getting more and more exasperated at the shameless frauds practised upon the exchequer even by his own officers. Yet, notwithstanding this apparently modern introduction of the word, it is to be feared that some grants, purporting to be Altamghá of his reign, have been released by our officials.

We find frequent mention of the word Tamghá in his time, but so far from conferring a privilege or immunity, it meant only a tax, or tribute, when applied fiscally.

In the following passage Báj باج "tax," is coupled with Tamghá:—"And it was ordered that the Báj and Tamghá were not to be collected except from arms and horses, elephants and camels, cows, sheep and goats and silken cloth, on which a small sum was to be levied in each Suba."

Tamghá is again called a tax which is raised in excess of the land revenue:—"Umr levied a tax on foreigners in three classes . . . . . which they called Jazia, and in every kingdom they demand something from every man's property except peasants, and that they call Tamghá; and in Irán and Turán they take some little in proportion to the wealth of the taxed."

In one of the general Farmáns issued by him in the 37th year of his reign, by which he justly earned the love of his subjects and admiration of posterity, he remits the Tamghá, Báj, and Zikát, on all articles, with a few exceptions.*

و دیگر اشیا و اسباب و امتعه و اجناس که مدار معاش جمهور انام

* It appears that previous to Akbar's time the tamghá had been remitted by Jahángír, and before that by Bábar. Possibly the remission of a tax by any sovereign was considered to hold good only during his reign, and to require a fresh act of remission on the accession of another emperor. Jahángír's veracity, however, is not beyond suspicion.—E. *add.*

و ملاك معيشت خواص و عوام است سواي اسپ و فيل و شتر و گوسفند و بز و اسلحه و قماش كه در تمامي ممالك محروسه تمغا و باج و زكوة و صد يك و انچه از قليل و كثير گرفته اند معاف و مرفوع القلم بوده باشد

"And other goods and chattels which are the means of livelihood of the people in general, except horses and elephants and camels and sheep and goats and arms and silk, which in all my dominions are liable to Báj and Tamghá and Zikát, and that which they took from small and great, are entirely remitted and struck off."

This is differently translated by Dr. Bird in his "History of Guzerat," in which he calls Tamghá "vested interests," and it must be confessed it is used in that sense in one of Akbar's letters to Abdu'llah Khan Uzbek.

In "Timúr's Institutes" (Book II., p. 308) Tamghá is spoken of as pay, or personal allowance of a soldier, and therefore approaches nearer to our modern meaning.—See also "Bábar's Memoirs," p. 354.

In the following passage it also means a stipend, according to "White's Translation," p. 361: or, a body-mark, according to Colonel Galloway's "Law and Constitution of India," p. 87. The context shews that either may be correct:—

و عمر نمودم كه هر مملكتي كه مسخر گردد گدايان آن ملك را جمع ساخته و ايشان را تمغه كنند كه ديگر گداي را برطرف سازند و اگر بعد از تمغه گدائي نمايند ايشان را به بلاد بعيده بفروشند

"And I commanded that whatever country was conquered they should collect the beggars thereof and make them an allowance that they should beg no more, and if, after being allowanced, they should beg again, they should be sold into distant countries," etc. There is apparently no reason to suppose with Galloway that the beggars were to be branded: it is more in consonance with the lavish generosity of an eastern monarch to pension them, as the natural translation of the text says.—B.

These passages serve to shew that the word Tamghá must have somewhat altered its meaning since its first importation into Hindústan; but they do not enable us to determine at what period Tamghá, or Altamghá, grants were first made.

We have already seen that they do not appear to have been introduced up to Akbar's time; and with respect to his successor, Jehangír, we find him in his autobiography, so far from asserting that a *red* seal was exclusively devoted to Altamghás, saying expressly that he changed the seals of Jagír patents from mixed gold and *vermilion* to gold alone.

جاي مهر را بطلا و دورش را بشنگرف ساختند من تمام را بطلا فردًا

"Instead of the seal which they made of gold with a rim of *vermilion*, I used one of gold only."

From these remarks it is to be gleaned that the period of the introduction of even the word Altamghá is a problem in Sphragistics which still remains to be solved; and though it appears to have been used in its present sense in Persia and Turkistan before the establishment of the Mughal dynasty in India, yet there seems reason to conclude that some time elapsed before the term was generally introduced into this country; and we are therefore justified in looking on any Altamghá grant older than Shahjahan with strong suspicion.

That it was not necessarily a rent-free grant, the British Government themselves had incontrovertible evidence, in that they stipulated to pay 26 lacs per annum for their Altamghá Farman from Shah Alam, A.D. 1765. It was, nevertheless, proclaimed by our Government that a grant of this nature was rent-free, and conveyed, moreover, an hereditary and transferable right. That the native subordinates of our Government were anxious to persuade us to that effect was naturally to be expected, and that the European functionaries were glad to assent to any opinion uttered by men who professed to have a knowledge of the laws and customs of the country, was also to be expected; but that the same opinion should have been entertained and confirmed when the regulations came subsequently to be enacted, is somewhat surprising, for there was much to make us pause before we committed ourselves to so positive a declaration. In several instances evidence had been given which was opposed to the construction finally adopted by the Government.

In the case of Jalálu'd-dín *versus* Mihru'n-nisá Begam, tried before the Provincial Council of Patna, in September, 1774, the Amánat officer, whose authority should have carried with it some weight, says, "from the reign of the kings of old, the orders of one king have continued valid, but it is now the ancient custom for the possessors of Altamghás and Madad Máshes to be turned out or removed." And we know that Nawwáb Muhammad Raza' Khan resumed several Altamghá grants in the year 1766, after the Diwání was granted to the Company; which he would scarcely have ventured to do, had he not been authorized by the practice of the country.—(See "Colebrooke's Digest," III., 238, and "Extracts from Official Records regarding Máfí," p. 16), It is therefore the more remarkable that we gave such ready acquiescence to representations not only entirely opposed to our own interests, and to the customs, laws, and records of the country, but frequently to the very language and tenor of the documents which purported to be Altamghá.

Amání, اماني अमानी

Land managed by a collector on the part of Government:—called also Kham and Khas. The Regulations have given the word greater currency in the Benares Province than elsewhere.

'Aml paṭṭá, عمل پٹه अमल पट्टा
'Aml sanad, عمل سند अमल सनद
'Aml dastak, عمل دستک अमल दस्तक

A deed appointing an agent, or granting authority to collect rents. From the Arabic عمل action, practice, rule.

Áná, آنا and آنہ आना

A native land measure equal to 16 Rúsís. Sixteen Anas go to a Kancha.—Saugor.

The sixteenth part of a rupee—which is usually written by Europeans, *anná*.

Ankbandí, انکبندي अंकबन्दी

An adjustment of rents asanúwár by the Malgúzár at the close of each harvest.—See under Ank.

Antarbed, انتربيد अंतरबेद

The old name for the Lower Doáb, extending from about Etawah to Allahabad. Occasionally it is used to signify the whole Doáb—thus, Kachwahas are said by the poet Chand to be in Antarbed; and it does not seem probable that they were in any numbers except in the Upper Doáb (see Kachwahas). The word is now seldom used, except by Sanskrit scholars. In that language it bears much the same meaning as Doáb, signifying the level country intervening (*i.e.* between the Ganges and Jumna), from अन्तर within, and वेदि an altar, a hearth, an earthen platform in the courtyard of a house.

Áolí, آولي आओली

Mode of estimating by the ascertained produce of a Biswa that of a Bígha.—E. Oudh. The rule is very simple. Take the number of seers yielded by a Biswa, halve it, and you have the produce per Bígha in maunds. The produce of a Biswah is ascertained from the produce of a Bígha, by doubling the latter, in maunds, and calling the product seers.

Aṛáṛí, اڑاڑي अडाडी

The old-established measurement of a field. A man says his Aṛáṛí is so much, say two bíghas, and though modern measurement may rate it higher, he will not consent to any change.—Benares. The term is, perhaps, derived from Aṛáṛá اڑاڑا, a high bank of a river or tank, which may therefore be supposed to enclose an unalterable area.

Arází, اراضي अराजी

Lands; plural of Arz عرض land. In revenue language, the word is chiefly applied to detached portions of land, which are generally either rent free, or recovered by the recession of rivers. It is therefore nearly synonymous with Chak.

Arsaṭh, ارسٹھ अरसठ

A kind of account which the author of the "Zubdatu'l Ḳawánín" says is the same as a monthly Jama' kharch.

ارسٹھ که عبارت از جمعخرچ ماهواري و مجمل وازخام است

"The arsaṭh, which is an expression for the monthly Jama' kharch and abstract of the Wázkhám."

The "Diwan Pasand" also says it is a monthly entry or abstract of several accounts, called Wázkhám, and that it is in reality only another name for Jama' kharch: بطور جمعخرچ که ارسٹھ نیز گویند. This is the meaning the word bears in the Printed Glossary, and the word Arsotta (Arsaṭhá), which precedes it, is probably an error.*

* This word is common all over the eastern part of the provinces, and is said to be so called from containing sixty-eight (arsaṭh) columns.—B.

'Arzdásht, عرضداشت अरजदास्त

An address or memorial, so called from its initial words.

Asámí, اسامي असामी

Literally names. A cultivator, a dependant, a culprit—all of which meanings we may suppose to be derived from such persons being entered in registers and tabular forms under the head of Asámí. It has been supposed, as Asámí frequently means a criminal, that it is derived from اثم *ism*, a crime; and the practice commonly adopted by Káyaths of writing the word اثامي with a *se* ث instead of *sin* س, gives some colour to this opinion. Asámí is the plural of the plural of Ism اسم a name (De Sacy, "Grammaire Arabe," II. 275).

There are two words, one with a ث *se* means a criminal, and the one with a س *sín* means a cultivator; but both words are Indian inventions in their present significations, and rather barbarous inventions too, though they have become so common as to be quite indispensable.—B.

An Asámí Chhaparband is a resident cultivator, that is, an Asámí who has a Chhapar چهپر or thatched house.

An Asámí Maurúṣí is an hereditary cultivator, that is, an Asámí who has Irṣ ارث or inheritance.

An Asámí Páhíkásht is a man who cultivates land of a village different from that in which he resides.—See Páhíkásht and Khudkásht.

An Asámí Shikmí is one who cultivates the land of, and pays the rent to, another Asámí.

Asámíwár, اساميوار असामीवार

Including all the names; usually applied to statements, and to revenue settlements made with the proprietors in detail.

Aslí, اصلي असली

A registered village—literally, original, from اصل *asal*, a root.

Dákhilí داخلي is the term applied to hamlets included in the Aslí village. It is not known at what particular time these words originated, but it must have been subsequent to Todar Mal's settlement. Our new settlements have swept away the distinction, which there was no occasion for preserving in the revised register.*

Áwárijá, آوارجه आवारिजा

A diary, a rough note-book, an abstract account of collections, remittances, etc. etc. The "Zubdatu'l Ḳawánín" says the word is derived from Awára, scattered, wandering, unfixed, because the Awárija is a collection of detached notes which would otherwise be dispersed. It is applied generally to an account of any description.

The work above-quoted says—

اوارجه اطلاق و آن در حقيقت جمعخرچ

It would seem, therefore, to be much the same as the Arsath, except that the latter is more strictly confined to a monthly account.

The "Farhang-i Rashídí" also states that the word is derived from Awára, scattered. The same work adds that Abar, Abara, Awára, and Awárija, mean not only an account, but an office of account, an exchequer :—

آواره دفتر حساب كه حساب پراگنده ديوان برآن نويسند و اوارجه گويند و بارگاه كه ديوان در آن كنند و بهردو معني بغير مدالف نيزآمده

"Awára, an office of account, so called because they write there the scattered accounts of the Díwán and call them Awárija: also the office in which they transact the revenue business, and in both meanings it is written without *madda* over the *alif.*"

* This is not quite correct: the terms *aslí* and *dákhilí* are still retained in many districts, not merely in the mouths of the people, but on the registers.—B.

See Awerja in the Printed Glossary, which appears a mistake for Awárija, though closely following Awárija Jama Kharch.

Bád, باد बाद्

A remission on account of deficient produce. One of the many meanings of the word in Persian is "annihilated," بمعني نابود و هيچ باشد according to the "Burhán-i Kátiʻ" and "Haft Kulzam," and has thus been extended in the revenue language of India to signify remissions occasioned by annihilation (of crops).

Bádsháhí, بادشاهي बादशाही

Literally, royal, from بادشاه a king. In the language of revenue officers it is generally applied to royal grants of rent-free land. Thus we say, "Bádsháhí Sanad," "Bádsháhí Tenures." The conditions of their validity are given in Reg. XXXVI. of 1803, and the corresponding enactments Reg. XIII. of 1795, and Reg. VIII. of 1805: the first being applicable to the Ceded Provinces, the second to Benares, and the third to the Conquered Provinces.

Benáwat, بيناوت बेनाउत

See above, under Benaudha.

Bhábar, بهابر भाबर

The forest under the Sewalik Hills. The tract varies in breadth from ten to twenty miles, and the slope of the ground varies from fifty to seventeen feet per mile, diminishing rapidly after the first few miles. Cultivation is confined only to the vicinity of the rivers issuing from the Himalayan range, but the soil in many parts is good, and consists of a rich black mould at the extreme verges of the tract, north and south. There are occasional patches also free from trees, but covered with high grass, and many spots afford good pasturage. With these exceptions, the Bhábar is a dense forest, but almost destitute of trees valuable for timber; and water is at such a depth below the surface, that all attempts to dig wells have been fruitless.—See "Printed Report on Rohilkhand Canals," p. 107.*

Bhábar is also the name of a light black soil in Baitúl, in Central India.

Bháíbánt, بہائي بانٹ भाईबांट

A term equivalent to Bhayachara, *q.v.* It is derived from **भाई** a brother, and **बांटना** to divide.

Bhág, بہاگ भाग

Tax; duty; share in kind. Also fortune, destiny.

Bhágnar, بہاگنر भागनर

The name given to the rich alluvial lands under the banks of the Jumna.—Central Doáb.

Bhej, بہیج भेज

Rent; a proportionate share; an instalment. Bhej is in common use, but is not noticed in any of the Dictionaries. It may be a corruption of the Sanskrit Bhág, a portion.

Bhej-barár, بہیج برار भेजबरार

A tenure frequently met with in Bundelkhand, in which the shares of the brotherhood are liable to periodical, or occasional, adjustment; and in which balances of revenue and village expenses, occasioned by the fraud or insolvency of a sharer, are made good by a rateable contribution from the other sharers. Strangers are often introduced in over-assessed estates on condition of paying the barár, but their admission by no means,

* See "Selections from Rec. N. W. P.," IV., 374.

as is sometimes supposed, forms a necessary incident of the tenure, of which the chief characteristic is the re-adjustment of the barár. At the late settlement of Bundelkhand it was stipulated in many instances that this liability to re-adjustment should cease; and practically, for some time previous, the re-adjustment had not been demanded, except upon occasions of a new settlement. It is probable that in a short time, as the value of property increases, the Bhej-barár tenure will altogether cease to exist.

Bhúngáí, بهونگاي भूंगाई

Is the name of a tax levied by the Raja of Bijaypúr on part of the forest produce of Tappa Saktísgaṛh, in zillah Mirzapúr. In the Official Report of the Settlement of the Tappa, the word is said to be derived from Bhúnga, a mallet.

Tangáí is another of these taxes; from Tanga, an axe.

Bharaí, بهرئي भरई

A cess levied in the Province of Benares, of which one-half was given to the Amil for charges of remittance, and the other carried to the credit of Government.—See Sec. 6 and 7 of Reg. II. of 1795.

Bharat, بهرت भरत

Amount of revenue paid by an individual or party. The word is chiefly used in Dehli, and is frequently pronounced Bharit and Barat. It is derived from Bharná, to pay.

Bhaṭṭíáná, بهتّيانه भट्टीआना

Is the name given to a large tract of land between the Hissar district and the Garra, which is tenanted chiefly by Bhaṭṭí Rajputs. Bhaṭṭíáná, or Bhaṭṭia, is a country of growing importance, the population and cultivation having greatly increased since our occupation.

It will be observed, by referring to the map of Dastúrs, that the Western boundary of Sirkár Hisár Feroza has been extended only to the bed of the War river, which runs not far to the Westward of the Ghaggar, the new Parganah of Wattu and Bhaṭṭíáná being altogether excluded: for this tract, full of sandy plains and Thals,* seems to have been little known in the time of Akbar, nor, with the exception of Malaud, which was in Múltán, does it appear to be included in any Sirkár of the adjoining Súbahs. It is to be observed, that Abu'l Fazl, in mentioning the breadth and length of the several Súbahs, measures from Hisár in the Dehli Súbah, from Ferozpúr in the Múltán Súbah, from the Satlaj in the Lahore Súbah, and from Bíkanir in the Ajmír Súbah. He appears, therefore, with the above exception, to leave the tract between all these places as neutral ground. To be sure, the Rev. Mr. Renouard, in his article on Dehli in the "Encyclopædia Metropolitana," includes Fattihabad in Ajmír, on the sole authority, apparently, of Hamilton's Gazetteer; but Abu'l Fazl certainly places it in Hisár Fírozá, and it was included in Hisár before his time, as we learn from the 5th chapter of the 2nd book of Shamsi Siráj's Táríkh Fírozsháhí, where he says—

پیش ازین در عهد سلاطین ماضیه آن سمت را در دفاتر دواوین شق هانسي مي نِشیند چون شهر حصار فیروزه بنا کردند سلطان فروز فرمود ازین تاریخ باز شق حصار فیروزه نویسند اتطاعات هانسي و اگروه و فتح‌آباد و سرستي تا سالوره و خضرآباد وِ اقطاعات دیگر بتمام داخل شق حصار فیروزه کردند †

* Thal or thar is the name given to the various deserts in Rajputána, and is probably a corruption of the latter half of the word मरुस्थली *marusthalí*, or desert region, applied to this tract.—B.

† This passage, as it stood in the original work, puzzled me considerably, and even now, after a comparison of three manuscripts, I am not quite sure how the text should really stand: the reading given above is, however, the most probable. In Sir H.

"Before this, in the times of the ancient kings, that district in the records of the revenue officers stands as Shaḳḳ Hánsí. When he built the city of Hisár Fírozá, Sultan Fíroz commanded that from that time forth they should write is as Shaḳḳ Hisár Fírozá, and the kitta's of Hánsí, Agroha, Fattihábád, Sirsútí as far as Sálaurah, and Khizrábád, and other entire kitta's, were included in Shaḳḳ Hisár Fírozá." This Shaḳḳ must therefore have included Akbar's Sirkár of Sirhind, as well as Hisár, for Sálaurá is under the Sewalik Hills and Khizrábád is on the Jumna.*

Elliot's own copy of Shamsi Siráj's work, the first doubtful passage reads دفاترو ابين the last word, though without the diacritical notes, is clearly meant for ائين *áín*; but in MS. No. 1002 of the India Office Library, I find دواسن (also without dots), which is probably for دواوين *dawáwin*, plural of *diwán*, which seems to me the best reading of the two. The copy lately purchased by the India Office at the Marquis of Hastings' sale wants forty or forty-five pages at this point, and the next page begins in the middle of this very quotation. The passage as it stood in former editions went on شق هاسى نوشته and in the author's copy the words are مي هشتد which has no meaning. In MS. No. 1002 we have the correct reading مي نشيند "it sits" (or as we should say "stands"): further on, for the reading of the first edition, اگروه *agroh*, we have in the author's copy اكره *akrah*, in No. 1002 اكروده *akrodah*, and in the Hastings' MS. by an evident error اكر فيروزه *akar firoza*. Lastly, for بنام in the first edition, which made nonsense of the passage, we find in all the other MSS. بتمام *batamám*, "entirely." These variations, though slight in themselves, are noticed here as an example of the very corrupt state in which we find many Persian MSS. of great historical value, and to shew the necessity for a reconstruction of our texts in accordance with principles of sound and enlightened criticism.—B.

* It was from the vicinity of these towns that the famous Fíroz Shah's Lat was taken and placed in its present position in Dehli. A very particular and interesting account of the removal of the Lat, and of the first discovery of Indian osteological remains in the neighbourhood is given by the same author; who, notwithstanding the adulatory tone of his history, gives us more valuable details respecting the condition of Hindústan in his time than any other historian of that or any subsequent period.

Sálaurá and Khizrábád are two places on the road from Ropar to Sirhind. The two places mentioned in the text are quite different, and have nothing to do with the matter.—E. *add.* And as the MSS. generally have تا instead of و there is no reason to suppose that Sálaurá was included.—B.

We may, perhaps, attribute the little knowledge entertained of these tracts by Abu'l Fazl to the depopulation caused by "the firebrand of the universe," Timúr. There is not a place in these parts which was not the scene of his wanton cruelty. Bhatnír, Ahrúní, Fattihabad and Tohana, all suffered at his hands. Sirsa was also attacked and plundered, if we may be allowed, as there seems reason, to look upon Sirsa as the town of Sirsutí. Indeed, it is still called Sirsútí by men that come from these parts; and Timúr's Sirsútí is represented as being precisely the same distance and direction from Bhatnír, Fattihabad, Tohana and Ahrúṇí, as Sirsa is. If this really be the old Sirsútí, the town must have changed its name before Akbar's time, as he only mentions Sirsa, stating that Fíroz Shah's canal passes near the town of that name.

It does not appear that the extensive desiccation which this country has undergone, and the further progress of which it is now hoped will cease (our attention being directed to improving the means* of irrigation), had proceeded to such an extent as we now view it, when Timúr invaded India. Mirkhond, Abdu'l Razzák, Sharfu'd-dín, and all the other historians of his time, though they mention that he had to cross one continuous desert from the Satlaj to Bhatnír, yet describe the great populousness of that town in terms which but ill accord with its present state. Sirsútí is also said to be on the banks of the *river* of the same name, so that it had not ceased to flow in those days, and had not yielded to the Ghaggar, by which the dry river bed under Sirsa is now known. A short time before, also, Ibn Batuta,† while he states he had to cross a desert to Abohar,

* One of the first measures should be the opening of the dams in the native states. There are at this time no less than twenty-four Bands on the Sirsútí from Thanesar to Sagara, where it joins the Ghaggar.

† It is much to be regretted that we have not a perfect copy of this enterprising traveller's work. The abridgment translated by Dr. Lee increases the desire to see the entire work as well edited. Professor De Gayangos, in a note to the first volume

"the first city in Hindústan," says of Sirsútí, "It is large, and abounds with rice, which they carry hence to Dehli;" so that neither in his time could the means of irrigation have been deficient. The river, indeed, up to the commencement of Akbar's time, seems to have been flowing, and to have been still called Sirsútí, for in the "Akbarnama" we read that in Humayún's re-conquest of Dehli, he bestowed upon the young Prince Akbar the Government of Hisár, and the provinces on the river Sirsútí; which, had they been the provinces on the modern Sirsútí, would most probably have been called Sirhind. Yet it must be confessed that Abu'l Fazl, in his detailed description of the Súbah of Dehli, gives prominent notice to the Ghaggar river, and he may therefore have considered the Ghaggar and Sirsútí to be the same.

Major Brown, in his survey of Hisár, fell in with a part of that which is now called the old Sirsútí. "The Sirsútí river was come upon quite unexpectedly. The best maps shew this river as joining the Ghaggar, between Murak and Samánah in the Patiála state. As the survey approached Tohanah, the zamíndárs and native officers brought it to notice, and directed

of his "Mahomedan Dynasties in Spain," states that he has obtained a perfect copy, and that he has it in contemplation to publish a translation of it,—a declaration which it is to be hoped he will shortly fulfil. The period of Ibn Batuta's visit to India (A.D. 1332-1342) is highly interesting, and makes us regret the more that the geographical details have been much confused by the epitomator. After leaving Dehli he goes to Biana (Baran?)—thence to Kol,—thence to Jalalí, a place seven days' journey (?) distant from Kol—back to Dehli—back again to Kol,—thence to Yieh Barah (Mainpúrí?) thence to the shores of a lake called "the Water of Life" (Talgram?)—thence to Kanauj,—thence to Merwa (?)—thence to Gwalior. The Chinese Embassy which he accompanied on its return, appears to have come with a view to the restoration of some Buddhist place of worship below the Hills, and perhaps in the district of Sambhal, which had been destroyed by the Mahometans; who "had also prevented the Hindus from cultivating the plains which were necessary to their subsistence." Hence we may perhaps obtain some information of the precise period when the depopulation of the country below the Sewalik Hills commenced; a question which has been cursorily noticed in the article Des.

our enquiries to this subject. It was stated that formerly this river flooded and enriched the lands to a great extent, and that even within the last ten years many villages derived great benefits from it. The bed of the river, however, has for some years been lost sight of altogether, and it was only in a few villages near Hansdaha that any vestige of it could be found; the remainder of its track was laid down from information from the zamíndárs as far as it could be depended upon." (Reports on Projected Canals in the Dehli Territory, p. 120.)

As this bed of the Sirsútí is nearly parallel with the course of the Ghaggar river, and with the Ghaggar Nalla, or Choya, there seems little room for doubt that it combined with the latter, and formed the river of Sirsútí, which was flowing under the walls of Sirsa (Sirsútí) in the time of Ibn Batuta and Timúr. Whether the Ghaggar* and Sirsútí were originally two entirely different streams, or whether they were originally one and the same; or whether, as is the case now, it has always been that the Sirsútí is merely a tributary of the Ghaggar, are questions that would lead us into too long a discussion, and are irrelevant to the present inquiry.

I am aware that it is usual to ascribe the deterioration of this tract solely to the Chalísa famine of A.D. 1783, but there seems sufficient ground for believing it commenced before that period. That the tract to the east of the Hyphasis was a desert at the

* Wilford says that the famous Drishadwati is the name of the Ghaggar, but in the "Tirtha Yatra" of the "Mahábhárat," where it is mentioned as forming one of the boundaries of Kurukshetra, it is said, "those who dwell *South* of the Saraswati and *North* of the Drishadwati, or in Kurukshetra, dwell in heaven." So that if Wilford's surmise is correct, what is now the Sirsúti was formerly the Ghaggar, and *vice versâ*; which would supply us with a fourth subject of enquiry. See further "Vishnu Purana," p. 181.—E.

This river, which Elliot writes Cuggur, is now generally called Ghaggar, and is usually admitted to be the Drishadwati. It is a few miles to the West of Amballa, and is generally dry. See also Edgeworth, "Botanic Agricultural Account of Protected Sikh States."—B.

period of Alexander's invasion, we learn from Diodorus and Quintus Curtius, and though they differ from Arrian in this respect, there is no doubt they represent truly the condition of a great part of this country in the time of that conqueror. Succeeding events must have increased the natural sterility of this region. The first Mahomedan invasions, which were frequently accompanied by extermination of the old inhabitants, may be considered one of the original causes of depopulation. As these occurred for 200 years, more or less, there was ample time for the desert to extend its reign. These were, after a short space, succeeded by reiterated Mughal invasions up to the time of Timúr, who crowned them by his ravages. The tract could have been but little improved up to the time of Akbar, and whatever prosperity it subsequently attained was reversed* by the Chalísa famine. It is perhaps to that period, when the deficiency of water was so grievously felt, that we are to attribute the drying up of many of the streams† which used to flow up to a late period in the Western Desert. It is a curious fact that the stream (Sankar or Sankra) which in 1739 was of sufficient volume to form the Treaty‡ Boundary between

* All notice of the ravages of the B'hattís is omitted, which was of itself no inconsiderable cause of depopulation.

† With respect to the Sirsútí, it may be doubted if at any time it ever reached the Indus or any of its affluents. From the earliest periods it is recorded as being absorbed by the sand. Some of the oldest legends of the country relate to this peculiarity, and allusions are constantly made to it by the ancient poets: "sicut samim arborem, in qua ignis latet, sicut *Sarasvatim* fluvium, cujus aqua sub terra fluit." "Stenzler's Raghuvansa," p. 17.—See also "Harivansa," pp. 507, 509.

‡ The words of the Treaty are—

تا حدیکه دریاي‌سند و نالهٔ سنکر بدریاي محیط اتصال دارد و آنچه
سایر جات و مهمات در سمت غربي دریاي سنده و نالهٔ سنکر واقع
شده باشد مخصوص اندولت نادره و ضمیمهٔ ممالک محروسه آن
سلطنت قاهره نمودیم

the possessions of Nadir Shah and Mahomed Shah, has not now even a puddle to moisten its arid bed. The further examination of this interesting question is foreign to the immediate subject of this enquiry, which is to consider the condition of Bhaṭṭíáná in Akbar's time, so as to shew what place it should occupy in the Dastúr Map; and, all circumstances considered, there can be no great error in having limited the boundary of Sirkár Hisár to the neighbourhood of the modern Ghaggar.

Bhaiyáchárá, بهیاچارہ भैयाचारा

The definition in the Printed Glossary is for the most part correct.

Bhaiyáchára is a term applied to villages owned by descendants from a common stock. From भाई brother, and आचार usage.

In such villages the whole of the land is occupied by the proprietary brotherhood, and the revenue assessed by a rate, or *bachh*; and if there be non-proprietary cultivators, they are not responsible to the general body, but are introduced by some individual sharer, and pay him rent for land on which he pays by rate, or *bachh.*

In many of these holdings are sub-divisions paying an ascertained amount of Jama, levied by the proprietors of each subdivision among themselves. They are called *thok, paṭṭi,* and various other names; but the existence, or non-existence, of the interior sub-divisions does not affect the general character of the holding of proprietors paying by a rate.

There are also various ways of assessing the rate, as on ploughs, on the actual cultivation of each year, on wells, on the amount of cultivation ascertained at the settlement, etc. etc., but the general distinction continues unchanged.—See Par. 199–201 of the Revenue Board's Printed Circular Order on Settlements.

Bhaibaṭ, بهيبت भैबट

See Bhaiwad.

Bhaihissí, بهي حصي भैहिस्सी

Bhaipansí, بهي پنسي भैपंसी

The shares of a brotherhood, especially in the lands of a village or township.

Bhaiáns, بهي انس भैग्रंश

Division of property or interests among brothers.

These three words are chiefly used in Bundelkhand, E. Oudh, Benares, and Lower Doáb.

Bhaiwád, بهي واد भैवाद

To pay and receive on the footing of one of the brotherhood.

Bi'lmuktâ, بالمقطع बिलमुकता

A Patta or lease under which a ryot pays a certain fixed sum at so much per plough or per Bíghá, not being liable to any further demand.

An engagement stipulating to pay a fixed money rent for the lands under cultivation, not subject to enhancement during the currency of the lease. See the Glossary under Bilmugta. The word is Arabic, and means "at a fixed or determined (rate)." It is often used to mean "in a lump sum," or "on the whole."

In Benares it signifies consolidated rate, including Mal and Abwab.—See Reg. LI. of 1795.

Birrábarár, برابرار बिर्राबरार

Collection in kind.—Central Doáb.

The expression seems derived either from Birah بره separation, division, on account of the crops being divided before appropriation; or from the Birra of the Patwarí's account books, which is applied to the entry of every crop under a distinct head. The proper word in book-keeping is Beora بیورا explanation; detail; knowledge; which is frequently corrupted into Birra.

Birt,* برت बिर्त

A tenure held on condition of the performance of offices, whether religious or secular. Proprietary right. The tenure in Gorakhpúr, under which the Birtías pay a fixed yearly sum equivalent to twenty per cent. of the Government revenue, on account of the Raja or superior; but are the owners of the soil, entitled to the entire management of the Mauzas, not liable to be ousted, holding a hereditary and transferable tenure, and subject to enhancement of the rent only when the Government Juma should be increased.

The Sankalap (सङ्कल्प "expectation of advantage from a holy work." Benfey) Birt is a religious grant made to a Brahman, in order to secure the merit of sacrifices and ceremonies performed by him, and held at first free, but in almost all these cases the necessities of the Raja of Gorakhpúr had compelled him to demand a small rent from the holder.

The Marwat (मर्वत) Birt was a compensation made by the Raja to the family of any man who was killed in his service in open fight, either with a neighbouring chief or in resistance to the Government, and is also called Khún Bahá (*i.e.* "washing away blood," from خون "blood," and بہانا to "wash away"); it was chargeable, according to the custom of the Raj, with half the rent demandable for a regular Birt village.

Jewan (जेवना "to eat") Birt is an assignment made by the Raja of the day to a younger son, of a certain number of villages in the Talúka for subsistance, to be held by such son and his

* From the Sanskrit व्रत *vrata*, a vow, according to some, but Wilson derives it from वृत्ति maintenance.

descendants as Jewan Birt for ever. The assignee was accustomed to take a Patta from the Raja for these villages, paying a certain sum as rent.—See Talúkdar.

The term Birta is applied in Nepal to rent-free land, of which there are four kinds in that principality, Jagír, Manachaul, Bekh, and Birta. By the last a perpetual title is conveyed, and the land is at the absolute disposal of the grantee and his heirs.

Birtiyá, برتيا बिर्तिया

A tenant who holds his land upon a fixed annual assessment which cannot be altered, except on certain conditions previously stipulated; nor can the land held by him be claimed by the donor. The definition in the Printed Glossary is correct.—See Birt.*

Biswábarár, بسوہ برار बिसवाबरार

Collecting by the Biswa.—Central Doáb.

The Biswa, from بيس twenty, is the twentieth part of a Bígha; and besides being a measure of land, is also used to signify the extent of proprietary right in an estate. Each estate or village is considered an integer of one Bígha, which is subdivided into imaginary Biswas and Biswansís, to shew the right of any particular party. Thus, the holder of five Biswas is a holder to the extent of one-fourth of the entire village.

Biswádárí, بسوہداري बिसवादारी

A name given to the tenure of independent village communities holding under a superior Talúkdar; as in Aligarh, Main-

* I am not sure that this definition is correct; in Behar, certainly, a *birt* grant can be resumed. Elliot himself seems to have had doubts on this subject, and refers to Buchanan's "India," II. 546.—B.

púrí, and Gorakhpúr. It is in some places, as in Dehli, used as equivalent to Zamíndárí and Pattídárí. If a man's share in an estate is sold, he says his Biswa is sold. (See Sel. from Rec. N.W.P. i. 119.)

Biswí, بسوي बिसवी

The alienation of land assessed at low rates on the payment of fines in advance.—E. Oudh.

In the North-west it generally means two Biswas deducted from each Bígha cultivated by under tenants, which are taken by the landlord as his right.—See Dobiswí.

Bolá, بولا बोला

The verbal agreement (from بولنا to speak) between the village lessees and the Asámís, either Páhikásht (non-resident) or Khúdkásht (resident). Any agreement between the Lumberdár (head man of the village) and Asámí (cultivator).—Dehli.

Bolans, بولنس बोलंश

Making over one's share to another.—Benares and E. Oudh.

Bolansí, بولنسي बोलंशी

The holder of another's share or inheritance. An adopted heir.—Benares and E. Oudh.

These words are derived from बोलना to speak, and अंश portion, share.

Bolahdár, بولهدار बोलहदार

An occupant of land under a verbal agreement with the proprietor or tillage community. In Hisár the bolahdárs are of two kinds; the *band-bolahdár*, who pays a fixed rent per annum for the land he cultivates, and the *bolahdár bi'l mukta'*, who pays a quit-rent for a certain amount of land whether he cultivates it or not. Both classes are entered in the settlement record or *band*, and both hold their lands at the stipulated rates during the present settlement (Sel. Rec. N.W.P. iv. 15).—W.

Búṛh Gangá, بڑہ گنگا बूढ़गंगा

Búṛh Gangá, from बूढ़ा old, is the name given to the bed of the old Ganges where it has shifted its stream; more especially to the two old courses, of which one is traced below Hastinápúr, and the other below Soron and Kampil. These changes appear to have occurred since the time of Akbar, and I have therefore in the Map of Dastúrs restored the old stream as it probably ran in his time.

This has not been done without cause. The reasons for restoring the Hastinápúr stream, and throwing Tarapúr to the eastern side of the Ganges are the following.

When Timúr marched from Mirath, he is said in the "Matla' us Sa'dín," and "Zafarnama," and other histories nearly contemporary, to reach Ferozpúr, which is distinctly described as being "on the banks of the Ganges." The course of the Ganges, then, in his time must have flowed in the bed of the present Buṛh Gangá. In the "Khulásatu'l Tawáríkh" also, written in the fortieth year of Aurangzeb's reign, copied by Shere Ali Afsos in the "Araish-i-Mahfil" (which professes to be a more original work than it really is), the Ganges is described as flowing under Barha, which would show that at a much later period the Ganges preserved its old course; for this does not mean indefinitely that it flowed under the extensive tract of country in the possession of the Barha Sadat, *q.v.* but literally, under the town of Barha, which was then in a flourishing condition, before it was sacked in A.D. 1748, by the rabble army of Safdar Jang. Moreover, in the Revenue Board's Records of the year 1819, there is a correspondence respecting several villages then within the area of Tarapúr, but included originally in Azampúr Báshta, which is still on the Eastern side of the Ganges.

From the Dastúr Map it will also be seen that the Soron and Kampil branch has been restored, by giving Faizpúr Badaria to Saheswán, and Nidhpúr and Aolái to Badaon: to which I have been led by the following considerations. They may be thought perhaps of no great force, but where, as in Oriental History, we are never indulged with topographical details, and have no accounts of the habits and pursuits of the people, nor of the intercourse and relations of social life, we must be content with the remotest allusions, and rejoice if, after a whole day's perusal of some almost illegible volume, we can extract a single fact worthy of record.

When the heroic Pirthí Raj retreats from Kanauj, he is represented in the "Kanauj Khand," as following the course of the Ganges, till he reaches Soron.

In the somewhat apocryphal biography of Shah Azízu'd-dín, contained in one of the many collections of the lives of Mahomedan Saints, he is represented as being aided by the Emperor Shamsu'd-dín in the capture of Kasba Khor, in a naval battle under the walls of that town with the Raja, who after his defeat fled to Kamaon. Now we know that Khor is on the bank of the Buṛh Gangá, close to Shamsabad, which city was (it is said) built by Shamsu'd-dín from the ruins of Khor. There may possibly be a shadow of truth in this account, which is also preserved in the traditions of the common people; though, as Khor is mentioned later than the time of Shamsu'd-dín, his building Shamsabad may be doubted.

Let us come to a later period, and we find the Emperor Muhammad Tughlak in one of his mad schemes removing his capital to Sargdwárí, "near Kampil and Patiálí on the banks of the Ganges," according to "Ferishta;" and "near Kasba Khor on the Ganges" according to "Ziáu'd-dín Barní." Either way it shows that the course of the river was then unchanged.

Still later, in the reign of Sayyid Khizr Khan, when there was unusual communication with Katehar, or Rohilkhand, we find the following allusions which may assist us in our investigation. Táju'l-mulk, after subduing Rai Harsingh of Katehar, "arrived at the ferry of Sargdwárí, and passing the Ganges, punished the Kafirs of Khor and Kampil."

The same General, after another campaign, marching from Badáon and Etawah, passes the Ganges at Pachlana.

In the same year the Emperor himself, after plundering Sambhal, crossed the Ganges near Patiálí.

نزديک پتيالي از آب گنگ گذشته

These quotations are taken from the "Tabaḳát-i-Akbarí."

The "Táríkh-i-Badáoní" uses precisely the same expression in two of these instances: and it is important to observe it, for the author was himself a great traveller, and was constantly on the move between Agra, Sambhal, and Badáon. Both he and the author of "Tabaḳát-i-Akbarí" were contemporaries of Akbar, and could not fail, if any changes in the course of the Ganges had occurred up to their time, to give prominent notice of the circumstance.

All the places noted above are on the right bank of the old Ganges, and would most probably not have been mentioned had the Ganges not run under them. At least in these days there are no such ferries as those of Pachlana, Patiálí, and Sargdwárí. But as it may perhaps be said that, notwithstanding the change in the river's bed, the expressions quoted above would not altogether have been inapplicable, other more decisive testimony may be adduced from a document in an old "Dastúru'l-'Amal," in which mention is made of a Mauza in Tappa Aúláí, Parganah Badáon, which, though the document may not be an exact copy of one publicly issued (it being merely inserted as a model for imitation), may yet serve to show without further question, that Aúláí was once an integral part of Parganah* Badáon. If it be remarked that the change in the course of the river is too great to have occurred within the period which has elapsed since the compilation of the Ÿín-i Akbarí, it may be replied that in our own time the change is almost every year perceptible, and that the Ganges has shifted its bed so much since the two opposite banks were measured, that although only five years elapsed between the surveys, they cannot be combined with any accuracy.

It is to be hoped therefore that the reasons given above may be considered to justify the innovation which has been ventured in the map.

Bujhárat, بجهارت बुझारत

Adjustment of accounts. From बुझाना bujháná, to cause to comprehend. In some districts it has a special significance.

"This audit of accounts (or Bujhárat as it is called) is a most important process to the whole of the community. The right of admission to the audit is the criterion of proprietary right" (Sel. Rec. N.W.P. iv. 143, from report on Azimgaṛh by Thomason).—B.

Búrá, بورا बूरा

Redeemable mortgage.—Eastern Oudh.

Britá, برتا ब्रिता

A grant, generally of land, to a religious person, or to a tenant on certain stipulations. See Birt, and the Printed Glossary under Burt.

* Moreover, in the book entitled the "Aḥwál-i Subaját," a new Parganah under the name of Nidhpúr, is entered as "in the time of the Sirkár of Badaun." This work was written before the final disruption of the empire, and is a highly interesting memorial of the state of India at the time of its composition. It was obtained from the library of Nawwab Muhammad Mír Khan, whose family has had close connection with the house of Timúr since its decline.

Brittántpattar, برتانت پتر ब्रितांतपत्तर

The record of a decision given by a Panchayet. From वृत्तांत circumstance, narration; and पत्र a leaf, a deed.

Bachhaunṭá, بچھونٹا बछौंटा

Distribution of an aggregate sum on several individuals. (See Behrí).—Upper Doáb.

Bahí, بہی बही

An account book; a register; a ledger.

Thus, Bahí Khata is the day book kept by merchants, and Bahí Patwárí, the village accountant's, or Patwárí's register.

Bakár, بکار बकार

Amount fixed by the appraiser.—See Bak.

Bakhshnámá, بخشنامه बखश्नामा

A deed of gift: from بخش gift, and نامه a letter, a document.

Bá farzandán, با فرزندان बाफरजंदान

Bá aulád, با اولاد बाऔलाद

Literally, with sons, with children: words inserted in a grant, when it was intended that the land should be inherited by the heirs of the grantee. The opinion of the Supreme Government (in the famous case of Farzand Ali) was that these terms refer to the immediate heirs of the grantee's body, whether male or female, not to descendants generally; and this, no doubt, is correct; but according to the lenient interpretation of the officers concerned in the investigations respecting Maafi tenures, the words are now generally declared to convey an hereditary title, without any restriction.

The Judges of the Sudder Dewanny Adaulat have also ruled

that a Bá farzandan grant is descendable to the heirs general (Reports, Vol. IV. p. 222): being opposed to the opinion of their law officers, who declared that the words in themselves, and apart from other expressions in the grant, created a joint interest with benefit of survivorship in the grantee and his children; or in the event of his having at the time of grant no children, but only grand-children, in the grantee and his grand-children.—(See "Macnaghten's Precedents of Mahomedan Law," p. 332, and pp. 48–52 of "Extracts from Official Records on Maafí Investigations.")

Baiṭh, بَيٹھ बैठ

Value of Government share of produce. The amount *settled* on the land, from *baiṭhná* بيٹھنا to sit: thus bearing the same etymological meaning as assessment. The word is used in many varieties of application in commercial transactions; thus, *kitná baiṭhtá* is "how much does it come to" (in reckoning or apportioning various items).

Bájantarí, باجنتري बाजंतरी

Bájantarí, or rather Bájantarí Mahal, was an item of collection under the Mahomedan regime, derived from H. बाजा a musical instrument; Sanskrit वाद्य.

Bák, باک बाक

Bák is used in the North West to signify an estimate of the produce without measuring the field.

There are men who make a profession of this, and it is wonderful with what accuracy they will guess the probable outturn of a crop by merely looking at it. In cases in my own experience it has happened that when the crop has been cut and threshed the valuer has not been more than one or two seers out.—B.

Bakíotá, بقيوتا बकीयोता

A list of arrears of revenue due from farmers.—Behar.

Bálúburd, بالوبرد बालूबुर्द

From بالو sand, and Persian بُرد cut: a term applied to a tract of land which is covered with a deposit of sand after an inundation. An item of remission of revenue on this account.

Bángar, بانگر बांगर

High ground, or uplands. Thus, "Pánípat Bángar," "Sonpat Bángar," are the elevated portions of those parganahs, in distinction to "Pánípat Khadir," "Sonpat Khadir."

Bárah, بارہ बारह

Land next to, or surrounding, the village, generally enriched by manure. The term is chiefly used in Dehli and the Upper Doáb, and is probably derived from بار or باڑ an enclosure.*

Báráni, باراني बारानी

Unirrigated land; land dependant on the seasons; from the Persian باران *bárán*, rain. Also a coat or cloak for keeping off rain, which Europeans usually corrupt into "brandy."

Barát, برات बरात

*** In addition to its numerous other meanings, it is used in the provinces, under the perpetual settlement, to imply an order to pay issued by a zamíndár on a mustájir ṭhíkadár or lessee. It is in this way:—Say a zamíndar wants to buy a lot of shawls, jewels, or such things, instead of paying the merchant in cash, he gives him a Barát or order on one of his lessees, the lessee pays the merchant, and at the next audit of accounts produces the Barát as a set-off against the rent due from him. In this

* Called Gohán in Oudh, and Goenḍ or Gwenḍ in Behar.—B.

way some of our zamíndárs contrive to anticipate the whole of their rents for several years to come.—B.

Bárbaṭáí, بارٻتائي बारबटाई

Division of the crops by sheaves or shocks, before the corn is trodden out. From the Persian بار *bár,* a load. In Rohilkhand it is more usually called by the Hindí synonym of Bojh-baṭáí.

Bárambá, بارنبه बारंबा

Literally, fruit of mangoes. Revenue derived from the lease of mangoe-groves. From بار fruit, and آم a mangoe.*

Bágam, باگم बागम

Said, in the Printed Glossary, to be the most productive lands in the Southern Division of Dehli, situate on the banks of canals; but this must be a mistake, as there are no canals in the Southern Division. The word, whatever it is, is most probably derived from *bágh,* a garden, or any richly cultivated and irrigated spot.

Ba'ẓí zamín daftar, بعضي زمين دفتر बाजी जमीन दफतर

An office established in A.D. 1782, before the enactment of the Regulations, for the purpose of enquiring into improper alienation of land. Literally, "the office of certain lands." The plan for the institution of this office is given at p. 224 of "Colebrooke's Digest of the Regulations," Vol. III.

Bebáḳ, بےباق बेबाक

Without arrears; paid up in full.—See Baḳí.

Bíáj, بياج बिआज

Interest on money. Bíájú is the capital put out to interest.

* This would be more correctly written as two words.—B.

Bíḍh bandí, بیڈہ بندي बीढ़ बन्दी

This is a peculiar system of calculating the amount to be paid by a cultivator. It is peculiar to Chibráman, a parganah of Farrakhabad, in the Central Doáb. It is thus described by Mr. Wynyard, the settlement officer, "By this system the Asámí pays his rent for the land in the aggregate, no matter whether he cultivates it or not." Kali Rai calls it बीड़ *biḍ*.—E. *add.*

Bídhá, بیدها बीधा

Synonymous with Bandobast. Determination of the amount to be paid as Government revenue.—Upper Doáb and Rohilkhand.

Bíghá, بیگها बीघा or बीगहा

A measure of land, subject to local variation. In the Upper Provinces it is usually considered in the English surveys to be 3,025 square yards, or ⅝ths of an acre. In Bengal it is 1,600 square yards, or little more than ⅓rd of an acre. A Kachcha Bíghá is in some places ⅓rd, in others ¼th, of a full Bíghá.

Akbar's Bíghá contained 3,600 Ilahí Gaz (see that article).

The following are some of the local variations of the Bíghá in the Upper Provinces:—

		BIGHAS.	B.	C.
In Farrakhabad, 100 acres,	=	175	12	0
In the E. and S. parts of Gorakhpúr,	=	192	19	7
In the W. and N. parts the Bíghás are much smaller.				
In Allahabad and part of Azimgaṛh,	=	177	5	15
In part of Azimgaṛh and Ghazipur,	=	154	6	8
In Bijnor,	=	187	19	15

In the Upper Doáb it was found that the average measurement of the side of a Bíghá, deduced from the paces of 148 zamíndárs, who were accustomed to practice this kind of mensuration, amounted to $28\frac{834}{1000}$ English yards; making the local (kachcha) bíghá equal to 831$\frac{4}{10}$; and 100 statute acres equal to 582 kachcha bíghás, 3 biswas.

It is needless to continue the comparisons; but see for further information "Prinsep's Useful Tables," p. 89.—E.

*** There seems to be some connection between the size of the kachcha, or local, bíghá and the value of land in different districts. The official bíghá consists of twenty cottahs or biswas, each side of which is measured by a rod of four cubits in length, thus called the chahár dasti, or chár háth ke kattá; but in the remoter parts of Gorakhpúr and the wild tracts bordering on Nepal the bíghá increases in size, till in some places we have it consisting of twenty kattás of as much as ten cubits in length each! and returning from the frontier back again to the more thickly peopled parts of the country, the cottah sinks by degrees to 9, 8, 7, 7½, and 6 háths in the various parganahs.—B.

Bighoto, بگھوتو बिघोतो

The name given to a tract of country bordered by Mewat on the East, Lohárú on the West, Hariána, Dhundhotí, and Chandán on the North, and Rath on the South. It includes Rewarí, Bawal, Kanon, Patodí, Kot Kasim, and a great part of the Bahraich Jagír. The word is only of local application, and does not appear to be known much beyond its own limits.

बिघोतो को द्वे धनी खोरो और चौहान

That is, "Bighoto has two lords, Khoros (amongst Ahírs), and Chauháns (amongst Rajputs)."

The name of Bíghoto, or Bíghota as it is sometimes called, is derived from Bígha Raj, a worthy descendant of the illustrious Chauhán, Pirthí Raj.—See Dhundhotí and Chauhán.

Bigahṭí, بگہٹی बिगहटी

Rent fixed on lands per bíghá. The same as Bigoti in the Glossary, which is also correct.

Bíjak, بيجک बीजक

A memo. deposited with grain when stored, specifying its amount; an invoice, a list; also an inscription.

The derivation is probably वेदयक, the causal form of the Sanskrit विद् to know.

Bísí, بيسي बीसी

A term peculiar to Kamáon.

Mr. Trail, the English Commissioner of the Province, reduced all the miscellaneous measures of quantity of land to nominal (not actually measured) Bísís. The Bísí is equal to twenty Pathas of Gaṛhwál, or twenty Nalís of Kamáon. The Patha, or Nalí, represents a measure of seed with a capacity of about two seers, and the number of Pathas in any area is estimated by the quantity of seed (generally wheat) required to sow it. The actual extent varies according to the quality and position of the land. The grain is sown much wider in the poor Uparáṅw lands near the summit, than in the rich Taláṅw lands near the base.—See As. Res., xvi., 178.

Behrí, بيهري बेहरी

A subscription; an assessment on a share. Instalments paid by under tenants to the landlord. Distribution of an aggregate sum on several individuals. A monthly collection according to their respective circumstances. Term given to a division of a Bhayachara estate. The share or interest of one of the brotherhood in an estate. The Persian Bahra has the same meaning, and is probably the origin of the word.

Behrídár, بيهريدار बेहरीदार

Holder of a share, denominated Behrí.—See Glossary, Beraidar.

Benaudhá, بنودها बेनौधा

A name commonly given by the natives to the country between Allahabad and Sarwar, *i.e.* Sarjúpar, the other side of the Sarjú (ancient Sarayu), the present district of Gorakhpúr; and between the Ganges and the Chhúab Nala, by which it is separated on the North-West from Baiswara. Benaudha appears to include the Western parts of Jaunpúr, Azimgaṛh, and Benares, and the Southern part of Oudh. Indeed, some authorities make it extend from Baiswara to Bijaypúr, and from Gorakhpúr to Bhojpúr. The common saying is that Benaudha, or Benáwat as it is sometimes called, contained twelve Rajas, who comprised one Paut, and were considered to have common interests. 1st, the Gaharwár of Bijaypúr; 2nd, the Khánzada Bachgotí; 3rd, Bais; 4th, Sarnet; 5th, Haiobans of Hardí; 6th, Ujjain of Dúmráñw; 7th, Rajkumar of Teorí Bhagwanpúr; 8th, Chandel of Agorí; 9th, Kalhans of Sarwár; 10th, Gautam of Nagra; 11th, Hindú Bachgotí of Karwar; 12th, Bisen of Majhaulí. These dimensions would imply that Benaudha was an extensive province, including the whole of Benares and Eastern Oudh; but I believe the limits first mentioned are the correct ones, and out of this narrower space it would be easy to construct the fifty-two parganahs, of which Benaudha is said to consist.

Bakhshíát, بخشيات बख़शीआत

The name of a division of the Jaunpúr Sirkár mentioned in Regulation II. of 1795. This Parganah no longer exists as a separate division. Its former history and the derivation of its name are very obscure; apparently, however, the designation of "Bakhshíát," or "Dihát Bakhshígarí," prior to the Cession, applied only to certain villages which were assigned to the Bakshí of the Fort at Jaunpúr, for repairs and other necessary expences, and it was not till after we got possession of the country, that the Talúkas of Soetha, Kariáwan, Nawáí, and Bhadí, all of which are Peshkashí Mahals, were included in the Parganah called Bakhshíát. Under these circumstances, there was no objection at the late settlement to absorb the sub-division in the manner most convenient, and the villages were accordingly distributed between Ghisuá, Havelí, Karákat, and Angli Mahul.

Baldiháí, بلدهائي बलदहाई

Compensation for pasture ground.—Rohilkhand.

It is usually called Bardaihí to the Eastward.—See Ang.

Balkaṭ, بلكٹ बल्कट

Rent taken in advance.—Lower Doáb, Bundelkhand, and Benares.

The word is also applied to the cutting of ears of corn without going through the usual process of reaping. Katáí is likewise used in this sense in Benares.

From this word is derived the name of the old Mahomedan tax bálkaṭí, which used to be demanded on commencement of reaping. From बाल an ear of corn, and काटना to cut.

Bandbehrí, بندبيهري बन्दबेहरी

Statement of the amount of each money instalment or share of a village. The word Band is used in many other combinations in the sense of statement, account, ledger; thus Bandbardasht or Bandbatáí is a statement of the amount of each instalment in grain. Band-hisáb is an abstract account. Bandphántah is a paper like the Bandbehrí which shows the liabilities of each sharer of a village.

Bapans, بپنس बपंश

Father's share.—Benares and Eastern Oudh.

Bapautí is more usual in the N. West and Bundelkhand.

The word is derived from बाप a father, and अंश share.

Baḳáyá, بقايا बकाया

Old balances of Revenue; plural of the Arabic باقي an arrear, a residue.

Barárí, براري बरारी

A shareholder paying his portion of the Jama according to the Barár.

Baráwurd, برآورد बरावुर्द

An estimate; calculating; casting up. From the Persian بر above, and آوردن to bring.

Baṛhí, بڑھي बढी

Profits, a corruption of Baṛhotarí: from بڑھنا to increase.

Barmhotar,* برمهوتر बरमहोतर

A free grant given to Brahmins for religious purposes.

Batnan-bád-batnan, بطنا بعد بطنا बतनन बाद बतनन

Literally, "body after body,"—words frequently inserted in grants, after the corresponding expression of Nasalan ba'd Nasalan, to signify that the tenure is heritable by lineal descendants in the male line. Under the present interpretation of the resumption laws, the expression is construed to convey the right of perpetuity, without this restriction.

Baṭṭá, بٹّا बट्टा

Difference of exchange; anything extra; an extra allowance; discount on uncurrent or short weight coins: usually called Batta. The word has been supposed to be a corruption of Bharta, increase, but it is a pure Hindí vocable, and is more usually applied to discount than premium.

Baidár, بيعدار बैदार

A proprietor by purchase; from the Arabic بيع selling. Hence Bainàma, a deed of sale.

* Also spelt ब्रह्मोत्तर and बम्होतर.

Bai'bi'l wafá dár, بيع بالوفادار बैबिलवफादार

A person having the possession and usufruct of a property on its conditional sale to him; the stipulation being that if a sum of money borrowed from him be not repaid by a fixed period, the sale shall become absolute; from بيع sale, and وفا performance of a promise.

Cháhí, چاهي चाही

Lands irrigated from wells (from the Persian Cháh چاه a well), as distinguished from باراني Báráni, or land dependent on rain for its moisture; Cháhí land pays a higher revenue than Báráni, because it has a certain supply of water, while the supply from rain is of course uncertain.

*** The extreme uncertainty of the supply of rain is the cause of the terrible famines to which India is peculiarly subject; and which it is now proposed to combat by a larger system of irrigation derived from canals. The system of irrigation from wells is defective in many ways. It necessitates the keeping by each cultivator of extra bullocks to work the well. Besides which to dig a well is a costly operation, and can therefore only be done by rich men or by the joint act of the community. A well is like an estate, the joint property of a large body of men, each of whom has his stated number of hours in the week for using the water. In the hot weather the necessity of getting water for the fields is so great that the wells are kept at work all day and all night, the water being led along conduits of earth sometimes for miles. When worked so incessantly the well will sometimes dry up for a time, because the water is taken out faster than it runs in, and the ryot has to stop working till it fills again. All the uncertainty, expense, and other inconveniences of the cháhí system will be obviated by canals.

In many parts of Behar there are no wells for agricultural

purposes, and the people are entirely dependent on rain or tanks.

It is curious to observe how the wells vary in size in different parts of the country. In the Panjáb the wells are often from fifteen to twenty feet in diameter, there is one at Amritsar which admits four rahaṭs or Persian wheels at once. Lower down, in the N.W. Provinces, six or seven feet is the average diameter, and the well is generally worked by the charas or charsá, a large leathern sack, which is drawn up by bullocks walking down an incline. This requires two men to work it, one to drive the bullocks and another to tilt the charas when it comes up; whereas the rahaṭ requires only a man or boy to drive the buffalo round (*v.* Arhaṭ).

Lower down again in Behar the wells diminish to two or three feet in diameter, and are worked by a kuṅr or small bucket of iron or earth, fastened by a long rope to a pole, the pole works on a pivot in a post four or five feet high and is balanced at the other end by a heavy log or mass of earth. This also requires only one man to work it. It is chiefly used by Koerís (or Kachhís) to irrigate their fields of poppy or other rare and costly crops. The labour of using it is hard, and the amount of water raised is less than by any other process; but in Behar, especially in the eastern parts of it, the soil is often so loose that a permanent well cannot be made, and the little temporary wells are therefore more economical. In Purneah they are very small, often not above a foot across, and are supported by rings of burnt clay called páṭ. A well of this kind costs two rupees only, and lasts a couple of years.

It is the western part of these Provinces and in the Panjáb that canal irrigation is peculiarly needed; in the eastern districts and in Bengal the land is low and full of marshes, tanks, and rivers, and the main staple is rice, which grows in three or four feet of water, and during the rainy season, when the country is generally submerged; but in the upper provinces the land is high and dry, and the wheat and other staples require constant irrigation to make them grow at all.—B.

Chákarí, چاكري चाकरी

Grant for personal services in the village; from چاكر a servant.

Chhír, چهير छीर

The lessee's own cultivation; corrupted from Sír.—Saugor.

Chhuṭautí, چهٹوتي छुटौती

Remissions allowed either on the Bíghá, or in rupees, by Malgúzárs, after forming an estimate of a field. Also, generally, any remission of Revenue by Government; from छुटना Chhutná, to be dismissed, to escape.

Chhut, Chhut Má'fí, or Mujráí, are terms specially applied in Benares to the reductions which have been made in the assessment of 1197 Faslí. Some of these have been authorized by the Government, but most of them have been granted without any such authority. Some of those in the former category are alluded to in Sect. 22, Reg. II. of 1795.

Chhoṛchiṭṭhí چهوڑچٹهي छोडचिट्ठी

A deed of release, from छोडना chhoṛná, to abandon, and चिट्ठी chitthí, a note.

Chiṭṭhí, چٹهي चिट्ठी

A note; a paper containing an order or demand. From this word are formed chiṭṭhí talab or talab chiṭṭhí, meaning a process or precept; a summons; from the Arabic طلب search, demand; and Chiṭnavís (written Chiṭnís in the Printed Glossary), a writer of notes or precepts; a secretary; from the Persian نوشتن to write.—E.

Chiṭṭhí taksim is a note or memorandum of allotment or partition of an estate by Baṭwára.—W.

Chiṭṭhí tankhwáhí, is a note containing a demand for payment of rent; also the same as Barát *q.v.*—W.

Chukárá, چکارا चुकारा

Customs duty.—Saugor.

Chukautá, چکوتا चुकौता

Field rates of rent; money rate; from चुकाना Chukáná, to settle or complete. Also an agreement for the delivery free of cost of a stipulated share of an estimated crop to the principal shareholder on the part of the rest.—Moradabad.—W.

Chukrí, چکري चुकरी

A fractional division of land.—Garhwál and Kamáon.

Chukat, چکت चुकत

A settlement; from चुकाना Chukáná, to settle.—Dehli and Upper Doáb.

Chungí, چنگي चुंगी

Illegal abstraction of handfuls of market produce. It is frequently, however, given voluntarily as a sort of rent for the use of market conveniences, such as booths, sheds, etc.; and in this sense is equivalent to the Baitak of the Deccan.

Chungí is also sometimes given to Fakírs, Zamíndárs, or Banias, for the establishment of new markets.—E.

In the Panjáb it is the name of a tax levied in kind on all produce that enters the city gates, an octroi in fact; and has been continued under British government.—B.

Chungí mahál, a place where grain may be landed from boats and stored on payment of a portion of it to the owners of the ground.—Behar.—W.

Chaubáchhá, چوباچهه चौबाछा

A levy of Revenue on four things, under the ancient regime, in the Dehli territory; namely, *pag*, *tag*, *kori*, or *kudi*, and *púnchhi*: i.e. *pagṛi*,* a turban, *tag*, a rag or thread worn by a child round its waist, *kori*, a hearth, and *púnchhi*, animals' tails, as of buffaloes, bullocks, etc.

As *tag* may be considered to be included in *pag*, another tax is substituted for it according to some authorities. Thus *palkaṭi* a cess on the *pala* cuttings (see Jharberí), or a cess on the *daranti* or sickle, or on the *khurpa* or grass-scraper; but the insertion of *tag* is correct, for the tax upon the *pag*, or men, was double of that upon the *tag*, or children.

Chaubísá, چوبيسه चौबीसा

From Chaubís, twenty-four; is a name applied to a tract of country containing that number of villages in the occupation of a particular tribe. There are several of them scattered over our Provinces, but they may perhaps be considered more frequent in the neighbourhood of Mathurá than elsewhere. Thus, we have within a circuit of about thirty miles round that city—

A Chaubísa of Jaes Rajputs.
A Chaubísa of Jadon Rajputs.
A Chaubísa of Bachhal Rajputs.
A Chaubísa of Kachhwáha Rajputs.
A Chaubísa of Jaiswar Rajputs.—See Chaurásí.

Chaudharáí, چودهرائي चौधराई

The jurisdiction of a Chaudharí, whose occupation has been correctly described in the Printed Glossary.

* Called by our early travellers *puckery*. "To scold lustily and to pull one another's *puckeries* or turbats off, being proverbially termed a banyan fight."—"Fryer's Trav." Lett. III. Chap. 3.

Chaudharáít, چودهرایت चौधराईत

A Chaudharí's fees of office.

Chaugaḍḍá, چوگڈّا चौगड्डा

The place where the boundaries of four villages meet. It is known also by the names of Chauhadda, Chausinghá, Chaukhá, Chauráha, and Chompta.

Chaumás, چوماس चौमास

Lands tilled from Asarh to Kúar, that is, during the Chaumása (four months), or rainy season, and prepared for the Rabí sowings.

Chaumásá, چوماسا चौमासा

The Indian seasons are, according to the Shasters, six in number, each comprising two months. These divisions are more fanciful than real; and the common people are content to adopt the more definite division of three. Chaumása, or Barkha, constitutes the four months of the rainy season. The rest of the year is comprised in Syálá, Járá, or Mohása, the cold season; and Dhúpkál, or Kharsá, the hot season.

Chaumasiyá, چومسیا चौमसिया

A ploughman hired for the season.—Saugor.

Chaur or Chaunr, چونر चौंर

A long low marsh lying between high banks, fit for growing rice, and generally full of water in the rains.—Behar.—B.

Chaurásí, چوراسي चौरासी

The word means, literally, eighty-four: and is territorially applied to a sub-division of a parganah, or district, amounting to eighty-four villages. Tod, in his "Annals of Rajputana," where Chaurásís are numerous, remarks that they are tantamount to the Saxon Hundreds (Vol. I. p. 141). This may be the case in some respects, but it is evident that Hundreds rarely contained a hundred *villages*, and sometimes not even half a hundred. Spelman, in his Glossary, says, "*Nusquam quod scio, reperiuntur* 100 *villæ in aliquo Hundredo per totam Angliam. Magni habentur qui vel* 40, *vel* 30, *numerant. Multi ne* 10*: Quidam duas tantum.*" Hallam also observes ("Middle Ages," Vol. II. p. 390), that the great divisions of the Northern counties had originally a different name, and that in course of time many of them have *improperly* acquired the name of Hundreds, which is conjectured to be a mere political division more peculiarly belonging to the South of England. Lingard also (Vol. I. p. 335) gives an extract from Doomsday Book to show how little uniformity prevailed with respect to the area and number of manors contained within each Hundred. Thus we see that Hundreds were never originally equally partitioned, and in this respect they differ from Chaurásís; for there is no Chaurásí, even though it may have dwindled down to ten or twelve villages, of which every originally component village could not, according to local tradition, be pointed out by the neighbouring zamíndárs; so that Chaurásís once comprised—theoretically, however inexactly in certain cases,—as the name implies, eighty-four villages.

I took occasion, when reporting the Mírat Settlements, to remark that I had discovered some Chaurásís in that district, and expressed my surprise that their existence had not been previously observed. The assertion, I well remember, was received with some degree of incredulity, and the existence of Chaurásís in any part of these Provinces was altogether denied. I have therefore taken some trouble to ascertain if I was deceived, and the following list, which is the result of my enquiries, will perhaps be considered to establish their existence beyond a question, not only in Mírat, but in almost every district in this Presidency.

In Deolí, now included in the Parganah of Bíbamíyú in Etawah, there is a Chaurasí of Tilokchandi Bais Rajputs.

The Parganah of Kuraolí, in Mainpúrí, constitutes a Chaurásí of Rathor Rajputs.

In Jewar of Bulandshahr, the Chaukarzada Jadon Rajputs have a Chaurásí.

In the Parganah of Chandaus in Aligaṛh, there is a Chaurásí of Chauhán Rajputs.

In Parganah Kantit, of Zillah Mirzapur, there is a Chaurásí of Gaṛhwár Rajputs, of which most of the villages are now in the possession of Brahmans.

In Parganah Khairabad, of Zillah Allahabad, there is another Chaurásí of Gaharwár Rajputs.

The Loháín Játs have a Chaurásí in Hariána.

One of the Tappas in Atraulí of Aligaṛh is a Chaurásí.

The Parganahs of Malaut and Bharangí in Bhattíána are each a Chaurásí.

There is also in the neighbourhood of Karsána, Sirpána, and Saháwar a Chaurásí of Balde Brahmans, and in Saheswan and Ujhani one of Tuar Rajputs.—See also article Janghára.

The Solankhí Rajputs have a Chaurásí in Nidhpúr and Saháwar, on the borders of the Mainpúrí and Badáon districts. They are the descendants of the princes of the sacred Soron, before the Rathors conquered Kanauj.

From Allahabad to Karra there is a Chaurásí of Johya Rajputs, who have been for a long time converted to Mahomedanism.

In the Parganah of Hansi there is a Chaurásí of Játs, comprising the Gots of Seil, Rongí, Bora and Satraungí.

In Parganah Sheolí of Cawnpore there is a Chaurásí of Chandel Rajputs.

In Oudh, opposite to Sheorajpúr, there is a Fattihpúr Chaurásí tenanted by Bisen Rajputs.

There is a Chaurásí of Chandel Rajputs in Kariat Dost, in Zillah Jaunpúr.

There is a Chaurási of Tuar Rajputs in Dasna and Jalalabad, Zillah Mírat.

There is half a Chaurási of the same tribe in Puth, in the same district.

The Nagrí Gújars have a Chaurási in Dankaur, Zillah Bulandshahr.

The Parganah of Loni was formerly a Chaurási.

The Parganah of Ghazipur, in Fattihpúr, was formerly a Chaurási.

In Mahomedabad Gohna, of Zillah Azimgaṛh, there was also formerly a Chaurási.

The Baláin Játs, the Salakláin Játs, and the Kalsean Gújars, have each a Chaurási in the Western Division of the Muzaffarnagar District.

The Nirwal Játs have a Chaurási to the South of Dehli.

In Baghpat the Gaur Tagás had a Chaurási, of which but few villages now remain in their possession.

Garra Kota in Damoh of Saugor is a Bundela Chaurási.

In the same Parganah the Deswal Ahírs had half a Chaurási.

Parganah Jhillo in Saugor is a Chaurási.

The Títwal Tagas of the Upper Doáb had formerly a Chaurási.

There is a Talúka Chaurási to the North of the Son (Soane), in Agorí Barhar of Mirzapur.

There is a Chaurási of Baḍgújar Rajputs in Mahendwar, the local name of a tract of country between the Mewat Hills and the Jumna.*

There is also a Chaurási of the same clan of Rajputs, now Musulman, on the banks of the Hindan, to the South West of Muzaffarnagar.

This branch of Rajputs had also a Chaurási in Rajpúra, and in Neraulí, Parganahs of Rohilkhand, and another on the opposite side of the Ganges at Anúpshahr. These, however, are

* More correctly the name of a small river now dammed up.—E.

only sub-divisions of the much more extensive possessions they had on either side of the Ganges.

There is a Chaurásí of Rangars in Parganah Kata of Seharañpúr.

There is a Chaurásí of Khúbar Gújars in Rampúr in the same District.

The Bunáphar Rajputs have a Chaurásí in Garra Mandla.

There is a Chaurásí of Gautam Rajputs, now Musulman, in Tappa Jar, Zillah Fattihpúr.

There is a Chaurásí also in Hatgaon, in the same District.

The Mahesara Tagas have a Chaurásí in Kithor, Zillah Mírat.

The Basían and Datean Tagas have each a Chaurásí in Puth and Síana, on the borders of Bulandshahr.

There is a Chaurásí of Sakarwal Rajputs in Parganah Chainpúr of Arrah.

The Parganah of Rohtak is a Chaurásí.

The Parganah of Tezgarh, in Damoh, is a Chaurásí.

There is a Chaurásí of Chauháns in Aonla, a Parganah of Bareilly.

There is a Chaurásí of Thukarel Játs in the Western parts of Aligaṛh.

There is a Chaurásí near the Cantonment of Urái in Jalaun.

The Sabaran Brahmans have a Chaurásí in Parganah Etawah.

The Ahírs have a Chaurásí in the Northern parts of Shekohabad, in Mainpúrí.

There is a Chaurásí near Bhojpúr, at a short distance from Farrakhabad, known generally by the name of the Chaurásí of Siraulí.

There is a Chauhán Chaurásí of Jhilmilí in Sirgúja.

There is a Chuk Chaurásí between Ghiswa and Jaunpúr.

There is a Chaurásí of Palwar Rajputs in Anaula of Gorakhpúr.

There is also another kind of Chaurásí in Anaula. When Chandersen, the Sarnet Raja, divided his acquisitions among his three sons, he gave a Chaurásí (in Koss) to his eldest son, constituting the Raj of Gorakhpúr; half a Chaurásí (in Koss) to his second, constituting the Raj of Hasanpúr Maghar; and a quarter Chaurásí (also in Koss) to the third, constituting the Raj of Anaula.

There are two Chaurásís in Parganah Chandpúr, Zillah Bijnor.

There are also two Chaurásís of Mewátís, one called the Kamú Chaurásí in Bhurtpúr, and the other the Dehli Chaurásí, near Sonah.*

Súrajpúr, in Ghosí of Azimgaṛh, is a Chaurásí Talúka, belonging to Kurhanya Bhúínhars.

The Suksena† Kayeths had formerly a Chaurásí around Sankisa, on the Kalínadí, between Mainpúrí and Farrakhabad.

* The existence of this Sonah Chaurásí is doubtful.—E. *add.*

† The Suksena Kayeths have now entirely deserted Sankisa (Sankasya). From this place have also sprung the Suksena Naís, Kachhís, and Bharbhúnjas; and it is highly interesting as being mentioned in the Rámáyana, and by the Chinese traveller Fa-Hian (A.D. 400), who speaks in terms of high approbation of Seng-kia-shi and its neighbourhood.

" Ce royame est fertile et abondant en toutes sortes de productions. Le peuple y est nombreux, riche, et sans comparaison plus joyeux que partout ailleurs " (p. 126). There is nothing in the present appearance of the country to warrant this high eulogium.

In the 14th Number of the Journal of the Royal Asiatic Society, there is an interesting account of a visit paid to Sankisa by the Múnshí of Lieutenant Cunningham, Bengal Engineers, which seems to call for a few remarks. The ruins of Sankisa (not called now Samkassa) can enter into no comparison with those of Kanauj, even if we include the ancient khera of Saraí Agath. The Gosaín's Temple, moreover, can scarcely be said to be built of the ancient large bricks; as there are but very few in the whole structure. There is also an important misapprehension to be corrected, as Lieutenant Cunningham and Colonel Sykes both lay too much stress upon it. It is stated as an extraordinary fact that the worship of the identical Naga mentioned by Fa-Hian is still annually performed; but the truth is, that the mound where this worship takes place is nothing more than the common heap of bricks, or earth, which we see in every village, erected for worship during the Nag-Panchamí. The only local Deity of Sankish is Bisarí, whose favour is supposed to be efficacious in removing diseases of the eyes.

The Elephant, mentioned at page 242, is the most interesting object at Sankisa. It is carved out of precisely the same description of stone as the Lat of Dehli and Allahabad. The body, which is about three feet high and on a pedestal sunk into the ground to the same depth, is well formed, but the snout has been knocked off by some

There is a Chaurási of Chauhán Rajputs in Bhopal.

There is a Chaurási of Sakarwal Rajputs in Pahargarh in Gwalior.

There is a Chaurási of Jatraní Játs in Khera Bijwasan.

There is a Chaurási in the Northern parts of Gadarpúr, Zillah Bareilly. It belonged to the race called Gobrí; but the space is, perhaps, too small to have comprised a Chaurási of villages, and it may therefore have represented a Chaurási of

zealous iconoclast. It bears inscriptions, or rather scratches, on its two flanks, and on the front of the right thigh.

The outer wall of the town, which does not appear to have a greater circuit than five miles, has been washed down, and nothing of it is now left but a succession of sloping mounds with several large gaps, which appear to represent the old gates. Saraí Agath, which is indebted for its name to the famous Muni Agastya, the fabled regenerator of the Dekkhan, is about a mile to the North of Sankisa, and has every appearance of being equally old. In 1843 about 20,000 rupees worth of coins were found at Saraí Agath, but there were none among them of any type previously unknown. Saraí Agath appears to have been an outwork of Sankisa, for it is beyond the wall above-mentioned. There are mounds beyond the wall in the same direction, which seem to have been rather fortifications than Stupas, though it is not improbable that close search will reward the enquirer with Buddhist remains. Several images of Bodhisatwas, and beautiful specimens of double-glazed pottery, strew the ground in various directions. It was in a vase of this description that the coins lately discovered were enclosed. Lieutenant Cunningham is probably correct in thinking that Sankisa was destroyed in the wars between Prithí Raj and Jaichand, but there seems reason to conclude that the town must have belonged to the latter when it was captured, for it is to the East of the Kalínadí, and is familiarly known as one of the gates of Kanauj. Hence, perhaps, we derive the story of the area of Kanauj being so large as to contain 30,000 shops of betel-sellers.

As the determination of the site of Seng-kia-shi confirms the truth of Fa-Hian's narrative, the European public are much indebted to Lieutenant Cunningham for his communication. It is only strange that Professor Wilson, who must have travelled close to, or over, its remains, and must have heard of the Suksena division of Káyeths and their original abode, should have doubted at all respecting its position, for Sankisa is generally recognized amongst the learned natives of these provinces to be the site of the Sankasya of the "Rámáyana;" and it is not unimportant to add that, when any inhabitant of Sankisa visits Nepal or Kamáon, he is treated with marked respect by the Pandits and men of influence, as a traditional story of some original connection with this ancient city is still preserved in those remote regions.

tanks, which are in that spot very numerous. There is one village in the tract which still goes by the name of Chaurási. But here we appear to have a Chaurási within a Chaurási; for the whole tract from the Píra Naddí to the Sardah, when it was under Hill-jurisdiction, was called the Chaurási Mal (*i.e.* sub-montane region—see Des), because it extended eighty koss in length and four in breadth, or, according to some authorities, because it extended eighty-four koss in length.

The old Parganah of Alamgúpúr, in the district of Amballa, in the Cis-Satlaj states, of which the modern district of Mani majra was a portion, was a Chaurási.

The Parganah of Gohana, in the Dehli Territory, constitutes a Chaurási.

Kariat Síkhar, in the Province of Benares, also constitutes a Chaurási.

The Jaurásis have, no doubt, the same origin. There is a Parganah Jaurási in Seharanpúr, a Jaurási Khalsa in Panípat, and a Jaurási near the Maha Balí temple in Gaṛhwál. There is a Jaurási range in the Himalaya (J.A.S.B. No. 138, p. 469).

In Jaunpúr, the Parganah of Byálsí is an abbreviation of Byálísí, or half a Chaurási, of Raghubansí Rajputs.

The Parganahs of Kútia and Gúnír in Fattihpúr also form a Byálísí,* or half Chaurasí.

Parganah Dariabad in Oudh contains five Byálísís, of which three belong to Sayyids, Kurmís, and Bisen Rajputs respectively.

Besides those enumerated in the North West, and those which are known to exist in Rajpụtana, we find indications of Chaurásis in several distant parts of the country.

There is a Parganah Chaurási in Surat, and a Síam Chaurási between the Bíah and the Satlaj.

There is a Chaurási of Dhákará Rajputs in Fattihpúr of Hoshangábád, and in Sobhapúr of the same district there is one of Gújars.

* From ब्यालीस "forty-two."

Chaurási is one of the seven districts into which the hill state of Sukat is divided.

The Kyarda Dún is said formerly to have contained eighty-four villages.

The Upades prasád says there are eighty-four cities in Gújar Das, or Guzerat.

In the Dekkan, eighty-four villages constitute a Desmukh, or Parganah. This can scarcely be universal, but it is so stated ("Journ. R.A.S." No. IV. p. 208) on the authority of Colonel Sykes. Elphinstone, on the contrary, says the Dekkan Parganahs contain 100 villages ("Hist. of India," Vol. I. 120).

There is a Chaurási Jurah in Orissa ("As. Res." XV. 213).

Captain Blunt ("As. Res." VII. 92), in Parganah Mahtin, on his way to Rattanpúr, meets with a Kauhair chief, of whom he says, "All that I could collect from this chief was, that in these mountains there are seven small Districts, called Chaurásís, containing nominally eighty-four villages, but that, in reality, not more than fifteen were then in existence."

There is a Chaurási marked on the Surveyor-General's Map at a short distance to the South of Kabul, which shews that all vestiges of ancient Hindu occupation are not yet erased from that country.

I proceed now to adduce instances of the existence in these Provinces, or a least the traditionary remembrance, of the still larger division of 360 villages, which number, as will hereafter be shewn, bears an intimate relation to the Chaurási, and is based on the same principle of computation. I will merely premise here (what is well worthy of remark) that for territorial subdivisions there is no intermediate number between 84 and 360.

Amongst the six Cantons of Játs on the borders of Hariana and Bikanír, there are no less than four which have each 360 villages, viz., Punya, Kassúa, Saran, and Gadarra.

Panípat Bangar and Khadar are considered to constitute 360 villages.

Sonepar Bangar and Khadar are also considered to constitute 360 villages.

In and around Sirsa in the Bhattí territory, there are, or rather were, 360 villages of Chauhán Rajputs.

The Bisen Rajputs have 360 villages in Oudh.

The Parganah of Barah, in Allahabad, is reckoned to comprise 360 villages.

The Parganah of Bhoelí, in the Province of Benares, consisted of 360 villages.

The Ahírs of Bíghoto have 360 villages.—See Bíghoto.

The Parganah of Mírat is said to have consisted of 360 villages.

The Bhattí Gújars have 360 villages in the Western side of the Bulandshahr District.

The Pundír Rajputs, most of whom are now Musulman, have 360 villages in the North East of Saháranpúr.

The Kachhwaha Rajputs had formerly 360 villages in the Northern Doáb.

The Chandel Rajputs in Bithúr and the neighbourhood, formerly had 360 villages.

The Ráthí Gújars are said to have had 360 villages in the Upper Doáb; but though they claim this number for themselves, it is questionable if they ever had so many.

In the old Province called Nardak, to the West of Karnál, the Mundáhar Rajputs (now Musulman) have 360 villages.

In Parganah Katehar, of Benares, the Raghubansí Rajputs have 360 villages.

The Katherya Raja of Madhar, in Serauli, of District Moradabad, claims as the ancient possession of his tribe 360 villages in Rampúr. This, however, could only have been a sub-division, as the Katheryas had many more villages in their possession.

Raja Ram, Baghel, is said to have given 360 villages to the Brahmans of Arail.

The Dhangal Mewatís, who were formerly Kachhwaha Rajputs, have 360 villages.

The Dulaut, and the Sarban Mewatís have also each 360 villages.

The larger division of 1,440, or 360 × 4, such as the Mohils have at Aurínt ("Annals of Rajasthan," Vol. I. p. 627), does not seem to exist anywhere in these Provinces, though it is claimed by the Pundír Rajputs near Hardwar, the Juria Ladhís of Rámgarh in Jubbulpúr, the Gaur Brahmins and the Jutú Rajputs of Hariana, and sometimes by the Bais of Baiswara.—(See Gautam.)

The Konkan or country between the Western Ghats and the sea, in the Bombay Presidency, is said to contain 1400 villages ("As. Res." I. 361).

It is not, however, with respect to the occupation of land only that the numbers of 84 and 360 are regarded with such favour. We find them entering into the whole scheme of the Hindú, Buddhist, and Jain religions, cosmogonies, rituals, and legendary tales; so much so, as to shew that they are not taken by mere chance, as arbitrary numbers to fill up some of their extravagant fictions, but with a designed purpose of veiling a remote allusion under a type of ordinary character.

Thus, within the sacred precincts of Brij there are considered to be 84 Forests ("Smyth's Dict. *v.* Banjatra.")

Chitterkote (Chittor) is the chief among 84 castles, and has 84 bazars (Khaman Rasa).*

The country of Brij is 84 † Koss round Mathura. When Maha-

* See Tod's "Western India," pp. 156, 204, 213, 248, 268, 326.—E. *add.*

† There appears to be a double Chaurásí in Brij. The Parkarma, or annual perambulation, extends in circumference 84 koss, and does not come nearer to Agra than Gao-Ghat: but the "Bhágavata" says that Brij is shaped like a Singhara, or pignut; and the three corners of it are thus given in a familiar couplet,

इत बरहद इत सोनहद उत सूरसेन का गांव
बिर्ज चौरासी कोस में मथुरा मंडिल मांह

That is, the Chaurásí of Brij extends on one side to Sonah; on another to the lake of Barra (on the Isan, near Bijaygaṛh); and on another to Sursen ka Gaṅw, or Batesar. It is strange, that notwithstanding the mention of Sursen ka Gaṅw in these trite ines, Colonel Tod should so often take credit to himself for being the discoverer of deo stole Sri Krishna's cows, the sportive God created new ones which grazed within this precise limit; and from that period, according to the Indian legend, the boundaries of Brij have been fixed, and to this day they are annually perambulated in the month of Bhadon (Brij Bilas).

The Mercantile tribes are 84 (Tod's "Raj." Vol. I. p. 120).

The Tribes of Sudras are also 84* (Price's "Hindí and Hindústaní Selections," Vol. I. p. 265).

Mount Meru is described as being 84,000 Yojans above the earth (Bhagavata; 5th Khand; and As. Res. Vol. VIII. pp. 273, 353).

The important places of Hindú Pilgrimage are reckoned to be 84. It is the popular belief, which does not appear to rest on written authority.

this capital, which he identifies with the Cleisobaras of Arrian ("Trans. R. A. Soc. Vol. III. p. 145). Even in the "Táríkh-i-Sher Shahí" (and Musulmans are rarely antiquarians) "Sursení, opposite to Raprí," is spoken of as the scene of an important engagement. In the first volume of the "Transactions," Colonel Tod announces his discovery in these words: "By the acquisition of this coin of Apollodotus, I made a double discovery, namely, of the coin itself, and of the ancient capital city. Conversing with the principal disciple of a celebrated Jain priest of Gwalior about ancient cities, he related to me an anecdote of a poor man, about thirty-five years ago, having discovered, amidst the few fragments left of Surapura on the Yamuná, a bit of (what he deemed) glass: shewing it to a silversmith, he sold it for one rupee; the purchaser carried his prize to Agra and sold it for 5,000, for it was a diamond. The finder naturally wished to have a portion of the profit, and on refusal, waylaid and slew the silversmith. The assassin was carried to Agra to be tried, and thus the name of Surapura became known beyond its immediate vicinity. This was a sufficient inducement to me to dispatch one of my coin-hunters, and I was rewarded by an Apollodotus and several Parthian coins. The remains of Surapura are close to the sacred place of pilgrimage, called by us "Batísur," on the Yamuná, between Agra and Etawah. Tradition tells us that it was an ancient city, and most probably was founded by Surasena, the grandfather of Krishna, and consequently the capital of the Suraseni of the historians of Alexander."—See also Vol. II. p. 286.

* I know no other authority for this statement than the one quoted, which is very poor. The whole Jatimala in the "Selections" is entirely wrong; and though it must be confessed that it would be no easy matter to compile a correct one, yet the more obvious errors should be expunged, as the work is intended to be educational.

Vallabha, the founder of the Rudra Sampradáya sect, had 84 followers (As. Res. Vol. XVI. p. 95).

There are 84 Gurus, or spiritual chiefs, of the sect of Rámánuj (Buchanan's Mysore).

There is an ankle ring called a Chaurásí, from that number of bells upon it (Kánún-i Islám).

The same name is given to the bells on an elephant's howdah cloth (A'ín-i Akbarí).

The temples of Mahadeo at Ujjayin are 84 (Journ. A.S.B. Vol. VI. p. 289).

The Hindú Hell is called Chaurásí, signifying that 84 places of punishment exist in Narak lok.*

The grand palace at Dattiah, which was built by Nar Singh Deo, was a series of ascending Chaurásís (on pillars). (Badshanama, by Abdú'l Hamíd Lahorí : 9th Jalús).

A Chaurásí of minor fortifications is said to have been contained within Rhotas (Jehangírnama, Vol. I).

The different postures of Jogís are 84 (As. Res. Vol. XVII. p. 184). These are called Asan; and the same name and number is given to the attitudes illustrated in the Koh Shastras (Tohfat-ul Hind).

The perfect Jogís, or Siddhas, are 84 (As. Res. Vol. XVII. p. 191).

The Gotras of the Gújars are 84 (Bansaolí).

The Gotras of the Ahírs are 84 (Tashríh-ul Akwám).

There are reckoned to be 8,400,000 species of animals; and these are comprised in four grand divisions, containing each a

* This is the popular belief; but it is not confirmed by the Shasters. In the "Vishnu Purana," p. 207, a list of twenty-eight Narakas is given. The "Bhâgavata" also enumerates twenty-eight, but the names differ from those of the "Vishnu Purana." In the "Márkandeya Purana" and in "Menu" (B. IV. V. 88-92) a list of twenty-one is given, *i.e.*, a quarter Chaurásí. In the same Puranas a list of forty-two is given, or half a Chaurásí. Wilson, in his "Sanskrit Dict." Art. नरककुण्ड, says there are eighty-six pits in Tartarus, and the same is asserted by Radha Kanta Deo in the "Sabda Kalpa Druma," on the authority of the "Brahma Vaivartta Purana."

quarter Chaurásí, or 2,100,000—viz. *jaráuj*, those which are produced from the belly; *andaj*, from eggs; *seodaj*, from perspiration; and *udbhid*, from the earth (Garuda Purana,* Pret Khand).

The third grade of Bengal Brahmans is divided into 84 families (Colebrooke's Misc. Essays, Vol. II. p. 188).

There is also a Chaurásí division among the Gaur Brahmans.

There are 84 different sects of Brahmans in Central India (Malcolm's Central India, Vol. II. p. 122).

The Bháts have a Chaurásí ṣub-division.

There is a Chaurásí sub-division also among the Hindu Kambohs of Upper India.

The Kahars, or bearers, of Parganahs Khair and Koel constitute a Chaurásí.

There are 84 Nayat, or families of Brahmans, in Guzerat (Enc. Metrop. Vol XXIII. p. 33).

There is a Chaurásí sub-division among Tambolís (Martin's Buchanan, Vol. I. p. 164).

There is a Chaurásí sub-division also among Baráís, or betel-sellers (Ib. p. 165).

There is another among Koerís (Ib. Vol. II. p. 470).

Amongst the 12 divisions of Káyeths, the Mathur and Bhátnagar have each 84 sub-divisions. The Siríbastam say they also have 84, but this is not confirmed.

Siva has, like Krishna, 1008 names, *i.e.* 12 × 84 (Linga Purana).

In the Vayu Purana we are told that the water of the ocean, coming down from heaven on Meru, encircles it through seven

* The usual sub-division is somewhat different—9,00,000 fish, 10,00,000 birds, 11,00,000 reptiles, 20,00,000 plants, 30,00,000 quadrupeds, and 40,00,000 different species of men. This division is confirmed in popular credit by the following memorial verses:

नौलाष जीव जल मैं बसै दश पक्षी परिवारा
ग्यारह लाष कीट करम बीस अस्थावर विस्तारा
तीस लाष पशु जीव चारि लाष नर प्राणी ॥

channels for the space of 84,000 Yojans (As. Res. Vol. VIII. p. 322; see also p. 353).

One of the four Vikramas lived, or reigned, 84 years* (As. Res. Vol. X. p. 43).

The following Musical Chaurásí may be considered more artificial than natural, notwithstanding Sir W. Jones' opinion to the contrary.

"Now, since each of the tones may be divided, we find twelve semitones in the whole series; and, since each semitone may in its turn become the leader of a series formed after the model of every primary mode, we have seven times twelve, or *eighty-four*, modes in all, of which seventy-seven may be named secondary; and we shall see accordingly that the Persians and the Hindus (at least in their most popular system) have exactly *eighty-four* modes, though distinguished by different appellations and arranged in different classes: but, since many of them are unpleasing to the ear, others difficult in execution, and few sufficiently marked by a character of sentiment and expression, which the higher music always requires, the genius of the Indians has enabled them to retain the number of modes which nature seems to have indicated, and to give each of them

* Col. Wilford considers this Vikramaditya to be the same as the Sáliváhana mentioned below; and adds, "It is not obvious at first why Sáliváhana is made to have lived *eighty-four* years; but it appears to me that this number was in some measure a sacred period among the Christians, and also the Jews, and introduced in order to regulate Easter day; and it is the opinion of the learned that it began five years before the Christian era, and the fifth year of that cycle was really the fifth of Christ, but the first only of his manifestation to the world, according to the Apocryphal Gospels: and it was also the first of the Christian era. In this manner the cycle of *eighty-four* years ended on the seventy-ninth of the Christian, which was the first of Sáliváhana's era, and was probably mistaken for the period of his life. It is mentioned by St. Epiphanius, who lived about the middle of the fourth century."—(As. Res. Vol. X. p. 93.)

It is scarcely to be wondered at that this imaginative writer should have noticed the very questionable existence of Chaurásís amongst Christians and Jews, and should have altogether passed over their obvious prevalence amongst the Hindus.

a character of its own by a happy and beautiful contrivance" (Sir W. Jones on the Musical Modes of the Hindus).

It may not be unimportant to add, with reference to the particular purposes of our enquiry, that the year is distributed by the Hindus into six Ritus,* or seasons, each consisting of two months, *i.e.* two Springs, Summer, Autumn, and two Winters; and an original Rag, or God of the mode, is conceived to preside over a particular season. "By appropriating a different mode to each of the different seasons, the artists of India connected certain strains with certain ideas, and were able to recal the memory of autumnal merriment at the close of the harvest, or of separation and melancholy during the cold months; or reviving hilarity on the appearance of blossoms, and complete vernal delight in the month of Madhu, or honey; of languor during the dry heats, and of refreshment by the first rains which cause in this climate a second spring. Yet farther: since the lunar year, by which festivals and superstitious duties are constantly regulated, proceeds concurrently with the solar year, to which the seasons are necessarily referred, devotion comes also to the aid of music, and all the powers of nature, allegorically worshipped as gods and goddesses on their several holidays, contribute to the influence of song on minds naturally susceptible of religious emotions. Hence it was that Pavan, or the inventor of his musical system, reduced the number of original modes from seven to six" (Ibid.). And here we cannot but invite attention to the assertion of Dion Cassius, that the planetary theory from which the denomination of the days of the week has been derived (see note to p. 73) is itself founded upon the doctrine of musical intervals. A highly curious exposition of this idea has been given in the "Mémoires de Trévoux," A.D. 1770 and 1771.

The following are a few instances of the use of 360.

* See Chaumasa; and note to p. 53 of Babington's "Guru Paramartan."

The Sun's car is 3600000 Yojans long, and the yoke is a quarter of that amount (Bhagavata, 5th Khand).

Revati, the wife of Bala Ram, was so tall that her stature reached as high as the hands clapped seven times could be heard, and her age at the time of her marriage was 3,888,000 years. Her age, therefore, was 360 × 10800 years (Coleman's Hind. Myth. p. 49).

The wives of Sálivâhana, the founder of one of the most noted Indian eras, were 360.—See Bais.

There are 360 chief places of pilgrimage at Gya (Gya Mahatmya).

There are 360 chief places of pilgrimage at Misrakh Nímkhar, Oudh (Nímkhar Mahatmya).

There are also 360 at Sambhal, in Moradabad (Sambhal Mahatmya).

The respirations of a healthy man are said by the Jogís to be 360 in the course of a Gharrí (Muáliját-i Dara Shekohí; and Sarode, 1st Khand).

A Chakravartí Raja has 360,000,000 cooks in his dominions, and 360 for his special use (Áín-i Akbarí).

Raja Bikramajít is said to have raised 360 temples near Ajudhya on the places sanctified by the extraordinary actions of Rama (Buchanan's Eastern India, Vol. II. p. 334).

In the Mahábhárata we read, "Oh twin Aswinas! There are 360 milch cows. There is a wheel without an axis, which revolveth without decay. It hath one name, and its felloes are fixed 720, *i.e.*, 2 × 360, spokes" (Annals Or. Lit. p. 287).

Again, "In this wheel, furnished with twenty-four critical divisions, and turned in perpetual motion round about this axis by six boys, are placed in the midst of it 360;" (ib. 294), which is afterwards (p. 450) explained to mean, that the wheel with twelve spokes, turned by six boys, signifies the year divided into six seasons.

Rama's auxiliaries, in his attack on Lanka, amounted to 360,000 monkeys (Râmâyana).

But, to revert to Chaurásís:* amongst the Buddhists there is a still more systematic use of them than we have seen to prevail amongst the Hindus.

Thus, in a translation by the Honorable Mr. Turnour (Journ. As. Society for 1837, p. 526) we read, "How does it by the Dhamma Khando division consist of 84,000 portions?"

"It comprises the whole of Buddho. It has been said by Anando, I received from Buddho himself 82,000, and from the *bhikkhus* 2,000; these are the 84,000 Dhamma maintained by me. By this explanation of the Dhamma Khando it consists of 84,000 divisions." Again (at p. 792), "Having learned that there were 84,000 discourses on the tenets of Buddha, I will dedicate a *viharo*, or monastery,† to each."

"Then bestowing 6,000 Kotis of treasure on 84,000 towns in Jambudipo, at those places he caused the construction of temples to be commenced by the Rajas" (Ibid. p. 792).

Again, "From 84 cities despatches were brought on the same day, announcing that the *viharos* were completed" (Ibid. p. 793).

Asoko raised also 84,000 columns throughout India. These are supposed by M. Remusat to have been the same as the *viharos* above-mentioned; but the two seem quite distinct (Nouveau Journ. Asiatique, Tom. XII. p. 417; Fa Hian, Ch. XXIII. and XXVII. and As. Res. Vol. VII. p. 423).

* It is extremely doubtful whether the Chaurásís mentioned in the text did always consist of exactly eighty-four villages. In the cases of which I have had personal cognizance, I have had reason to doubt the fact. I think the most reasonable supposition is that as the territories of some powerful clans did really contain eighty-four villages, it grew to be a habit with others who had a large settlement in one place to call it a Chaurásí also.—B.

† Viharo is rather a temple or pleasure ground than monastery. See a definition by Wilson (Journ. R.A.S. No. IX. p. 110); by Mr. Joinville (As. Res. Vol. VII. p. 422), and by B. Hodgson (Trans. R.A.S. Vol. II. p. 246). This word Viharo is the origin of the name of the city at Behar, an important seat of Buddhism (see Sadik Isfahani, p. 24).

In the extracts from the Dípavansa, we read:

"The last of these was Ajitajano; his descendants, 84,000 in number, ruled in Kapilanagaram" (Journ. Asiat. Soc. Vol. VII. p. 926).

The descendants of Makhádeva were 84,000 monarchs, who reigned supreme at Mithilá (Ibid. p. 926).

Asoko's descendants were 84,000 rulers, who reigned supreme in the capital Báránasí (Ibid. p. 927).

In the opinion of Buddhists the life of man reached at one period 84,000 years. This was the highest it attained after successive augmentations (Enc. Jap. Cap. IV. p. 32. See also note 14 by M. Landresse to Ch. XXXIX. of Fa Hian's Travels).

Maitreya was to live 84,000 years, and the law which he was to deliver after his *nirvan* was also to endure for 84,000 years (Ibid. Ch. VI. note 8).

In the third heaven they lived to the number of 1344,000,000 years; *i.e.* 16 × 84,000,000 (Alphab. Tibet. p. 484, and Journal Asiatique, Tom. VIII. p. 44).

The life of other gods in the Buddhist mythologic hierarchy was equal to 360,000,000 years (Ibid.; and As. Res. Vol. VI. p. 210).

Buddha had 84,000 wives (Sieon hing pen kei King, quoted by Remusat).

The Buddhists assign to Brahma a life of 1008,000,000 years; *i.e.* 12 × 84,000,000 (Foe-tsou-toung-ki, quoted also by Remusat in the Foe koue ki).

The fourth kind of Arúpa, a species of spirit residing in the uppermost heaven, live 84,000 Mahákalpas (Trans. Royal A. S. Vol. III. p. 91; and As. Res. Vol. VI. p. 214).

The Cingalese historians say that 84,000 rocks encircle the great rock Mahámeru. The height of this rock is 168,000 (*i.e.* 2 × 84,000) Yadúns (Annals of Orient. Lit. pp. 385, 386).

Meru is generally considered with the Cingalese, as with the Hindus, to be 84,000 Yojanas high, and its ranges, according to the following progressive scale, shew the value attached even to sub-divisions of the Chaurásí.

Sumeru, or Meru, is in height	84,000	Yojanas
1st. Yokhunthara, the first hill, is in height	42,000	,,
2nd. Isinthara, the second ditto	21,000	,,
3rd. Káraveka, the third ditto	10,500	,,
4th. The Hill Sudhatsana....................	5,250	,,
5th. Ditto Nimethara	2,625	,,
6th. Ditto Vimantaka	1,312	,,
7th. Ditto Atsakána........................	656	,,

(Trans. R.A.S. Vol. III. p. 78.)

The Cingalese fabulous histories also treat us with periods regulated according to this mysterious number. The "Rajavali" says the most powerful king amongst them was called Mahá Dewa, who remained in the wilderness for 84,000 years. There were also, notwithstanding this pre-eminence, 84,000 kings who had this title (Annals of Or. Lit. p. 392).

Four brothers of king Mahálinde had 84,000 children and grandchildren (Ib. p. 391).

Amongst the Burmese also, the mountain Mienmo is 84,000 *jazina* high. The Jagánto is also 84,000 high, and the first river 84,000 *jazinas* wide and deep. The seas, in the midst of which the great islands lie, have a depth of 84,000 *jazinas*. The seats of the Nát are placed one above the other at the distance of 42,000 (84,000 ÷ 2) *jazinas*. The second chain of mountains is 42,000 *jazinas* high, and the second river 42,000 *jazinas* wide and deep. The eastern and western islands are each 21,000 (84,000 ÷ 4) *jazinas* in circumference, and so on (Tandy's Birman Empire, Chap. 2 and 3; and As. Res. Vol. VI. pp. 175–186).

The Buddhists of Nepaul assert that the original body of their sacred Scriptures amounted, when complete, to 84,000 volumes (As. Res. Vol. XVII. p. 42).

The Shastras, or brief aphorisms of Buddha, comprise half a Chaurásí, or 42; and the book in which they are contained is the first which was translated from the Sanskrit into Chinese (C. F. Neumann's Catechism of the Shamans, p. 150).

This is, perhaps, the Book of Foe, contained in forty-two chapters (Foe koue ki, pp. 44 and 263).

In the Jain religion, also, the prevalence of Chaurásís is surprisingly great. Thus, Rishabdeo sent 84 teachers to instruct other countries in the principles of his faith (Ward's Hindús, Vol. II. p. 244).

Near him were 84,000 Jains (Ibid. p. 244).

The Boy Buddha taught 42,000 boys, *i.e.*, 84,000 ÷ 2 (Ibid. p. 261).

The same holy personage retained 84,000 concubines (stated above to be wives), and he lived 84,00,000 great years (As. Res. Vol. XVIII. p. 250).

Sakra, the regent of the north in the Jain Mythology, has 84,000 fellow gods (Ibid. p. 275).

In their cosmogony also, as in the Cingalese, the height of the mountains bears an evident reference to this mystic number. Himavat is twice as broad as Bharata varsha (*i.e.*, omitting fractions, 1052 yojanas): the valley beyond it is double its breadth (2105); the mountain Mahá Himavat is twice as much (4210); its valley is again double (8421); and the mountain Nishadha has twice that breadth (16,842). (Colebrooke's Misc. Ess. Vol. II. p. 223.)

The Swetambaras have 84 Siddhántas (As. Res. Vol. XVII. p. 242).

There are 84 points of difference between the Digambaras and Swetambaras, regarded as of infinite importance (Ibid. p. 289

They have 84 Gachchos, or Gotes, of which a list is given in detail (Ibid. p. 293; and Trans. R.A.S. Vol. III. p. 337).

Mahavira, in one of his births, reigned victoriously 84,00,000 years (As. Res. Vol. XVIII. p. 251).

Rishabdeo lived 84,00,000 great years (Colebrooke's Misc. Essays, Vol. II. p. 208).

The ages of many other Jinás, besides Rishabdeo and Mahávira, are based on the number 84. Thus, the eleventh lived 84,00,000 of common years; the eighteenth lived 84,000; the nineteenth was deified 65,84,000 years before the close of the fourth age; the twentieth 11,84,000 ditto; the 21st 5,84,000 ditto; the 22nd died 84,000 years before the close of the fourth age (Ibid. pp. 310–312).

It is to be hoped that these many instances of the use of 84 will not be considered to rank with the Trinads, Septads, and Enneads of Varro, Bungus, Fabritius, Morel, and a host of other laborious triflers, who have occupied themselves in philosophising about the properties of numbers, and have exercised their time and talents in endeavouring to prove that *Numero Deus impare gaudet.* The thought may not improbably occur to some, that if works on Indian History and Antiquities were ransacked, it would be as easy to trace a predilection for any other number as for 84; but a little examination would soon end in disappointment. *Seven* and *twelve*, as might reasonably be expected, and will be hereafter shewn, come in for a good share of attention; but any higher numbers it would be in vain to look for. Popular sentiment has, to be sure, invested the numbers 24, 32, 52, 60, and 64* with some slight degree of favour, and a

* There is also a very remarkable use of seventy-four in epistolary correspondence. It is an almost universal practice in India to write this number on the outside of letters; it being intended to convey the meaning that nobody is to read the letter but the person to whom it is addressed. The practice was originally Hindu, but has been adopted by the Musulmans. There is nothing like an intelligible account of its origin and object, but it is a curious fact that, when correctly written, it represents an integral

commune of villages comprising one of these numbers is occasionally to be found, but very rarely; and there are also two instances of 87; that is, if the large tracts of Satási in Badaon and Gorakhpúr derive their names from that number, which may be doubted; but to get any number that can be at all considered to rival 84, it must be shown that it pervades not only the tenures of land, but the mythology, theogony, and literature of India. That this is the case with 84, must be considered sufficiently established from the concurrent proofs collected from different parts of India. It is evident from the frequency of its adoption that these manifold coincidences are anything but fortuitous; and we cannot therefore resist the cumulative evidence here adduced to show that they must have had some esoteric meaning, and been designed with a view to impress the initiated with peculiar veneration for this number.

It becomes, then, a question to consider what is the cause of the selection of the number 84 for such a marked preference; and in doing so it will first be necessary to revert to the number 360, with which it stands in a kind of reciprocal relation.

It is evident that the selection of 360 rests upon astronomical considerations, and it is important to observe what a clue this interpretation affords to unravel some of the chief difficulties of Hindu chronology, which so perplex the student at his first contemplation of the subject, as frequently to deter him altogether from the further prosecution of his enquiries.

number of seventy-four and a fractional number of ten; thus, ७४ ॥ = .* These additional strokes being now considered, except by well-educated men, merely ornamental, we find it frequently written ॥ ७४ ॥. The Musulmans usually write the seventy-four with two strokes across, or after, the number, with the addition of the words بديگران *ba digarán*, which makes it assume the form of an imprecation. May not, then, after all, this seventy-four and ten have been originally intended to convey a mystic symbol of Chaurási?

* These four lines represent ten anas in the Hindu mercantile system of notation, the two upright strokes stand for four annas each, and the two horizontal ones for one anna each.—B.

Thus we have the following astounding numbers assigned to the four ages :—

Sătya Yug......................	17,28,000	years.
Treta...........................	12,96,000	,,
Dwapara	8,64,000	,,
Kali	4,32,000	,,
Making a Mahayuga of...	43,20,000	

But it has been declared (Manu, Chap. I. 67 to 71) "That a year of mortals is a day and night of the gods." Hence, if we divide each of the numbers mentioned above by 360, we obtain the following more rational periods.

Satya Yug	4,800
Treta	3,600
Dwapara	2,400
Kali.........................	1,200

which gives a regular decrement in arithmetical progression, according to the notions of diminishing virtue in the several ages (Wilson's Note to Mill's India, Vol. I. p. 157).

Here the actual divisor* is evidently based on the days comprised in the lesser equal year, which was adopted by most eastern nations,† and founded, as Scaliger‡ conceives, on the natural lunar year, before the exact period of a lunation was fully understood. It is true that the Indians were acquainted with the equinoctial year, but, in their arbitrary and fanciful

* F. Schlegel is of opinion that the numbers in the Yugs decidedly possess an astronomical import (Philosophy of History, Vol. I. p. 98). Wilson, however, says it does not seem necessary to refer the invention of these periods to any astronomical computations, or to any attempt to represent actual chronology (Vishnu Purana, p. 24).

† The great year of these nations was also, according to Anquetil du Perron, composed of 360 ordinary years. "Or les Astronomes Arabes, particulièrement Albumasar, comme les Chaldéens, les Grecs, reconnoissent de grandes années du Monde, composées chacune de 360 années solaires; celles-ci n'en faisant alors qu'un jour" (Antiquités de l'Inde, Introd. XXII. See also pp. 549, 589).

‡ (De emendatione Temporum).

computations, they might, nevertheless, on account of the roundness of the number, and its possessing so many convenient divisors, have adopted the luni-solar, the first approximation to a true solar year, and the one with which they first became acquainted; particularly as they had divided the circle into 360 degrees,* and had assigned a degree, or Mandala, to each day of the year (Maurice's History of Hindústán, Vol. I. p. 91). In other countries, besides India, we find the concurrent use of these two years; and occasionally we find one used to the supersession of the other, either by interpolation, or by some other mode available to those in search of the means of correction.

A remarkable instance of the endeavour of the Chaldeans to reconcile the periods of the two years is given in the second Book of Diodorus Siculus, and shows how astronomical periods influenced even the architectural designs of the early ages. He says that Semiramis is stated to have built the walls of Babylon of the extent of 360 stadia, to mark *the number of days of the year*. Yet he states that, in Alexander's time, the circuit of the walls was 365 stadia; shewing that a subsequent correction had been applied, after the annual revolution had been more accurately ascertained.

Another curious instance of this system of accommodation occurs in the Egyptian year. A fable respecting the birth of

* It must be borne in mind that this division of the circle is a matter purely conventional, and the 360 parts into which it was divided by the Indians, as well as the Greeks, are evidently dependent on the number of the days of the early year; just as the Chinese, with a more perfect knowledge, divide their circle into 365 parts and one-fourth. "The division of the circle into 360° seems to have been pointed out to the earlier astronomers, by its being an articulate number nearly equal to the days in the year; and consequently one of the degrees was nearly equal to the portion of the ecliptic described by the sun in one day. Whatever, however, were the grounds on which this division was adopted in the first instance, it was adhered to afterwards in the most improved methods of ancient and modern astronomy, from a sense of the convenience presented by the number 360 in the great number of its divisors."—"Peacock's Arithmetic" (39).

three gods and two goddesses was devised, in order to account for the insertion of the five intercalary days, which were superadded to the 360 contained in the old year of twelvemonths.* We may therefore readily admit the supposition that the knowledge of the true year is not incompatible with the occasional application of the lesser year in such instances as those under discussion.

After this instance from Jablonski, it may be needless to add that the Egyptian theology was replete with these allusions to siderial revolutions; and the Gnostics, who frequently borrowed from the Egyptians, apply the mystic numbers of their predecessors, without, probably, being aware of the original purpose for which they were framed. Thus, in the system of Basilides the number of primary Æons is, as in the Persian system, seven; these went on producing and multiplying, till they reached the number 365.† The total number formed, according to the Grecian numeration, the cabalistic‡ word *Abraxas* (Milman's History of Christianity, Vol. II. 116). This number has evidently an astronomical reference, as much as the 360 has in the Indian System. In the system of Bardesanes, there were 36 Decani, who ruled the 360 days of the year (Ib. 125). Other instances need not be adduced to shew the value attached to 360, in consequence of its being connected with the supposed period of the year, and therefore based on siderial computation. Let us now see whether the mystical number 84 may not be found to rest on a similar foundation.

* "Jablonski Panth. Ægyp." Lib. II. C. I. p. 143.

† This is not an exact multiple of 7, but 7 is more nearly than any other short term an aliquot part of 365.

‡ The Romans adopted a strange conceit of representing the period of an annual revolution by indigitation. Pliny tells us the image of Janus was so placed as to indicate with his fingers the number 365.

Janus geminus a Numa rege dictus, qui pacis bellique argumento colitur, digitis ita figuratis, ut trecentorum sexaginta quinque dierum nota per significationem anni temporum et ævi se Deum indicaret.—"Hist. Nat." Lib. XXXIV. 7.

As 360 is the multiple of the number of months in a year, with the number of days in a Savana, or solar, month, or the number of lunations, or tithis, in a Savinya, or lunar, month; so is 84 the multiple of the number of months with the number of days in the week;* the multiple of the number of the planets with the signs of the zodiac; or the multiple of the days of a quarter lunation (in which period the moon passes through seven Nakshatras, or asterisms) with the years of Jupiter's siderial revolution (Bentley on Hindu Astronomy, p. 129). That this is no extravagant supposition may be seen in Colonel Warren's "Kala Sankalita" (212), where he says, "In the cycle of 60 years are contained 5 cycles of 12 years each, sup-

* We are so accustomed to regard the week as a natural division of time, that, if there were room, it would be useful to consider the speculations of the learned on its origin. The question is not unimportant as regards the time of the introduction of Chaurásís, and it may therefore be as well to mention that it is to the quarter lunations that Bailly ascribes the origin of the Indian week. Prof. Wallace, on the contrary, says it was most probably fixed with relation to the number of planets." "British India," III. 79. The following passages from A. W. Schlegel's Preface to "Prichard's Egyptian Mythology" are also subjoined for consideration:—

"Among the Greeks and Romans the observation of the days of the week was introduced very late: although the custom had made some iuroads even before the Christian era, through the influence of Egyptian and Chaldee astrologers, and also of the Jews, who were dispersed here and there throughout the Roman Empire. Ideler, in his excellent Manual of Chronology, remarks that the week had a natural origin in the accidental duration of the phases of the moon. Ideler passes over the Indians, and with good reason; for they had not the week, and could not have had it, since they divided the *nychthemeron* into thirty hours."

"Besides the twelve signs of the zodiac, the Indians had also from early times another division of it into the seven-and-twenty *Nakshatras*, or houses of the moon. In order to fill up the breach, which had been neglected, they were increased, as often as was necessary, to eight-and-twenty by an intercalation."

It may be also proper to add that the order in which the names of the days of the week follow each other is dependent, not upon the size, period, or distance of the planets respectively, but solely upon an astrological conceit. The doctrine was that a planet presides over each of the hours, according to the natural order from Saturn down to the Moon, and that planet to which the first hour belonged was also regent of the whole day.

posed equal to one year of the planet Jupiter:" shewing that Jupiter's revolution was used in counting cyclar periods.

It is needless to particularize all the instances in which the partiality of the natives of India for the numbers 7, 12, and 30 is shewn.* It will be sufficient to adduce in detail only two instances of the allegorical uses to which the numbers 7 and 12 are applied.

In Masudi's valuable Historical Encyclopædia, entitled "The Meadows of Gold and Mines of Gems," he says, "In the reign of Bálkít, king of India, the game of chess was invented. He studied the numbers (of the product of the squares) of this game, and wrote a work on the subject for the Hindús, which is known under the title طرق حنگاتيدا. He laid also an allegory of the higher bodies in the chess, that is to say, of the stars of the heavens, observing the numbers 7 and 12. Every piece was consecrated to a star." . . . . . . "He preferred it to backgammon (النرد), in which game the 12 points of the tables answer to the 12 months of the year, and the 30 tablemen are expressive of the 30 days of the month." Here, then, we have not only a Chaurásí on a chess-board, but the larger symbolical number of 360 on a backgammon board. Masudi wrote in the early part of the tenth century, and as he frequently exercises a critical acumen which is highly commendable, his statements may be received with confidence, though it is not quite evident what potentate may be meant by Bálkít.

Let us take also the emblematical figure of Surya, the Indian Sun. He is represented with 12 spokes to his wheel, indicating, as the Bhágavata expressly says, the number of months, and

* See "Ward's Hindus," Vol. I. Preface 98, and pp. 55, 56, 266; Vol. II. pp. 70, 74, 75; Vol. III. Proleg. p. 24, Introd. Rem. p. 4, and pp. 7 and 40; and Vol. IV. pp. 17, 20, 315, 457. "Coleman's Hindu Mythology," pp. 196 and 209. "Moor's Pantheon," p. 303. "As. Res." Vol. VI. p. 210; VII. p. 274; and VIII. pp. 289, 290. "Foe Koue Ki," pp. 125, 150, 165, 176, 186, 238. "Wilson's Oxford Lectures," p. 55. "Vishnu Purana," Book II. c. 2 and 4; Book III. c. 1 and 2, and pp. 214, 233, 236.

sitting under a canopy formed by the 7 heads of the Coluber Naga. He is also represented driving 7 steeds, or one steed with 7 heads, and also has 12 titles, forms, or manifestations, which denote his distinct powers (*Ádityas**) in each of the 12 months throughout his passage through the ecliptic. (See As. Res. Vol. I. p. 263, and "Brahma Puran," quoted by Vans Kennedy in his Ancient and Hindu Mythology, p. 349). The allegorical import of this Chaurásí is so evident, that we need go no further to assign causes for the selection of this multiple of 7 and 12, to represent territorial sub-divisions in India : no numbers being considered more appropriate for that purpose than those which bear reference to the motion of the earth, the revolving seasons, and the succession of seed-time and harvest ; especially † among

* आदित्य m. sol. (Aut ab आदि et त्य, aff. quo adjecc. formantur e præposs. et adverbb. localibus, ita ut sit initium anni faciens vel a cujus constellatione anni initium factum sit; pro mensium enim numero sol duodena nomina accipit, et in duodenos *Aditjas* discernitur ; primus *Aditjas* धातु est, quo nomine Brahmâ, primigenius deorum, dicitur ; Mahâbhâr : I., v. 2524, hunc deum solarem ab initio *Aditjam* dictum fuisse suspicor, nomine ad ceteros posthac extenso ; aut vera est Indorum derivatio ab अदिति quæ est cunctorum deorum mater ; est आदित्य etiam deus in universum).—Lassen's "Anthologia Sanscritica," p. 172.

† That this multiplication of numbers having in themselves a rational basis, and founded on observation, is at the root of all the extravagant epochs of the Hindus, has been well shewn in an article on their Astronomy in No. II. of the "Calcutta Review." In shewing that the factors which enter into the period of the *Kali-Yug* are derived from the cycle of precession, the author observes :—

"The amount of this precession is, according to the best modern observations, somewhat more than 50″ annually ; but, according to the Hindu system as stated by Bailly and all other writers on the subject, it is taken as 54″. Whether this is owing to any actual change in the amount since their epoch, or is due to errors in their observations, we shall have to consider immediately ; at present we have only to do with the fact. This precession being observed, it would naturally occur to every astronomer to enquire into the length of the period in the course of which this point would make a complete revolution of the whole equinoctial circle. At the Hindu rate of precession this period will be immediately found to be 24,000 years, the quotient resulting from dividing the whole circle, or 360° by 54″, the assumed precession for one year. Now, the duration of the Kali-Yug is just 18 times this period of 24,000 years ; or the Kali-Yug is the period during which the equinox will have been 18 times at each point of the a people whose worship was directed towards physical objects, and the manifold powers and departments of nature; and who in their contemplative moments were fond of marking

"The mighty hand
That, ever busy, wheels the silent spheres;
And as on earth this grateful change revolves,
With transport touches all the springs of life."
—*Thomson's Seasons.*

equinoctial circle. Why 18 should have been chosen as a multiplier rather than any other number, we are not able positively to determine. It might have been chosen arbitrarily, merely on the ground that 24,000 years being too short a period to satisfy Hindu notions, some number must be chosen as a multiplier; or it might be selected as being the greatest common measure of 360 and 54; or it might be for the following reason:—The position of the moon's node, or the point in which her orbit cuts the ecliptic, goes round the ecliptic in a little more than 18 years, just as the intersection of the earth's equator with the ecliptic goes round it in about 25,700 years in reality, but according to the Hindu estimate of the precession, in 24,000 years. If, then, the Hindu rate of precession were correct, and if the period of the revolution of the moon's node were 18 years, instead of about 18 years and 7 months, then if the sun and moon were in conjunction at any point in the ecliptic, they would be in conjunction again at the same point in the ecliptic after a period of 432,000 years. . . . . . The length of the Kali-Yug being thus determined, a short process would lead to the assignment of its commencement. If a point was assigned from which to measure the precession, as we measure it from the first point of Aries, the commencement of the epoch would be at once determined by dividing the distance between that first point and the actual position of the equinox at the period of observation by the annual precession, say 54″. Now it is obvious that any point might be assumed arbitrarily as the first point of the zodiac, or the astronomer might be led by some peculiar coincidence to fix upon some particular point in preference to all others. The latter was the fact in the actual case before us. On calculating backwards the position of the planets, they found that on a particular day in the month of February, in the year 3102 B.C., the Sun, Moon, Saturn, Mars, Jupiter, and Mercury were, not indeed in actual conjunction, but at least in the same quarter of the heavens, the greatest distance between any two of them probably not exceeding 17° or 18°. . . . It is true that at this period Venus was in a different quarter of the heavens, being about 62° in longitude apart from Saturn; but what theorist would allow a single planet to stand in the way of the establishment of so grand an epoch? Not, certainly, the framers of the Hindu Astronomy; and accordingly they did determine that, at the commencement of the Kali-Yug, all the planets were in conjunction at the first point of the zodiac, and thus was the famous epoch fixed."

This is not the place to enter, as fully as the interesting nature of the subject demands, into the enquiry when Chaurásís were first introduced into the mythology and administrative details of India; but it is obvious to remark that the Buddhists and Jains are more partial to the number than the Brahmans; and that the Rajputs, of whom the Agnikula portion appear to have been supporters of the Buddhist doctrines (see Gaur Taga), as well as their congeners, the Gújars and Játs, more particularly affect that number than any other tribes at present found in occupation of the soil. It does not necessarily follow that the Buddhists introduced Chaurásís; but it may fairly be conceded that, if we deduct from the Chaurásís mentioned above, those which may perhaps be considered exclusively Brahmanical, the greater part may be ascribed to Buddhism, and may have been readily adopted and incorporated at some subsequent period by the Hindus, according to the usual accommodating spirit of polytheism. Even the emblematical solar Chaurásí may have been a subsequent importation, as it is questionable if Súrya's chariot is represented in the Vedas* as it is in the Puranas.

It is, moreover, very remarkable that Manu (VII. 115) uses

* It must be confessed, however, that the Sun has 7 steeds and 7 rays, according to the Rig Veda. "Seven yellow mares bore thee in a chariot, Oh shining Sun!" (Chap. IX. Hymn VII.)—according to the numbering in Dr. Rosen's translation of the Rigveda Sanhita. Again, the Sun has seven rays, "These are the seven rays of the Sun, and my abode is in the midst of them" (C. XV. H. XII.). There is also possibly some indication of a quarter Chaurásí in an address to Agni. "Thrice seven secret names the priests have found in thee" (C. XII. H. VIII.). According to the Vedas, also, 21 pieces of Pulas wood are to be got ready against a sacrifice (Stevenson's "Sanhita of the Sáma Veda," p. vii. and "As. Res." VII. 274). A fast of 21 days also is enjoined as an austerity previous to singing the Sama Veda (Stevenson's Sanhita, p. ix.), and 21 milch cows "yield the true milk in the super-excellent place of Sacrifice" (Ib. p. 217). See also another instance of a quarter Chaurásí from the Vedas, in "As. Res." VII. p. 252. In the Puranas, as might be expected, the number is very common (See Langlois' Harivansa, I. p. 112, and II. pp. 68, 440; Stenzler's Raghuvansa, C. II. 25; and Surya Narayan Upanishad, quoted by Vans Kennedy, in his "Ancient and Hindu Mythology," p. 346).

only the *decimal* division when speaking of the civil administration. "Let him appoint a lord of 10 towns, a lord of 20 towns, a lord of 100, and a lord of 1000."

It must not be forgotten also, in the attempt to fix the time of the introduction of Chaurásís into India, that in the compilation of Parásara, who, by the position of the colures recorded by him, is ascertained to have lived not earlier than 1200 years before Christ, the estimate of the lunation is erroneous, nor is any mention made of the days of the week, or of the twelve signs, which seem to have been introduced into India at a much later period; so that if Chaurásís do depend on the astronomical basis which has been assigned to them, they could not have existed in his time.

As, therefore, neither in the time of Parásara, nor in that of Manu, who is supposed to have flourished about three centuries after Parásara, or in the ninth century before Christ, is there anything which can be construed into the remotest allusion to Chaurásís, we must look for their introduction to some subsequent period; and in the midst of so much uncertainty, it seems lawful at least to conjecture, that the most probable date is that, when the Buddhists from Scythia, following that tide which from the earliest ages has been setting in towards the South East, immigrated to India, and became incorporated with the tribes who were in previous occupation of the country.

Chaus, چَوس चौस

Land four times tilled.—Rohilkhand.

Chausinghá, چوسنگھا चौसिंघा

A raised mound indicating where the boundaries of four villages meet.—See Chaugadda.

Chauthiyá, چوتھیا चौथिया

A measure in general use for grain, and about equal to a seer of wheat; Chaukarí is a quarter, and Adhelı is a half, Chauthiyá. Five Chauthiyás are equal to a Kuro or Pasera (*i.e. pánch ser*, five seers), and twenty Kuros to one Khanṛí. These words are equally used in superficial measures. Thus, an area which would require five Paserí of seed to sow it, is about equal to a Bígha (which in Hoshangabad is a little more than a statute acre, being 4,900 square yards), and was rated at about a Rupee of revenue. A Khanrí would be about equal to four rupees, and a Máni to twice that amount.—Saugor. See Bísi and Jaríb.

Chak, چک चक

A portion of land divided off. It is applied to detached fields of a village, and to a patch of rent-free land. In old revenue account books it is the name given to that part of the township which is taken from the residents of the village and assigned to a stranger to cultivate. A passage in the "Zubdatu'l Ḳawánín" runs as follows:—"And in a village the whole of whose area is not really cultivated by the máliks and mustájir, they leave them as much as they can manage, and make the rest into a 'chak' under a complete sanad, giving it into the possession of some one else to cultivate."

Chak bandí, چک بندي चकबंदी

The fixing or registering the boundaries of a chak, showing the corners or points where it abuts on other lands.

In Dakhiní Hindí the equivalent is चतुर्सीमा or "four boundaries" (see Journal R.A.S. VI. 368).

Chakbarár, چک برار चकबरार

Collecting rents according to the size or productiveness of chaks.—Central Doáb.

Chakkat, چکّت चक्कत

The loss of a whole plot of ground by diluvion: the contrary of *ritkat*.

Chaklá, چکله चकला

A Chaklá is a sub-division of a Sirkár, comprising several parganahs. The only Chaklás familiarly known in these Provinces are those of Azimgaṛh and Korah. The designation is not uncommon in Oudh.

Chaklás were first instituted in the reign of Shahjahán, by Sa'dullah Khan, the minister (see Karorí), and therefore there is reason to apprehend that the Sanads given at p. 253, Vol. III., of "Harington's Analysis," are forgeries. Much stress was laid upon these documents at the time of their publication, but as they purport to be of the time of Akbar, and at the same time mention Chaklás, they are open to dispute.

Chaknámá, چکنامه चकनामा

A deed, or statement, shewing the area and boundaries of a Chak. The word is as old as the time of Akbar. It is mentioned in his instructions to Amilgazars.

Chalán, چلان चलान

An invoice; an announcement of despatch (from चालाना to cause to go).

Chanchar, چانچر चनचर

Land left untilleḍ for one, two, or three years.

Chaniyádá, چنیاده चनियादा

Land under a crop of Chana, or gram.—Rohilkhand. In Dehli the same is called Chanial and Umri, and in some other Provinces Chanara; in Lower Doáb, Onr.

Charhwí, چڑهوی चढवी

Raising rent (from चढाना to raise).

Dáin, داين दाइन

The eight Dáins in the Dún are hill estates, each containing a certain number of hamlets, of which the fields and the lands of one adjoin to, and mix with, the fields of another. The Mokaddams of these Dáins are probably the ancient zamíndárs of the Dún.

Dákhilá, داخله दाख़िला

A receipt (from the Arabic دخل *dakhl*, arriving, entering). In the Printed Glossary it is called Dachela, as well as Dakhila.

Dákhilnámá, داخلنامه दाख़िलनामा

A warrant of possession; also derived from دخل *dakhl.*

Dám, دام दाम

The Dám in the "Áín-i Akbarí," and consequently in most revenue accounts, is considered to be the fortieth part of a rupee; but to the common people it is known as the fiftieth part of a Taka: twenty-five therefore go to a Paisa, and twelve and a half to an Adhela.—See Damrí and Chhadam.

Dámí wásilát, دامي واصلات दामी वासिलात

Gross assets of a village (from the Dám of account, mentioned above, and the Arabic root وصل joining, arriving).

Dánabandí, دانهبندي दानाबन्दी

Cursory survey, or partial measurement, or weighment, to ascertain the produce of each field. The usual method of Dánabandí, under the Native Governments, was to divide the crop into three or four kinds, and then for the Government Officer to select from each kind a biswa of the best looking crop, and for the cultivator to select a biswa of the worst looking crop. The produce of the two was carefully cut and weighed, and the average produce estimated accordingly. This would go on as long as there was any variety of crop, or quality of produce, which could occasion dispute.

زرعتِ آنجا چهار قسم سازد اول دوم سوم چهارم بعد ازان بموجه
رعایا ازیک قسم یک بسوه بهتر خود بگیرد و رعایا از همان قسم یک
بسوه که زبون دانند خود بگیرند * (Kitáb-i Ḳánún)

"Let him divide the cultivated land into four kinds, first, second, third, and fourth, after that in presence of the ryots let him select himself one biswah of the best of one kind and let the ryots themselves select from the same kind one biswah which they consider worst."

Dánadár, دانه‌دار दानादार

Apportionment of Jama, or of any other contribution, according to the actual produce.—Benares.

Dánpattar, دان‌پتر दानपत्र

A deed of gift by which land is conveyed to Brahmans.

Dánpattardár, دان‌پتردار दानपत्रदार

Grantee of Brahman caste, to whom lands have been assigned for religious purposes.

Dastúr, دستور दस्तूर*

As this word, which is perhaps a mere abbreviation of Dastúr ul 'Aml, has been fully explained under Sirkár, this article will be devoted to a detailed consideration of the Map

* The author's principle of keeping strictly within the limits of the North-Western Provinces as then constituted, renders this article imperfect, as it refers to an earlier political division of the country. The map will be found in some cases not to tally with the lists given in the article. For instance, under Sirkár Agra, we are told that it contains four Dastúrs, but in the map only three are given, the fourth, that of Mandáwar, not being in the N.W.P., but in a native state.—B.

of Dastúrs, and of the territorial changes which have occurred since Akbar's time.

SUBA AGRA.

SIRKÁR AGRA.

حويلي آگرا.	1 *Havelí Agrá.*	دهولپور	17 *Dholpúr.*
اتاوه	2 *Eṭáwah.*	راپري	18 *Rápri.*
اود	3 *Od.*	رجوهر	19 *Rajohar.*
اودهي	4 *Odhí.*	سونکهرسونکهري	20 *Sonkhar - Sonkhrí.*
اول	5 *Ol.*	فتح پور	21 *Fattihpúr.*
بجواره	6 *Bajwárah.*	کهتومر	22 *Khatomar.*
بيانه	7 *Biánah.*	مهابن	23 *Mahában.*
باري	8 *Bárí.*	متهرا	24 *Mathurá.*
بهوساور	9 *Bhosáwar.*	مهولي	25 *Maholí.*
بناور	10 *Banáwar.*	منگوتله	26 *Mangoṭalah.*
توده بهيم	11 *Todah Bhím.*	منداور	27 *Mandáwar.*
بهسکر	12 *Bhaskar.*	وزيرپور	28 *Wazírpúr.*
جليسر	13 *Jalesar.*	هندون	29 *Hindaun.*
جنوار	14 *Janwár.*	هتکانت	30 *Hatkánt.*
چوسټهه	15 *Chausaṭh.*	هيلک	31 *Hílak.*
خانوه	16 *Khánwah.*		

This Sirkár is said to contain thirty-three Mahals, but none of the copies of the "Áín-i Akbarí" give the names of more than thirty-one. The discrepancy is cleared up by referring to the Dastúr Statement, where we find the Baldah and Havelí Agra, and the Baldah and Havelí Bianah, given each as two Mahals.*

* Havelí and Baldah mean respectively "home" and "abroad," or literally, "house" and "country:" the former alludes to the district close to the capital, and the latter to that at a distance.—B.

There are four Dastúrs in this Sirkár, viz., Havelí Agra, Etawah, Bianah, and Mandáwar, of which the only perfect one which we retain is Etawah.

It will be observed that there are in this list several names of which we have now no knowledge, and Agra is consequently a very difficult Sirkár to restore. The changes which have affected Agra more than other Sirkárs are attributable to the different dynasties to which this portion of the country has been subjected. Játs, Imperialists, and Maráṭhas have at different times imposed names of their own creation on their acquisitions, and have served thus to confuse the records of Akbar's reign.

After excluding the Parganahs which belong to the now foreign* territories of Bhartpúr, Jaypúr, and Dholpúr, we have in our own dominions the following of which the name no longer exists—Numbers 1, 5, 14, 16, 18, 25, 26, and 30.

1.—Havelí Agra was divided by the Játs into several Chaklas, the distribution of which will be explained hereafter. Many of them appear as separate Parganahs in the records of our first settlements.

5.—Ol is a large village in the Parganah of Farrah, held rent-free with others in the neighbourhood, in virtue of a Sanad given by Maharaja Daulat Rái Sindhiá to Múnshí Chait Singh. This tenure is sometimes known as Parganah Berí. Ol no longer gives name to a Parganah, Farrah having succeeded to its importance, as Súraj Mal removed the Tehsíldarí Katcherry to it, after he had plundered Ol, on account of the opposition he experienced from the Zamíndár of that place. A portion of the Parganah of Ol is included in the Bhartpúr territory.

* By this expression must be understood those states which formed part of the Mughal empire, but are now ruled by native feudatories, and whose internal affairs are not managed directly by British officials.—B.

14.—Janwar. All the copies concur in writing the word thus, but there can be no question that it is properly Chandwár.. It has been succeeded as a Parganah by Ferozabad. Chandwár was built among the ravines of the Jumna by Chandar Sen, a Chauhán, whose fort is still to be seen on the banks of the river, and is early conspicuous in Musulman annals. The "Táju'l Ma'áṣir"* tells us that it was near this place that Jay Chand encountered his fatal defeat. Shortly after the invasion of Timúr, we find the Chandwár Rajputs in occupation of Jalesar, from which they were not expelled again till A.D. 1413. The precise date of the decline of Chandwár cannot be ascertained. The legends of the neighbourhood are completely contradicted by authentic history.

16.—Khánwah. The greater part of Khánwah is in Sirhindí, but the town of Khánwah is in the Bhartpúr territory. As the Ját 'Amil resided at Sirhindí, the name of that town was imposed on the Parganah.

18.—Rápri has been superseded as a Parganah by Shikohabad, its position on the Jumna being more calculated for defence than for controlling collections. In all the copies of the "Áín-i Akbarí," Rápri is recorded as in the Dastúr of Biánah; but as this is impossible, on account of the intervention of Chandwár and Hatkánt, we must presume it is a mistake; more particularly as a Dúmrí is inserted in the Etawah Dastúr, which should of course be Rápri. In the early Mahometan History of India, Rápri obtains frequent notice, and appears usually to have been united with Chandwár under one government. The ruins of Rápri opposite to Batesar still remain to testify its former importance, but they are more of a Mahometan than a Hindu character.

25.—Maholí is now included in the Parganah of Mathurá

* There is some doubt as to this reference. It is probably a mistake for "Tabaḳát-i Násirí.—E. *add.*

(Muttra); and the village of Maholí is still extant about four miles to the South of that city.

26.—Mangotlah is still the site of a Thana in the Southern angle of Aríng. The Talúkas of Sonk and Sonsa were included in it.

30.—Hatkánt is on the left bank of the Chambal, and has been noticed in the article Bhadauria. On account of its inconvenient situation, the Játs removed the Tehsíldarí Katcherry to Bah.

The Parganahs now included within the boundaries of Sirkár Agra, and of which no mention occurs in the "Áín-i Akbarí," form an unusually long list.

سعدآباد	1	*Sa'dábád.*	بيبامو	13	*Bíbámau.*
فتح آباد	2	*Fattihábád.*	باه پناهت	14	*Báh Panáhat.*
ارادت نگر	3	*Irádatnagar.*	فيروزآباد	15	*Fírozábád.*
حضور تحصيل	4	*Hazúr Tahsíl.**	مصطفي آباد	16	*Mustafábád.*
كهندولي	5	*Khandaulí.*	ارينگ	17	*Aríng* (part).
فرح	6	*Farrah.*	سونئي	18	*Sonei.*
سيكري	7	*Síkrí.*	رايا	19	*Ráyá.*
جانب راست	8	*Jánibrást.*	هاتهراس مڑسان	20	*Háthras Murṣán.*
لكنان	9	*Laknán.*	مات	21	*Mát.*
شكره آباد	10	*Shikohábád.*	سرهندي	22	*Sirhindí.*
گهرور	11	*Gihror.*	سهپو	23	*Sahpo.*
كرهل	12	*Karhal.*			

* It is perhaps hardly necessary to explain that in all districts in the N.W.P. the Hazúr Tahsíl is that in which the chief town of the district lies, and which is therefore in the Hazúr, or "presence," of the Collector and other Government officials. It is sometimes also called the Sadr, or "chief," Tahsíl.—B.

Sa'dabad.—In the time of Sa'dullah Khan, Wazír, who has acquired notoriety for his proceedings in Afghanistan, and the general ability of his administration during the reign of Shahjehan, this Parganah was formed from about 200 villages of Jalesar, and eighty from Mahaban, with a few from Khandaulí; and a town was built in the centre of them, which he called after his own name, Sa'dabad.

Fattihabad, known also by the name of Zafarnagar, was included in the Havelí of Agra, and formed part of the Tappa of Shamsabad. The town and saraí of Fattihabad were founded by Aurangzeb in 1067 A.H., in commemoration of the victory obtained by him over his brother Dara Shikoh.

Iradatnagar is formed from part of Shamsabad, and from Sanya, one of the Tappas of Havelí Agra. The towns of Sanya and Shamsabad are both within the Parganah.

Hazúr Tahsíl is formed from part of Gaoghat and of Kakáraul, or Paltaura, and from Merhakar, Tappas of Havelí Agra.

Khandaulí was one of the Chaklas, or Tappas, of Havelí Agra. It is frequently entered in the old records as little Kábul, or Tappa Kábul Khúrd. More than half of the present Parganah of Khandaulí has been taken from Chandwar.

Farrah is formed from Ol and part of Gaoghát, a Tappa of Havelí Agra. Achnera, one of the many Parganahs intermediately formed from Havelí Agra by the Játs, is included in Farrah.

Síkrí, or Fattihpúr Síkrí, contains the Parganah of Fattihpúr, and parts of Karaulí and Karahra, Tappas of Havelí Agra. It is a mistake to suppose that Síkrí was a mere village before Akbar built his palace there. We find mention of Governors of that place long before his time. Thus, in the "Tawárikh-i-Mubárik Sháhí" we find Malik Khairu'd-dín Tuḥfa recorded as Governor of Síkrí, even as early as the time of Sayyid Mubárik; and we find it also mentioned in that voluminous compilation, the "Akbarnama," that shortly before the battle of Khanwa, which established the empire of the Mughals, Bábar, having obtained in the neighbourhood of Síkrí some important advantages over Rana Sanka, directed that the name should be changed from Síkrí to Shukarí, or "place of thanks." It is strange that the addition of Fattihpúr should have been imposed upon it by his son on similar grounds.

Janibrast.—This Parganah, so called from being on the right bank of the Jumna, and known also as Bareipúra, comprises other inferior Pattís and Talúkas. Kamait Pattí, opposite the town of Etawah, and Chakarnagar were included in Indawa and Bakípúr, Tappis of the Havelí of Etawah. The Talúka of Sandaus, known also as Parhára, will be treated of under Írij.

Laknan remained attached to Etawah up to the time of Govind Pandit. It was separated when this tract of country came into the hands of the Nawab Wazír. The Havelí of Etawah comprised seven Tappas—1, Khás Havelí; 2, Sataura; 3, Indawa; 4, Bakípúr; 5, Dehli; 6, Jakhan; and 7, Karhal. Laknan is composed of portions of the two Tappas of Indawa and Bakípúr. Sataura, as well as Havelí Khás, are included in the present Parganah of Etawah.

Shikohabad is composed of Rápri and parts of Tappas Dehli and Jakhan in Etawah. Shikohabad was not founded till the time of Dara Shekoh, the eldest brother of Aurangzeb.

Gihror, now a Parganah of Mainpúrí, was included in Rápri.

Karhal, also a Parganah of Mainpúrí, was one of the seven Tappas of Havelí Etawah.

Bíbamau is composed of parts of the Tappas of Dehli and Jakhan in Havelí Etawah. Bíbamau (Bibameyú), where the Tahsíldar's Katcherry is fixed, is a small village situated on the Sarsú river, in the Parganah of Jakhan. Dehli (Deolí) lies between the Sarsú and the Saingur Naddís. Jakhan is now uninhabited, but the ruins of the Khera are on the Jumna. I should have been disposed to give the whole of Jakhan to Rápri, in which it certainly was included before the time of Akbar, for we find it expressly said to be a Parganah of Rápri at p. 336 of "Bábar's Memoirs," but the local records distinctly state that Jakhan has been from time immemorial considered a Tappa of Havelí Etawah.

Báh Panáhat was originally Hatkánt.* Báh and Panáhat were rated as two separate Parganahs during the early period of our administration.

Ferozabad succeeded to Rápri, being in a more convenient position to control the collections. It was built in the reign of Shah Jahan by a nobleman called Feroz Khan, on the lands of the five Mauzas, Pempúr, Rasúlpúr, Dataulí, Muhammadpúr, and Sukhmalpúr; and the Játs subsequently raised a fort here to the South of the town,—one of the bastions of which has now been converted into a Trigonometrical Survey Tower.

Mustafabad, sometimes called the second division of Shikohabad, forms part of Rápri.

Aríng (part).—About one-third of the present Parganah of Aríng was originally included in Mangotlah. The remainder has been noticed under Sirkár Sahar.

Soneyí was originally a portion of Mahaban,—or Maháwan, as it is generally written by the Musulmans.

Raya.—The same remark applies. Both these Talúkas were subsequently included in the Mursan Talúka.

Hathras and Mursán were detached from Jalesar chiefly. They were till lately considered as two separate Parganahs.

Mát formed part of Mahaban.

Sirhindí has been formed from portions of Khánwah and Havelí Agra.

Sahpo formed part of Jalesar. It has lately been increased by annexations from Sa'dabad.

* For Hatkánt, see article Bhadauriá in Part I.—B.

Sirkár Kanauj.

بهويگانو 1 *Bhúígáṅw.*
بهوجپور 2 *Bhojpúr.*
تال‌گرانو 3 *Tálgráṅw.*
بٹهور 4 *Biṭhúr.*
بلهور 5 *Bilhúr.*
پٹيالي 6 *Paṭiálí.*
پٹي علي‌پور 7 *Paṭṭí 'Alípúr.*
پٹي نکهت 8 *Paṭṭí Nakhat.*
برنه 9 *Barnah.*
پهپهوند 10 *Phaphúnd.*
سکيت 11 *Sakít.*
سونج 12 *Sonj.*
شيولي 13 *Sheolí.*
سکت‌پور 14 *Sakatpúr.*
سکرانو 15 *Sakráṅw.*
سهار 16 *Sahár.*
سورکهه 17 *Saurakh.*
سکندرپور اودهو 18 *Sikandarpúr Údhú.*
بيرور 19 *Bírwar.*
سکندرپور اتريجي 20 *Sikandarpúr Atrejí.*
شمس‌آباد 21 *Shamsábád.*
چهبرامو 22 *Chhabrámau.*
ديوها 23 *Deohá.*
کنوج با حويلي 24 *Kanauj ba Havelí.*
کنپل 25 *Kampil.*
کراولي 26 *Karáolí.*
ملکونسه 27 *Malkonsah.**
نانامو 28 *Nánámau.*
بارا 29 *Bárá.*
سهاور 30 *Saháwar.*

Sirkár Kanauj contains 30 Mahál̀s, and is divided into the three Dastúrs of Kanauj, Bhúígáṅw, and Sakít.

The Parganahs of which there is now no longer any mention are—Numbers 8, 18, 20, 23, 27, 28, and 29.

8.—Pattí Nakhat is now included in the North of Parganah Uriyá, and was considered a separate Parganah till the commencement of our administration. The chief town was Babarpúr, near Sarái Ajít Mal.

* Kali Rai writes this مالکون سا *málkon sá*, in two words.

18.—Sikandarpúr Udhú is now included in Chhabrámau, and is mentioned as a separate Parganah in the reports of the three first Settlements. The town of Sikandarpúr still exists.

20.—Sikandarpúr Atrejí, which one copy says was called also Malikpúr Sikandarpúr, was subsequently known by the name of Karsanah, and is now included in Saháwar. The remains of Atrejí still exist in Parganah Marehra on the right bank of the Kálí Nadí; and Sikandarpúr on the opposite bank is now known as Sikandarábád. It is reported in the neighbourhood, that in consequence of some quarrel between the Zamíndars, a Government Officer was sent from Dehli to institute enquiries into the cause, and the result of his mission was that 60 villages of Solankí Rajputs were detached from Saháwar, and made into a separate Parganah by the name of Sikandarpúr Atrejí.

23.—Deoha is included in Bilhaur, and was mentioned in the early Settlements as a separate Parganah, under the name of Dewa. The town of Dewa still exists near Bilhaur.

27.—Malkonsá is the old name of Rasúlabad. The names are still frequently united, as Rasúlabad Malkonsá.

28.—Nánámau is on the Ganges, and was the head town of a Parganah, till it was included in Bilhaur by Almas Ali Khán.

29.—Bárá is now included in Akbarpúr.

The new parganahs within the old Sirkár of Kanauj are—

تروا	1 *Tirúá.*	بیلہ	6 *Belah.*
تھتّیا	2 *Thaṭṭiá.*	اکبرپور	7 *Akbarpúr.*
رسول آباد	3 *Rasúlábád.*	کشني نبي گنج	8 *KishníNabíganj.*
شیوراج پور	4 *Sheorájpúr.*	پیپرگانو	9 *Pipargánw.*
اوریا	5 *Uriyá* (part).	محمدآباد	10 *Muḥammadábád*

تپه پهارا 11 *Tappa Pahárá.*	مہرآباد 15 *Mihrábád.*
حضور تحصیل 12 *Hazúr Taḥsíl.*	بان گانو 16 *Bángáṅw.*
قایم گنج 13 *Káimganj.*	اسلام گنج 17 *Islámganj.*
سونہار 14 *Sonhár.*	اعظم نگر 18 *A'zamnagar.*

Tirúá and Ṭhaṭṭia.—These were not rated as separate Parganahs till the commencement of our administration, and have now been thrown again into a single Parganah. They were formerly within the Parganah of Talgrám, or Talgráṅw (the village of lakes).

Rasúlabad has been explained under Malkonsá.

Sheorájpúr was formerly within the area of Bithúr.

Uriyá (part) has been explained under Pattí Nakhat.

Belah was originally merely a village of Sahár, and was for a long time the seat of a Sub-Collectorship.

Akbarpúr gave name to a Parganah, when it was made the chief town of Sirkár Shahpúr; and now frequently goes by the name of Akbarpúr Shahpúr, in consequence. See further, under Shahpúr, Sirkár Kálpí.

Kishní Nabíganj was formerly in Bhúígáṅw. As on the British accession it was held by Chandharí Uday Chand under a different tenure from the rest of Bhúígáṅw, it was constituted a Parganah, and has so remained.

Pípargáṅw.—The villages included within Píparganw were given in Jagír by Mahomed Khán Bangash to his wife, and detached for that purpose from Shamsabad. On her death they continued under separate management, and so remained till the British accession, when they were permanently formed into the separate Parganah of Píparganw.

Muḥammadabad, usually pronounced Moḥamdabad, was also a Zillah of Shamsabad.

Tappa Pahara, within which the City of Farrukhabad (Farrakhabad) and Station of Fattihgarh are situated, was originally a portion of Bhojpúr, from which it was detached by Mahomed Khán Bangash, and its revenue assigned for the expenses of his Zenana.

The Hazúr Taḥsíl is a large tract, detached in the year 1217 Faslí, for the convenience of collection, from Shamsabad, and united with Píparganw, Muhammadabad, Bhojpúr, and Tappa Pahara under the charge of a separate Tahsíldar.

Káímganj.—Part of Kampil and part of Shamsabad were taken to make this Parganah. Certain villages of these two Parganahs were held in farm by Jahán Khán, and other Patháns of Maú and Káímganj (called after Káím Jang, the son of Mahomed Khán Bangash); and as these villages had thus for a long time been held separate from the other two Parganahs, they were formed into the Parganah of Káímganj, when the British administration commenced.

Sonhár formed at one time a portion of Barna. It is said in the annals of the Rathors, that on Jay Chand's defeat by Mahomed Ghorí, the remnant of his family, which chose not to seek their fortunes in Rajputana, took up their abode in Barna, and after residing there for several generations, gave the present Parganah of Barna as a Sankalap (or grant for the performance of religious ceremonies, *v.* Birt) to Brahmans, and making Sonhár their residence, it became in course of time a separate Parganah.

Mihrabad was formerly included in the large Parganah of Shamsabad. Its name is said to be derived from Mihr-Parwar, the wife of Shamsu'ddín, King of Dehli.

Bángáńw was a Zillah of Mihrabad, and therefore originally in Shamsabad.

Islámganj was also formerly a Zillah of Mihrabad.

A'zamnagar* was constituted a Parganah at the commencement of the British administration. It was formerly a Tappa

* Kali Rai calls this Aliganj, and it is so called in the map of zamíndárí possessions.

of Shamsabad, and was for some time the residence of the Amil of that Parganah.

SIRKÁR KÁLPÍ.

اورئي	1	*Urai.*	سوگن پور	8	*Súganpúr.*
بلاسپور	2	*Biláspúr.*	شاه پور	9	*Sháhpúr.*
بهدهيک	3	*Bhadhek.*	کالپي	10	*Kálpi.*
ديراپور	4	*Derápúr.*	کنار	11	*Kanár.*
ديوکلي	5	*Deokali.*	کهنڈوت	12	*Khundaut.*
راتهه	6	*Ráth.*	کهريله	13	*Khurela.*
راي پور	7	*Ráipúr.*	محمد آباد	14	*Muhammadábád.*

همير پور 15 *Hamirpúr.*

The Sirkár of Klápí contains 16 Mahals, the Havelí and Balda of Kálpí being divided in the Dastúr Table into two Mahals. These constitute only one Dastúr. It is strange that the area is omitted from No. 7 to 12, but as there is no doubt about their present position, the omission is of no consequence.

It will be observed that in the list above given, there are but few which are recognized in the present day in our own Provinces; the missing ones being Numbers 1, 2, 3, 4, 5, 7, 8, 9, 11, 12, 13, and 14.

1.—Uraí is in Jalaun, and the site of a British cantonment.

2.—Bilaspúr still exists on the banks of the Jumna, about six miles South from Sekandra. The Parganah of Bilaspúr is now generally known as Sekandra, or Bilaspúr Sekandra.

3.—Bhadhek now forms a portion of the Parganah of Kalpí, and is included in part of the long strip of land which runs between Jalaun and the Jumna. The word is difficult to read in all the copies I have consulted. It assumes the various forms of Badhalsa, Badhasabad, Babban, Badangola, and Badhatasta.

4.—Derapúr forms part of Dera Mangalpúr in Cawnpore.

5.—Deokalí is now contained within Uriya. The old town is about two miles South from Uriya, on the bank of the Jumna.

7.—Ráipúr is on the right bank of the Jumna, and extensive ruins proclaim its former importance. Only a small portion is included in the Hamírpúr District, the rest is in Jalaun.

8.—Súganpúr is now in Uriya, between Deokalí and Pattí Nakhat. Súnganpattí still exists in the centre of Uriya.

9.—Shahpúr is now a deserted village in Bhognípúr, on the bank of the river Jumna, a short distance South-West from Bhognípúr. It was formerly the residence of the Amil, till the Nawab of Oudh removed it to Akbarpúr. In the Registers of the later Empire, as in the "Hakikat-i-Jama" of Hardí Rám Kayath, we find Sháhpúr giving name to a separate Sirkár, which comprised 25 Mahâls, among which were the Parganahs of Pattí Nakhat, Súganpúr, Bilaspúr, Derapúr, and Mangalpúr. The Sirkár was frequently held in Jagír by a prince of the royal family. When Sháhpúr was much injured by the encroachments of the Jumna, the chief station was removed to Hajípúr on the Sengár, and in the course of time, in consequence of alarms inspired by the malice of a sprite called Bhúra Deo, it was removed to Akbarpúr. Hence it has retained the name of Akbarpúr Shahpúr; but at the commencement of our administration, Bhognipúr was separated from Akbarpúr, and formed into a separate Parganah.

11.—Kanar is a large Parganah of Jalaun. The old town of Kanar, being now in ruins, is called Kanar Khera. As Jagmohanpúr is built near the site, the chief of the Sengár Rajputs is frequently known as the Raja of Kanar Khera.

12.—Khandaut is included in Jalálpúr, in the Hamírpúr district. The village is on the south bank of the Betwa, about two miles west of Jalálpúr.

13.—Kharela is also in Jalálpúr, and the town is at the southern extremity of that Parganah.

14.—Muhammadabad is a Parganah of the Jálaun District, skirting the northern bank of the Betwa.

The Parganahs of which we have no trace in the "A'ín-i Akbarí" are—

بهوگني پور 1 *Bhognipúr.*	سكندره 4 *Sikandrah.*
منگل پور 2 *Mangalpúr.*	جلال پور 5 *Jalálpúr.*
أوريا 3 *U'riyá.*	كهركه 6 *Kharka.*

پنواري 7 *Panwári.*

Bhognípúr was formerly contained within Sháhpúr. It was constituted a Parganah at the commencement of our administration, and now includes within its area another new Parganah, called Músánagar.

Mangalpúr was formerly a village called Nera in Parganah Bilaspúr. It was bestowed along with fifty-two villages upon Mangal Khan, by Muhammad Ahmad Khan, the Jagírdar of Sirkár Sháhpúr. Mangal Khan changed the name of Nera to Mangalpúr, and thenceforward the fifty-two villages constituted a separate Parganah. In the year 1216 Faslí, it was united with Derapúr into one Parganah, now known as Dera Mangalpúr.

U'riyá. About two-thirds of U'riyá are in this Sirkár, containing the two Parganahs of Súganpúr and Deokalí. The remainder of U'riyá formed Pattí Nakhat in Sirkár Kanauj. The three were united into the Parganah of U'riyá in 1216 Faslí.

Sikandrah was formerly Bilaspúr.

Jalálpúr, sometimes called Jelálpúr Kharela, contains two old Parganahs—Khandaut on the North, and Kharela on the South. The town of Jalálpúr, which is called after Jalál Shah, a Fakír, who lies buried there, is built within the lands of Khandaut.

Kharkah was formed from parts of Muhammadabad, U'ráí, Khandaut and Rath.

Panwárí was a portion of Rath, which has an area of no less than 580,000 Bíghas. But no certain information respecting this Parganah can be gleaned, except that it was originally called Parhárpúr; still, this gives us no clue to its position, unless we assume it to be the Parihár in Sirkár Írij. But the probabilities are in favour of its having been a part of Rath.

SIRKÁR KOL.

اترولي	1	*Atraulí.*	خورجه	11	*Khúrja.*
اكبرآباد	2	*Akbarábád.*	دبهائي	12	*Dabhái.*
اهار	3	*Ahár.*	سكندرا راو	13	*Sekandrá Ráo.*
پهاسو	4	*Pahású.*	سورون	14	*Soron.*
بلرام	5	*Bilrám.*	سيدهوپور	15	*Saidhúpúr.*
پچلانا	6	*Pachláná.*	شكارپور	16	*Shikárpúr.*
تپل	7	*Tappal.*	كول	17	*Kol.*
تهانه فريدا	8	*Thána Farídá.*	گنگيري	18	*Gangerí.*
جلالي	9	*Jalálí.*	مارهره	19	*Márehra.*
چندوس	10	*Chandaus.*	ملكپور	20	*Malikpúr.*

نوح 21 *Noḥ.*

This Sirkár contains 21 Maháls, divided among the four Dastúrs of Kol, Márehra, Akbarábád, and Thána Farídá.

There are but few lost names in the above list, viz., Numbers 6, 15, 18, and 20; and three even of these have only very lately been absorbed into other Parganahs.

6.—Pachláná forms the eastern portion of Atraulí.

15.—Saidhúpúr.—There has been great difficulty in restoring this Mahál, but it appears to be no other than Siṛhpúra. In some copies, indeed, it is written Siṛhpúr.

The chief objections to consider Saidhúpur as Siṛhpúra, arise from its being separated from the rest of the Dastúr of Márehra by Sikandarpúr Atrejí and part of Sakít; and from its being combined with Pachláná, the most distant Parganah of the Dastúr, as two Mahals; but on closer examination it is found that only by taking a portion of Sakít into Márehra and Siṛhpúr, can the true area of all the neighbouring Parganahs be restored according to the "Áín-i Akbarí;" and when this is done the old status is represented with surprising correctness. The second objection vanishes when we find other distant Parganahs, about which we can entertain no doubt, grouped as two Mahals; as in the instance of Tilbegampúr and Jelálpúr, Sirkár Dehli, and Seohára and Jhalú, Sirkár Sambhal. Under these circumstances, coupled with the consideration that Saidhúpúr has Solankhí Zamíndárs, we may safely assume Siṛhpúra to be in the Dastúr of Máṛehra.

There was another cause of hesitation. In the Sirkár of Kanauj, Bírwar (بیرور) occupies the alphabetical place of, and is written like, Sarwar (سرور); and had there not been other instances in that Sirkár of the alphabetical arrangement being disregarded, we might have supposed that Siṛhpúra was meant.

18.—Gangerí forms the South-Eastern portion of Atraulí. Gangerí and Pachláná have been absorbed since the last Settlement.

20.—Malikpúr has now been converted into Anúpshahr. The village of Malikpúr is about five miles South-West from Anúpshahr. In the first few Settlements it is spoken of as a Parganah, generally in conjunction with Ahár.

The new Parganahs are also few—

کهیر 1 *Khair.*	گورئی 3 *Goraí.*
حسن گڑہ 2 *Hasangaṛh.*	انوپ شہر 4 *Anúpshahr.*

Khair, Hasangaṛh, and Goraí have been detached from Kol.

Anúpshahr.—The town and fort of Anúpshahr, after which this Parganah is called, were built by Anúp Singh, who was honoured with the title of Raja Aní Raí Singh Ahmad Khání, by Jahangír, and invested by him with a Jagír of 84 villages on each side of the Ganges, tenanted by Baḍgújars of his own tribe. Raja Aní built Jahangírábád also, and called it after the name of his royal patron, as well as Ahmadgaṛh in Pítámpúr, in honour of his dignity of Ahmad Khání. The present incumbent has succeeded to the title, but not to the extensive possessions of his ancestors; for Rája Sher Sing, who was the incumbent at the time of the cession, sold nearly the entire Estate, except the Talúkas of Jahángírábád and Ahmadgaṛh, which were then possessed by another branch of the family. Anúpshahr was formed from the area of Malikpúr, but it is only of late years that the entire area of Malikpúr has been absorbed into Anúpshahr, for in the first Settlements of Aligaṛh and Moradábád we find them recorded as separate Parganahs.

Sirkár Tijárah.

اندور	1	*Indor.*	بيگوان پور	4	*Begwánpúr.*†
اوجينه	2	*Ujína.*	بيسرو	5	*Bisrú.*
اومري اومرا	3	*Umri Umrá.**	بهسوهرا	6	*Bhasohrá.*

* Mr. C. Gubbins says Umrí Umrá are in the Noh according to the old arrangement, but in the map they are in Hatín.—E. *add.*

† There is some confusion in the text, not only in the spelling of certain names, but also as to the situation of the mahàls. Begwánpúr is an anomalous looking word, and is probably a corruption of Bangwán, a mistake which might easily occur in Persian writing (بنگوان and بيگوان). The termination *púr* does not belong to the word, which, on the authority of Mr. C. Gubbins, should be Paningwán (پَنِنگوان). "It is an old city surrounded by ruins and tombs and tamarind groves and fine old wells. It used to be one of the chief head-quarters of the Khanzádas. The houses there are roofed for the most part with slate set on edge." It is not in Hatín but in Púnáhána.—E. *add.*

تجاره	7	*Tijárah.*	فتح پور مونگرتا	13	*Fattihpúr Múngartá.*
چمراوت	8	*Chamráwat.**	کوتله	14	*Kotila.*
خانپور	9	*Khánpúr.*	گهاسیره	15	*Ghásera.*
ساکرس	10	*Sákras.*	کهوا کاتهانا	16	*Khawá Káthánú*
ساتهاداري	11	*Sáthádárí.*	نگینان	17	*Naginán.*
فیروزپور	12	*Fírozpúr.*			

This Sirkár consists only of one Dastúr. It contains 18 Mahâls; but the name of one between Tijárah and Chamráwat remains blank in all the copies which have been consulted. By referring, however, to the Dastúr table, it appears that the name of the omitted Mahál is Púr, which, as it is not within our territory, requires no further notice.

Of the old Tijárah Parganahs within the district of Gurgáńw there are eight which no longer exist, viz., Numbers 1, 2, 4, 5, 10, 14, 15, and 17.

1.—Indor is a Parganah of which the chief town still exists on the Western brow of the Mewat Hills, near the source of the Indorí river, one of the streams which fall into the Sábí. It lies between Noh and Kotila. The area is represented as containing 1,30,450 Bíghas, of which the British portion is included in Parganah Noh, the remainder in the Tijárah country.

2 and 4.—U'jína and Begwánpúr are included within Hatín.

5.—Bísrú is included in Púnáhána.

10 and 17.—Sakras and Nagína (Nagínán) are included in Fírozpúr; but were considered separate Parganahs till the lapse of the Fírozpúr Jagír to Government.

14.—Kotila contained 71,265 Bíghas, of which the greater part has gone to form the Parganah of Noh, and the remainder to form the Parganah of Hatín. Kotila still exists, eight miles South from Noh, but scarcely ranks above an ordinary village.

* Or Jhimráwat.

It was formerly a place of very considerable importance, and was one of the chief strongholds of the turbulent Mewatís. We learn from the "Tawáríkh-i Mubarikshahí" that it was taken and destroyed by the Sayyid King, Khizr, in A.D. 1421.

15.—Ghasera has been thrown into Noh. It is still a respectable town, encircled with a strong wall with bastions.

The present Parganahs included within this area, and not mentioned in the "Áín-i Akbarí," are—

نوح 1 *Noh.*	هتين 2 *Hatín.*

پوناهانه 3 *Púnáhánah.*

Noh was formerly a Mauza within the area of Parganah Indor. In A.D. 1764 theJát chief, Súraj Mal, after killing Rao Bahádúr Singh, who had previously seized upon the Parganahs of Indor and Kotila, and after plundering the town of Ghasera, established his own Amil in Noh, and placed under his charge the collections of Indor, Ghasera and Kotila; since which time it has remained a separate Parganah.

Hatín, which lapsed to the British Government in 1231 Faslí, on the death of Faizulláh Beg Khan, was originally named after a Mauza of Bhagwánpúr, and now includes within its area Ujína and Bhagwánpúr,* and parts of Sonah and Kotila. In the time of Mohamed Shah, Rao Badan Singh, the father of Súraj Mal, held a lease of this Mahál from the Jagírdars in possession. His son, taking advantage of the weakness and decline of the Mahomedan Government, refused to fulfil the conditions his father had entered into, and maintained by force of arms possession on his own account: and building a mud fort in Hatín, included his acquisitions within a new Parganah of that name, which has been retained to this time.

* Or Paningwán.

Púnáhánah, which was formerly included in Nawwab Shamsu'd-dín's Jagír, was originally a small Mauza in Parganah Bisrú. In A.D. 1717 Súraj Mal built a mud fort in Púnáhánah, and established it as the head quarters of a new Parganah, formed out of Bisrú and parts of Chamráwat and Paháṛí.

Sirkár I'rij.

The only Parganahs of I'rij in our territory (excluding Jalaun, which, having lately lapsed to us, I have not considered), are—

كونچ 1 *Kúnch.*	پريهار 2 *Parihár.*

Kúnch retains its name in the district of Hamírpúr, and is isolated by Parganahs of the Jalaun territory.

Parihár, so called from the tribe of Rajputs who are its zamíndárs, includes in a portion of its area the Talúka of Sandaus, now contained in the Parganah of Janibrast in Etawah. Its position in the midst of the ravines of the Kúárí and Chambal has always fostered the turbulence of the zamíndárs, and in the early period of our administration a military party sent out to control them was severely handled, and the officer in command lost his life.

Sirkár Sahár.

پهاري 1 *Pahárí.*	كامه 4 *Kámah.*
بهدولي 2 *Bhadaulí.*	كوه مجاهد 5 *Koh Mujáhid.*
سهار 3 *Sahár.*	نون هيره 6 *Núnherah.*

هوڈل 7 *Hoḍal.*

This Sirkár, which is sometimes called Pahárí, contains seven Mahâls forming one Dastúr; but in some copies Núnhera is recorded as a separate Dastúr. Only two of these Parganahs are in our territory—numbers 3 and 7,—but the dimensions of the former are much curtailed, on account of the formation of other Parganahs from part of its large area. We find it stated in the history drawn up by Sarúp Chand, for the use of Sir J. Shore, that Shahjahán, in the twentieth year of his reign, gave Kámah, Pahárí, and the other Parganahs of this Sirkár, to Kírat Singh, the father of Raja Jai Singh, as the imperial authorities were not strong enough to control the turbulence of the Mewatís; but I do not find it mentioned among the transactions of that year in the "Shahjahán-náma."

The new Parganahs within this area are—

شیرگڑہ 1 *Shergaṛh.*	کوسي 2 *Kosí.*

ارینگ 3 *Aríng (part).*

These three Parganahs were formerly included in Sahár. The two first were separated by the Játs, but for a long time retained the single name of Kosí, and the latter, at the commencement of our administration; since which time the three have continued separate Parganahs. Aríng includes also the Parganahs of Govardhan and Sonsa; and Kosí includes that of Shahpúr; but as they were intermediately formed, and no mention is made of them in the "Áín-i Akbarí," they require no notice.

In the Hakíkat-i-Jama of Hardí Rám Káyath, which was written about the time of the decline of the empire (the precise year is not mentioned), there is no such Sirkár as that of Sahár, and we find it succeeded by Islampúr (called by Aurangzeb, Islamábád) Muttra (Mathurá), containing 12 Mahâls. There is also the new Sirkar of Biana Hindaun formed according to the same work, containing 29 Mahâls, while the Sirkár of Agra is reduced to the mere Havelí round the city.

II.—*SUBA ILAHÁBÁS.*

SIRKÁR ILAHÁBÁS.

الهاباس با حويلي	1 *Ilahábás bá Havelí.*	سکندرپور	6 *Sikandarpúr*
بهدوي	2 *Bhadoí.*	کنتت	7 *Kantit.*
جلال آباد	3 *Jalálábád.*	کیواي	8 *Kewáí.*
سورانو	4 *Soránw.*	کهیراگڑه	9 *Khairágaṛh.*
سنگرور	5 *Singraur.*	مہه	10 *Mah.*
		هادي آباس	11 *Hádíábás.*

This Sirkár is said to contain only **11** Mahál̇s, though Jalálábád is reckoned as 4. They are divided among the three Dastúrs of Ilahábás, Bhadoí, and Jalálábád.

The Parganahs now no longer extant are Numbers **1**, **3**, **5**, and **11**.

1.—Ilahábás.—The name of the fort and Parganah were subsequently, according to the Chár Gulshan and several other authorities, changed by Shah Jahán to Ilahábád, as the termination of *bás* was presumed to savour too much of Hinduism.* The Parganah is now known by the name of Chail, which is itself a place of some antiquity, as it is mentioned in the "Latáif-i Ashrafí."—See Harbong ka Raj.

3.—Jalálábád, or Jalálábás, is the name of Arail, which was imposed on it by Akbar, in commemoration of his own title of Jalálu'd-dín.—See note to Harbong ka Raj.

During the time of the Nawwáb Wazír's Government, Arail was included in Sirkár Tarhár,† and is so mentioned in the

* It is far more probable that the name Ilahábád was the original name as imposed by the Musulmans, and that the final syllable "bád," which they did not understand the meaning of, was changed by the lower orders to "bás," as it is to this day always pronounced "Ilahbás" by them."—B.

† Sirkár Tarhár appears to have occasionally varied its bounds. It seems at one

Schedule of Revenues given in the "Appendix to the 5th Report." It is strange that we find this Parganah, which forms a separate Dastúr, intervening between the Parganahs which form the Dastúr of Havelí Ilahábás. The position of Bara would point it out as a component part of Jalálábád, but, for the considerations given in the article Ghora, I have recorded it in that Sirkár. There is no measurement to guide us in this case, but the Revenue yielded is so small—being 7,37,220 Dams, with the small contingent of only 10 Sawárs and 400 Infantry—that it does not admit of the addition of Bara.

5.—Singraur is the old name of Nawábganj. Singraur is a very ancient place, and is spoken of in the "Rámáyana," as Sringavera.* The town of Singraur is still extant on the left bank of the Ganges, a few miles above Allahábád.

11.—Hadíábás was the name of the Parganah now called Jhúsí.—See Harbong ka Raj.

The new Parganahs are—

اريل 1 *Arail.*		تپه کون 5 *Tappah Kon.*
نواب‌گنج 2 *Nawábganj.*		تپه چوراسي 6 *Tappah Chaurásí.*
جهوسي 3 *Jhúsí.*		تپه اوپرودہ 7 *Tappah Upraudh.*
چايل 4 *Cháil.*		سکتيس‌گڑہ 8 *Saktísgaṛh.*

Arail.—See Jalálábád.

Nawábganj.—The Parganah of Singraur received its new name of Nawábganj from Nawáb Mansúr Ali Khan, who built a ganj and town near Singraur, which he established as the chief station of the Parganah.

time to have included part of Chanár. In the "Ahwál-i Súbaját," mentioned in the article Budhganga, Sirkár Tarhár is said to contain nine mahâls, amongst which are to be recognised Jalálábás and Chaukandí.

* Wilson, "Theatre of the Hindús," I. p. 300; "Rámáyana," I. i. 28; Carey and Marshman, Vol. III., p. 247.—E. *add.*

Jhúsí.—See Hadíábás.

Cháil is the old name of Ilahábás bá Havelí. The town of Cháil is situated in the centre of the Parganah.

Tappah Kon is a portion of Bhadoí, from which it was detached when Sakat Singh married the Maunas Raja's daughter, to whom it was given in dowry, and thenceforward became a Tappah of Kantit, to which it did not belong when the "Ín-i Akbarí" was written.

Tappah Chaurásí is a portion of Kantit. Probably but a very small portion of this Tappah was known in Akbar's time, but we have no measurement to guide us.

Saktísgaṛh. This, too, was in Kant t, and was also, perhaps, mostly unknown. The country was previously called Kolana, in consequence of the residence of the Kols in this neighbourhood; and it was not till Raja Sakat Singh of Kantit destroyed their stronghold, and built Saktísgaṛh on its site, that the Tappah obtained its new name.

The Talúka of Mirzapúr Chauhárí, which is in the Allahábád district, was formerly in the Parganah of Jalálpúr Bilkhar in Sirkár Manikpúr, the rest of which Sirkár is in Oudh. It has been included in Allahábád since the time of Raja Madárí Lál, Ámil.

Sirkár Karra.

اينچهي	1	*Enchhí.*
اتهربن	2	*Atharban.*
اياه ساه	3	*Ayáh Sáh.*
حويلي كرا	4	*Havelí Karrá.*
راري	5	*Rárí.*
بلده كرا	6	*Baldah Karrá.*
كراري	7	*Karárí.*
كوتله	8	*Kotilah.*
كونرا عرف كرسون	9	*Kuṅrá,* alias *Karsoṅ.*
فتح پور هسوا	10	*Fattihpúr Haswá.*
هتگانو	11	*Hatgánw.*
هسوا	12	*Haswá.*

This Sirkár has 12 Maháls comprised in one Dastúr.

The numbers which are obsolete are 1, 4, 5, 6, and 9.

1.—Enchhí.—This Parganah is now represented by Ghazípúr. The modern histories of India convey to us this information by calling the famous rebel Bhagwant, Khíchar, a Zamíndár of Parganah Enchhí (see further under Gházípúr). The village of Enchhí is still extant on the bank of the Jumna. The old fort, which is the theme of popular story, is not to be seen, but the people of the neighbourhood delight in telling a marvellous tale how Raja Palbhan Deo was slain in it, with all his family, by a demon called Brimha Dano; from which time it has been deserted; but the site is visited during the Dahsehra, when the superstitious villagers come from afar to make their annual offering at the shrine of the demon.

4 and 6.—Havelí Karrá and Baldah Karrá. The distinction has now been lost between them as separate Parganahs. They are both included in Parganah Karrá.

5.—Rárí has now been changed to Ekdalla, in which place Nawwáb Shuja'ud-daulah established his Tahsíldarí, but the Parganah retained its name of Rárí till the cession. The town of Ekdallah is on the Jumna, about two miles to the West of Rárí. Dhátah is also a Zillah of Rárí.

9.—Kúṅrá, *alias* Karson.—This is the old name of Mutaur, which it appears to have acquired from the course which the Jumna takes in this neighbourhood. The projecting patches of alluvial land which are formed near the banks of the river are called by the Zamíndárs Kunda, probably from their shape, which they might have conceived to bear some resemblance to a Kuṇḍa,* a vessel for kneading bread in; a platter. The Mauza of Kunda, or Kunra, still exists on the bank of the Jumna, at the North-Western angle of Parganah Mutaur.

* See "Dabistán," II. 79.—E. *add.*

The new Parganahs included within Sirkár Karrá are—

ایکدله 1 *Ekdallah.*	غازي پور 3 *Gházípúr.*
دهاته 2 *Dhátah.*	متور 4 *Mutaur.*

Ekdallah.—See Rárí.

Dhátah.—In consequence of the disturbances which arose between two parties of Kurmís in this neighbourhood, the Nawwáb Wazír was compelled to establish a separate Zillahdar in this place, in the year 1197 Faslí, and about fifty villages taken from Rárí were placed under his charge. Since the cession, Dhátah has been considered a separate Parganah.

Gházípúr may be considered to have been established as a Parganah in lieu of Enchhí, from the time that Bhagwant Rai Khíchar built his fort here, and killed Ján Nisár Khan, the general of Muhammad Shah; of which a full account is given in the "Taríkh-i Muzaffarí," and most other modern histories of India. The "Hadíkatu'l Akálím" assures us that he retained possession of the entire Sirkár of Kora for several years, and was only at last subdued by the strenuous efforts of Nawwáb Sa'ádat Khan. Dunyápat, the worthy descendant of the family, opposed our government shortly after its accession, but did not lose much by it, as he was subsequently rewarded with a handsome pension. After the death of Bhagwant Rai, the Amil continued to reside in Gházípúr; but Gházípúr was not recognized as a Parganah till the commencement of our administration in 1803, when for the two first settlements it is recorded as Enchhí, 'urf Gházípúr.

Mutaur.—Nawwáb 'Abdu's Samad Khan, who performed a conspicuous part in the time of Aurangzeb, was presented by that monarch with the Jagír of Kuṅra. Shortly after his investiture, he built a fort and dug a handsome tank at Mutaur, which succeeded to the importance of Kuṅra; but Wásilbáḳí papers are in existence which show that the Parganah retained its old name to as late a period as 1188 F.S.

Sirkár Korá.

جاجمو 1 *Jájmau.*	کوتیا 5 *Kútiá.*
کورا 2 *Korá.*	گنیر 6 *Gunír.*
گهاتمپور 3 *Ghátampúr.*	کیرتپور کنانده 7 *Kíratpúr-Kanánda.*
مجهاون 4 *Majháwan.*	

محسنپور 8 *Muhsanpúr.*

This Sirkár has eight Mahâls, divided into the three Dastúrs of Korá, Kútiá, and Jájmau.

The missing Parganahs are numbers 4, 7 and 8.

4.—Majháwan, which is reported as a separate Parganah during our first settlements, is now included in Jájmau and Saṛh-Salímpúr. The town of Majháwan is still extant on the Pandu river, in the South Eastern angle of Jájmau.

7.—Kíratpúr-Kanánda is the old name of Parganah Bindkí.

8.—Muhsanpúr, called also Rawatpúr Muhsanpúr, is now included in Saṛh-Salímpúr, and is reported as a Parganah in our first settlements. The village of Muhsanpúr is still extant near the Arind river, in the Southern angle of Saṛh-Salímpúr. Its position is pointed out in the interesting letters of Naunít Rai, who styles himself "one of the Amlá of Muhsanpúr, a Parganah of Kora."

The new Parganahs are—

تپه جار 1 *Tappah Jár.*	بندکی 2 *Bindkí.*

ساره سلیمپور 3 *Sarh-Salímpúr.*

Tappah Jár belonged to Parganah Kora, from which the Wásilbáḳís show it to have been separated from the year 1180 F.S.

Bindkí.—See Kíratpúr Kanánda.

Saṛh-Salímpúr.—This Parganah has been formed from Muhsanpúr and Majháwan. There have been several intermediate changes in the size and constitution of all these Parganahs, owing to the various jurisdictions to which Sirkár Korá has been subject; but there is no occasion to record them here, as they have no concern with the comparison on which we are at present engaged.

Sirkár Kálinjar.

اوگاسي	1	*Ugásí.*	رسن	6	*Rasan.*
اجيگڑه	2	*Ajaigaṛh.*	كالنجر	7	*Kálinjar.*
سهوندا	3	*Sihondá.*	كهنده	8	*Khandeh.*
سموني	4	*Simauní.*	مهوبا	9	*Mahobá.*
شاديپور	5	*Shádípúr.*	مودها	10	*Maudhá.*

This Sirkár contains eleven Mahals, Kálinjar ba Havelí being counted as two. It comprises a single Dastúr.

The Parganahs either extinct or beyond British Bundelkhand are the following—Numbers 2, 5, 6, 7 and 9.

2.—Ajaigaṛh.—This Parganah lies to the South of Kálinjar. The fort is garrisoned by British troops.

5.—Shádípúr is the old name of Parganah Pailání. The large village of Shádípúr is still extant on the bank of the Jumna. When the Bundelás built their fort in Pailání, and made it the residence of their Tehsíldar, the name of Pailání was gradually substituted for Shádípúr. From the Sanad appointing Bhím Sen Chaudharí of the Parganah, it appears that in the year 1121 F.S. the name of the Parganah was Shadípúr Pailaní.

6.—Rasan is the old name of Parganah Badausa. The town still exists about seven miles to the South of Badausa. Tieffenthaler gives us a clue to this Mahál by telling us it is seven miles N.E. from Kálinjar.

7.—Kálinjar ba Havelí.—See Badausa.

9.—Mahoba is in the Jalaun territory.

The new Parganahs are—

بدوسا	1 *Badausá.*	باندہ	3 *Bándah.*
پیلاني	2 *Pailáni.*	سميرپور	4 *Sumerpúr.*

Badausá.—See Rasan. This was established by the Bundelas as the site of a new Tehsíldarí, in consequence of Harbans Raí, a Raghubansí Rajput, being in independent occupation of Rasan. The greater portion of Kálinjar is included in Badausá.

Pailání.—See Shádípúr.

Bándah was originally a portion of Sihonda, but has been considered a separate Parganah since the time that Raja Gumán Singh, the Bundela, took up his residence here. Briggs, in his translation of Ferishta, says that Sikandar Lodi penetrated to Bándah,—which would imply that the town was older than the time of Akbar; but "Bándah" has been written by mistake for "Bándhú," or "Bándúgaṛh," as is evident from the "Táríkh-i Afághana," where a more detailed account of this difficult and unsuccessful expedition is given.

Sumerpúr was originally a portion of Maudha.

Sirkár Bhatghora.

See Ghora in a separate article.

Sirkár Jaunpúr.

الديمو	1 *Aldímau.*	جونپور	6 *Jaunpúr.*
انگلي	2 *Anglí.*	چاندي پور برهر	7 *Chándípúr-Birhar.*
بهتري	3 *Bhitarí.*	چاندہ	8 *Chánda.*
بهدنو	4 *Bhadanw.*	چريا كوت	9 *Chiria Kot.*
تلهني	5 *Tilhaní.*		

چکیسر	10	*Chakesar.*	قریات سویتهه	25	*Kariát Soethah.*
خرید	11	*Kharíd.*	کوله	26	*Kolah.*
خاص پور تانده	12	*Khášpúr Tánda.*	گهسوا	27	*Ghiswá.*
خانپور	13	*Khánpúr.*	گهوسي	28	*Ghosí.*
دیوگانو	14	*Deogánw.*	گڑواره	29	*Garwárah.*
راري	15	*Rárí.*	کوڑیا	30	*Kauriá.*
سجهولي	16	*Sajhaulí.*	گوپالپور	31	*Gopálpúr.*
سکندرپور	17	*Sikandarpúr.*	کراکٹ	32	*Karákaṭ.*
سگري	18	*Sagrí.*	مریاهو	33	*Mariáhú.*
سرهرپور	19	*Surharpúr.*	محمدآباد	34	*Muhammad-ábád.*
شادیاباد	20	*Shádíábád.*	مونگرا	35	*Múngrá.*
ظفرآباد	21	*Zafarábád.*	مجهورا	36	*Majhaurá.*
قریات متو	22	*Kariát Mittú.*	مو	37	*Mau.*
قریات دوست پور	23	*Kariát Dostpúr.*	نظام آباد	38	*Nizámábád.*
قریات میندہ	24	*Kariát Menda.*	نیگون	39	*Negún.*
			نتهوپور	40	*Nathúpúr.*

The Sirkár of Jaunpúr has 41 Mahála, Jaunpúr bá Havelí being considered as 2; and 2 Dastúrs, which in size are very disproportionate—one comprising only the 2 Mahála of Múngrá and Garwárah.

This large Sirkár has descended to us in a more perfect shape than any other which we have to examine. Exclusive of those within the Oudh territory, namely, Aldemau, Chandípúr Birhar, Chándah, Khášpúr, Tándah, Sajhaulí, Surharpúr, and Majhaura, the only Mahála not now extant within British jurisdiction are Numbers 10, 25, 26, and 39.

10.—Chakesar was in existence till the late settlement; when, under the arrangements then made for improving Parganah Boundaries, it was included, with a newly-formed Parganah, called Surajpúr, in Ghosí; where the two united still constitute the Tappah of Chakesar.

25.—Ḳariát Soethah is now included in Parganah Anglí of Jaunpúr. It formed one of the Talúkas of Bakhshíat, which was broken up and distributed amongst several Parganahs at the late settlement.

26.—Kolah is the old name of Kol Aṣlá.

29.—Negún is included in the modern Parganah of Máhul.

The new Parganahs are also very few.

ماهل 1 *Máhul.*	گذارا 4 *Guzára.*
اترولي 2 *Atraulí.*	كول اصلا 5 *Kol Aṣlá.*
بادشاهپور 3 *Pádsháhpúr.*	سنگرامو 6 *Singrámau.*

Máhul is formed from Parganah Negún, and parts of Anglí and Surharpúr. Although at the time of the cession Máhul is entered in the registers as one of the four portions into which the province of Gorakhpur was divided, it received no higher denomination than that of Talúka, which has been changed by us into Parganah. In the middle of the last century, two Sayyids of the name of Sher Jehan and Shamshád Jehan, acquired possession of Negún and parts of Surharpúr and Anglí, as well as a few villages of Jaunpúr, and taking up their abode in Máhul Khás, gave their usurpations the name of Talúka Máhul. The town of Negún is now known as Ḳasba Khas, on the Eastern border of Máhul.

Atraulí was a Parganah formed a short time previous to the cession out of Balwant Singh's acquisitions from Tilhaní, but was originally included in Kauria. It has now been included again in Tilhaní, and the Parganah goes by the united name of Atraulí Tilhaní.

Badshahpúr is another name for Múngra. The Parganah is also known by the name of Múngra Badshahpúr.

Guẕára.—Tappa Guẕára, including Bhainsa, was originally in Karakat; and Sultánípúr, which is in the western angle of Bhainsa, is a Talúka of Katehar.

Kol Aṣlá is the modern name of Kolah, derived from the village of Aṣlá, which was formerly the site of a Tehsíldarí Katcherry.

Singramau is a Talúka of Parganah Chanda, the rest of which is in Oudh.

See further under Sirkár.

Sirkár Gházípúr.

بليا 1 *Balliá.*

پچوتر 2 *Pachotar.*

بلهابانس 3 *Bilhábáns.*

بهرياباد 4 *Bahriábád.*

برايچ 5 *Baráich.*

چونسا 6 *Chaunsá.*

دهمه 7 *Dihmah.*

سيدپور نمدي 8 *Sayyidpúr Namdí.*

ظهورآباد 9 *Zahúrábád.*

غازي پور 10 *Gházípúr.*

قريات پلي 11 *Ḳariát Palí.*

كوپا چيت 12 *Kopá Chít.*

گڑها 13 *Gaṛhá.*

كرينده 14 *Karendah.*

لكهنيسر 15 *Lakhnesar.*

مدن بنارس 16 *Madan Benares.*

محمدآباد پرهاباري 17 *Muhammadábád Parhábárí.*

Sirkár Gházípúr comprises only one Dastúr. It has nineteen Maháls, Havelí Gházípúr and Muhammadábád Parhábárí being each counted as two.

This Sirkár, after all the ill-written names have been verified, is also found to have descended to us in a perfect shape. In the above list we miss now only the following Parganahs, viz., 5, 6, 11, and 16.

5.—Baráich.—This Parganah has caused more doubt than any other; but I believe it to be represented by the present Mauza Baráich in the Mahál of Bhataulí on the Gangí Naddí, which falls into the Ganges between Karendah and Gházípúr. Baráich is a small Parganah, containing only 2,000 Bíghas, and the place I have assigned to it is not altogether an improbable one for a Parganah.

6.—Chaunsá is in the Shahábád district in the Bengal Presidency, noted for being the place where two battles have been fought which have decided the fate of India, viz., that of Buxar in 1765, and the one which led to the expulsion of Humáyún from India; in describing which, by the way, some translator or compiler, whose name I do not now remember, has been led into a ludicrous mistake. In translating Ni'amat ullah, he says Humáyún when retreating from Chaunsá across the Ganges recognized Nizám, his water-carrier, by a strong smell of *musk*, whereas the original merely informs us that he saved the emperor by seating him on an inflated mashak (a leather water bag).

11.—Ḳariát Palí was included at the late revision of boundaries in Muhammadábád Parhábárí.

16.—Madan Benares is the old name of Zamania.

There is only one new Parganah in this Sirkár.

زمانیه 1 *Zamánia* (now generally written and pronounced زمنیه).—B.

Zamánia has succeeded to Madan Benares. During the decline of the empire we find it combined with Gházípúr in giving name to the Sirkár. Thus, "Sirkár Ghazípúr Zamánia, 17 Maháls."

Doába is a Tappah of Parganah Fattihpúr Bahia, which is recorded as being in the Sirkár of Rohtas, and the Súbah of

Bihár. It has only been noticed here because its position would appear to point it out as a portion of this Sirkár.

Sirkár Benáres.

افراد 1 *Afrád.*	پندره 4 *Pandrah.*
بنارس با حويلي 2 *Benares bá Havelí.*	كسوار 5 *Kaswár.*
بيالسي 3 *Byálisí.*	كتيهر 6 *Katehar.*
	هرهوا 7 *Harhúá.*

This Sirkár, which comprises only one Dastúr, has 8 Mahàls, Havelí Benáres being counted as two.

The extinct Parganahs are Numbers 1, 2, and 7.

1.—Afrád (*i.e.* pieces) consisted chiefly, as the name would imply, of several detached Mauzas in different Parganahs, and had therefore, perhaps, no determinate boundary. There are Mauzas, for instance, in Katehar and in Kaswár, which are still recorded as having been once in Parganah Afrád. I have assigned to Afrád a position between Katehar, Kaswár, Benares, and Kola, but the greater portion has been taken from Kaswár, in which Afrád Khas is situated.

2.—Benares bá Havelí contained the modern Parganahs of Lotha, Dihát Amánat, and Sheopúr, the two former to the South, and the latter to the North, of the little river Barná.

7.—Harhúá is the old name of Aṭhgáṅw. The village of Harhúá is still extant in this Parganah, on the high road from Benares to Jaunpúr. It is said that there were formerly only eight villages in Harhúá, and hence the name of Aṭhgáṅw.

The new Parganahs within Sirkár Benares are—

جالهوپور 1 *Jálhúpúr.*	مجهوا 4 *Majhowá.*
شيوپور 2 *Sheopúr.*	اٹهگانو 5 *Aṭhgáṅw.*
لوتها 3 *Lothá.*	دهات امانت 6 *Dihát Amánat.*

Jálhúpúr is a Talúka detached from Katehar by Raja Balwant Singh.

Sheopúr was originally in Havelí Benares, from which it was detached by Raja Chait Singh.

Lothá is a portion of Havelí Benares. It was subsequently included in Dihát Amánat; but is now considered a separate Talúka.

Majhowá is a Talúka of Kaswár.

Aṭhgáṅw.—See Harhúá.

Dihát Amánat was originally in Havelí. It comprehends the city of Benares and the tract immediately around it.

It is strange that in the Benares Mahals, Bhúínhárs are not mentioned as Zamíndárs by Abu'l Fazl. The difference between them and Brahmans does not appear to have been fully comprehended; for that it did not exist two hundred and fifty years ago, it is difficult to suppose.

SIRKÁR CHANÁR.

اهيرواره	1 *Ahirwárah*	قريات اين روي اب	8 *Ḳariát in rúi áb.*
بهويلي	2 *Bhúelí.*	مجهواره	9 *Mujhwára.*
بڑهول	3 *Barhaul.*	مهايچ	10 *Maháich.*
تانده	4 *Tánda.*	مهواري	11 *Mahwárí.*
چنار با حويلي	5 *Chanár bá Havelí.*	موئي	12 *Mawaí.*
دهوس	6 *Dhús.*	نروں	13 *Narwan.*
رالہوپور	7 *Rálhúpúr**	هنوا	14 *Hanwá.*

There is only one Dastúr in Chanár, comprising 14 Mahals;

* This is entered in the best copies as Rághúpúr راگهوپور. It is certainly now written and pronounced Ráhúpúr.

though the Parganah tables concur in saying there are only 13 Maháls. The two last are omitted from most of the copies of the "A'ín-i Akbarí," but are requisite to complete the Sirkár. In those copies, indeed, in which they are entered they are nearly illegible.* It is evident from history that this part of the country was but little known, and we must therefore allow for some error and confusion.

We retain the names of all the Parganahs in the above list, except those of Numbers 1, 4, 8, and 14.

1.—Ahírwárah, so called after the original Zamíndárs of those parts, has now been corrupted and abbreviated into Ahrora.

4.—Tándah is the old name of Parganah Barah. The Mauzas of Tándah Kalán and Tándah Khúrd still exist on the right bank of the Ganges, at a short distance from each other.

8.—Ḳariát ín rú-i áb (*i.e.* the villages on this side of the water) is now known as Ḳariát Síkhar.

14.—Hanwá.—See Bhagwat.

The new Parganahs, of which we find no mention in the "A'ín-i Akbarí" as belonging to this Sirkár, are—

برہ 1 *Barah.*	بھگوت 3 *Bhagwat.*
قریات سیکھر 2 *Ḳariát Síkhar.*	اھرورہ 4 *Ahrorah.*

کیرامنگرور 5 *Kera Mangror.*

Barah.—See Tándah.

Ḳariát Síkhar.—See Ḳariát ín rú-i áb. It does not appear when the name of the Parganah was changed, or for what particular reason the strange title of Ḳariát ín rú-i áb was given originally to this Parganah.

Bhagwat.—This Parganah, previous to the conquest effected

* In them, moreover, they are entered as being entirely Siyarghal, or rent-free, which may be perhaps the cause why they are omitted in so many copies.

by the Gautams, was held by Jamí'at Khan, Gaharwár, whose defence of the fort of Patíta is a favorite theme with the people. The old name of this Parganah was Hanoa, which was extinct before the time of Jamí'at Khan, when it was known only as Bhagwat.

Ahrorah.—As much of this Parganah as was known in Akbar's time was called Ahírwára.

Kera Mangror.—Mangror is entered in the "Áín-i Akbarí" as a Parganah of Sirkár Rohtas, Súba Behar, and in the later periods of the empire, as belonging to Sirkár Shahabad, which is now the district of Shahabad in Southern Behar, under the Lieutenant-Governor of the Lower Provinces.

SÚBA OUDH.

Sirkár Gorakhpúr.

اترولا	1 *Atraulá.*	رسولپور غوث	11 *Rasúlpúr Ghaus*
انہولا	2 *Anhaulá.*	رام گڑہ گوري	12 *Rámgaṛh Gaurí.*
بنایکٹ پور	3 *Bináikpúr.*	گورکھہ پور	13 *Gorakhpúr.*
بمہني پاره	4 *Bamhnípárah.*	کٹہلا	14 *Kaṭihlá.*
بہاواپاره	5 *Bháwápára.*	رہلاپاره	15 *Rihlápára.*
تل پور	6 *Tilpúr.*	مہولي	16 *Mahaulí.*
چلوپاره	7 *Chilúpára.*	مندوا	17 *Mandwá.*
دھریاپاره	8 *Dhuriápára.*	منڈله	18 *Mandla.*
دھیواپاره کہانا	9 *Dhewapára Kuhání.*	رتن پور مگہر	19 *Ratanpúr Maghar.*
رہلي	10 *Rihlí.*		

This Sirkár forms only one Dastúr, containing twenty-four Maháls; Gorakhpúr bá Havelí, Rasúlpúr Ghaus, Ratanpúr

Maghar, Binaikpúr, and Rámgaṛh Gaurí, being each reckoned two Mahāls.

This is a difficult Sirkár to restore, and, even after verifying all the illegible names, we have in the list of extinct or foreign Parganahs numbers 1, 4, 9, 10, 12, 14, 15, 17 and 18.

1.—Atraulá is in Oudh.

4.—Bamhnípárah.—This is the South-Eastern angle of Parganah Nawwábganj, which we gave up to Oudh in 1817.

9.—Dhewápára Kuhána is the old name of Salímpúr Majhaulí, Shahjahánpúr, and Sidhoa Jobna, which were part of the great Majhaulí Raj. In some old writings the name of the Mahál is entered Nawápár Kuhánά Dhewápár. The popular name of the village of Salímpúr is Nawápár; (Buchanan, "Eastern India," Vol. II. p. 361, says Nagar); and the Parganah would have been restored as Kuhánά Nawápár, had it not been for the alphabetical arrangement requiring an initial *d* in this place. The name Dhewápár is now nearly extinct. Nawápár is common.

10.—Rihlí is the Northern and Western part of Nawwábganj, ceded to Oudh.

12.—Rámgaṛh Gaurí—We are assisted in this name by being told it is on the Raptí. It is the old name of Balrámpúr, in Oudh.

14.—Katihlá is the old name of North Bansí. When the Katihlá Raja was defeated and slain by the Bansí Raja, the old name of the Parganah became extinct. Bansí, South of the Raptí, was called Ratanpúr, which Mahál is combined with Maghar in the "Áín-i Akbarí."

15.—Rihlápára.—At the suggestion of Mr. Reade, the late collector, I have entered this Parganah as the old name of Aurangabad Nagar; but I confess some doubt on the subject, for all the copies give distinctly Kihlápára, and the substitution of the *r* for *k* displaces the alphabetical order usually preserved.

17.—Mandwá is the ancient name of Bastí.

18.—Mandla.—No trace can be had of this Mahál. Mr. Reade suggests that it may be the old name of Amorha; but Amorha is itself an old Parganah, and is included, in the "Áín-i Akbarí," in Sirkár Oudh.

The new Parganahs in Sirkár Gorakhpúr are—

سليمپور مجهولي	1	*Salímpúr Majhaulí.*
سدهوا جوبنا	2	*Sidhuá Jubná*
شاهجهان پور	3	*Sháhjahánpúr*
سلهٹ	4	*Silheṭ.*
منصورنگر بسي	5	*Mansúrnagar Bastí.*
اورنگاباد نگر	6	*Aurangábád Nagar.*

Salímpúr Majhaulí.—This is a portion of the old Parganah of Dhewápára Kuháná.

Sidhuá Jubná.—Ditto.

Sháhjahánpúr.—Ditto. I have somewhere seen it mentioned that these Parganahs were in Sáran, but the statement appears to rest on no authority.

Silhet was detached from Parganah Havelí about the year 1633 by the Majhaulí Raja, and was recovered by the Satásí Raja about fifty years afterwards. It has since this period been rated as a separate Parganah.

Mansúrnagar Bastí.—See Mandwá.

Aurangábád Nagar.—See Rihlápára.

Sirkár Oudh.

Amoṛha (Amoḍh) is the only Parganah of this Sirkár in British territory. It is in the Dastúr of Havelí Oudh.

Sirkár Khairábád.

The only portion of this Sirkár in our jurisdiction is Khákatmau, which probably included also the modern Parganah of

Paramnagar, although the local officers are unanimous in representing that Paramnagar was originally a portion of Shamsabad. Kháhatmau is in the Dastúr of Palí.

III.—*SUBA DEHLI.*

Sirkár Dehli.

اسلام آباد پاکل	1 *Islámábád Pákal.*	جلال آباد	19 *Jalálábád.*
اڈه	2 *Aḍh.*	جلال پور بروت	20 *Jalálpúr Baraut.*
پاني پت	3 *Pánípat.*	حويلي قديمي	21 *Havelí Ḳadímí*
پالم	4 *Pálam.*	حويلي جديدي	22 *Havelí Jadídí.*
برن	5 *Baran.*	دارالملک دهلي	23 *Dáru'lmulk Dehlí.*
باغپت	6 *Bághpat.*	داسنه	24 *Dásnah.*
پلول	7 *Palwal.*	دادري طاها	25 *Dádrí Táhá.*
برناوه	8 *Barnáwah.*	دنکور	26 *Dankaur.*
پوتهه	9 *Púth.*	روهتک	27 *Rohtak.*
دوبلدهن بيري	10 *Dobaldhan Berí*	سونيپت	28 *Sonípat.*
تلپت	11 *Tilpat.*	سفيدون	29 *Safídún.*
تانده پهوگانه	12 *Tánda Phúgánah.*	سيکندرآباد	30 *Sikandarábád.*
تل بيگم پور	13 *Tilbegampúr.*	سراوه	31 *Saráwah.*
جهجهر	14 *Jhajhar.*	سينته	32 *Sentah.*
جهارسه	15 *Jhársa.*	سيانه	33 *Siánah.*
جيور	16 *Jewar.*	شکرپور	34 *Shakarpúr.*
جهنجهانه	17 *Jhinjhána.*	کرنال	35 *Karnál.*
چهپرولي	18 *Chhaprauli.*	گنور	36 *Ganaur.*

گڑہ مکتیسر 37 *Garhmuktesar.*		لوني 43 *Loni.*
کتانہ 38 *Kutánah.*		میرتھہ 44 *Mírath.*
کاندھلہ 39 *Kándhlah.*		ماندوتھي 45 *Mándauthí.*
کاسنہ 40 *Kásnah.*		مسعودآباد 46 *Masa'údábád.*
کھرکھودہ 41 *Kharkhauda.*		هستناپور 47 *Hastinápúr.*
گنگیرو 42 *Gangerú.*		هاپور 48 *Hápúr.*

The Sirkár of Dehli consists of forty-eight Mahåls, divided into the seven Dastúrs of Havelí, Pánípat, Baran, Mírath, Jhajhar, Rohtak and Palwal.

This large Sirkár has descended to us in a very perfect form. Excluding the foreign Parganahs of Jhajhar, Dádrí Táhá, and Safídún, we miss in the above list only numbers 11, 12, 21, 22, 23, 32 and 46.

11.—Tilpat.—The greater part of Tilpat was included by Nawwáb Faríd Khan, a nobleman of Jehangír's time, in Farídabad, now a Parganah of the Balamgaṛh Jagír; but the town of Tilpat is included in the Southern Parganah of Dehli. It is a place of great antiquity, and is one of the five towns demanded by the Pánḍava brothers, the refusal of which was one of the causes of the "Great War." Authorities do not concur in the names of the five towns, but Tilaprastha (Tilpat) is generally one ("Wilson's Hindu Theatre," Vol. II. 337).

12.—Tánda Phúgánah.—This Mahál is generally written Tánda Bhagwán, and we are led to the identification of it by learning that it has a fort on the Jumna. There is a Tánda on the Jumna, and the Parganah attached to it, although it consisted of only four or five villages, was considered a separate one till the late revision of Parganah boundaries, when it was aborbed into Chhapraulí. Tánda and Phúgánah continued to form one Parganah till the time of the Maráṭhas, when Phúgánah was separated, and given in Jagír to Nijábat Ali Khan, Bahraich.

21, 22, and 23.—The three next Mahâls comprise the environs of Dehli, and the names sufficiently point out their relative position.

32.—Sentah is the old name for Parganah Agauta in Bulandshahr. It would have been difficult to identify this, had not Agautá been called a Chauhán Battísá, or commune of thirty-two villages of Chauháns. There are now not very many Chauhán Zamíndárs here, and as the Parganah of Sentah is represented in the "Áín-i Akbarí" to have Chauhán Zamíndárs, I was disposed to think that it was meant for Somna in Aligaṛh; and in many copies the word more resembles Somna than Sentah; but this local designation of the Battísá establishes that Sentah is the proper reading. Sentah, moreover, is considered in the neighbourhood to have been the chief town of the Parganah.

46.—Masa'údábád.—The old traveller, Ibn Batuta, has helped me to verify this, as he mentions at p. 110, that he stayed at Masa'údábád on his way from Hánsi to Dehli, reaching it after two days, and receiving there a complimentary visit from the minister. Now, Masa'údábád on that road is the old name of Najafgaṛh, which is a late erection, being built by Ghulám Husain Khan, and called after his patron Najaf Khan. Masa'údábád had, however, previously changed its name to Afzalpúr, which was built by Chaudharí Afzal Khan in the time of Alamgír. The old mud fort of Masa'údábád is still to be traced about a mile to the East of Najafgaṛh.

The new Parganahs included within Sirkár Dehli are the following:

دادري	1 *Dádrí.*	بهادرگڑه	5 *Bahádurgaṛh.*
اگوتا	2 *Agautá.*	سنبهالكا	6 *Sambhálká.*
فريدآباد	3 *Farídábád.*	كتهور	7 *Kithor.*
پالي	4 *Pálí.*	گوره	8 *Gorah.*

اجراره 9 *Ujrárah.*	دهلي پرگنه جنوب 11 *Dehlí S.*
دهلي پرگنه شمال 10 *Dehlí N.*	*Parganah.*
Parganah.	بهواني 12 *Bhiwání.*

Dádrí was not formed into a Parganah till 1231 Faslí, when Rao Dargahí Singh of Chatahrá, a Bhaṭṭi Gújar, who was appointed Faujdár of Dásna, Sikandarábád, etc., under Najíbu'd daulah, took advantage of the disorganization of the country during the decline of the Moghul monarchy, to obtain possession of certain villages of Sikandarábád, Kásna, Tilbegampúr, and Dásna, of which 70, including Dádrí Khás, were acquired from Kásna alone; and his family were retained in possession on a Mukarrarí Jama when our rule commenced. The Talúka lapsed to Government on the death of Rao Ajít Singh.

Agautá has succeeded to Sentah, which still exists as a village on the right bank of the Kálí Naddí, about four miles West from Agautá. Before the establishment of the name of Agautá, the Parganah was known by the name of Sentah Partábpúr: Partábpúr being a large village in the Northern angle of the Parganah.

Farídábád has been explained under Tilpat. The Parganah is in the Balamgaṛh jurisdiction. Balamgaṛh is itself only a modern fort, having been built by a Ját, called Balú, *alias* Bilram, a relative of Súrajmal of Bhartpúr, within the boundary of his own village of Sahípúr, in Tilpat.

Pálí is included within the area of Pákal, or Islámábád Pákal, as it is called in the "Ā'ín-i Akbarí." The united Parganah is now generally known as Pálí Pákal.

Bahádurgaṛh.—This Parganah is composed of about an equal number of villages from Pálam and Jhajhar, which the Emperor Muhammad Shah, in A.D. 1728, bestowed upon Bahádur Khan, Beloch, who built the fort of Bahádurgaṛh within the area of Sharifábád, a village of Pálam. Bahádurgaṛh is still held in Jagír.

Sambhálká was detached from Pánípat in the fourth year of the reign of Farúkhsír, and held as a royal demesne for his own private expenses. It continued subsequently to be held as a Jagír, and when on the death of the last incumbent it escheated to Government, it was again included in Pánípat.

The Parganah of Sambhálká was more usually known amongst the natives as Farrukhnagar.

Kithor was originally a Tappah of Sirává, from which it was detached in the time of Najíb Khan by Jít Singh Gújar, the founder of the Gújar family of Príchatgaṛh.

Gorah was formerly in Hápúr. The Gújar Raja of Paríchatgaṛh, Nain Singh, formed it into a separate Tappah.

Ujrárah was also detached from Hápúr. Fattih Ali Khan, the ancestor of Khwájah Basant, in whose Jáidád it was comprised, formed it into a separate Tappah, and it now, small as it is, ranks as a Parganah.

Dehli, Northern Parganah. This Parganah was formed in the year 1838. It includes part of Havelí and Pálam. The Parganah of Báwana, or Boana, which is included in it, was itself a new formation from villages of Palam, which Aurangzeb detached for the purpose of paying certain expenses of the Royal household, and as they comprised fifty-two villages (Báwan) the tract, as well as the chief town within it, was designated Báwana.

Dehli, Southern Parganah, was also formed in 1838. It includes a part of Palam, Havelí, and Masa'údábád, and a few villages of Tilpat. Najafgaṛh, which has been already mentioned, was subsequently formed from Masa'údábád, and included, besides the villages of that Parganah, twenty-four villages from Jhajhar, and twelve from Jharsa. The two modern Parganahs of Dehli, therefore, comprise the old Parganahs of Havelí Ḳadím, Havelí Jadíd, Dáru'l-mulk Dehli, Pálam and Masa'údábád. The three first were subsequently united into the Parganah of Havelí, and when Palam was afterwards added, it was known as one Parganah under the name of Havelí Palam. This name it retained under our administration, till the new division took place, which has been particularized.

Bhiwání was originally a portion of Dádrí Táhá.

SIRKÁR REWÁRÍ.

باول	1 *Báwal.*	رتاي جتاي	6 *Ratáí Jatáí.*
پاتودهي	2 *Pátaudhí.*	كوٹ قاسم علي	7 *Koṭ ḲásimAlí.*
بهوره	3 *Bhorah.*	گهلوت	8 *Gahlot.*
تاورو	4 *Táoru.*	كوهانه	9 *Kohánah.*
ريواري با حويلي	5 *Rewárí ba Havelí.*	سهنه	10 *Suhnah.*
		نيمرانه	11 *Nímránah.*

This Sirkár contains eleven Maháls, divided into four Dastúrs. Only four of these Maháls are in British territory, and as they retain their ancient names, they require no notice, except to observe that Sonah (Suhnah) is out of its place in the alphabetical list, and might therefore give rise to some suspicion of its correctness, but Abu'l Fazl mentions it also in the text, in such a manner as to enable us to identify it as the Sonah which still gives name to a large Parganah.

The only new Parganah within this Sirkár is,

شاهجهانپور 1 *Sháhjahánpúr.*

This small Parganah, containing only eight villages, is isolated from the rest of Gurgáṅw by territory belonging to the Tijara Raja. The popular story runs that it was formed by Sháhjahán, in compliance with a vow which he made when he was retiring in anger from his father. He met with favorable omens in this neighbourhood, and vowed, if they were accomplished, he would raise a town and constitute it the head of a Parganah.* The new Parganah was taken chiefly from Lohana, and in the "Aḥwál-i Súbaját" the Parganah is entered as Lohana, 'urf Shahjahánpúr Chaubára.

Sirkár Sahháránpúr.

اندري	1 *Indrí.*	چرتهاول	15 *Charthâwal.*
امبهته	2 *Ambihtah.*	حويلي	16 *Havelí.*
بدهانه	3 *Budhánah.*	ديوبند	17 *Deoband.*
بدولي	4 *Bidaulí.*	رام پور	18 *Rámpúr.*
بهت كنجاور	5 *Bahat Kanjáwar.*	رورکي	19 *Rúrkí.*
بهوگپور	6 *Bhogpúr.*	راي پور تاتار	20 *RaípúrTátár*
پور چپار	7 *Púr Chapár.*	سيكري بهوكرهيري	21 *Síkrí Bhukarherí.*
بهومه	8 *Bhúmah.*	سرساوه	22 *Sarsáwah.*
بگهرا	9 *Baghrá.*	سروت	23 *Sarwat.*
بنت	10 *Banat.*	سردهنه	24 *Sirdhanah.*
تهانه بهيم	11 *Thána Bhím.*	سنبل هيرا	25 *Sambalherá.*
تغلق پور	12 *Tughlakpúr.*	سورن پلري	26 *Soran Palrí.*
جوراسي	13 *Jaurásí.*	كهاتولي	27 *Khátaulí.*
جولي	14 *Jaulí.*		

* Another origin is ascribed to Sháhjahánpúr, which is perhaps more probable than the one mentioned above. Ihlád Sing, a relative of the Chauhán chief of Nímranah, was held in high consideration in the Court of Sháhjahán, and obtained leave from the Emperor to rebuild Lohana, which had been destroyed in consequence of its harbouring notorious robbers. Ihlád Sing called the new town after the name of his patron.

If Sháhjahán was himself the founder, and ever occupied the spot, it was most probably visited by him when his army was encamped at Belochpúra in A.D. 1623, and was in possession of the passes of the Mewat Hills.

كهودي 28 *Khúdi.*	مظفرآباد 32 *Muzaffarábád.*
كيرانه 29 *Kairána.*	منگلور 33 *Manglaur.*
گنگوه 30 *Gangoh.*	ملهي پور 34 *Malhaipúr.*
لكهنوتي 31 *Lakhnauti.*	نكور 35 *Nakor.*

نانوته 36 *Nánautah.*

This Sirkár contains thirty-six Mahâls, divided into four Dastúrs—Deoband, Kairána, Sirdhanah and Indrí. The last is on the right bank of the Jumna, and is not within British jurisdiction, its villages being distributed amongst the Sikh lords of Jagadrí, Ladhoa, Thanesar, etc. etc., while Indrí Khas is included within the Kanjpúra Nawwáb's 'Iláka.*

The Parganahs in the above list, which are no longer recorded as such, are Numbers 5, 6, 8, 11, 12, 16, 20, 23, 28, 31, and 36.

5.—Bahat Kanjáwar was in the time of Sháhjahán converted into Sultánpúr Bahat. In the time of Najíbu'd daulah, Bahat and Sultánpúr became separate Parganahs, and have so remained since. The Mauzá of Kanjáwar is in Muzaffarábád.

6.—Bhogpúr is on the Ganges, and the Parganah comprised the Eastern portion of Jawálapúr, including Hardwár. Bernoulli states, indeed, that Bhogpúr is another name for Hardwár, but this is, I believe, not correct. At any rate there is a Bhogpúr about ten miles South of Hardwár, which is no doubt the head town of the old Parganah of the same name.

8.—Bhúmah has only within the last ten years lost its name as a separate Parganah. Baisúmhah has now succeeded to it, but Bhúmah is still a very respectable town, and in Akbar's time is spoken of as chief of the Barha Sadat villages.

11.—Thánah Bhím.—All the copies concur in writing it Bhím, which is the name derived from the founder of the town,

* This territory is now part of the Ambála district of the Panjáb. As much of Súba Dehli as lies to the West of the Jumná is also under the Government of the Panjáb.—B.

who is represented to have been a mace-bearer to the king. In later times, the place has been known by the name of Bhaun, so called from a famous Bhaun (Bhawan), or temple, of Deví, near the town.

12.—Tughlaḳpúr.—The Timúrnáma mentions that Tughlaḳpúr, where the Indians opposed the conqueror in naval combat, is situated twenty-five koss above Ferozpúr (in Hastinápúr). Tughlaḳpúr still exists in Núrnagar, and was formerly the chief town of a Parganah, to which Núrnagar has now succeeded.

16.—Havelí has become the Parganah of Sahâranpúr.

20.—Raipúr Tátár.—Within the area of Faizábád, in the old Parganah of Raipúr Tátár, Shahjahán built his palace of Bádsháh Mahal, and changed the name of the Parganah to Faizábád. The Mauza of Raipúr still exists on the banks of the canal.

23.—Sarwat is the old name of Parganah Muzaffarnagar, and the village of that name still exists about a mile N.E. from Muzaffarnagar.

28.—Khúdí is the old name of Shikárpúr, which is not yet altogether dropped by the common people. It is said to be the name of the Raja who founded the town.

31.—Lakhnautí.—The greater part of Lakhnautí has within the last three years been thrown into Gangoh, and part into Bidaulí.

36.—Nánautah.—The greater part of Nánautah was at the same time thrown into Gangoh, and parts of it into Rámpúr and Thánah Bhaun.

The new Parganahs present a long list, chiefly owing to the changes effected by Najíbu'd daulah and the Gujar Talúkdars.

کهیري	1	*Kherí.*	جوالاپور	5	*Jawálápúr.*
سکرودہ	2	*Sakraudah.*	فیض آباد	6	*Faizábád.*
نورنگر	3	*Núrnagar.*	پتیہر	7	*Patehar.*
جمال گڑہ	4	*Jamálgaṛh.*	جہانگیرآباد	9	*Jahángírábád.*

سلطان‌پور 9 *Sultánpúr.*		تهانه بهون 12 *Thánah Bhaun.*	
مظفرنگر 10 *Muzaffarnagar.*		شاملي 13 *Shámlí.*	
کاتهه 11 *Káthah.*		جانسته 14 *Jánsath.*	

بیسومها 15 *Baisúmhá.*

Kherí.—This was formed into a separate Tappa in the time of Zabit Khan, through the influence of the Púndír Zamíndárs, who are Rajputs converted to Mahomedanism. It was formerly a part of Rurkí.

Sakraudah was originally in Jaurási, and formed into a Parganah by Rao Kutbu'd dín, in the time of Zabit Khan.

Núrnagar is called after the famous Núr Jahán Begam, who took up her abode there for some time. Núrnagar, or rather Govardhanpúr—by which name the Parganah is now more generally known, since Núrnagar Khas has been transferred to Sahâranpúr—has succeeded to the old Parganah of Tughlakpúr.

Jamálgaṛh, or Jamál Kherah, was originally in Gangoh, and was formed into a Parganah by Jamál Khan, the Amil of Gangoh in the time of Najíb Khan. By late arrangements Jamálgaṛh has been thrown into Nakor.

Jawálápúr.—This is the new name of the greater part of Parganah Bhogpúr. In records written previous to the British accession, the Parganah is denominated Bhogpúr, 'urf Jawálápúr, but is now known only as Jawálápúr.

Faizábád.—See Raipúr. In the time of Shahjahán Faizábád became a place of great importance, and gave name to an entire Sirkár. In the "Hakíkat-i Jama," by Hardí Rám Káyeth, it is said to contain 24 Mahâls; while Sahâranpúr was reduced to 17.

Patehar.—Anwar Khan, an Afghan of Patehar, in the time of Najíb Khan, established this as a separate Tappa, or Parganah. It was a part of Bahat Kanjáwar.

Jahángírábád was originally in Ráipúr Tátár, and was formed into a Parganah at the same time as Faizábád.

Sultánpúr.—See Bahat Kanjáwar.

Muzaffarnagar.—See Sarwat.

Káthah was originally included in Deoband, from which it was detached by Najíb Khan, who was compelled to establish a separate collector in Badgáṅw, on account of the turbulence of the Zamíndárs of the neighbourhood.

Thána Bhaun.—See Thana Bhím.

Shamlí was originally a portion of Kairana. We learn from the collection of letters of Nand Ram Mukhlis* that a village in Kairana, called Mahomedpúr Zunárdar, was included in the Jagír bestowed by Jehángír upon Hakím Muḳarrab Khan. A Chela of the Nawwáb's (Shaman) built a ganj, or market, in the village, and after otherwise improving it, called it after his own name, Shamlí. The Jagír remained in the family of Muḳarrab Khan till it was resumed by Bahadur Shah, who also formed Shamlí, with a few other villages, into a separate Tappa, which in course of time has acquired the title of a Parganah.

Jánsath is now included with Jaulí in one Parganah, called Jaulí Jánsath. It was formed into a separate Parganah in the time of Farrukhsír, through the influence of the famous ministers Hasan Ali Khan and Abdullah Khan.—See Barha Sadat.

Baisúmhá has attained the dignity of a Parganah, by the town of Baisúmhá having been one of the head-quarters of the Gújar confederacy in the time of Raja Gulab Sing. The old Parganah of Bhúmhá is included in it.

Sirkár Hissar Feroza.

اگروهه	1	*Agrohah.*	بهنگيوال	4	*Bhangiwál.*
اهروني	2	*Ahroni.*	پونيان	5	*Púnián.*
اتهكهيره	3	*Aṭhkhera.*	بهارنگي	6	*Bhárangi.*

* I doubt if this is the correct authority. I think it is in the "Jahángír-náma."—E. *add.*

بروالا	7 *Barwálá.*	سرسا	17 *Sirsá.*
بهتو	8 *Bahtú.*	شيورام	18 *Sheorám.*
بروا	9 *Birwá.*	سيدهمكه	19 *Sídhmukh.*
بهتنير	10 *Bhaṭner.*	سيواني	20 *Sewání.*
توهانه	11 *Tohánah.*	شانزده دهات	21 *Shánzdah Dihát*
توشام	12 *Toshám.*	فتح آباد	22 *Fattihábád.*
جيند	13 *Jínd.*	گوهانه	23 *Gohána.*
جمال پور	14 *Jamálpúr.*	كهانڈه	24 *Khánda.*
حصار	15 *Hissár.*	ميهم	25 *Mihim.*
دهاترت	16 *Dhátrat.*	هانسي	26 *Hánsí.*

There are twenty-seven Mahâls in this Sirkâr (Hissâr being counted as two), and four Dastúrs—Havelí Hissâr Feroza, Gohâna, Míhim, and Sirsâ. There are, however, several Parganahs excluded from the Dastúr list, for what reason does not appear.

Of these Mahâls, those which do not retain their old name in our territory are numbers 2, 3, 4, 5, 6, 8, 9, 10, 11, 13, 14, 16, 18, 19, 21 and 24.

2.—Ahroní is partly in Ratiyah and partly in Fattihabad. The historians of Timúr point out its position, by saying it is on the road from Fattihabad to Tohana. The place was burnt and pillaged by the conqueror, merely because the inhabitants did not come out to pay their respects (مراسم استقبال بجا نياوردند). Ahroní has now reverted to its original name of Ahírwan; whereas in Sirkár Chanár, Ahírwara, which derived its name from the same tribe, has now been corrupted into Ahrora.

3.—Aṭhkhera is under the Raja of Jhínd, and is known now by the name of Kasonan.*

* Aṭhkherá is in the Parganah of Mirwâna, in Patiâla, and Kasonan or Kasun is four miles off, in Jhínd.—E. *add.*

4.—Bhangíwál, so called from the tribe of Játs which inhabited it, is the old name of Darbah, in which place the officers of the Raja of Bíkaner built a fort, and thenceforward it came to be considered the chief town of a Parganah.

5.—Púníán, called also after a tribe of Játs, is in Bíkaner, but is now included in another Parganah.

6.—Bharangí is also in Bíkaner.

8.—Bahtú is partly in Fattihabad and partly in Darbah. Bahtú Khas is in the former Parganah.

9.—Birwá is the protected Sikh territory.

10.—Bhaṭner.—The old town of Bhaṭner is in Bíkaner, but part of the Parganah is now included in Raniyah.

13.—Jhínd gives name to one of the protected Sikh states.

14.—Jamálpúr is included in the late cession from Patiála. The old town of Jamálpúr is near Tohana.

16.—Dhátrat was in Jhínd, but is now in British territory.

18.—Sheorám is in the Bagar country, in the Jagír of Nawwáb Amír Khan. Two-thirds of Sheorám are now in Loharú, the remainder in Dadrí.

19.—Sídhmukh is in Bíkaner.

21.—Shánzdah Dihát, or Ḳariát (*i.e.* the sixteen villages), is included in Ratiyah Tohana amongst the late cessions from Patiála. The Ilaka is generally known by the name of Garhí Rao Ahmad. I have heard it stated that it is in Jhínd, and not in Ratiyah Tohana.

24.—Khanda is in Jhínd.

The modern Parganahs are—

بہل 1 *Bahal.*	رتیہ 3 *Ratiyah.*
رانیہ 2 *Ràniyah.*	دربہ 4 *Darbah.*

Bahal was originally in Sewání, from which it was separated in A.D. 1758 by Jawání Singh, a Rajput, who built a mud fort at Bahal, and maintained possession of a few neighbouring villages.

Ràniyah was in Bhaṭner. The old name of the village was Rajabpúr. The Rání of Rao Anúp Sing, Rathor, took up her abode here, built a mud fort, and changed the name of Rajabpúr to Ràniyah, which it has since retained.

Ratiyah is now included in one Parganah with Tohana. It was composed of villages from Ahroní, Jamalpúr, and Shánzdah Ḳariát.

Darbah.—See Bhangíwal.

Some considerations respecting the Western boundary of this Sirkár have been offered in the article Bhaṭṭíáná.

Sirkár Sambhal.

امروهه	1	*Amrohah.*	جهالو	15	*Jhálú.*
اعظم پور	2	*A'zampúr.*	جدوار	16	*Jadwár.*
اسلام پور بهرو	3	*Islámpúr Bahrú.*	حويلي سنبهل	17	*Havelí Sambhal.*
اوجهاري	4	*Ujhárí.*	ديوره	18	*Deorah.*
اكبرآباد	5	*Akbarábád.*	ڈهاكه	19	*Dhákah.*
اسلام پور درگو	6	*Islámpúr Dargú.*	دبهارسي	20	*Dabhársí.*
اسلام آباد	7	*Islámábád.*	دوديله	21	*Dúdilah.*
بجنور	8	*Bijnor.*	راجپور	22	*Rájpúr.*
بچهراون	9	*Bachhráon.*	رجب پور	23	*Rajabpúr.*
بروي	10	*Biroí.*	سنبهل	24	*Sambhal.*
بساره	11	*Bisárah.*	سيوهارا	25	*Seohárá.*
چاندپور	12	*Chándpúr.*	سرسي	26	*Sirsí.*
جلال آباد	13	*Jalálábád.*	سهسپور	27	*Sahaspúr.*
چوپله	14	*Chauplah.*	سرساوه	28	*Sirsáwah.*

شيركوت 29 *Sherkot.*

شاهي 30 *Sháhí.*

كندركهي 31 *Kundarkhí.*

كيرتپور 32 *Kíratpúr.*

كچهه 33 *Kachh.*

گندور 34 *Gandaur.*

كابر 35 *Kábar.*

گنور 36 *Ganaur.*

كهانكري 37 *Khánkarí.*

لكهنور 38 *Lakhnor.*

لسوه 39 *Liswah.*

مغلپور 40 *Moghalpúr.*

مجهوله 41 *Mujhaulah.*

منداور 42 *Mandáwar.*

نگينه 43 *Nagínah.*

نهتور 44 *Nahtaur.*

نيودهنه 45 *Neodhanah.*

نرولي 46 *Neraulí.*

هتمنه 47 *Hatmanah.*

This Sirkár contains forty-seven Maháls and three Dastúrs—Chándpúr, Sambhal, and Lakhnor.

The missing Parganahs exceed those of any other Sirkár, amounting to more than half of the entire number, viz., Numbers 3, 4, 6, 7, 9, 10, 11, 13, 14, 16, 17, 18, 19, 20, 21, 22, 23, 33, 34, 36, 37, 38, 39, 41, 45 and 47.

3.—Islámpúr Bahrú is now contained in Thákurdwara. The town is still is existence. The Jesuit Tieffenthaler leads us to this information by giving its name correctly, which cannot be said of any other copy which I have consulted. Salímpúr Bahrú, by which name it is now more usually known, has the credit in the neighbourhood of having been the head town of a Parganah.

4.—Ujhárí has only lately been absorbed into Hasanpúr.

6.—Islámpúr Dargú is now included in Bachhráon, one of the Parganahs of Hasanpúr. In the revenue accounts of 1166 F.S. it is recorded as Islámpúr Dargú, shamil Bachhráon.

7.—Islámábád.—This Parganah was retained till the year 1209 F.S., and was absorbed into Nagína at the commencement of our administration. The village of Islámábád is abandoned.

9.—Bachhráon is now in Hasanpúr.

10.—Biroí is in the Rámpúr Jagír.

11.—Bisára is also in Rámpúr.

13.—Jalálábád.—This is the old name of the Parganah of Najíbábád. The town of Jalálábád is still in a flourishing condition.

14.—Chauplah is the name of Morádábád. Rustam Khan, Dekkání, founded Rustamnagar in this Parganah, which in the time of Farrukhsír was changed to Morádábád, and the name of Chauplah became extinct. Sirkarah was also formed from Chauplah.

16.—Jadwár remained as a Parganah till 1153 F.S. Part of Jadwár is included in Bahjoí, and part in Islámnagar and Asadpúr. The village of Jadwár is in the Southern angle of Bahjoí.

17.—Havelí Sambhal is included in the Parganah of Sambhal.

18.—Deorah is the old name of Seondarah, and the village of Deorah is about five miles to the south of Seondarah. Seondarah was occupied by a Tehsíldárí Katcherry before the time of the Patháns, but the name of Deorah was preserved till the cession, and began to be called Deorah Seondárah only in the Second Settlement. The name of Deorah is derived from the Dor Rajputs, who were the Zamíndárs of the Parganah.

19.—Dhákah, } These two Parganahs have also lately been
20.—Dabhársí, } absorbed into Hasanpúr—the intermixture of villages being so great as to render this arrangement convenient.

21.—Dúdílah is in Rámpúr.

22.—Rájpúr is also in Rámpúr.

23.—Rajabpúr is now included within Amroha, and is held chiefly in rent-free tenure. The village of Rajabpúr is about ten miles to the S. W. of Amroha.

33.—Kachh is the old name of Parganah Tigrí, now included in Hasanpúr.

34.—Gandaur is the old name of Bashta, which is now combined with Asampúr. Bashta, indeed, used frequently to be called Gandaur Bashta.

36.—Ganaur.—The town of Ganaur still exists in Asadpúr. The greater portion of the Parganah is in Asadpúr—a part is in Rajpúra.

37.—Khánkarí is in Rámpúr.

38.—Lakhnor is also in Rámpúr, and is more generally known as Shahábád on the Rámganga. This, being the seat of the old Katherya Rajas, may be considered the capital of the country, and is so spoken of by the ancient historians. As the place is now but little known, transcribers generally confound this town with the more celebrated Lakhnau, and English translators have not been free from the same error. Bernoulli gives Lakhnor as a separate Sirkár, and alters its dimensions greatly from those given to the Dastúr in the "Á'ín-i Akbarí."

39.—Liswah is included in Rámpúr.

In these, and other similar instances I have not attempted to verify the names. It was sufficient for me to find these Maháls in the Dastúr of Lakhnor to make me include them in the Rámpúr territory. All that we have of Lakhnor is easily identifiable, and as nothing is wanting to complete our boundary, and as it will be observed from the Map there is ample space in Rámpúr, we may fairly presume the missing Maháls to be in that Jagír.

41.—Majhaulah.—The greater part of Majhaulah is now included in Bahjoí—part is in Rájpúra and Islámnagar. Majhaulah Khás is still a large village, about five miles to the East of Bahjoí.

45.—Neodhanah is the old name of Islámnagar. Here again we are assisted by Tieffenthaler, when all Persian copies fail. He calls it Neudhana (Bernoulli I. 133). The two instances mentioned in this Sirkár are almost the only ones where I have found this enterprising Jesuit traveller of any use; and it is strange it should be so in Sambhal, for his list of that Sirkár is the worst he has given, being filled with names which have either been ill-transcribed, or fabricated. It does not appear that he ever visited these parts himself, but sent natives to pick up information. The name of Neodhanah being given correctly we are able to connect it with the traditions of the Gautam Rajputs of Núrpúr in Islámnagar.

47.—Hatmaná has gone to form part of Richhá and Chaumahalá. Hatmaná Khás is in Chaumahalá.

The following list shows the new Parganahs of Sirkár Sambhal—

دارانگر	1	*Dáránagar.*	سیونداره	9	*Seondárah.*
نجیب آباد	2	*Najíbábád.*	تهاکر دوارا	10	*Thákurdwárá.*
رجپوره	3	*Rajpúrah.*	تاراپور	11	*Tárápúr.*
اسدپور	4	*Asadpúr.*	رچها	12	*Richhá.*
بهجوئي	5	*Bahjoí.*	حسن پور	13	*Hasanpúr.*
اسلام نگر	6	*Islámnagar.*	چومحله	14	*Chaumahalah.*
سرکره	7	*Sirkarah.*	باشته	15	*Báshtah.*
مرادآباد	8	*Murádábád.*	افضل گڑه	16	*Afzalgaṛh.*

Dáránagar.—This Parganah was formed from portions of Bijnor and Jhálú by Ráo Jet Singh, Ját, in the time of Muhammad Shah.

Najíbábád.—The town of Najíbábád was founded by Najíb Khan, within the Parganah of Jalálábád, the name of which has now been superseded by Najíbábád.

Rajpúrah is formed from parts of Majhaulah and Ganaur.

Asadpúr is formed from parts of Ganaur and Jadwár.

Bahjoí comprises parts of Majhaulah and Jadwár.

Islámnagar is formed from Neodhanah and parts of Jadwár

and Majhaulah. The name of Islámnagar is said to have been given to Neodhanah by Rustám Khan, Dekkání.

Sirkarah was originally a portion of Chauplah, but it does not appear when it was established as a separate Parganah.

Murádábád (Morádábád).—See Chauplah.

Seondárah.—See Deorah.

Thákurdwárá.—This Parganah was established about the time of Muhammad Shah, by Katheryas, of the name of Mahandí Singh and Surjan Singh. The greater part of Thákurdwárá has been obtained from Islámpúr Bahrú. The Northern portion was originally within the jurisdiction of Kamáon. In Thákurdwárá are also included about fifty villages of Seohara, and nearly 150 of Moghalpúr.

Tárápúr.—This Parganah has been restored to the Eastern side of the Ganges.—See Budhganga.

Richhá.—Part of this Parganah is formed from Hatmaná; but the greater portion we may presume to have been under the jurisdiction of Kamáon. Part is also taken from Baláí.

Hasanpúr* was originally in Dháká; but now comprises six old Parganahs—Kachh, Bachhraon, Dháka, Dabhársí, Ujharí, and Islámpúr Dargú.

Chaumaḥlá is a modern Parganah, formed by Nawwáb Faizullah Khan from the four Parganahs of Sirsawa, Richhá, Kabar and Rudrpúr. The old Parganah of Hatmaná, which was extinct before this Parganah was formed, is for the most part comprised in the Northern angle of Chaumaḥlá.

Báshtah is the new name of Gandaur.

Afzalgaṛh.—I have restored Afzalgaṛh to Sherkoṭ and Nagína,

* An Altamgha grant, said to have been given by Shahjahán in favor of Mubariz Khan, ancestor of the present Zamíndárs of Hussainpúr, places Hussainpúr in Havelí Sambhal, but it is not easy to conceive how that Parganah could have penetrated through Dhaka and Ujharí. The grant, therefore (it was resumed by the Pathans), must either be a forgery, or Sambhal is alluded to rather as a Sirkár than a Parganah.

as far as the Ramganga. The rest has been concluded to have been within hill jurisdiction; though it is usual to consider the whole of Afzalgaṛh and Rehar as belonging to Sherkoṭ.—See Des.

Sirkár Badáon.

اجاؤن	1 *Ajáon.*	بلئي	7 *Balaí.*
انوله	2 *Aoṅla.*	سہسوان	8 *Saheswán.*
بداون با حويلي	3 *Badáon bá Havelí.*	ستاسي مندیا	9 *Satásí Mundiyá.*
بريلي	4 *Barelí.*	سنیا	10 *Suneyá.*
برسير	5 *Barsír.*	کانت	11 *Kánt.*
پونر	6 *Púnar.*	کوت سالباهن	12 *Koṭ Sálbáhan.*
		گوله	13 *Gola.*

This Sirkár consists of thirteen Mahála, which constitute only one Dastúr.

The extinct Mahála are numbers 5, 6, 7, 9, 11 and 13.

5.—Barsír is the old name of the Parganah of Saraulí, which it retained till the time of the cession. The village of Barsír, which is still inhabited, is about six miles to the South of Saraulí, and is on the borders of Aoṅla. Saraulí is still called by the common people Barsír.

6.—Púnar.—Púnar Khas is a deserted Mauzah in Púranpúr Sabna. Púnar forms only a small portion of the present Parganah of Púranpúr Sabna, since it is represented as containing only 5,749 Bíghas.

7.—Balaí.*—When Mírak Ján, Amil in the reign of Shahjahán, founded Jehanabad, the name of the Parganah was changed from Balaí to Jehanabad, in honor of his new town. The Khera of Balaí is still to be seen near Jehanabad.

* Also called Bilahtí.—E. *add.*

9.—Satásí Mundiyá.—This is a very difficult Parganah to restore. It assumes all kinds of shapes in the various copies,—Mokudduma Sunas, Munala Sunasun, Sunanut Mudrusa; and Bernoulli increases our doubts by calling it Mandia, *surnommée* Saniassi. If it had not been for the present existence of the Parganah of Satásí, on which word many of the changes seem to ring, we might not have been able to identify it at all; and even now it might be considered open to suspicion, because the Mahál is said to have Tagá Zamíndárs, whereas Satásí has none; but then neither is there a single Tagá Zamíndárí throughout the district of Badáon, and scarcely any in its immediate neighbourhood,—so that this is no real objection. It only shows that the Tagá Zamíndárís have become extinct. The ruins of Satásí are said to be near Bírkhera, four miles to the South of Bisaulí, and Mundiya is a large inhabited village about six miles to the North West of Bisaulí. The position of the two chief towns renders it very probable that they were combined into a single Parganah. I was at one time disposed to call it Satásí Manaunah, because Manaunah was the seat of a Native Collector at one period, but its close proximity to Aoṅla, which is itself the head town of a Mahál, would not admit of this construction. Guided by all these considerations, I believe I have not been wrong in calling the Mahál Satásí Mundiyá.

11.—Kánt.—This was originally the name of Shahjahánpúr. When that city was founded by Bahadur Khan, in the time of Farrukhsír, the name of Kánt became extinct. Tilhar is also formed from Kánt.—See Bachhal.

13.—Gola has been considered in its alphabetical place.

The new Parganahs within this Sirkár present a list of unusual length.

بسولي	1 *Bisaulí.*	بليا	3 *Baleá.*
كرور	2 *Karor.*	جهان آباد	4 *Jahánábád.*

نواب گنج	5	*Nawwábganj.*	جلال پور	15	*Jalálpúr.*
بیسلپور	6	*Bísalpúr.*	کهیرا بجهیرا	16	*Kherá Bajherá.*
شاهجهان پور	7	*Sháhjahánpúr.*	کتره	17	*Katra.*
پیلی بهیت	8	*Pílíbhít.*	پواین	18	*Pawáín.*
سلیم پور	9	*Salímpúr.*	بڑاگانو	19	*Baŕágánw.*
اوجهانی	10	*Ujhání.*	پورن پور سبنا	20	*Púranpúr Sabná.*
فرید پور	11	*Farídpúr.*	کهوتار	21	*Khotár.*
اوسهت	12	*Usahat.*	فیض پور بدریا	22	*Faizpúr Badariyá*
تلهر	13	*Tilhar.*	ندهپور	23	*Nidhpúr.*
نگوهی	14	*Nigohí.*	اولای	24	*Aúláí.*

Bisaulí is a portion of Satásí Mundiyá, the remainder being represented by the present Satásí, with the addition of Tappa Rotah of Badáon.

There seems no reason why Bisaulí should not have given name to a Parganah in Akbar's time. It is an old town, and though it is indebted for its chief improvements to the generous and gallant Nawwáb Dúndí Khan, who lies buried, as well as many other members of Ali Mahomed's family, at Bisaulí, yet it had been for a long time previous a place of some consideration. In our eyes it possesses interest as being the first cantonment of a British brigade in Rohilkhand.

Karor is included in the old Mahál of Bareilly.

Baleá was originally in Saneyah, but subsequently in Karor, from which it was detached at the fourth settlement.

Jehánábád.—See Balyí.

Nawwábganj was originally a portion of Bareilly. It was not formed into a new Parganah till the fourth Settlement, when a Tehsíldárí was established at Nawwábganj. The town was founded on the lands of Bichorea, in the time of Nawwáb Asofud-Daulah.

Bísalpúr was also in Bareilly. It derives its name from an Ahír of the name of Bísú, who lived in the time of Sháhjahán.

Sháhjahánpúr.—See Kánt.

Pílíbhít, or as much of it as was known in the time of Akbar, was taken from Balyí.

Salímpúr was originally in Saneyah.

U'jhání.—From the old settlement records we find that when the Parganah of Badáon was annexed at the fourth settlement to Bareilly, it comprised seven Tappas. U'jhání comprises Tappa Jalálpúr, and is separated from its parent Parganah, along nearly its entire Eastern border, by the river Sot.* The

* Sot means any small stream in Rohilkhand.—E. *add.*

The same word is applied in Gorakhpúr and the adjoining parts of Bahár to the old bed of a river in which there is only a small quantity of water with a feeble current. It is probably derived from the old Hindi स्रुत, which means trickling, oozing; connected with which are the Marathi words स्रव, स्राव, स्रवण, etc., with a similar meaning, from the Sanskrit स्रु to trickle, ooze.—B.

This river is now generally known by the name of Yárwafádár, or "the faithful friend." As various origins are ascribed to this name, it may be as well to subjoin the correct one from the "Táríkh-i Muhammad Sháhí" of Khushhál Chand:—

از مضافات سنبهل بصوب سرکار بدایون لواي فیروزي انتماے متوجه گشتند دراثناء راه بسبب اشتداد تموز و کمیابي آب روزے چند تکالیف بر عسکر منصور میگذشت وعالمے بعلت حرارت وامراض دیگر مبتلا گشته وپیکر عنصري حضرت جهانبانے نیزتکسل کشیده بارے درین راه سوت نام دریاچه که پیچ درپیچ میگذرد همراهي رکاب سعادت نموده در هر منزل خدمت آبداري لشکر بحر پیکر بجا آورده ابروے تمام حاصل نموده حضرت آنرا بنام یار وفادار موسوم فرموده چون چشمه سلسبیل شهره افاق فرمودند

On their way from Sambhal to Badáon His Majesty and the royal army suffered much from heat and thirst, till they came to the little river Sot, which kept winding in and out by the side of the road, and supplied them with water at each stage. In gratitude for this service His Majesty honored it with the name of "Yár-i Wafádár," or "the faithful friend."—B.

village of Jalálpúr is about ten miles to the South of U'jhání. When Rohilkhand was under the administration of the Patháns, U'jhání became the residence of Nawwáb 'Abdullah, and thenceforward it was constituted the chief town of a Parganah.

Farídpúr was originally a portion of Bareilly, known as Tappah Khalílpúr.

U'shat, or U'sahat, includes Tappah Mahánagar of Badáon.

Tilhar was a portion of Kánt. When Raja Tilok Chand, a Bachhal Rajput, founded Tilhar, he included the surrounding villages in a new Parganah.

Nigohí.—This Parganah was originally a portion of Golah.

Jalálpúr was a portion of Bareilly, known as Tappah Charkholah. The town of Jalálpúr was founded by Raj Deo, son of Raja Básdeo, Katherya, who lived subsequent to the time of Akbar.

Kherá Bajherá.—This Parganah was formed from portions of the new Parganahs of Jalálpúr, Tilhar, and Farídpúr, and therefore was originally a part of Kánt and Bareilly.

Katrah was originally in Bareilly, and it was not till the time of Kamál zaí Khan, the son of Muzaffar Khan, who in the time of 'Alamgír founded Katrah on the ruins of the old town of Míránpúr, that the Parganah of Míránpúr Katrah was established.

Pawáín was originally a portion of Golah. The old village of Golah is in this Parganah, and is still inhabited.

Barágáṅw was also a part of Golah.

Púranpúr Sabná.—Púranpúr is the chief town of the Parganah. Sabná, which was taken by the Rohillas from the Dotí Ilaka, which has been carried away by the Sardah.

Parganah Púranpúr is formed from parts of Golah and Púnar, and the village of Púranpúr was in the former Parganah. The portion near the Sardah was not known in Akbar's time, and has therefore been excluded from the map.

Khotár was originally a portion of Golah, but the greater

part has been excluded from the map for the reasons stated under Golah.

Faizpúr Badariya was originally included in Saheswán.

Nidhpúr was a portion of Badáon.

Aúlái was also a portion of Badáon.—See Budganga for further information respecting the boundary of this Sirkár.

Dahsanní, دهسني दहसन्नी

Belonging to ten years. A book comprising the collections, accounts, registers, etc., of ten years.

The book generally known as the "Dahsanní Kitáb" was compiled in the year 1210 F.S. with the aid of the Ḳánúngoes, Mútawallís, and Ḳázís, assembled at Bareilly for the purpose of shewing the quantity of land in occupation of the Mafídárs. In it the name of the occupant was sometimes recorded, sometimes that of his son, and sometimes, when neither could be ascertained, the name of the original grantee.

The "Dahsanní Kitáb" was compiled with a view of meeting the changes of property attendant on two revolutions: the usurpation of the Rohilla Patans, and the conquest by the Nawwáb Wazír. Two columns of this register exhibit, under the description of Málik Ḳadím and Málik Hál, the ancient proprietor known to the Kánúngo records, and the more recent occupant.—"Bengal Revenue Sel." Vol. I. p. 319.

Da'wí, دعوي दावी

A demand; a claim; a plaint.

Ḍeoṛhá, ڈيوڑھا डेवढा

One-and-a-half; used to express interest in kind on grain, at the rate of 50 per cent.—See under Bengat.

Des, ديس देस

Literally country; a term applied in Rohilkhand to cleared

villages on the borders of the Taráí. In the Dekkan it is used much in the same way to signify a champaign country. See "Journal R.A.S." Vol. II. p. 212, and the Printed Glossary, under Des and Desh.

It will be seen by referring to the map of Dastúrs, that a large tract has been excluded from Sirkárs Sambhal and Badáon which might be supposed to have belonged to them. The fact is, that the districts on the Northern boundary either belonged to Kamáon, or were altogether unknown. Even those which are entered in the ancient Registers as being in Sirkár Kamáon, have no recorded area: such as Gadarpúr; Sahajgír, now Jaspúr; Dauázda Kot, now Kota; Chinkí, now Bilherí and Sabna; Bhuksár, now Kilpúrí and Rudarpúr. A great portion of this tract was included in the Chaurási Mál, of which the boundaries are given in the article Chaurásí. It was known also as the Naulakhí Mál;* but what portion of the present Des was included in, or excluded from it, is very doubtful. The idea of this tract ever yielding, as its name implies, nine lacs of rupees, is surprising to us who view it in its present state; and the name of Naulakhí Mál notwithstanding its avowed prosperity from the time of Akbar to Aurangzeb, particularly in the reigns of Tremal Chand and Báz Bahadur, may with some reason be deemed an exaggeration.

That these wild regions yielded, not long before our accession, more revenue than they do at present, is easily accounted for by the intestine troubles of Kamáon on the North, and of Rohilkhand on the South, which induced a large refugee population to resort to them for security; and that they have somewhat deteriorated of late years may be accounted for by our early assessments having been too high, which has necessitated present deductions; and by a withdrawal of some portion of its popula-

* I suspect this to be a corruption of Mahál, "estate," but not being personally acquainted with the district in question, I hesitate to alter it on a presumption.—B.

tion, which has been induced by the quiet and security which prevail in more favoured spots in the neighbourhood. Notwithstanding, however, their apparent deterioration, there can be little doubt that the Des is gradually encroaching upon the Taráí, and that there is prospect of further improvement by a judicious application of the abundant means of irrigation which nature has placed at our disposal.

We may be pretty certain that, even in the most palmy days of the Naulakhí Mál, the Des had not advanced into the Taráí so far as it now has, and that it was chiefly the Northern portion of the Taráí which was so prosperous under the rule of the Kamáon Rajas.

The fact of the Mahomedans not being able to extend their dominions to the foot of the hills, proves that the portion beyond the Des must have been nearly, if not quite, as inhospitable and insalubrious as it is now; for we cannot but conceive, that nothing would have protected it against aggression but a thick belt of jungle on its Southern border, which would have invested that tract with more terror than thousands of armed men. That there was no indisposition to acquire territory in that direction we know from two invasions of the time of Akbar, though he professed to have given a Sanad to the Kamáon Raja, Rudar Chand;* and that there was no strength in the Kamáonís to oppose them, if the Mahomedans had determined on it, we know from their appeals to Rustam Khan for assistance against the Katheryas; from the easy occupation which was effected for a short time by the Imperial general, 'Azmatullah Khan; from the purchased retreat of the Rohillas after their first invasion; and from the feeble resistance offered at a later period to the Gorkhas. Indeed, from the establishment of the Mahometan Empire down to the present time, we cannot contemplate any period when the Des, or the cleared plain, was

* Rudar Chand was the son of Kalyán Chand, who established Almorah as the capital. Rudarpúr was founded by Rudar Chand.

cultivated so far North as it now is. What the Taráí may have been in olden time it is not possible to say; but there are many symptoms of the tract having enjoyed a prosperous state long antecedent to the times of the Chand dynasty, when there was probably no Taráí, but what was marked by rich cultivation and populous abodes of man.

The occasional remains of ancient buildings and aqueducts assure us that it enjoyed an early period of prosperity, and the allusions in the drama of Sakuntalá to the scenery in the neighbourhood of the Málin, which falls into the Ganges near Bijnor, could scarcely have been applicable, had the features of the country not been greatly changed since the time that Kálidása wrote. We cannot be far wrong in supposing that it followed the fate and fortunes of the Gorakhpúr jungle, which from the Chinese Travels lately published, we know to have been the site of flourishing towns before the fourth century, and to have presented signs of growing deterioration in the seventh, when the Buddhist religion was approaching the period of its extermination in India. From this time to the occupation of the Mahomedans, the history of India is a complete blank, and scarcely can we extract a single fact from the voluminous Puranas, which, notwithstanding Colonel Vans Kennedy's emphatic denial, are now pretty well acknowledged to have been compiled at this comparatively late period.

In the Mahomedan histories the gloom is but little dispelled; but whenever we have allusions to these districts, we find every cause to suppose that the country was at least as wild as it is now. All beyond Amroha, Lakhnor, and Aonla is spoken of as a desert, which the Imperial troops fear to penetrate.

The most northerly position ever mentioned is that of Kábar, when it is marked as the boundary of cultivation at the close of the thirteenth century, in allusion to some revenue reforms introduced by Jalálu'd-dín, the first of the Khiljí dynasty. But, beyond this, there is not anywhere to be found the remotest allusion to crossing even the Ramganga, except when Feroz Shah is represented to have come for several successive years to Sambhal, to carry his inroads into the country of the Katheryas; and, in another instance, when we hear of an Imperial commander having pursued the Katheryas from Badáon to the hills, but not till they had endeavoured to secure their safety in the Jungles of Aonla, which are said by Abdu'l kádir Badáoní to extend round that place *no less than twenty-four Koss.** The exaggeration is evidently great, but if the statement is even partially true with respect to Aonla, we may be sure that the country under the hills was not in a much better condition.

We then come to the period alluded to at the beginning of this article, when, during a few years of the Moghul dynasty, the prosperity of the tract in some measure revived; but it was not long before it again declined, for even in the time of Muhammad Shah, we find the neighbourhood of Kashípúr thus described by Shaikh Yar Muhammad, an acute observer, who wrote an amusing account † of his embassy of condolence to the Kamáon Raja, Deví Chand, in A.H. 1130:

هر آينهٔ از صعوبت راه و رنج صعود و نزول گهاتي و شعب جبل و دامنگريهاي خار زار و كوه و بيابان چگويم اين همه شورش و مستي و جرش و خروش آغاز مشغولي كه شاهصاحب بملاحظه آن سير كوهستانرا تجويز فرموده بودند فرو نشست ليكن ذوق شوق بار و باد پيوست در عرصه چهار روز الموره كمايون منزل گاه شد *

* جنگل انوله كه تا بست و چهار كروه محافظ آنست

† This appears in a collection of letters entitled "Insha-i Kalandar," which has been printed in quarto in Calcutta, under the title of "Dasturu'l Insha." There are some interesting allusions in this work to the early progress of the British in India
I cannot find this in the India Office Library.—B.

Not long after this, we find the Jesuit Tieffenthaler thus describing the commencement of the route from Rudarpúr to Almorah—"On traverse d'abord *un desert long de 20 milles,* dans le quel on trouve des arbres extrêmement hauts," etc.

So that, after all, these districts do not present a very unfavourable contrast with their condition under the preceding administration. Enough, at any rate, has been adduced to shew, that there was no occasion to place the Des boundary of Badáon and Sambhal in a more advanced position than has been represented in the map.

Dhálá, دهالا धाला

Collections levied from Asámís to cover village expenses, generally at the rate of one anna to every rupee, or a seer of grain to every maund of actual produce.—Rohilkhand.

In the Central and Lower Doab and Saugor it is generally used in combination with Jama, as Jama-Dhala, and is synonymous with Dhár-báchh, *q.v.*

Dhárbáchh, دهارباچهه धारबाछ

Dhárbáchh means any even or general distribution; but the term is chiefly in use in the central portion of these provinces to denote an imperfect Pattídarí tenure, in which part of the village lands is held in common, and part in severalty; the profits of the land held in common being first appropriated to the payment of the Government revenue and village expenses; and the balance, whether under or above, being distributed among the proprietary body according to the extent of their respective holdings.

Dhárbáchh, in short, is synonymous with the meaning most generally given to Báchh in the Western Provinces, and Bíghádam in the Eastern: under which latter term the tenure has been properly described in the Printed Glossary.—See Dhála and Dhár.

Dhárdhúrá, دھاردھورہ धारधूरा

The boundary formed by a stream. The changes in the course of streams form a frequent subject of disputes, which are settled on this principle, especially in Rohilkhand, by determining where the deep stream flows; from *dhár*, or *dhála*, a stream, and *dhúrá*, a boundary.

The principle is very good where land is gained by gradual accretion, but is open to objection where the lost lands are capable of identification, and is opposed not only to the sensible maxim, "*Quod vis fluminis de tuo prædio detraxerit et vicino prædio attulerit, palam tuum remanet*"—but to Regulation XI. of 1825, which was based on the decisions of the Sudder Dewanny Adawlat, and the replies of the law officers, and which regulates the principle to be observed in such disputed cases, wherein a law of immemorial usage does not prevail. The consequence is, that even where the Dhárdhúrá law is acknowledged, the decisions in these extreme cases are not found to be uniform. Note to p. 251, Vol. III. of "Harington's Analysis;" and p. 146 of "Notices of Suits," by Maulavi Muhammad Bakar.

Dhonchá, دھونچا धोंचा

Four-and-a-half. The word is found in arithmetical tables of the multiplication of fractions, which are in constant use with our surveying Amíns, when reducing their linear measurements to Bíghas. The words used by them in fractional multiplication are—

Ḍeorhá,	डेवढा	ڈیوڑھا	$1\frac{1}{2}$
Dhamá,	धमा	دھما	$2\frac{1}{2}$
Hontá,	होंटा	ھونٹا	$3\frac{1}{2}$
Dhonchá,	धोंचा	دھونچا	$4\frac{1}{2}$
Ponchá,	पोंचा	پونچا	$5\frac{1}{2}$

Khonchá,	खोंचा	کھونچا	$6\frac{1}{2}$
Satonchá,	सतोंचा	ستونچا	$7\frac{1}{2}$

The size of the fields rarely requires Amíns to go beyond this.

Dhúr, دھور धूर

The twentieth part of a Biswa, and therefore equal to a Biswání. The word is little used in the Upper Provinces, except in Benares; but is common in Behar.

Dhurá, دھرا धुरा

A boundary. The word is used chiefly in the Doáb and Rohilkhand, and is sometimes pronounced Dhúra.—See Dhárdhúra.

Dhúrkaṭ, دھورکٹ धूरकट

An advance of rent paid by Asámís to Zamíndárs in the month of Jeth and Asarh.—Benares and E. Oudh.

Dhaurí, دھوری धौरी

A corruption of Adhaurí (from *adha*, half); a bull's hide cut into two pieces.—Dehli.

Dharah, دھره धरह

A percentage on all weighments of goods imported into the city. The word is peculiar to Núrpúr, in the Panjáb.

Dhaṛí, دھڑی धड़ी

A measure of five seers.

Dharaukí, دھروکی धरौकी

To ascertain by guess, in case of a dispute, as to the quantity of land in actual cultivation, on which to estimate the Jama.—Eastern Oudh.

Dhartá, دهرتا धर्ता

Discount and commission. Applied to increase of demand upon land; also to an item entered according to usage by bankers in excess of cash advanced; being generally about three per cent.—Saugor.

Dishṭbandhak, دشتبندهک दिष्टबनधक

The pledge of real property, being that which the debtor can keep in view, such as land, houses, etc., from Sansk. दृष्टि *dṛishṭi*, sight, and *bandhak*, pledge. Hypothecation. It is not much used in the North-West, except in Benares.—See Bhogbandhak.

Dubsí, دبسي दुबसी

The percentage allowed to Government farmers on the revenue paid to Government; formerly 10 per cent, *i.e.* two *biswas'* produce out of twenty—Saugor.—See Dobiswí, from which it is contracted.

Dofaslí, دوفصلي दोफसली

Land producing two crops a year. It is also known by the names of Dobar, Dosáí, Dosáhí, and Juthelí.

Ḍúhí, ڈوهي डूही

Alluvial formations. A mark of village boundaries.—See Dúdha.

Dobiswí, دوبسوي दोबिसवी

An allowance, reduction, or cess of two Biswas out of twenty; or ten per cent. The right of the Zamíndár in land, as Malikana is in money. Dobiswí is frequently given by Mafídars to Zamíndárs, particularly when they are not confident of the validity of their tenure.

Dohlí, دوهلي दोहली

Service land; applied in the Dehli territory as Baunda in the Doáb.—See Bhúndarí. But in many places within that territory it is only that land which is given to Brahmans. Dohlí, or Dohrí, is also applied there to the perquisite of Fakírs at harvest time.

Daul, ڈول डौल

Estimate of assets for the purpose of assessment. Daulnama was the name given to the extract from this estimate, which was made over as a *Potta* to the party who was to pay the revenue.

ڈولنامہ کہ آنرا پتہ گویند برعایا بدهد و قبولیت از رعایا بگیرد

—Extract from the "Kitáb-i Ḳánún."

Ḍaul properly means a form, and is used in parts of Behar to express the formal application made by a ryot to a Zamíndár for permission to cultivate land. This application, with the word "granted," or the signature of the Zamíndár alone written on it, is given back to the ryot, and does duty for a *Potta*.—B.

Don, دون दों

A fractional division of an estate.—Gaṛhwal.

Dungání, دنگاني दुंगानी

A small fractional division of an estate.—Kamáon.

Dar, در दर

A rate; whence Darbandí, used to express the rate of rent of each field in the township.—See Darbandí.

Dariyáburd, دریابرد दरियाबुर्द

Dariyáshikast, دریاشکست दरियासिकस्त

Lands cut away by encroachments of a river; from *daryá,* a river, and *burdan,* to bear away, and *shikastan,* to break.

Dariyábarámad, دریابرآمد दरियाबरामद

Alluvion. Lands reclaimed from a river; from *daryá,* a river, and *barámadan,* to accrue, to come up.

Dariyábarár, دریابرار दरियाबरार

See Dariyabaramad.

Dahotará, دهوتره दहोतरा

Tithes. An allowance, or tax, of ten per cent.; from *dah,* ten.—See Dahaik.

Darámad, درآمد दरामद

A term in keeping the *Itláḳ;* an account of fees paid for serving processes; the return of a process: from the Persian درامدن to come in.

Darbandí, دربندي दरबंदी

A statement of the different rates of a village; also, assessing the price or value of crops or produce.

Dastúru'l-'aml, دستورلعمل दसतूरउलअमल

A body of instructions and tables for the use of revenue officers under the Native Government. Notwithstanding the frequent appeal by Ḳánúngoes and our early European officials to the Dastúru'l-'aml, no two copies can ever be found which correspond with each other, and in most respects they widely differ. Those which profess to be copied from the Dastúru'l-

'aml of Akbar, are found to contain on close examination sundry interpolations of subsequent periods.

Besides the Dastúru'l-'aml, another book, called the 'Aml Dastúr, was kept by the Ḳánúngoes, in which were recorded all orders which were issued in supersession of Dastúru'l-'aml. It is probable that the Dastúru'l-'amls in use, shortly before our administration, were compiled from both these books, and hence have arisen the variations noted above.

Fárighkhatána, فارغخطانه फारिगखताना

A fee on writing a Fárigh-khattí, sometimes taken by Patwárís. The term Fárigh-khattí is correctly explained in the Glossary to signify a written release or acquittance.

Fárigh-khattí means a receipt given at the close of the year by the Zamíndár to the ryot, stating that all rent and demands of all sorts have been paid for that year.—B.

Fautínáma, فوتي نامه फौतीनामा

A document reporting the death of an incumbent and the names of his heirs; from the Arabic فوت *faut*, death.

Fard, فرد फर्द

A list, a sheet, a statement. Thus Fard-i-Kásht is a statement of a ryot's cultivation, from *kásht*, cultivation; and Fard-i Tashkís is a settlement record, from *tashkís*, specification, assessment.—See Fird in the Printed Glossary.

Farmán, فرمان फरमान

A royal mandate; an order; a patent. In English it assumes various shapes, as Firman, Pharmaun, and Phirmand.

Farod, فرود फरोद

Literally down, descending, alighting. A term used in the

customs' department to express the arrival and deposit of goods within certain defined limits.

Faryádí, فريادي फरियादी

A plaintiff; from فرياد *faryád*, a complaint, lamentation.

Fasl, فصل फसल

A season, crop, harvest; and hence the term *faslí* is applied to the era established with reference to the harvests of Hindústán. These harvests occur twice in the course of the year; one is known by the name of Kharíf, and the other by the name of Rabí'. The former is correctly explained in the Printed Glossary, under "Fusly Kheruf," to signify the autumnal harvest of rice, millet, etc.

Rabí' signifies the spring crop, or dry harvest, comprising peas, wheat, barley, gram, etc. The common people sometimes denote these harvests by other names.—See Asarhí.

Kharíf is derived from the Arabic خرف, the falling of autumnal rains, the gathering of autumnal fruits; and thus it came generally to mean the gathering of harvest: whence the term Al-Mukhárif (not noticed by either Golius or Richardson) a tribute gatherer.

Rabí' literally means spring (Pocock, Spec. Hist. Ar. p. 181), and it may therefore appear strangely applied to a Muhammadan lunar month, which in course of time makes a revolution of all the seasons, occurring sometimes in winter, sometimes in summer, sometimes in spring, sometimes in autumn. But the false prophet cared little for chronological propriety, and adopted in his new calendar the names of the old Arabian months of the solar year without any reference to their meaning, or more probably without reflecting that in a short time they would become exceedingly inappropriate. In the same way, Jalálu'd-dín, when he reformed the Persian calendar, introduced similar anomalies, and the names of many of the months, as at present applied, depart widely from their original meaning. Mardád, for instance, is the presiding angel of winter (Farhang-i Jahángírí), but the present month of Mardád is July.*

With respect to the period during which the harvests last, authorities are by no means agreed; some, like the Díwán Pasand, give eight months to the Kharíf, and four to the Rabí'; others, like the Zubdat-ul ḳawánín, and Raj Rúp,† give six months to each harvest. It is not easy to define the exact period of each, as the occupations of both harvests are, during some months, carried on simultaneously. Thus the sowing of the Rabí' and cutting of the Kharíf, and very frequently the ploughings for both harvests, are carried on at the same time, and it becomes difficult to say to which harvest most labour is devoted.

There is an attempt made to explain the cause of this difference of opinion respecting the duration of the two harvests in the second book of an anonymous Dastúru'l-'aml. The author says, "Some writers assign different periods to the Rabí' and Kharíf. In the Súbah of Bengal the Kharíf has nine months, and the Rabí' three. In Orissa the Kharíf has ten months, and the Rabí' two;" so that, if this be the real cause, we must always regard the country of the writer, when we consider his accounts of the periods of Rabí' and Kharíf.

* And Murdád is always July according to Richardson. The words in the Farhang-i Jahángírí are موکل بر فصل زمستان, and Rashídí repeats the statement in the same words, but also says it is the name of the fifth month of the solar year. Perhaps the anomaly may arise from the harvest alluded to being that of the crop which is sown in the winter, and reaped in the summer like the Rabí.—B.

† He observes that the Indians begin their year at the new moon of the month of Mihr, which is the commencement of the rainy season; and their year is divided into two parts: the Kharíf, from the new moon of Mihr (the seventh Persian month—September) to Sipandármuz (the twelfth month—February), 6 months and 178 days; and the Rabí, from the new moon of Farwardí (the first month—March) to Shahriwar (the sixth month—August), 6 months and 187 days—total, 365 days. At the same time he observes that the people of Irán and Turán continue to reckon Rabí first.—B.

Faisala, فيصله फैसला

Adjustment, decision, decree, settlement. It is an Arabic word, derived from the *fasl* mentioned above, which signifies cutting, separating, disjoining; and hence applied to a season. Hence also *faisal* is a judge, because he discriminates between right and wrong, and the decision given by him is a *faisala*. Ibn-i Arab Sháh calls the Day of Judgment يوم الفصل. The word Mufassil, so familiar to our ears, is similarly derived, signifying districts, or territory separated from the seat of Government.

Gachh, گچهه गछ

Portion of an estate, held separately.—Purneah, Behár.—B.

Gánwbaṭ, گانوبٹ गांवबट

A division of a Talúka into separate villages, or of the several Dákhilí Mauzás of an Aslí village: from गांव *gáṅw*, a village, and बटना *baṭná*, to be divided.—See Gátábandí.

Gánw kharcha, گانوخرچه गांवखरचा

Expenses incurred in the municipal administration of a village; from *gáṅw*, a village, and *kharach*, expenditure. This item is called also Malba in the Western part of these provinces. The literal meaning of that term is refuse, sediment, dirt; and is applied, like Ghúrbarár, *q.v.* in the sense of Gáṅw kharcha, on account of the many small items thrown into it, which could not be included under any other more specific head.

In the Panjáb this fund is often applied to the entertainment of travellers in a Musulman village; defalcations not exceeding ten rupees are also paid from it.

Gánwtí, گاونتي गांवटी

Of, or belonging to, a village; especially applied as Gáṅw

kharcha to the several expenses of municipal administration, such as wages of accountants, craftsmen, and police.—Saugor.

Gauhán, گوهان गौहान

A village made over by its proprietors to any person on a permanent Jama, with all the privileges of Zamíndár.—Eastern Oudh.

Gaunṭá, گونٹا गौंटा

Village expenses.—Bundelkhand.—See Gaṅwkharcha.

Gaunṭiyá, گونٹیا गौंटिया

A small hamlet. All these words are derivatives from *gáṅw*, a village.

Gauṭíká, گوٹیکا गौटीका

The head manager of a village, equivalent to a muḳaddam elsewhere.—Sohágpúr.

Gáṭábandí, گاٹابندي गाटाबन्दी

The division of a village by Gáṭás, corresponding with Khetbat. The opposite of Gáṭábandí is Pahábandí.

Gáṭábandí is a peculiar kind of tenure under which the fields of individual proprietors are not found in juxta-position, but scattered through many villages. Thus the boundaries of one village are frequently found to contain lands belonging to other villages, while some of its own fields will be included in the boundaries of another village, and that, perhaps, not contiguous. The tenure assumes various forms of complexity, being sometimes exceedingly intricate. It is found to prevail extensively in the Central and Lower Doab, Bareilly, and Benares. The mode of recording it is detailed in paragraphs 225 to 237 of the Board's Settlement Circular.

We owe the discovery of this kind of complex tenure to late years, when a more perfect system of registration was established at the Settlements made under Reg. IX. of 1833; but it is by no means such a rarity as it was considered when first brought to notice. It is found to prevail over various parts of India.

Gaṭhá, گتها गठा

The twentieth part of a Jaríb, or measuring chain. Each Gaṭhá contains three Iláhí gáz, *q.v.* The word is derived from गठना *gaṭhná*, to join, to unite by knots.

Gaz, گز गज

A yard. 3 Gaz = 1 Gathá, and 60 Gaz = 1 Jaríb.—See Iláhí gáz, and the Printed Glossary, under Guz and Gudge.

Gayál, گيال गयाल

The land of deceased Biswádárs lying unclaimed; land coming under the management of the Malguzár after an Asamí deserts his village.—Rohilkhand, Dehli, and Upper Doab. It is called also Uṭh; both derived from words signifying departure—the former from गया gone, and वाला a person; the latter from उठना to rise up (and depart).* It is equivalent to the Gatkul of the Dekkán; from the Sanskrit गत *gata*, gone, passed away, and कुल *kul*, family, lineage.

Gáṭewár, گاٹيوار गाटेवार

Is also synonymous with Khetbat.—See Gáṭábandí.

Ghardwárí, گهردواري घरद्वारी

An illegal cess from shopkeepers and householders; from घर *ghar*, a house, and द्वार *dwár*, a door.

* This derivation is from Col. Sykes, in J.R.A.S. No. IV. p. 208, but as the word is sometimes written and pronounced *ghaṭkul*, may it not be from घटना to decrease? —E. *add.*

Gharí, گھڑی घड़ी

An hour; or the instrument for measuring time. As a revenue word, it is applied to the sub-division of a village; thus, Khandígáṅw in Dehli is divided into 144 Lángrís, each Lángrí containing 8 Gharís.

Gharphánt, گھرپھانت घरफांत

An arrangement made by the manager of an estate, or by the shareholders themselves, for the payment of the Government revenue by each village, when more than one is included in a lease.—Kamáon.

Gharpattí, گھرپتی घरपत्ती

A house-tax, now abolished.—Kamáon.

Gharwára, گھروارہ घरवारा

The local name of a sub-division of a portion of Bundelkhand, extending from about Tirohan to the Jumna, said to have been bestowed rent-free on Kanaujiya Brahmans by Raja Ram, Baghel. It may perhaps be derived from the Ghora mentioned above, *q.v.*

Ghair mazrú'ah, غیرمزروعہ गैरमजरूआ

Uncultivated land; from the Arabic غیر *ghair*, not, and مزروعہ *mazrú'ah*, cultivated.

Ghátání, گھاٹانی घाटानी

The name of a toll levied on crossing rivers or hill-passes; from Ghát, a pass or ford.

Ghíkar, گھیکر घीकर

A tax for pasturage in the hills, chiefly in use in Kilpúrí; equivalent to Gobal in the plains.

Ghúnt, گھونت घूंत

Rent-free lands, assigned as endowments of religious establishments.—Gaṛhwál and Kamáon.—See Gúnth.

Ghúrbarár, گھوربرار घूरबरार

Dues levied on every sharer and under-tenant in proportion to the whole expenses incurred during the year.—Bundelkhand.

The word is derived from Ghúra, a dunghill, or sweepings; as all kinds of miscellaneous items are included.—See Gaṅw-kharcha.

Ghorá, گھورا घोरा

Ghorá, or Bhatghorá, subsequently known as Ahmadabad Ghorá, is the name of an old and extinct Sirkár, which, according to the register in the "Ấín-i Akbarí," contained 39 Mahála, and yielded a revenue amounting to 72,62,780 Dams. But it is evident that this Sirkár was almost entirely unknown, for the names of the Mahála are not given, nor is there any record of measurement; nevertheless, we may fairly presume that Tirohán, Chíbúmau, Darsenda, and Bara, and the greater part of the Rewah territory, were included in Ghorá. It might have been supposed that the Parganahs below the Ghats, bordering on the Jumna, would have had separate names and areas in the Imperial Records, but it appears from an examination of an ancient grant conferring rent-free lands on the Ḳáẓí of Darsenda, that the Parganah of that name is distinctly said to be included in Ahmadabad Ghorá. Bara, also, we know from the authentic records of our own history, was under the Rewah Raja till the time of Asafu'd Daulah, and the present Zamíndár of the Parganah is a Baghel, connected with the Rewah family.*

* "I have stated that Parganah Barah was included in the Sirkár of Bhatghora, on the authority of Sir H. Elliot's Glossary; but even that work does not contain much information respecting the territorial divisions connected with this Parganah.

Ghorá, moreover, still exists under the name of Ghorá Khás, on the borders of Tirohán and Chíbúmau. The patent above alluded to was issued by 'Alamgír in A.H. 1095. From about this period to the decline of the monarchy, Ghorá was better known, and even Singraulí is said to have been added to it. An Amil also was established in Tirohán, who used to reside in the fort built by Basant Ráí, but the whole Sirkár was subject to constant annexations and separations, according to the extension or diminution of Mahomedan influence in these wild parts.

If anything were wanting to show how little this part of the country between the hills and the Jumna had been subdued by the Mahometans up to the time of Akbar, we might satisfy ourselves by finding the Afghan emperors attacking Kantit, which is said to be "a dependency of Panna." Here, also, as in the case of Bandá, we have another mistake respecting names, which we can only correct by referring to other histories of the same period. Briggs, in his translation of Ferishta, speaks of

In fact, there are few parts of these Provinces regarding the early history of which less is known. In the "Áín-i Akbarí" the gross revenues and the number of mahâls in Bhatghora are merely given, the names of the mahâls are not specified. If Barah was included in this Sirkár, it must have ceased to belong to Rewah, especially if the latter territory were ma'f. But, at all events, after the downfall of the Empire, it would seem that Barah reverted to Rewah. . . . . It is generally believed in the Parganah that the Nawwâb Vazír's authority was established there previous to the time of Asafu'd-daulah, and that the Barrah Baghels, wishing to throw off their allegiance to Rewah, and to secure to themselves proprietary possession, sided with the Nawwâb Vazír, and offered to pay a small tribute. The Nawwâb accepted this offer, protected them from Rewah, confirmed them in their Zamíndârí position, and subsequently augmented the small tribute into a regular jama'. However this may be, there are complete accounts of the contest between Asafu'd-daulah and the Rewah Raja, from which it would seem that Barah was then for the first time fairly annexed to the Oudh dominions."—Mr. R. Temple's Report on Barah, Sel. Rec. N.W.P. Vol. IV. p. 412. He states in another place (p. 400) that, in 1778, when the Nawwâb's force, commanded by Mr. Osborne, proved victorious over the Raja, the Parganah was farmed out to Mr Osborne himself, and subsequently, in 1801, ceded to the British.—B.

"Balbhaddar Ray, Raja of Kutamba, a place dependent on Patna," instead of "Kantit, dependent on Panna," as it should be. Now, if Kantit was at that time dependent on Panna, even according to the shewing of Musulman histories, we must not be surprised if Chíbúmau, Darsenda, etc., were also little known till the time of 'Alamgír.

In a Dastúru'l-'aml of the later Empire, Panna is entered as containing 115 Mahály, and Ahmadabad as containing nine Mahály, and at this time there was a specification of Parganahs, which we do not find in Akbar's register.

The "Ḥadíḳatu'l Akálím" describes Tirohán as dependent on Sirkár Arail, or Tarhar (six Mahály); but this was at a period long subsequent, when Allahabad was under the Government of the Nawwáb Wazír.

Under all circumstances, we may perhaps consider that the limits which have been assigned to Ghorá in the Dastúr Map are not far wrong, but it is not easy to speak with confidence on the subject, as this part of the country was rarely, or never, visited by the Imperial generals, and we can only take advantage of such slight and incidental allusions as can be obtained in the absence of more satisfactory information.

Ghumáo, گهماو घुमाउ

A term applied to as much land as can be ploughed by one pair of bullocks in a day.—Dehli.

The Ghumáo, however, has in many places lost its original meaning, and is used as a measure of land of varying extent. In Jalandar it is stated to be one-fifth of a bigha only, while in Wadin it is three-fourths of an acre. Eight kanáls make a ghumáo, and two kanáls are rather more than one bígha.

Ghair mumkin, غير ممكن गेरमुमकिन

Barren waste; unproductive land; not capable of cultivation

(contracted from غیرُ مُمکِنُ آلزَّراعة *ghair mumkinu'l zará'at*, i.e., "whose cultivation is not possible").

Girdáwarí, گرداوري गिर्दावरी

Patroling, inspecting, going the rounds (from the Persian گرد *gird*, circuit, circumference, and آوردن *áwardan*, to bring).—See Girdáwar.

Grihasth, گرهَستھ गृहस्थ

A householder, a villager, a ryot. This word formerly indicated that stage in the life of a Brahman when he lived in a house discharging the ordinary duties of life; but is now applied to agriculturists generally, in which sense it is the equivalent of किसान peasant (from Sansk. गृह house, and स्था domain).

Grihasthí, گرهستهي गृहस्थी

Husbandry.—From the above.

Gola, گوله गोलह

The name of a tract of country which once comprehended a great part of the present district of Shahjahánpúr. It is said to have contained 1484 villages, and, before the time of the Rohillas, to have comprised ten Tappas.

Haveli. 268 Villages.	*Islámabad.* 277 Villages.	*Aurangabad.* 34 Villages.
Pilkhana. 70 Villages.	*Chakidpúri.* 347 Villages.	*Godarna.* 103 Villages.
Nigohi. 112 Villages.	*Majhwa.* 135 Villages.	*Mati.* 139 Villages.
	Murtaẓábad 'urf Jiwan. 103 Villages.	

Ṭhákúr Uday Singh of Pawáín seized upon the Tappas of Islamabad, Jíwan, Aurangabad, and part of Havelí, and formed the Parganah of Pawáín. Godarna, Nigohí, and part of Havelí went to form Nigohí. Baṛágaon was formed from Pilkhana and part of Havelí. Chakídpúrí and part of Majhwa went to form the Southern part of Púranpúr; and Matí and part of Majhwa went to form Khotar. I have been particular in my enquiries respecting this Mahál, both from its intrinsic interest as a "terra incognita," and because it cannot be concealed, that if so many large districts have been formed from Gola, the "Áín-i Akbarí" gives it a very inadequate area—only 24,540 Bíghas. The above sub-divisions are taken from a Zillabandí, dated as far back as 1119 Faslí, which is in the possession of the Ḳánúngoes. It is not easy to discredit this return, and we must presume, as is of course highly probable, that the greater portion of this modern Gola must have been uncultivated in Akbar's time, and that, the Northern and Eastern boundaries being undefined, new clearances, as they were made, were added to the original Mahál of Gola; so that when the Zillabandí was subsequently made, its limits had increased to an extent utterly inconsistent with the entry in the "Áín-i Akbarí." The greater portion of Khotar, and parts of Baṛágáṅw and Pawáín, have, therefore, been excluded from the Dastúr Map, as serving to represent more accurately the limits of Gola as known in Akbar's time.

It has been supposed that the first historical mention which we have of this remote region is in the "Akbarnáma," where that strange madman, Kumber Díwána, is represented as extending his ravages into Kant* Gola, until he was defeated by Rukn Khán; but it was in truth mentioned before this period, for it is evident that Gola is meant, when it is stated in Ferishta that Ḥisámu'l Mulk was, in A.D. 1377, appointed to the Government of Oudh, Sambhal, and Korla. His work was written subsequent to the "Akbarnáma," but, in writing of

* The name of this Mahál is frequently coupled with Gola in old histories.

past times, he never adopts modern territorial divisions, and, therefore, there is no reason to suppose that Gola was not in existence in the year mentioned;—in fact, we have positive proof of its existence before that period, for Zíáu'd-dín Barní distinctly mentions Gola in the reign of 'Aláu'd-dín Khiljí, A.D. 1296 to 1316.

We may also be allowed to indulge in the speculation that Gola is perhaps mentioned by Fa-hian (A.D. 399) under the name of Ho-li, in the following passage of the French translation:—"En passant la rivière *Heng*, et se dirigeant au midi l'espace de trois *yeou yan*, on arrive à un forêt nommée *Ho-li.*"

Now, as *g* is changed by the Chinese traveller into *h*—as in the instance of Gang (the Ganges) into Heng,—it would be no extravagant supposition to conceive that Gola is represented by the forest of Ho-li, notwithstanding that its position is not very correctly represented. Indeed, all his bearings between the Ganges and Gogra appear to be wrong.

Gonṭiyá, گونٹیا गोंटिया

The chief manager of a village; a Potel. In some places the term is applied only to Brahmans who have the management of villages.—Benares and Saugor.

Gunjáish, گنجایش गुनजाइस

A Persian word signifying capacity, and applied in fiscal language to the capabilities of a village, particularly with reference to a proposed increase of revenue.

Gurdachhná, گردچھنا गुरदछना

Rent-free land given to a spiritual teacher; from Guru, a teacher, and Dachhná, a fee or homage.

Gurkhaí, گرکھئی गुरखई

The name applied to a mortgage in Bundelkhand, which is

attended with the peculiar condition of leaving the mortgager to pay three-fourths of the revenue of the mortgaged land.

Gaṛá baṭái, گڑابٹاي गड़ा बटाई

A division of produce previous to the threshing, effected by stacking the sheaves in proportionated shares; from गड़ा a sheaf.—Rohilkhand.

Gaṛhíband, گڑھي بند गढ़ीबन्द

A description of Má'afí tenure in Bundelkhand, by which lands are held on paying a stipulated yearly tribute; but not one-fifth the amount which ought to be paid. These favourable terms have been made by the Gaṛhíbands themselves during the imbecile state of the former Government, which had not power or force sufficient to compel them to pay their proper quota. On its being demanded, they shut themselves up in their forts—hence the name—and if not the stronger party, were at any rate sufficiently powerful to withstand any attack on the part of the Government. After standing a siege for weeks, the Government were glad to come to terms, and let them off their revenue for a stipulated yearly sum. The title dates from the first advent of the Maraṭhas into Bundelkhand, when they found a large portion of the lands ceded by Chattarsál to the Peshwa, held by these petty Ṭhákúrs, related either by blood, or caste, to the numerous local Rajas, then in the country, to whom they were bound to pay a light quit-rent, or to perform military service when called upon. Some of them were younger branches of the reigning family, and others took advantage of the anarchy which followed the demise of Govind Pandit, to seize upon adjacent villages, and fortify them.

When the power of the Maráṭhas became consolidated, they soon perceived that the Gaṛhíbands were difficult to deal with in every way; slow and irregular in their payment of revenue; ready to take offence at the slightest insult which they might fancy had been cast on them, and capable, from their numerous ties of brotherhood and caste, of raising a formidable, and often successful, opposition to the Government, and making common cause whenever it was attempted to coerce even the weakest individual of their body. A continual struggle was therefore maintained between the Government and the Gaṛhíbands, which generally ended to the advantage of the latter; and hence we still find them in full occupation of the territory which they usurped, and from which they could not be dislodged (Public MSS).

Guzashta dár, گذشته دار गुजस्तदार

A ryot who holds his lands by prescriptive right—literally, "from time past," *az sálhá-i guzashtah*.—W.

Hál, حال हाल

Literally, the present state. The word is used in revenue accounts to represent the existing state of Collections [chiefly those of the current year, as opposed to *baḳáyá* بقايا, those of past years].—See Hál Tauzí'.

Hálá, حالا हाला

An instalment of revenue.—Dehli.

Hálí, حالي हाली

The Government assessment.—Dehli.

Hál tauzí', حال توزيع

An account of Collections for the current period.

This word is also written توجيه *taujíh*, in which case it would mean "examination." I am unable to say which is correct, both are used in the same technical sense.—B.

Hár, هار हार

A sub-division, or part of an estate. In Saugor it means the cultivated space immediately round a village, which is quite opposed to the meaning it generally bears in the North-West, where it is applied to the land most distant from the site of the village, *i.e.* beyond the *manjha.* In Bundelkhand, and some other places, it signifies a tract of land, but the term in no way indicates separate possession of the tract designated. All the sharers may hold land in one Hár. In the first and last sense, the word may be supposed to be derived from *hár*, a necklace, a chaplet; in the second, from *harná*, to tire out. However fanciful this latter derivation may be, the most unimaginative cultivator in Hindustan will declare that it is so called because both bullocks and men get fatigued (*har játe*) before they reach it.

Házir zámin, حاضر ضامن हाजिर जामिन

The person who becomes security for the appearance of another.

Habúbát, حبوبات हबूबात

Articles formerly furnished gratis to men in authority, consisting of sheep, milk, eggs, blankets, hides, etc. The system of Habúbát is not yet extinct, where European functionaries are negligent in the control of their establishments.

Had, حد हद

A boundary.

Hadbandí, حدبندي हदबन्दी

The settling and demarcation of boundaries. This has been most carefully done in the N.W.P. preliminary to the late Settlement. When they were not pointed out by the parties concerned, they were adjusted by arbitration. Wherever disputes were likely again to arise, it has been usual to bury some imperishable material in the earth, according to the instructions of the Hindu lawgiver Manu (Chap. VIII. 249–251). "The persons concerned reflecting on the perpetual trespasses committed by men here below, through ignorance of boundaries, should cause other land-marks to be concealed under ground. Large pieces of stone, bones, tails of cows, bran, ashes, potsherds, dried cowdung, bricks and tiles, charcoal, pebbles and sand, and substances of all sorts which the earth corrodes not, even in a long time, should be placed in jars not appearing above ground on the common boundary."—See also the "Mitákhshará" on the same subject.

Halbandí, هلبندي हलबन्दी

Is occasionally used in the sense of Halbarár and Halsarí, *q.v.*

Also a tenure in Ajaon, Sirsawah, and the North Western parts of Bareilly, in which a few Bíghas are assigned to each Asámí who has a plough, for the cultivation of cotton and Indian corn, for which he pays at the rate of one rupee per Bígha: for all other land in his occupation he makes payment in kind.

In Kamáon, Halbandí is applied, as Jot is in the plains, to signify the quantity of land under cultivation by any party.

Halḳa, حلقه हलका

A village circuit. A boundary line which comprises the lands and dwellings of a Mauza. The word, in Arabic, literally signifies a ring. Halka, says De Sacy in a note to his "Excerpta ex Abulfeda," p. 539, "proprie est annulus. Temporibus recentioribus Halḳa dicti sunt milites pretoriani, qui apud Sultanos Ægyptiorum corporis custodiæ inserviebant."

Halsárí, هلساري हलसारी

Sub-division and apportionment of revenue on ploughs. The

assessment of a certain amount on each plough in a village. The word is synonymous with Halbandí and Halbarár.

Haḳḳ, حق हक

Share or right.—See Haḳḳ Malikána in the Printed Glossary. This word enters into the composition of the seven following articles.

Haḳḳ bhent, حق بهينٹ हक भेंट

Presents frequently made half-yearly by the Malzugárs to native officers in authority.

भेंट means "meeting:" and the presents were made on meeting the great man who received the rent.

Haḳíyat, حقيت हकीयत

Right, share, proprietorship.

Haḳḳ hawáladár, حق حوالدار हक हवालादार

Haḳḳ Hawáladár, or correctly, Haḳḳ-i Hawáladár, is the grain given to Shahnas, generally at the rate of a seer and a half to every maund.—Rohilkhand.

Haḳḳ kamínchárí, حق كمين‌چاري हक कमीनचारी

Haḳḳ siyánchárí, حق سيان‌چاري हक सयानचारी

Haḳḳ thokdárí, حق تهوكداري हक थोकदारी

Dues and fees to Kamíns, etc., derived, according to old custom, from the inhabitants of villages, and varying in every Pattí, but generally equivalent to about three per cent. on the Government revenue.—Kamáon and Gaṛhwál.

Kamín in the plains is applied to village servants, but in Kamáon it is used synonymously with Búrha, to signify a superintendent of village management, whose office is in the gift of Government, and generally hereditary. Seana bears the same meaning in Gaṛhwál.

Haḳḳ zamíndárí, حق زميندارى हक जमीनदारी

A Zamíndár's proprietary right.

Hariyánw, هريانو हरियांव

A division of a crop, in which the ryot retains nine, and the zamíndár receives seven, parts. The word is derived from Har, a plough, because the ryot retains a ploughman's share (one-eighth) more than the half.

Harhamesh, هرهميش हरहमेस

The insertion of this barbarous expression into a grant is considered to imply perpetuity. The literal meaning of the word is "every always," *i.e.* for ever and ever.

Hasho minhái, حشو منهائي हसो मिनहाई

That which, after being deducted, is entered in the Hasho and excluded from the rent-roll. The term is therefore applied to rent-free, Nankar, or other assigned lands.

و انچه از جمله مواضع در وجه نانكار و معافي ايمه وغيره بوده باشد منها كرده باقي را درمقام حشو قلمي سازند

See Bariz for a description of the Hasho.

Hastobúd, هستوبود हस्तोबूद

The learned translator of the Institutes of Timúr says, at p. 367, that the meaning of this expression is not understood by him. It signifies a calculation on the data of the present (هست "is") and past (بود "was"). An estimate of the assets of a tract of land. Also, when corrupted into Hastnabúd, it signifies a remission granted by Zamíndárs for the portion of land failing in produce. The meaning of Hastobúd has been well explained in the Printed Glossary, under Hastabúd.*

Hawáladár, حوالدار हवालादार

One employed to protect the grain before it is stored; a steward or agent employed for the management of a village; corrupted by the English into Havildár.—See the Printed Glossary under Huwáludár and Havildár.

Hibadár, هبهدار हिबादार

A possessor of property by deed of gift; from *hiba*, a gift.

Hibanáma, هبهنامه हिबानामा

A deed of gift.

Hissadárí, حصهداري हिस्सादारी

Co-partnership; applied to a village in which a number of sharers have a proprietary right in the land. From *hissa*, a share, which has been explained in the Printed Glossary.

Hissa hákimí, حصهحاكمي हिस्साहाकिमी

The share of produce to which the king, or ruler, is entitled. It is needless here to enter on the controversies on this subject, respecting the amount, under the old law, Hindú and Muhammadan, to which he was entitled. It is pretty certain, however, that, even in the most favourable periods of Hindú rule, when they had to pay twenty other taxes besides that on land, less was never taken from the ryots than they are now called upon to pay—at least, in these Provinces.

Hissa hálí, حصه هالي हिस्सा हाली

A ploughman's share, or wages in kind; generally amounting to about one-eighth of the produce.

* In Purneah it supersedes the village Jama'bandí entirely.—B.

Hissa kashí, حصه کشي हिस्सा कशी

The distribution and apportionment of shares according to strict genealogical succession. Several collectors, during the time of the Settlement, used to make out laborious statements of this nature, under a misapprehension of the particular course of enquiry enjoined by Reg. VII. of 1822, for the purpose of registering and securing the rights of inferior sharers.

Hissait, حصيت हिस्सैत

A shareholder.

Ínch, اينچ इंच

Security.—Dehli.

Ikbáchhí, اکباچهي इकबाछी

Distribution of any sum or cess, levied upon all lands at an equal rate.—Central Doáb.

Ikotrá or Ekotrá, يکوترا इकोत्रा or एकोत्रा

Ekatrá, يکترا एकत्रा

The sum total.—Bundelkhand.

It is also applied generally to signify the numeral 101, as well as interest at the rate of one per cent. per mensem.

Ijmálí, اجمالي इजमाली

A tenure in which several persons hold an estate in common, each receiving a certain share of the rents, without actual division of the land.—B.

Iláhí gaz, الهي گز इलाही गज

The standard Gaz, or yard, of forty-one fingers, instituted by Akbar. After much controversy respecting its length, it was authoritatively declared by Government to be thirty-three inches long; and the declaration has been attended with considerable convenience to revenue officers, as a bígha measured by this yard constitutes exactly five-eighths of an acre. The several opinions respecting the length of the Ilahí Gaz, and the means instituted for determining the point, will be found given in detail in Thomas's "Prinsep," Vol. II. p. 88, and the Journal of the B.A.S. vol. VII. p. 42.—See Kos and Bígha.

'Ilákadár, علاقدار इलाकादार

The person who enters into engagements at the Settlement.—See Lumbardar, and Malguzar.

Inglis, انگلس इंगलिस

A pensioner.

Isti'mál, استعمال इस्तीमाल

Custom, usage. This word is employed to denote the peculiarities in the use and pronunciation of Persian words which occur in the official documents of the courts of India.

"I subjoin a few notes on the *Isti'mál i Hind.* Those who wish to study this important subject, ought to make themselves acquainted with the writings of Mírzá Qaṭíl, entitled چهار شربت, شجرة الاماني, and نهر الفصاحة; and a treatise by Anwar 'Alí on the spelling of Persian words, entitled *Risálah i Imlá i Fársí.* These works have been lithographed, and are easily obtainable.

"The *change* in spelling, form, meaning, and construction, which an Arabic word, apparently without any reason, undergoes in Persian, or which an Arabic or a Persian word undergoes in Hindustani, is called تصرف *taçarruf.* The taçarrufát of Persian words are included in the استعمال فرس *isti'mál i furs,* the usage peculiar to the Persians, and the taçarrufát of the Hindustani language, and of the Persian written in India, in the استعمال هند *isti'mál i hind.* A knowledge of the latter is of great importance, not only for those who read Persian books written or printed in India, but also for every Hindustani scholar; for although the Isti'mál i Hind is looked upon with suspicion by learned natives, we have to bear in mind that its peculiarities are *generally adopted*, and therefore correct. So at least for the Hindustani, according to the proverb غلط عام صحیح و فصیح.

"In its relation to Persian the Isti'mál i Hind will, of course, in most cases, appear as something faulty; for the peculiarities may no longer be a natural form of development, or a غلط عام, but the result of ignorance, a غلط عوام کالانعام. Nevertheless, the Isti'mál i Hind is visible in every Persian book written by Indians, from the works of their excellent historians down to a common dinner invitation (ضیافتنامه) of the daily life. Even the works of a writer like Abulfaszl, "the great Munshí," shew traces of it. Hence the truth of Mons. Garcin de Tassy's remark that every Persian scholar ought to be acquainted with Hindustani. If this be true for the Persian scholar, it is much more true for the compiler of a Persian dictionary; for a good dictionary ought to be based upon a thorough knowledge of the language in all its forms of development, and must be a history of the language as well as a vocabulary.

"But if we only understand by Isti'mál i Hind the influence of the Hindí and Hindustani upon the Persian, we would almost identify the term with "the usage of the Persian writers since the establishment of the Mogul dynasty." This would be wrong; for the Isti'mál i Hind includes peculiarities which once belonged to the Persian, as spoken in Persia, but which the modern I'rání, in the course of its progress, has entirely discarded. In early times Persian had become the court language of Túrán, and from Túrán it was carried to India by the waves of the Túránian immigrants and invaders. Hence on the whole, the Persian of India is Túránian. As Latin in the Middle Ages, so was the Persian in Túrán, and subsequently in India the language of the learned. The works of the pre-classical and classical periods were studied and imitated, and peculiarities have thus been preserved which have long since disappeared in the I'rání Persian.

The difference between the pre-classical and the modern Persian is, of course, not so great as between Latin and any of the Romanic languages; because the pre-classical Persian had already attained that logical simplicity to which our modern European languages happily tend; and though representing the growth of the Persian language during nine centuries, it is scarcely greater than the difference between the English of Fletcher and Beaumont and the English of our century. The Persian language has been compared to a bare tree, *stripped of all its leaves.* This stripping process, however, is going on in every spoken language, and shews that the copious and beautiful forms of languages like Sanskrit, Gothic, Greek, and many modern *savage* languages, are as many illogical incumbrances. The sequences of events and the order of things which the imitative genius of the modern languages expresses by the order of the words, are expressed in the ancient languages by the annexation of words and particles rather than by a logical order of the words, as if the speaker was afraid that the hearer could only understand those ideas for which there was an audible equivalent. Whilst many are apt to look upon *stripping off the leaves* as a matter of regret, I would consider it as a step towards delivering the human mind from the fetters of form. Perhaps I tread upon contestable ground. But a fact remains: it is this, that of all nations whose languages are preserved to us, the Persians are the first Arians that pitched the tent of speech on the elevated table-land of logical thought.

"Simplified, then, as the Persian language is, further change in terminations being impossible, the growth, as in modern English, is only visible in the pronunciation, the spelling and the meanings of words. For the study of this development a comparison of the works of the older writers with those of the modern, is essential; and as the Persian written and studied in India has hitherto been imitating the pre-classical and classical Persian of the early invaders, the importance of the Isti'mál i Hind is easily recognised.

"The following peculiarities are said by native writers to be common to the Persian of Túrán and India.

"*a.* Many words end in the Túránian Persian in ک (kaf) whilst the

I'ránian has a گ (gáf); as کبگ a kind of partridge, in Túr. کبک; مشگ *mishg*, musk, in Túr. مشک *mushk;* اشگ a tear, in Túr. اشک; سرشگ a drop, in Túr. سرشک. Similarly, بزشگ a doctor, رشگ jealousy, خلشگ, etc., in Túr. with a final káf.

"*b.* Also in the beginning of certain words: as گشادن, in Túr. کشادن (as every Muhammadan in India pronounces); گشنیز coriander seed, in Túr. کشنیز.

"This difference between the Túránian ک and the I'ránian گ becomes very apparent in dictionaries arranged according to the first and last letters. Thus in Surúrí اشگ stands in the فصل الف مع کاف فارسي, whilst in the Madár in the فصل الف مع کاف تازي.

"*c.* The Túránian has preserved a clear distinction between the واو and يا, when مجهول (ó, é) and معروف (ú, í). The modern I'ránian has only معروف forms (í, ú). The *words* which have a majhúl letter must be learned from the dictionaries; Indian Persian grammars specify the cases, when the *ending* ي is pronounced معروف.

"*d.* The Túránian has in all cases preserved the نون غنه. The I'ránian has given it up in some, especially after an alif. Thus, forms like ماندم, راندم, آن گاه, هرآنچه, etc., are pronounced in I'rán *mŭndam, rŭndam, ŭngáh, harŭnchĭ*, but in India still *mándam, rándam*, etc.

"*e.* The Túránian never adopted the interchange of *dál* (د) and *dzál* (ذ).

"*f.* Certain words are peculiar to the Túránians. Examples—وي *he*, for the I'ránian او; پور *son*, for پسر; سو *side*, for طرف; شو *husband*, for شوهر; پگاه *dawn*, for صبح; بيگاه *evening*, for شام; اري for بلي; يزنه *brother-in-law*, for شوهرخواهر; ينگاه or ينگا *sister-in-law*, for برادر زن; دادر *brother*, for برادر; خوش دامن *mother-in-law*, for مادر زن; خسر *father-in-law*, for پدر زن; خسر پوره for برادر زن; پاليدن and کافتن *to search*, for جستن; تير را برتافتن *to throw the arrow*, for انداختن تير را; شستن *to sit*, for نشستن; خاستن *to rise*, for برخاستن; دينه روز (cf. شبانه روز) *yesterday*, for ديروز; آب سوار شدن *to swell (water)*, for آب زياده شدن; روز سوار شدن *to pass away (day)*, for گذشتن روز;

فوت شدن *to die;* پائیدن for قرار نمودن ; خسپیدن *to sleep,* for خوابیدن ; رفتن, the same as شدن, *e.g.* قربانت روم *I am thy sacrifice;* پائین شدن for فرود آمدن ; خلانیدن for گائیدن ; ماندن 1. the same as نهادن *to put;* 2. the same as گذاشتن *to leave behind,* e.g. چیزرا بر طاق ماندو ام *I have left the thing on the shelf,* where ماندو is a Túránian form for مانده ; or این خانه‌را بمانید *leave this house* (بگذارید); 3. the same as طلاق دادن *to divorce;* 4. the same as نهادن *to leave behind;* etc.

"Although several of those words do occur in Íránian authors, yet we generally find them used in peculiar places, as in rhyme, where it was difficult to avoid them; or in order to prevent repetitions, etc.

"The following peculiarities appear to be limited to the Persian spoken and written in India.

"*a.* Words have peculiar meanings. Examples—آسوده, the same as سیر *satisfied;* پس خورده *leavings;* پس غیبت *absence,* for غیبت ; مثل misl, *a set,* the same as رده ; جامه *a* (made up) *coat;* حلال خور, the same as کناس or خاک‌روب *a sweeper;* برف *baraf,* often pronounced *barf,* ice (for *snow*); داماد, *vide* Vull. Dict.; خلیفه a flattering title applied to cooks, tailors, etc.; سبزي *hemp,* for بنگ ; سه‌پهر *afternoon;* ناچار for لاچار ; مایوس *despairing;* جاي‌ضرور *a closet,* for ضروري ; ولایت Kábul and Persia;* خالصه the royal exchequer; جارجه and ترک *tark,* the catch-word at the bottom of the page of a manuscript; سرکار, *vide* Vull. Dict.; جاگیر, *vide* Vull., *also* board given to a poor student who is to teach children in return; صوبه 1. a province, 2. the same as صوبه‌دار an officer in charge of a province; رساله, the same as رساله دار an officer commanding a troop; آبکاري *vide* Vull.; خواه مخواه without reason.

* Vullers has at least half a dozen blunders in his dictionary, all arising from his ignorance of the meaning of this word. Thus, under اصول, in his Corrigenda II. p. 1558, No. 2, in regione Kashmír کشمیر ولایت, a blunder for کشمیر و ولایت Kashmír and Persia; also sub جیقه جیقه کردن I. p. 546; s. چل دختران I. p. 578, etc. Now-a-days, in India, ولایت means *Europe,* esp. *England.*

"*b.* The word كه is pronounced *ké*, not *kĭ*. This seems to be the old form كے, still preserved in كاشكے. The Iszáfat is pronounced *ĕ*, not *ĭ*, and *é* in cases of words ending in ۂ, *e.g.* خانۂ من khanah *é* man. The word بادشاه is pronounced بادشاه *bádsháh*, as پاد *pád* in Hind. means *crepitus ventris*. Similarly do the Persians use the form انكژ (a prick to urge on an elephant), in order to avoid the Hind. انكس which sounds, as Rashídí observes, like آن كس. Other Indian pronunciations are—پلك *palk* and *palak*, for *pilk*, an eyelid ; فغان *fighán*, the same as ناله, for *fughán ;* قانزه for قيزه, already observed by Abul-Faszl in the Áín i Akbarí. Words of the same class as عفو *e.g.* سهو a mistake, هجو a satire, وحي a revelation, سعي exertion, have lost the jazm and are pronounced *'afó*, *hafó* with the واو مجهول, the accent being on the penultima, but *sa'ĭ*, *wahĭ* with the accent on the ultima.

"*c.* Peculiar forms are پيدايش, زيبايش, يارش (the first and last occur in Abulfaszl), for پيدائي , زيبائي, ياري, the ending *ish* being properly restricted to nouns derived from *verbs ;* ترشائي for ترشي acidity ; كسائي (derived from كس), for آدميت humanity ; سائس, سئيس, or سائيس a groom, for سائس ; a plural اجنه *ajinnah*, ghosts ; گنجيفه *a pack of cards*, for گنجفه ; سنجاف for سجاف, *vide* Vull. ; درستگي, مهربانگي, سختگي, (Abulfaszl), for درستي, مهرباني, سختي, the ending گي not leading to an adject. form in ۂ ; دوغله and دوخله *a mongrel ;* اسپ ماديه for اسپ ماده ; الا نه for الا ; باد الله for عباد الله, a proper noun ; پتيله for پاتله ; تالاش for تلاش ; جامداني *a wardrobe*, for جامدان ; جريبانه *a fine*, for جرمانه ; ربيع الثاني for ربيع الآخر ; جماد الاول and جماد الآخر for جمادي الاولى and جمادي الاخرى ; داوات for دوات ; دروغه for داروغه ; دوكان for دكان *a shop ;* دوانين for دواوين ; شوله for شله a *certain dish ;* ريشم for ابريشم ; صميمي *pure*, for صميم ; لازمي for لازم ; كمخواب for كمخاب ; معه for مع ; مفروغ for فارغ ; هرج for حرج.

d. In words beginning with آ, the Madd is often omitted ; as اچار

pickles, استر *lining*,* استين *sleeve*, ابفت *canvass*, اماده *ready*, التمغا *a royal order*, ابكار *a distiller*, for آچار, آستر, آبفت, آماده, آلتمغا, آبكار.

e. After a long vowel we often find a vowel elided; as آفرين *áfrín*,† for the Íránian *áfarín*; مولوي *maulwí*, for *maulawí*; امادگي *ămádgí*, for *ámádagí*; پوشيدگي *póshídgí*, for *póshídagí*; خالصه *khálçah*, for *kháliçah*; آژدن *ázhdan*,† for *ázhadan*.

"*f.* Two Sákins are avoided; as ارجمند *arjamand*, for *arjmand*.

"*g.* The Persian letters گ, چ, پ, are used instead of the Arabic ك, ج, ب; as in افگندن, شگوفه, شگافتن, for افكندن, شكوفه, شكافتن; اسپ, تپ, for اسب, تب; غنچه for غنجه; ديباچه for ديباجه; خرچ for خرج.

"*h.* The Tashdíd of many Arabic words falls away, as نواب *nawáb*, for *nawwáb*, an (Indian Nawáb); ذره, pl. ذرات *an atom*.‡

"*i.* The following pronunciations are very common, though generally *prohibited* in the dictionaries—خزان *khizán*, autumn, for خزان *khazán*; دراز *diráz*,§ for the Persian *daráz*, long; شنبه *shambah*, and even *shumbah*,‖ Saturday, for شنبه *shambih*; پلاو *puláw*, and even پولاو, a well-known dish of rice, meat, and spices, for پلاو *paláw*. The modern Persian and Turkish have پلاو *piláw*. درويش *durwesh*,¶ for *darwísh*, a beggar; نمک *nimak*, salt, for *namak*; نمكين *nimkín*, adj., for *namakín*; گواه

* Entered by Vullers as Persian. It is Indian.

† So in many Persian Dictionaries written by Indians.

‡ There is a curious mistake in Vull. Dict. I. p. 378. Burhán, whom Vullers copies, has پنده بمعني نقطه و ذرات هم بنظر آمده است; but Vullers does not observe that نقطة and ذرات (the Indian printer of the Burhán left out the Tashdíd) are synonymous, reads ذرأت for the A. ذرءت, and translates *canities in anteriore capitis!*

§ Vull. also has *diráz*, although Burhán gives clearly بروزن نماز *namáz*.

‖ Vull. also has پنجشنبه *panjshambah*, I. 375, b., and سه شنبه *sihshambah*, II. p. 354, whilst in other places he has correctly *shambih*.

¶ Adopted by some Indian Dicts., as the Ghias, on a mistaken etymology.

gawáh, a witness, for گواه *guwáh;* گره *girah*, a knot, for *girih;* مزدور *mazdúr*, wages, for *muzdúr;* كاغذ *kághidz*, paper, for كاغذ *kághadz*.

"*k.* A great number of Arabic words are universally pronounced wrongly in India; as قلعه *qil'ah*, a fort, for *qal'ah;* قيامت *qaiámat*, the resurrection, for *qiyámat;* قطعه *qat'ah*, for *qit'ah;* عروس *'urús*, a bride, for *'arús;* هجر *hijr*, separation, for *hajr;* عجز *'ijz*, weakness, for *'ajz;* رجا *rijá*, hope, for *rajá;* فضا *fizá*, space, for *fazá;* رضا *razá*, contentment, for *rizá;* جيب *jéb*, a pocket, for *jaib;* غياث *ghaiás*, for *ghiás*, help; شهاب *shaháb*, for *shiháb*, a meteor; عصمت *'açmat*, chastity, for *'içmat;* موقع *mauqa'*, for *mauqi';* موسم *mausam*, a season, for *mausim;* خيمه *khímah*, a tent, for *khaimah;* شجاعت *shujá'at*, bravery, for *shajá'at;* حماقت *himáqat*, for *hamáqat*, folly; قصور *qaçúr*, a fault, for *quçúr;* عقوبت *'aqúbat*, for *'uqúbat*, punishment; حشمت *hashmat*, pomp, for *hishmat;* جنت *jinnat*, paradise, for *jannat*.

"*l.* Peculiar spellings; as ازدهام for ازدحام; پيكار for پيگار; تعويز for تعويذ. Proper nouns are often written together, as حسينعلي for حسين علي. Similarly, صاحبدل for صاحب دل; انشاء الله تعالى* for ان شاء الله تعالى; مشتملبر for مشتمل بر consisting of; آنحضرت for آن حضرت; عنقريب, عليحده, ذيحجه, ذيقعده, for عن قريب, ذي حجه, etc. Reversely, خانه ها, ساده لوهي ها, for خانها, ساده لوحيها. Also, موسا for موسى; خورم happy, for خرم *khurram;* رحمان for رحمن.

m. Barbarous forms; as بهيات, پرگنات, دار الكچهري books, for كتابها; مرفه الحال for مرفع الحال; مچرب *mücharrab*, greasy; شب ليلة القدر, as we say, *the strait* of *Bab* el Mandeb; فريسد *firísad*, for فرستد he sends; قلف *qulf* for قفل *qufl*, a lock; قطع for قطعه; نماز خواندن, Hind. نماز پڑھنا, for نماز كردن."—From an Article by Mr. Blochmann, on "Contributions to Persian Lexicography," in J.A.S.B. Vol. XXXVII. Part I. p. 32.—B.

* Thus also in Persian MSS.

Itláḳ, اطلاق इतलाक

The term is applied to the office and records of Dastaks (demand, or summons), and Talabana (fees for the service of processes). It literally means freeing, liberating; and it is therefore difficult to say why it is so applied in revenue accounts; except it may be in the sense of forwarding, issuing, striking off.

Itláḳ navís, اطلاق نويس इतलाक नवीस

The person who keeps the Dastak accounts.

Jáedád, جايداد जाएदाद

Jáedad signifies a place; employment; also, assets, funds, resources. It signifies likewise the ability of any district or province in respect to its revenue; an assignment on land for the maintenance of troops, or of an establishment.

Jáedad now generally means, at least in Behar, landed property generally, also the crops as they stand.

Jeṭh ra'iyat, جيٹهه رعيت जेठ रइयत

The head ryot who conducts the village business, and acts as Chaudharí of the village; from Sanskrit *jeshṭha*, eldest, chief. The meaning is correctly given in the Printed Glossary. Where there is a Muḳaddam, the Jeṭh-ryot ranks below him, and is often known by the name of Chuḳaddam; but it is most usual to consider Muḳaddam, Jeth-ryot, Mahtoṅ, Mukhya, Mahetya, and Basít as synonymous terms.

Jewan* birt, جيون برت जेवन बिर्त

A stipend allowed to the family of an old deceased servant.—Eastern Oudh and Benares.—See Birt.

Jhánsá, جهانسا झांसा

An assessment formed without specific ground, and only by

* From जेवना *jewnā*, to eat, a word of the Bhojpuri dialect.—B.

general estimate.—Saugor. The word is, perhaps, derived from *jhansná*, to cozen, to flatter, to deceive.

Jhúnḍí, جهونڈي झूनडी

A clump of grass. It is also applied in Dehli, as Khewat is elsewhere, to signify the amount due from each sharer in a Bhayachara estate.

Jins-i-kámil, جنس كامل जिन्सकामिल

First-rate crops. The best crop that a field can produce.

Jinswár, جنس وار जिन्सवार

(A statement) relative to crops.—See Jamabandí.

Jiziya, جزيه जिजिया

A tax on infidels. Applied in Saugor to a house-tax on the inhabitants of towns not engaged in tillage, which is also called Pandrí, *q.v.*—See Jazea.

Júla, جوله जूला

A tract of land containing four Alí, or sixteen Bísís.—Gaṛhwál and Kamáon.—See Bísí.

"In Gaṛhwál, as in Kamáon, there are numerous denominations of land, but the Júla was, and is, the chief measure, differing in value according to local usage, and the various classes of landholders, but in every instance exceeding in quantity one Bísí, and measurable by it."—Gaṛhwál Settlement Report.

Jama', جمع जमा

The whole; total; revenue generally, and the Government demand in particular; amount assessed.

Jama'bandí, جمع بندي जमाबन्दी

A village rent-roll. A statement of the rents fixed on every field in the township. In Madras it signifies the annual settlement of the revenue, and bears this meaning in the Printed Glossary.

The term is very comprehensive, and, indeed, admits of so many meanings, that it is found to change, so as to accommodate itself to the prevalent system of revenue management. About fifteen years ago, a Jama'bandí was most commonly known as a daul, or estimate, on which to base an assessment. It is now applied chiefly to the annual rent-roll furnished by the village accountants. It is also used variously in villages, as well as in Government records. Jinswar Jama'bandi, for instance, is usually a detailed statement of the rent levied upon each kind of crop. In Brij it is more specially applied to a kind of tenure found in parts of that tract.*

Jama' jhartí, جمع جهرتي जमा झर्ती

A statement of receipts and expenditure. Periodical account of either cash or grain.—Saugor.

Jama' kharch, جمع خرچ जमा खर्च

Debit and credit. Cash account.

Jama' wásil báḳí, جمع واصل باقي जमा वासिल बाकी

An account of the revenue of Government, with entries of payments and arrears.

Jamnauṭá, جمنوٹا जमनौटा

Jamnauṭyá, جمنوٹیا जमनौटिया

A certain consideration given to a Zámin, or security; generally amounting to about five per cent.†

* The Jama'bandí in the Provinces under perpetual settlement is a very lengthy statement of each ryot's holding, his rent and other dues, the amounts paid, remitted, or due, and many other particulars. It is, in fact, the rent-roll of a whole village.—B.

† A Hindi derivative from the Arabic ضامن.

Jamog, جموگ जमोग

Transfer of liabilities by mutual consent. A conditional mortgage.—Benares, Eastern Oudh, and Lower Doáb.

Jamogdár, جموگدار जमोगदार

A person who lends a landed proprietor a sum of money, and recovers that money from the Ryots.—Benares, E. Oudh, and Lower Doáb.

Jaríb, جريب जरीब

A measuring chain or rope. Before Akbar's time it was a rope. He directed it should be made of bamboo with iron joints, as the rope was subject to the influence of the weather. In our survey measurements we use a chain. A Jaríb contains sixty Gaz, or twenty Gathas, and in the standard measurement of the Upper Provinces, is equal to five chains of eleven yards, each chain being equal to four Gathas. A square of one Jaríb is a Bígha. Till the new system of survey was established, it was usual to measure lands paying revenue to Government with only eighteen knots of the Jaríb, which was effected by bringing two knots over the shoulder of the measurer to his waist. Rent-free land was measured with the entire Jaríb of twenty knots.

A Jaríb, in Hebrew and Arabic, signified originally only a measure of capacity, equal to four Kafíz, or 384 Mad, and in course of time came to signify the portion of land which required as much to sow it as a Jaríb would contain (Asása-l-lughát). The Patha and Nalí of Ġaṛhwál and Kamáon have a similar origin.—See Bísí. This use of the term must have altered before the reign of Timúr, for in the Institutes we have the following injunction, which is evidently the foundation of Akbar's division of soil into three classes:

واگر رعیت بحاصل و قسمت سه توده راضي نشود اراضي مضبوط را
اول و دويم و سيوم جريب نمايند و جريب اول را سه خروار و

جریب دویم را دو خروار و جریب سیوم‌را یک خروار جمع بربندند و نصف‌را گندم و نصفي‌را جو اعتبار کنند وانچه جمع شود دو یک مال بگیرند

Jaziya, جزیه जज़िया

From the Arabic جزا subjugation; conquest; compensation. A capitation tax levied by the Muhammadans on their subjects of another faith. The correct word is Jizyat, but it seems usual in Hindústan to pronounce the word Jazya.—See Jazziah, Jezia, and Jaizeyeh in the Printed Glossary.

From the passage quoted from the "A'ín-i Akbarí," in the article Altamgha, it appears that the Khalífa Umar laid an annual tax upon every one who was not of the Muhammadan religion. A person of high condition paid forty-eight dirhams, one of moderate means twenty-four, and one in an inferior station twelve dirhams.—See "Hedaya," Book IX., cap. ii. and viii.

It does not exactly appear when this tax was instituted in India. Tod ("Annals of Rajasthan," vol. i. p. 403) thinks it was imposed by Babar in lieu of the Tamgha which he solemnly renounced on the field of battle, after the victory which gave him the crown of India; but we read of it long before this, for as early as the time of Alá-ud-dín, only a century after the final subjugation of Hindústan, we find it spoken of as an established tax. Thus, in the dialogue recorded by Ziáu'd-dín Barní and Ferishta, between that tyrant and Kaẓí Mughíṣ-ud-dín, we read, "From what description of Hindús is it lawful to exact obedience and tribute?" To which the obsequious Kazí replies, "The Imam Haníf says that the Jazya, or as heavy a tribute as they can bear, may be imposed instead of death on infidels, and it is commanded that the Jazya and Khiraj be exacted to the uttermost farthing, in order that the punishment may approach as near as possible to death." "You may perceive," replied the king, "that, without reading learned books, I am in the habit of putting in practice that which has been enjoined by the prophet."

But it would appear that up to the time of Fíroz Shah, Brahmins were exempted from the tax, for in a very interesting chapter of Shams-i-Siráj's work we find that monarch imposing it for the first time on this influential class.

و در عهد سلاطین پیشین البته از طایفه زناردارن جزیه نستیده جزیه ایشان معاف کرده بود هیچ وقتي این طائفه بکسي جزیه نداده سلطان فیروز شاه بتوفیق حضرت الله جمیع علماء دین‌دار و مشایخ نامدار را بدرگاه خود جمع کنانیده بگوش ایشان رسانیده که این غلط عام افتاده که از طائفه زناردار جزیه نستد و سلاطین گذشته که درین کار کوشش بسیار نکرده از سبب انکه کارکنان و غلامان انزمانه هوا خواهان یگانه غفلت ورزیده بر ایشان آگاهي نداده چون طائفه زناردار کلید حجره کفر اند و کافران بر ایشان مستقل اند اول از ایشان جزیه بستانند و معاف ندارند

"In the time of the former Sultáns certainly the Jazya was not taken from the tribe of thread-wearers (Brahmins), their Jazya was remitted, and at no time has this tribe ever paid Jazya to any one. Sultán Firoz Shah, by the divine guidance, collected all the Ulemá and Shaikhs into his darbár, and represented to them that this was a common fault into which all his predecessors had fallen, being misled by their servants, who were negligent and did not inform them of the omission, and that now as the thread-wearers were the chief of the infidels, they were the first from whom Jazya should be levied."

On this occasion, which was so much at variance with his usual spirit of conciliation, the Brahmins thronged him in his hunting-palace, and threatened to burn themselves alive before him; and at last were only dissuaded from their purpose by the other Hindús of Dehli taking upon themselves to pay the Jazya of the Brahmins. In his time, the highest class of Hindús was rated at forty, the second at twenty, and the third at ten Tankas per head; and these remonstrances had the effect of inducing the king to admit the Brahmins to the favorable terms of the lowest class.

After the death of Ratan Chand, the capitation tax was once more levied, as it is stated in the Tawáríkh-i Muhammad Shahí to have been again repealed by Muhammad Shah, at the intercession of Maharaja Jay Singh and Girdhar Bahadur.

Since that period, no Emperor was possessed of sufficient authority to enforce the Jazya, and this odious tax became extinct for ever; but not till it had operated as one of the most effectual causes of the decline of the Muhammadan power, by alienating the affections of the Hindú population, which the early Moghul Emperors had courted, and in some measure obtained.

We again learn that it was enforced with great severity in the time of Behlol and Sekander Lodi, which was perhaps no inconsiderable cause of the facility with which the empire was wrested from the hands of that family.

The tax was abolished by Akbar in the ninth year of his reign, and was not imposed again till the twenty-second of Aurangzeb, who with his wonted intolerance, directed that its levy should be attended with every circumstance of contumely which his ingenuity could devise.

A passage in the Zubdatu'l Akhbárát states that he ordered that the Jazya should be brought to the collector by the payer himself and on foot, and that the collector should sit, while the payer stood, the collector should put his hand *over* that of the payer and lift the money out of it, and that the tax must not be sent to a collector by a messenger, but brought in person. The rich were to pay the whole year's tax in one instalment, and the middle classes in two, the poorer in four. The Jazya is remitted on conversion to Islam or death.

It was at this time that admirable letter is said to have been written which is ascribed by Orme to Jaswant Singh, by Tod to Rana Raj Singh, and by the Mahrattas to Sevaji (Grant Duff, vol. i. p. 219, and Elphinstone's India, vol. ii. p. 458). Stewart (Hist. Bengal, p. 308) says that Shaista Khan, in A.D. 1679-80, enforced the Jazya in Bengal at the rate of 6½ per 1000 on all property, and that Christians paid one and a half per cent. additional duty on their commerce. The sick, lame, and blind were excused.

From this period it appears to have been regularly levied, and with particular severity in the time of Farrukhsír (in consequence of the appointment of Ináyat Ullah as financial minister, who had been secretary to the bigoted Aurangzeb), until the time of Rafíu'd-darját, when the Barha Sayyids abolished it, and the Hindús again recovered their consequence, Rattan Chand, a Hindú, being appointed financial minister, and being possessed even of such influence, as to be empowered to nominate the Mohamedan Kazís of the Provinces.*

Kúdá Bíghá, کودا بیگها कूदाबीगहा

A Bígha measured after a curious fashion in some of the Eastern parts of Rohilkhand. The Malguzar measures the breadth by the rope, or by the ordinary Kadams (steps), and then the cultivator, running by springs as great a space each time as he can stretch, measures the length: each spring being counted half a Kadam. The result is the area. The Bígha of this mode of measurement varies from 2½ to 3½ Kachha Bígha.

* Colonel Galloway (Law and Constit. of India, p. 27), states this on the authority of Ferishta: but Ferishta died more than a century before this period.

The meaning of the words is a Bígha measured by leaps, from کودنا Kúdná, to jump.

There is another curious Bígha of these parts, measured by the paces of a woman eight months gone with child.

Kos, کوس कोस

The itinerary measure of India, of which the precise value has been much disputed, chiefly on account of the difficulties which attend the determination of the exact length of the Gaz, or yard. The "A'ín-i Akbarí" lays down distinctly that the Kos consists of 100 cords (طناب tanáb), each cord of 50 Gaz; also of 400 poles (بانس báns), each of 12½ Gaz: either of which will give to the Kos the length of 5000 Gaz. The following particulars relative to the distances between the old Minars, or Kos pillars, may be interesting, and may be considered to afford an approximately correct means of ascertaining the true standard.

	Road distance in English yards.	Direct distance in ditto.
Octagonal Minar to Nurelah in Delhi ...	4,513	4,489
Minar between Ṅurelah and Shápúrgáṛhí	4,554	4,401
Minar opposite Alípúr	4,532	4,379
Minar opposite Siraspúr	4,579	4,573
Ruins of Miṇar opposite to Shalimar......	4,610	4,591
Average.................	4,558	4,487

Length of the Kos = 2 miles 4 furlongs 158 yards.

It is important to observe that the length of the Ilahí Gaz deduced from these measurements is $32\frac{818}{1000}$ inches, showing how very nearly correct is the length of 33 inches assumed by the British Government (See Ilahí Gaz).

The measurements taken to the South of Dehli, between the Minars in the Muttra district, closely correspond. Out of twelve distances it is found that eight give 2 m. 4 fur. 19 p. 1 yard, three give 2 m. 4 fur. 25 p. 3 yards, and one gives 2 m. 4 fur. 38 p. 2 yards.

It may be proper to remark that it is frequently supposed that the Minars are set up every two Kos, and that the Kos contained 2,500 yards; but the "Áín-i Akbarí" appears sufficiently explicit on the point. The same work gives the values of the local Kos. It says, the Guzerat Kos is the greatest distance at which the ordinary lowing of a cow can be heard, which is determined to be 50 Járíbs, or 15,000 Gaz. This Kos resembles the Chinese lih, *i.e.* the distance which can be attained by a man's voice exerted in a plain surface, and in calm weather. Another in Bengal is estimated by plucking a green leaf, and walking with it till it is dry. Another is measured by a hundred steps made by a woman carrying a jar of water on her head, and a child in her arms. All these are very indefinite standards.

The same may be remarked of the Oriental míl, as well as the European mile and league. The two former evidently derive their name from the Roman *milliare*, and the difference of their value in different places proves that the mere name was borrowed, without any reference to its etymological signification. According to the "Kamoos," the Oriental míl is a lax and vague measure, but it has been considered by Dr. Lee to be to the English one, as 139 to 112.

Kos is an Indian word: the equivalent word in Persian is Karoh, the same as the Sanskrit Krosa, of which four go to the yojan; about the precise value of which different opinions are held. Bopp ("Nalus," p. 213) says it is equal to eight English miles. Professor Wilson ("Sanskrit Dictionary," p. 689) estimates it at nine miles, and says other computations make it about five miles, or even no more than four miles and a half, and, in his commentary on the Chinese travels, estimates it at no higher than four. But these travels enable us to fix the distance with tolerable precision. By following Fa-Hian's route between places of which the identity is beyond question, as between Muttra and Kanouj, and between Patna and Benares, we find the yojan in his time to be as nearly as possible seven

English miles; and this agrees much better with what we find the yojan to be, if we resolve it into its component parts. Eight barley-corns equal a finger, twenty-four fingers equal a Dand, one thousand Dands equal one Krosa, and four Krosa one Yojan. Now, estimating the fingers' breadth at eight barley-corns, this makes the yojan equal to six miles, one hundred and six yards and two feet.*

Kroṛ, کروڑ कड़ोड़

Ten millions. The names of the higher numbers are thus given in the "Zubdatu'l Kawánín." 100 Kror = 1 Arab. 100 Arab = 1 Kharab. 100 Kharab = 1 Níl. 100 Níl = 1 Padam. 100 Padam = 1 Sankh. 100 Sankh = 1 Ald. 100 Ald = 1 Ank. 100 Ank = 1 Padhá.

The three last names are rarely met with in other account books, but Colebrooke (Hindú Algebra, p. 4) assigns names to seventeen orders of superior units in the decimal scale, ending with Parárdha. In one work, the name of which I cannot now

* क्रोश: In Böhtlingk and Roth two definitions are given. One is = 1000 daṇḍas = 4000 hastas = $\frac{1}{4}$ yojana; the other = 2000 daṇḍas = 8000 hastas, but still = $\frac{1}{4}$ yojana, showing that the values of the daṇḍa and hasta were undefined.

The actual kos of the present day in India is equal to two English miles in most places, but in the Panjab it is seldom more than a mile and a half or a mile and one-third. The further east the longer the kos, so that in Bengal it exceeds two miles; and I am told that in Bundelkhand it is as much as four miles. In Bahár and Gorakhpúr, and many other parts of India, there is also a kachá kos, which is not much more than a mile, and sometimes even less.

The calculations in the text are not exact. The table should stand apparently—

8 barley-corns = 1 finger.
6 fingers ...... = 1 hasta or hand (which is omitted in the text).
4 hastas ...... = 1 daṇḍa or rod.
1000 daṇḍas ...... = 1 kos.
4 kos .... = 1 yojan.

The other computation makes 8 hastas = 1 daṇḍa. It is probable that the lower amount of 4 hastas to the daṇḍa represents the kachá kos so prevalent in India, and the larger, the pakká or official kos. The same double system of pakká and kachá pervades all the weights and measures of India.—B.

remember, the grades in the ascending scale are carried much higher, and the names differ in some respects from those of Colebrooke. Thus 100 Sankh = 1 Udpada. 100 Udpada = 1 Maha Udpada. 100 Maha Udpada = 1 Jald. 100 Jald = 1 Madh. 100 Madh = 1 Parárdha. 100 Parárdha = 1 Ant. 100 Ant = 1 Maha-ant. 100 Maha-ant = 1 Shisht. 100 Shisht = 1 Singhar. 100 Singhar = 1 Maha-singhar. 100 Maha-singhar = 1 Adant-singhar, which in numerals amounts to 1,000,000,000,000,000,000,000,000,000,000,000,000,000. But it is evident that this advance should have been made by tens, and not by hundreds; by which the numerals would be reduced to twenty-four places—100,000,000,000,000,000,000,000. This luxury of names for numbers is without example in any other language, ancient or modern, and implies a familiarity with their classification according to the decimal scale which could only arise from some very perfect system of numeration; at a period, moreover, when the most scientific people of the Western world were incapable by any refinement of arithmetical notation of expressing numbers beyond one hundred millions.—See "Enc. Metrop." Arithmetic (12), and "Vishnu Purana," p. 631.

Karoṛí, کروڑي कड़ोड़ी

When Akbar introduced his revenue reforms, he appointed a collector for every Karoṛí of Dams (*i.e.* 2,50,000 Rs.) whom he designated by the title of Amil, or Amilguzar, and to that functionary the instructions are directed in the "A'ín-i Akbarí," the designation of Karoṛí being of subsequent introduction. This sum, which was placed under his management, agrees with the amount at present established under the resolutions of Government, dated 30th October, 1837, as that which should form the charge of a Tahsíldar.

A Karoṛí, however, on his first appointment had somewhat more power than is invested in our Tahsíldars. He received eight per cent. on the amount of his collections, besides perquisites: he was directed to see that lands were not suffered to fall out of cultivation; to scrutinise the rent-free grants; to report upon the condition of the Jágírdárs, and of the subjects generally in his neighbourhood; to forward an account of all remarkable occurrences; and to perform the duties of kotwal, if none were appointed within his jurisdiction; and whenever, on account of drought or other calamity, he thought it advisable to depute any one for local enquiries, he could avail himself of the services of the Amín of the Súbah. This system lasted till A.D. 1639, in the reign of the Emperor Shah Jahán, when his minister, Islám Khan, deputed a separate Amín to every Parganah for the purpose of fixing the Jama, and the Kaṛoṛí was left in charge of the collections, to which the duties of Faujdar were added, with an allowance of ten per cent. on the collections. But it was found that the powers of the Faujdar and Kaṛoṛí were too great to be united in one person, and to check the abuses which began to be prevalent, Raí Ráyán Jíswant Ram, the Peshkar of Islam Khan, suspended for a time the power of the Kaṛoṛís, and appointed subordinate collectors for each village, who were ordered to take exact account of the collections of the Kaṛoṛís, and the purposes to which they had been applied, to check all the fraudulent exactions of which they and their dependents had been guilty, and to resume all the extra cesses which they had illegally demanded from the people.

When that excellent minister Sa'dullah Khan succeeded Islam Khan, he combined the duties of Amín and Faujdar in one person, and appointed him superintendent of a Chakla of several Parganahs (see Chakla); and placing the Kaṛoṛí entirely under his orders, established five per cent. on the collections as the amount of the Kaṛoṛí's allowance, and of this, one per cent. was subsequently deducted. The business of assessment and settlement was left entirely to the Amín—with that the Kaṛoṛí had no concern, but it was his business to encourage agriculture, to make advances, station watchmen over the ripening crops, and report when any indulgence and leniency appeared expedient.

This system lasted during the time of Aurangzeb, and till the dissolution of the empire.

The following extract, taken from the patent of the Amín-Faujdar, written at the beginning of last century (the title خلد مکان* proves that the document is subsequent to Auranzeb's reign), will show how much the power of the Karorí had declined since his original appointment.

و زریکه از سنه چهل و دو عهد حضرت خلدمکاني نزد رعایا باقي باشد بکروري قدغن نماید که سریصد پنجروپیه برجمع حال که به تشخیص درآید درهر فصل تا وصول آن به تحصیل درآورده و انچه بصیغهٔ تقاوي درسالگذشته برعایا تنخواه شده باشد آنرا باباقي سالمذبور در اول توزیع سال حال بگیرد که درصورت اهمال بازخواست ازو خواهد شد و احتیاط بکار برد که کروري جرات باخذ ملبه و وجود ممنوعه بارگاه والا نکند

* * * * * * *

و برطبق قاعدهٔ معین از وجه حق التحصیل کروري یکروپیه عوض

* The lakabs or titles of honour of the six greatest Mughal Emperors are as follows :—

BABAR .........A.D. 1526	....	فِردَوس مکاني	...... Firdaus Makání.
HUMÁYÚN 1530	....	جنت آستاني	...... Jinnat Ástání.
AKBAR 1556	....	عرش آشیاني	...... 'Arsh Áshyání.
JAHANGÍR 1605	....	جَنت مکاني	...... Jinnat Makání.
SHÁHJAHÁN 1627	....	فردوس آشیاني	...... Firdaus Áshyání.
AURANGZEB 1658	....	خلد مکاني	...... Khuld Makání.

They are always mentioned after death by these titles in official and literary documents.—See J.A.S.B. Vol. XXXVII. Part I. p. 39.—B.

برآمد موقوف داشته داخل درجمع نماید که ثاني الحال در برآمد کروري مجرا خواهد شد و مابقي را بموجب سند حضور منجمله زر بقایا و تقاوي که بوصول رسد بتصدیق خود بکروري تنخواه میداده باشد و بر تقدیریکه زر مسطور به تنخواه حق التحصیل وفا نکند قدر زاید را از تحصیل سالحال تن نماید

"And as to the money which is still owing by the ryots from the forty-second year of his late majesty's reign, the Kaṛoṛí is charged to collect at every harvest five per cent. in excess of the present jama', according to assessment until the whole be collected; and the sums which were allowed to the ryots under the head of "takáví" in the past year are to be realised, together with the arrears of the said year, at the first audit. In case of negligence he will be held responsible, and let him beware of venturing to collect any sum on account of village expenses, or under any head prohibited by the government." . . . .

"And according to the established rule the Kaṛoṛí may keep back one per cent. as his haḳḳu'l tahsíl (*i.e.* his fee or allowance for collecting) but must enter it in his accounts under the head of jama', and credit will be allowed him subsequently to that extent; and the rest that he shall collect under his majesty's warrant under the heads of taḳáví and arrears is granted to him as salary; if it do not amount to what he is entitled to, he may make good the deficiency out of the collections for the current year."*

Kachwánsí, کچوانسي कचवान्सी

The twentieth part of a Tiswansí, of which twenty go to a

* The second passage I have translated freely, as it appears to have been incorrectly copied or carelessly worded by the original scribe, or both. I think, however, I have succeeded in catching the general import. The document itself is not in my possession, and no clue to its whereabouts is given by the author.—B.

Biswansí. The twentieth part of a Kachwánsí is an Unwánsí, or Nanwánsí. The word Kachwánsí is rarely used in account books; the more usual denomination is Pitwansí. But it must be confessed that great difference of opinion prevails respecting these fractions. It is even sometimes stated that a Kachwánsí is the twentieth part of a Biswansí, but as these denominations were, even under native governments, rarely used in practice, and are now less used than ever, it is a matter of little consequence what precise value is attached to them.

Sirkár, سرکار सरकार

This word is more correctly spelt Sirkár, but is more familiar to Europeans as Circar, in consequence, perhaps, of the geographical division of the Northern Sirkárs being so written. In other parts of this Supplement it will appear as Sirkár.

A Sirkár is a sub-division of a Súbah. The North Western Provinces, excluding the Saugor and Nerbudda territories, comprise no complete Súbah, but only portions of the four Súbahs of Agra, Allahabad, Dehli and Oudh. Each Súbah is divided into a certain number of Sirkárs, and each Sirkár into Parganahs or Mehals (which are used as equivalent expressions), and the Parganahs again are aggregated into Dastúrs or districts; and as the Parganahs of the same Dastúr are of course always contiguous, the Dastúr statement in old registers, if copied with any regard to correctness, frequently forms a very important means of the verification of doubtful names.

Súbah is an Arabic word, signifying a heap of money, or a granary. Sirkár is literally a chief, a supervisor. Dastúr besides signifying a rule is also a minister, a munshi; Parganah means tax-paying land:

پرگنه زمیني را گویند که ازان مال و خراج بگیرند

It is strange that the "Burhán-i Ḳáti'," while giving this Hindustani meaning, does not speak of it also as a sub-division of a province, for it is so given in the older lexicons, as for instance in the "Farhang-i Jahangiri;" and though it is omitted in the "Farhang-i Ibrahímí," the word was undoubtedly in use in the time of that compilation, being not only found in the almost contemporary memoirs of Baber, but in the "Tabakát-i Násirí," and the "Fatuhát-i Fírozshahí" (in which we find that about A.D. 1350, there were fifty-two imperial Parganahs in the Doáb) and even on an inscription dated A.D. 1210, discovered at Piplianagar in Bhopal ("Jour. A.S. Bengal," Vol. V. p. 377).

The other words do not appear to have been in use till introduced by the Moghuls, nor do any of them appear to be used in similar senses in foreign countries, except Sirkár, which is stated in the "Chiragh-i Hidayat" to be used in Western Asia also, in the sense of a territorial sub-division, the authority quoted being the translation of the "Mujalis-ul Nufais."

The words used before Akbar's time to represent tracts of country larger than a Parganah, were Shakk شق, Khitta خطه, 'Arsa عرصه, Diár دیار, Viláyat ولایت, and Iktá' اقطاع, but the latter was generally, though not always, applied when the land was assigned for the support of the nobility, or their contingents, and the presiding officer was called Mukta or Iktadar. Thus, in the early historical writers before the close of the fourteenth century, we find Shakk-i Sámánah, Khitta-i Oudh, Arsa-i Gorakhpúr (this term is rarely used for any other tract), Diar-i Lakhnautí, Viláyat-i Mián Doáb, and Ikta'-i Karrá.

Between Sirkár and Dustúr there appears a connexion; one meaning chief, and the other minister; between Súbah and Parganah a connexion may also be traced; one being a large, the other a small collection; but whether the words were chosen with reference to this connexion may be doubted.

The title of Súbahdar, or lord of the Súbah, is long subsequent to Akbar's time. Sipáhsálár was then the only designation of the Emperor's Viceroy in each Súbah.

I have endeavoured to restore the Sirkárs, Dastúrs, and

Parganahs as they stood in the time of the Emperor Akbar. The copies of the "Ãín-i Akbarí" vary so much, and such ignorance is frequently exhibited by the transcribers, that to verify the names of Parganahs has been a work of great labour, which is by no means to be estimated by the ease with which the eye runs over a coloured map.

The Parganahs which retain their own names have frequently occasioned as much doubt as those which have undergone a complete change. The annoyance may be easily estimated by those who know what various phases Oriental alphabets can assume; and those who do not, may be convinced by learning that in a single Sirkár one copy presents you with such complete disguises and metamorphoses as Kathal for Kampil, Sanani for Patiali, and Saniwarbarka for Saurakh; and the difficulty does not cease when, after frequent conjectures and comparisons, the name has been verified; for the adjustment of areas to meet those represented in the "Ãín-i Akbarí," has frequently been the source of much perplexity. But it is in separating the Sirkárs into Dastúrs that the ignorance of the copyists has been chiefly exhibited, for all the Parganahs are frequently mixed together, as if there were no meaning at all attached to Dastúr. It has been therefore thought proper to explain in some detail the principle of the construction of the map, premising that several copies of the "Ãín-i Akbarí" have been consulted for the occasion.—See Dastúr.

Explanation of the System adopted in the Arrangement of the Maps.

Should it be desired to ascertain the position and names of the Parganahs as at present constituted, they may be learnt by referring to the Modern Ethnographical Map, which has been drawn up for the purpose of illustrating several articles in this Supplement.*

* *Note.*—The Maps will be found in the fold of Vol. I.

An endeavour has also been made to represent the state of Zamíndárí possession in the time of Akbar—but in comparing the difference of colour in the modern and ancient map, it is not to be inferred that it is entirely occasioned by change of possession. There is reason to apprehend, as Abúl Fazl generally enters only one tribe as in possession of the Parganah Zamíndárí, and seldom more than two, that he has only mentioned those which had a predominance or clear majority; omitting all consideration of the others, whose number was inferior: now, the map of modern possession has been drawn out with a view of shewing as far as the scale would admit, all tribes of importance, so that if one particular class is found in possession of but a small part of a Parganah, it has been entered under its appropriate colour. As even in the same Parganah, the villages of each tribe are much intermixed, the colours of course represent the proportions, and not the positions, of each.*

The boundaries of the old Sirkárs appear for the most part well rounded off and defined. There are some which are somewhat doubtful, as will be seen by referring to the articles Bhattiana, Budhganga, Des, and Ghora. There is only one which appears to require notice in this place.

It will be observed from an inspection of the map of Sirkárs and Dastúrs, that the Parganahs of Sirkárs Gházípúr and Jaunpúr are strangely locked into each other near the confluence of the Gunti and Ganges. The fact of Sayyidpúr Namdí being in the old registers entered in the Sirkár of Gházípúr, while Bhítarí, which is between Sayyidpúr and Gházípúr, is entered in the Sirkár of Jaunpúr, would seem to show that the proper reading is Sayyidpúr Bhítarí, and that Bhítarí has been entered separately by mistake; but Sayyidpúr used formerly to be called Namdí; so that solution does not help us. The fact is,

* The original maps were on a large and legible scale; but it was found necessary to reduce them for the press; which could not, of course, be accomplished without throwing many of the limited tribes into the *miscellaneous* colours.

that Sayyidpúr and Bhítarí, which habit induces us now to couple together, were originally two distinct Parganahs, and in two different Sirkárs; nor were they regarded in any other light than as two distinct Parganahs, till they were given in Jágír to Babu Usan Singh, from which time as they were held under one Sanad (see the "Balwant-náma"), they began to be spoken of as one Parganah, and are so entered in the Regulation of 1795. In the Parwanah appointing Shaikh Abdullah Amil of Ghazípúr, amongst the twenty-two Parganahs mentioned in his Sanad, Sayyidpúr and Bhítarí are given separately; and this consideration throws much suspicion upon the Zamíndarí Sanad given in the Azimgarh Settlement Report, printed in the "Journal of the Asiatic Society" for 1838, and which might otherwise have been of some service in unravelling the difficulty. Sayyidpúr and Bhítarí are written together in the Persian Ziman, and (though they certainly appear to be enumerated as two) yet they occur without the intervention of the word Parganah; and in a manuscript copy of the Sanad, the entry of Sayyidpúr Bhítarí as one Parganah is beyond question. The same is observable in Kauria Tilhaní. Now, these are modern combinations, and could scarcely have been used in the fourth year of Jahangír, within twenty years after the compilation of the "Áín-i Akbarí," where they are entered with such marked distinction. Kauria and Tilhaní being in all respects separate Parganahs; and Sayyidpúr and Bhítarí not only separate Parganahs, but in two different Sirkárs. The entry of Maunát and Bhanjan as two separate Parganahs in the same Sanad, which are entered simply as Mau in the "Áín-i Akbarí" is also suspicious. These considerations, coupled with the loose wording of the document, lead us to put little faith in it as evidence respecting the mode in which Sayyidpúr and Bhítarí were entered at an early period in the imperial records, and justify the implication conveyed in that report, that the document is not authentic.

We must, therefore, notwithstanding the irregular appearance which this part of the map presents, consider that the entries are correct, and that the division was intentional.

PART IV.

TERMS ILLUSTRATIVE OF RURAL LIFE.

[Under this head I have thrown together all words which do not properly fall under the three preceding heads. This Part therefore is a very heterogeneous one. Names of trees and plants, rustic tools and implements, descriptions of soil when they have reference merely to agriculture and not to revenue purposes, and many other matters are here included.—B.]

A'bád, آباد आबाद

Literally, as stated in the printed Glossary, "abode, residence;" but more frequently used in the N.W. Provinces, as cultivated, flourishing, populous.

A'bádán is used in the same, but, as the "Farhang-i Rashídí" observes, in a somewhat intensive sense.—A'bádání signifies prosperity, population.—A'bádkár is a settler on waste land.

A'bád is frequently used in combination with a proper name to denote a city, as Haidar-ábád, Shahjahan-ábád. When used in construction with a Hindú name or vocable, it generally denotes that the termination has been changed from bás باس to A'bád آباد. Thus the Brahminábád, mentioned in the "Chachnama," and "Tuḥfatu'l Ḳirám," was originally Brahminbas, or Bamanwas.—See Harbong ka Raj.

Ábpáshí, آبپاشي

Irrigation of fields, from P. آب water, and پاشيدن to sprinkle.

Ábí, آبي आबी

Irrigated land; from آب water. The word, though of general application, is more exclusively applied in Central Doáb to land irrigated from tanks, jhíls, and streams. As the supply of water is generally precarious, the rent paid for such land is about one-half of that which is paid for land irrigated from wells.—See Cháhi, Part III.

Abíj, ابيج अबीज

Grain that does not germinate; the same as Nirbíj. From अ a, or निर nir, priv. and bíj बीज seed.*

Adhikárí, ادهكاري अधिकारी

Proprietor; holder of a right or privilege.

Ágal, آگل आगल

A long and heavy piece of wood to which the hill-men tie their buffaloes. The Ghikar, or grazing-tax, *q.v.* was formerly levied "fí ágal," or so much per log.—E. *add.*

Agar, اگر अगर

Aloe wood; lignum aloes (*Aquilaria agallocha*, Roxb.). It emits a pleasant odour when burnt, and forms one of the chief ingredients of native pastils.

* A distinction is sometimes drawn between these two words. Abíj being used to signify grain which has been produced in a withered and worthless state in the ear, while Nirbíj implies that which, though produced healthy, has been subsequently destroyed by weevil or damp, etc.—B.

Ágar, آگر आगर

A salt pit. Ḱharí is the name of the small compartment within it.

It is stated by some authorities that this word is the origin of the name of the imperial city of Agra, and from the brackish nature of the soil and water, there is no improbability in the statement; but Ni'mat ullah, in his History of the Afghans, gives a very different account. He says that Sultán Sikandar Lodi, after getting on board a boat at Mathura (Muttra), asked his steerer which of the two heights before them was fittest for building. On which the steersman replied, "That which is a-head (Agra) is the best." At this the Sultán smiled and said, "The name of this town, then, which I design to build, shall be Agra." This must be altogether an imaginary dialogue; besides which, it is not likely the steersman would speak Sanskrit to the Emperor. It is evident, moreover, that Sikandar was not the founder of Agra, as is generally reported, though he may have built the fort of Bádalgaṛh; for the capture of it is celebrated in the verses of a Ghazni poet in the time of Masa'úd, the son of Ibrahim, the grandson of the great Mahmúd; and it is even acknowledged to have been an old city before the time of the Afghans, in the autobiography of Jahangír, whose veracity need not be impeached in passages where he has no occasion to indulge in the "Ercles' vein" respecting the achievements of himself or his ancestors. There is in Ferishta mention of the conquests made in India during the reign of Masa'úd.

"In his reign Hajib Toghantagín proceeded in command of an army towards Hindústan, and being appointed Governor of Lahore, crossed the Ganges, and carried his conquests further than any Mussalman had hitherto done, except the Emperor Mahmúd. Like him he plundered many rich cities and temples of their wealth, and returned in triumph to Lahore, which now became in some measure the capital of the Empire."—Briggs' Ferishta.

Ágarí, آگري आगरी

A manufacturer of salt. See Ágar.

Agayá, اگيا अगया

A disease which affects rice, in which the whole plant is dried and burnt up, from Ág آگ fire. See Khaira.—E.

Also in Bahár, the lemon-scented grass (*audropogon muricatum*) which is used as a specific in some diseases of cattle, such as goti or small-pox.—B.

Agaund, اگوند अगौंद

The top of the sugar-cane cut up for seed; in distinction to Bel ka bíj, in which the whole cane is cut up into six or seven pieces. The division of the cane is much more minute in some places. Pát comprises the leaves at the top. Ag, Agáo, Agaurá, Agin, and Gaundí are the names given to a few inches below the Pát. Kánchá, called also Gulli, Palwa, and Phungí, consists of about a foot below the Ag, and is chiefly used for seed. The rest of the cane is called Gánde, Gandá and Ganná.

Agor, اگور अगोर

Agor, or Agoraiyá, is a man appointed to keep watch over crops; from agorná اگورنا to watch. The term is used chiefly in Benares, rarely in the North West.

Agwár, اگوار अगवार

The portion of corn set apart for village servants, so called because it is (áge) آگي—the first thing to be taken from the heap. In the East, it is used to signify the perquisites of ploughmen in kind. See Jeora and Thápa.

Agwásí, اگواسي अगवासी

The body of the ploughshare.—Eastern Oudh.

A'har, آهر आहर

A'harí, آهري आहरी

A small pond; smaller than a Pokhar and Talú, and larger than a Talaya and Marú. These two last words are chiefly in use to the Eastward. In Dehli, and the neighbourhood, Johar is a large pond, Jharí is a middling sized one, and Let* is a small one, more resembling a puddle. Thus, *Let páni barsá* means, "It has rained but little." Higher proportions are indicated by *Kuṅr páni barsá*, "It has rained a furrow full;" *Kiári bhár*, "To the extent of the bed of a garden;" *Naka tor páni barsá*, "It has rained enough to break the embankments."

Taláo in Dehli is applied generally only to such tanks as are lined with masonry.

In the Doáb and Rohilkhand, the words more generally known are, Ságar, Taláo, Pokhar, Dabrá, And, Liwár, Talárí, and Gaṛhaiya, or Gaṛhela—Ságar being the largest.

Ahar is also a salt-pit, a trough for watering cattle, a drain. —E.

In Amritsar the large pools which abound inside the city walls† are called *ḍáb*, probably meaning "depressions," from *ḍábná*, to press down. Another word used for a natural lake (*taláo* being often artificial) is सर *sar*, which forms the last member of the word Amritsar(= the lake of nectar). A pretty couplet, sometimes quoted in the Panjáb, runs—

ऐ सर हंस प्रीत न कर चोग चुग गहि उड़जाहि ।
कर कमलन सिउ दोस्ती सर सुके मुरझाहि ॥

"Love not the swan, o lake, for he feeds and flies away;
Give to the lotus thy love, tho' he wither and die, he will stay."
—B.

* Probably from *leṭná*, to lie down, to be flat.—B.

† I ought, perhaps, to have written "abounded," because I believe they are now nearly all drained off. At least, the authorities were at work on them so long ago as 1860.—B.

Ahíṭá, اهيتا अहीटा

A person appointed to watch the grain when it is ripe, and see that none of it is carried away before the demand is paid. The word is Hindi.

Áíndán, آئين‌دان आईनदान

From Áín آئين a law, and dánistan دانستن to know; a man who practises on the simplicity of his neighbours by his knowledge of the regulations of Government.

Aiwára, ايواره ऐवारा

A cow-shed in the middle of a jungle, according to the "Gharíbu'l-lughat" of Khan Arza. The "Tuḥfatu'l-lughát" does not notice it.—E.

The common words are Arár अड़ाड़ and Bathán बथान q.v.—B.

Ajmúd, اجمود अजमूद

Parsley *(Apium involucratum)*.

Ajwáín, اجواين अजवाईन

(*Ligusticum ajowan*, Roxb.). Aniseed.

Ák, آک आक

Gigantic swallow-wort *(Asclepias gigantea)*. It is a common shrub all over Upper India, and is celebrated in the Tálíf-i sharíf for its many valuable properties. It is of high repute amongst the Indian practitioners, and at one time much attracted the notice of European physicians. The plant is more commonly known under the name of Madár.

Ák is also a sprout of sugar cane.

Akaiá, اکیّا अकैया

One of the sacks or baskets of a pannier.

Akan, آکن आकन

Grass and weeds collected from a ploughed field.—See Godhar.

A'kás bel, آکاس بیل आकास बेल

The air creeper *(Cuscuta reflexa ?)*. It has no root, or leaves, but grows luxuriantly on the tops of trees. It is from this circumstance that the name is derived—आकाश A'kás meaning in Hindí, the sky, the atmosphere. It is also called अमर बौंरिया Amar baunṛiá, or the undying creeper, and under this name is much used in native medicine as a remedy for rheumatism, and in alchemy is considered very efficacious as a transmuter of metals. It is supposed by Hindús that the man who finds its root will become rich.

A'khá, آکھا आखा

A pair of grain bags used as a pannier.

Akor, اکور अकोर

A bribe. Hence it is applied in the North-West to the coaxing a cow or buffalo, which has lost its calf, to eat grain. The same process is called Toria in Benares.

Akor, or Kor, as it is sometimes pronounced, is also applied to the food which a labourer eats in the intervals of work in the open field.

Akrá, اکرا अकरा

A grass, or vetch, which grows in fields under spring-crop, creeping round the stem of the young plant, and checking its growth *(Vicia sativa)*. Akrá, or Ankrí, as it is often called, is something like the Masúr, and it is used as fodder for cattle.

A'l, آل आल

The *Morinda citrifolia*. Its roots give a permanent red dye to the well-known Kharúá cotton cloth. It is said in the Mu'álaját-i-Dárá Shikohí to be the same as Manjít; but the latter is the *Rubia tinctorum*, or, perhaps, more correctly, the *Rubia cordifolia*. The plant, which is very hardy and rarely ever affected by drought, is generally considered not to be productive till the third year of its growth. It is cultivated in several provinces of India. In the Peninsula, the best quality comes from Maisúr. In the North-West Provinces, the Ál of Hattá and Bundelkhand is the most prized; and the chief emporium of its sale is Músánagar in the Doáb. It is grown only in Már and Kábar soils, and, when ripe, is dug out of the ground with narrow pickaxes; every care being taken to prevent the small roots sustaining injury, from the bark of which the most valuable portion of the dye is extracted. It is not an exhausting crop, and is usually followed by gram.

Ál is also sometimes used in the North-West for a Páná, or division of a village.

Álá, آلا आला

Wet; moist; land saturated with water, especially with rain water. This is the correct word, but it is provincially pronounced Al, Ahal, Alí, and Ael.—E. Also in the Eastern districts for the ridge separating fields, especially in land irrigated from tanks, or which depends on rain water for its moisture. It is sometimes written आईल *áíl*, and under the forms *ahal* and *ali* is occasionally, though incorrectly, applied to the fields themselves.—B.

Almárí, الماري अलमारी

A chest of drawers; a book-case. The word is derived from the Portuguese *almario*, which comes from the Latin *armorium*, an armoury, or cupboard for keeping arms and clothes in; in old English *aumbry*.—B.

A'lo, آلو आलो

The word is in use in Benares in the same sense as Dadrí, *q.v.* to signify a portion of unripe corn.

A'ltá, آلتا आलता

Was formerly on our tariff. It consists of balls of cotton impregnated with lac dye, and manufactured in all large towns where jungle produce is procurable. It is more generally known by the name of Maháwar.

Anárdána, اناردانه अनारदाना

A species of millet, so called from its resemblance to the seed of the pomegranate.—See As. Res. XV. 473.

Andhí, آندهي आंधी

A hurricane, or storm. The word is pure Hindí, and extremely common everywhere in India; but M. Langlès in an amusing note on the travels of Mr. Hodges, presumes that the word is a corruption from the French. "Aoundy, *ouragans.* J'ignore l'origine de ce mot sur lequel toutes mes recherches ne m'ont procuré aucun renseignement. Je serais tenté de croire qu'il y a erreur de la part de M. Hodges; car plusieurs savans voyageurs que j'ai consultés m'ont avoué ne point connaitre ce mot, et ne se rappelaient pas l'avoir entendu prononcer dans l'Inde; peut-être est-ce une corruption du mot Francais *ondée!!*"

A'ng, آنگ आंग

Signifies the demand on each head of cattle for the right of pasture.—Dehli. This is paid to the proprietor of the land. Bít is that which is paid per head to the cowherd.

Angaḍḍiyá, انگڈيا अंगड्डिया

Said in the Glossary to be applied to persons in the Northern

Provinces, who carry money concealed in their quilted clothes. The word may, perhaps, therefore be derived, or somehow corrupted, from Angarkha; but it is used, I believe, only in Gujrát, and not in our Northern Provinces, where Rokaria is the term applied to such persons; from *rokar*, money.—E.

*** In Behar it is the name of a class of men who are employed by merchants and bankers to carry remittances of cash from one firm to another. They travel long distances with very large sums of money, and are never known to embezzle or act dishonestly, though they are poorly paid. The facilities for making remittances now afforded by the introduction of the money-order and other systems, will probably, in course of time, lead to the extinction of this trade. The men are, I believe, of no particular caste.—B.

Áṅgan, آنگن आंगन

A court yard. An enclosed area near a house—Angná is also used in the same sense.—E. Rather the courtyard, or "patio," as the Spanish call it, formed by the rooms of the house itself, which is usually built round the four sides of a square.—B.

Angwárá, انگوارا अंगवारा

The proprietor of a small portion of a village.—Eastern Oudh and Benares.

It is also applied in the former province to reciprocal assistance in tillage.

Anjan, انجن अंजन

A grass which grows in great abundance in the Upper Provinces, and is largely used as fodder for cattle.

Anjaná, انجنا अंजना

An inferior kind of rice.—See Dhan.

Ánk, آنک आंक

Figure, unit, number, amount, a share. Hence, Ankdár is used in the Central Doáb to signify a sharer.

The initial *A* is either long or short—both are correct; but the former is most usual in Hindí.

Áṅwlá, آنولا आंवला

(Phyllanthus emblica). A kind of myrobalan. The fruit is acid, and is stated in the "Tálíf-i Sharíf" to be of great use in cutaneous eruptions, and to be known also as بجي *Bijji* and دهابري پهل *Dhábrí Phal.*

The tree is worshipped by agriculturists on the 11th of Phagun, which day is therefore known by the name of आश्रोंला एकादसी, and on this occasion libations are poured at the foot of the tree, a thread (generally red or yellow), is bound round the trunk, prayers are offered up for its fruitfulness, and the ceremony is concluded by a Pranám, or reverential inclination of the head to the tree.

Áokán, آوکان आओकान

Straw and grain heaped up.—Benares. See Gantah.

Áokhal, آوکهل आओखल

Land reclaimed from waste, and brought under cultivation. Also spelt ऊखल *úkhal,* especially in the Northern Doáb and Dehli.

Áorí, آوري आओरी

Bank of a pond or rivulet to the water's edge; applied generally to signify a piece of dry land left uncultivated.

Ár, آر आर

Ladle used in sugar factories.—E. Oudh. The same word, or

rather आड़, is applied in Benares as an abbreviation of Arárá, the bank of a pond. And in Hindí generally *Ár* signifies a goad.

Arába, ارابه अराबा

A cart. It is usually spelt with an ع, but the "Burḥan-i Káti'" gives it correctly with an ا. The word being purely Persian cannot begin with ع. In the "Farhang-i Rashídí" and in the "Haft Kulzam," the king of Oudh's dictionary, I find no mention of it under either letter, but in the former, under the article Banádar, it is spelt with an ع. Arába is not much used in India, except in writing; but it is in common use throughout the Turkish empire. Richardson describes it as a two-wheeled carriage; but in Constantinople it has four wheels.

Arah, اره अरा

Cross-ploughing. The straight furrow is *khaṛá*, and ploughing from corner to corner is *nok-náka*. This is only when fields require three ploughings.—E. *add.*

Aṛáṛ, اڑاڑ अड़ाड़

Outsheds for cattle; harvest floor for Mahwa blossoms.—Eastern Oudh and Benares.—E.

Otherwise a small grass hut in the jungle, where the cowherds pass the night; it is usually on the edge of a cleared patch on which the cattle assemble. Fires are sometimes lighted round them to keep off tigers. See Bathán.—B.

Aṛáṛá, اڑاڑا अड़ाड़ा

Steep bank of a river, pond, or tank.

Araí, ارئي अरई

Goad at the end of a whip. The diminutive of Ar. *q.v.*

'Araḳ, عرق अरक

Juice; whence we derive our "Arrack."

Araṇḍ, ارنڈ अरंड

The castor-oil plant (*Palma Christi*).

Also रेंढ़ी reṅṛhí, which is more common.—B.

Ardáwa, ارداوہ अर्दावा

Ground meal. The mixture now known by the name of Ardáwa comprises equal portions of the chick pea and barley, and forms almost universally, in Upper India, the food of horses kept by Europeans.

Argaṛá, ارگڑا अर्गड़ा

An enclosure, or pound for cattle, in Puráṇiyá (Purneah). Elsewhere called Pháṭak.—B.

Arhar, ارهر अरहर

A species of pulse (*Cytisus Cajan*) called also frequently توار tuár.

The "Mirat-i-Aftabnama" says that tuár or túr, is only amongst the people of Shahjahánabad (Dehlí) synonymous with Arhar, and that elsewhere Túr is another species and larger than Arhar, having a stalk like sugar-cane. It is also called Rahar.

Arhaṭ, ارهٹ अरहट

*** Also and perhaps more commonly रहट rahaṭ. A machine for raising water from a well, usually called by Europeans the "Persian wheel." Its construction is rather complicated and may be thus described. Across the mouth of a well is laid a long beam or láṭh, one end of which projects six or seven feet beyond the edge of the well; this beam serves as an axis to a large heavy double wheel hanging over the well, and has at its other end a small wheel with cogs of wood, which fit into corresponding cogs in a horizontal wheel, whose axis is fixed into the ground below and at the top into a beam supported at either end by walls of mud. To this upright axis is attached a long branch of a tree to which a buffalo is harnessed, having his eyes blinded by little caps of leather. He walks round and round the horizontal wheel and sets the whole in motion. On the wheel that hangs over the well is a long string of little earthen pots called तिंड tinḍs which going down empty, and coming up full, tilt over at the top and discharge their contents into a trough which carries the water along an earthen conduit or aḍḍá to considerable distances. It is obvious that such a well cannot be worked where the water is very far from the surface, as the expense and difficulty of making a long string of pots or tinḍs would be very great. Accordingly the Persian wheel is not found much lower down than the Upper Doáb, and is more common on the Jamna side of the Doáb than near the Ganges. It is, however, almost the only kind of well-gear known in the Panjáb. The creaking of the wheels and the splash and sparkle of water, with the old mud walls under a spreading tree, form one of the commonest and most pleasing features in a Panjáb landscape. As regards supply of water it is a question whether the arhaṭ or the *charas* q.v. is the better. My own opinion is in favour of the former, as its supply is continuous, though each tinḍ holds but little water; the huge charas discharges more water, but much time is lost in its descent and ascent. I think it will be found that an arhaṭ worked for twelve hours—other things being equal—delivers more water than a charas worked for the same time. See Cháhí, in Part III.—B.

'Aríat, عاریت आरीयत

Borrowing anything which is itself to be returned—from the Arabic عار. It differs from Karẓ, inasmuch as in the latter, the articles borrowed are not to be identically returned.—See "Hedaya," Book XXIX.*

Arthiá, ارتهيا अर्थिया

A client, a broker, an agent, a dependant.

Arwí, اروي अरवी

A species of Arum, an esculent root called in the Eastern districts a कचालू Kachálú, and घूंइंयां ghuñiñyáñ.

Asharfí, اشرفي अशरफी

A gold mohar.—See "Prinsep's Useful Tables," p. 4.

More correctly Ashrafí. The gold mohar is not now a legal tender in British territory, though there are heaps of them in existence. The ordinary value is 16 Rs., but varies according to the character of the coin.—B.

Ashjár, اشجار अशजार

Trees; plural of the Arabic شجرة.

Ashráf, اشراف अशराफ

Plural of the Arabic شريف *Sharíf*, noble. A class of cultivators in Rohilkhand, and Oudh, and Benares, who designate themselves by this title, and claim certain privileges. The opposite of the term is ارذال, *i.e.* those of low degree, the vulgar.—E.

The term is generally used in speaking of Brahman, Rajput, or Bhúíñhár cultivators, as opposed to Kurmís, Kachhís, and the like, who are razíl. The privileges claimed by the Ashráf are principally that they should be assessed at a lower rate, and have better lands assigned them than the Irzál.—B.

* *e.g.* If you borrow an umbrella it is *'ariat*, if you borrow money it is *ḳarz*.—B.

'Ashrát, عشرات अशरात

Tens; plural of the Arabic عشر ten.

Asíchá, اسيچا असीचा

Unirrigated; from अ not, and सिचना to water.

Aṣíl, اصيل असील

A female servant amongst Mussulmans. It bears also a contrary meaning; as, noble by birth. The origin of both is from the Arabic. The former meaning is derived from a free servant being superior to a Launḍí or purchased slave; the second from the stem of an illustrious lineage. It is not uncommon amongst ill-educated people to call a slave Aṣíl, but it is proper to observe the distinction noted above.

Ason, اسوں असों

The current year; the word is not used much in the North-West, but when used is generally pronounced Eson.*

Asthán, استهان अस्थान

An abode, residence. From the Sanskrit स्थान a place.

Asthal, استهل अस्थल

A fixed residence; usually applied to the spot in which Fakírs remain; a hermitage, presided over by a mahant.

Aṭá, اٹا अटा

Aṭárí, اٹاري अटारी

An upper-roomed house; an upper story. The second of these words is a diminutive of the first.

* From Persian اِین سنّه *in sanna*, this year.

Aṭábú, اٹابو अटाबू

The local name given by the resident Ahírs to a tract of country between the Kálá Naddí and the Ratwá, including the greater part of the Parganah of Márehra.

Aṭhmás, اٹهماس अठमास

Lands constantly ploughed from Asáṛh to Magh for sugar-cane, from आठ eight and मास a month. See Chaumás.

Athmaná, اتهمنا अथमना

The West.—Dehli. The word used in opposition to Athmaná is Ugmana, the East. Athae अथये is also occasionally used to signify the West, but its more correct and universal meaning is "the evening."* Both words appear to be derived from Ast, *q.v.*

Atarpál, اترپال अतर्पाल

Land which has been once under cultivation, and then abandoned. The word is more correctly Antarpal.—Central a d Lower Doáb.

Áwá, آوا आवा

A furnace or potter's kiln. A brick kiln is پجاوه pajáwa, a corruption of پزاوه pázáwa, from پزانیدن pazánídan, to cook.

Awásí, اواسي अवासी

A word used in the province of Benares (See Dadrí).—E.

It means unripe corn picked from time to time and brought home to be eaten. In times of scarcity many of the poorer ryots are often obliged to forestall the harvest in this way to the detriment both of their health and pockets.—B.

* Under this sense it is given as a local word of Bundelkhand, in the Vocabulary printed in No. 144 of the "Journal of the Asiatic Society of Bengal;" but it is a common Hindí term, by no means confined to that Province. In the same Vocabulary there are some other words which do not appear to be correctly entered, either with regard to their meaning or local application.

Awáí, اوائي अवाई

A pickaxe.—Eastern Oudh.

Bábú, بابو बाबू

Formerly Bábú was used only as a title of respect; now, especially among Europeans, it is used also to designate a native clerk who writes English, such clerks being chiefly Bengalís, among whom the title of Bábú has a wider acceptation than in Hindústan.

In Gorakhpúr, the descendants of the younger brothers of the Sarneṭ Raja are called Bábú, and there the term, still maintaining its original dignity, is applied generally to any man of family or influence. Crossing the Gogra into Benaudhá, and Benares, we find it applied only to the younger brothers, or near relatives of Rajas. Thus in Reg. VIII. of 1795, Sec. X., Bábús are defined to mean "persons of the (Benares) Raja's blood and family." In the East, Bábú is also applied to Mussalmans, as Bábú Musharraf Ali Khan of Talúka Báz Bahádur in A'zamgaṛh.—E. *add.*

The term Bábú is now very generally used by Europeans and natives alike, especially in Bengal and Behar, as a title of Zamíndárs and native gentlemen of wealth and position who have no other special title. The Zamíndár of Madhoban in Parganah Mehsi of Champáran has the title of "Rájkumár Bábú," to indicate his descent from the family of the Rajas of Sheohar and Maharajas of Betiyá (Bettiah). This title has been confirmed by Government; but in most cases the title of Bábú alone is assumed and conferred at the pleasure of the people themselves.—B.

Bágh, باغ

Bághíchah, باغيچه

A garden. Bághíchah or Bághchah is the diminutive of Bágh.—E.

Baghíchah is generally used as synonymous with फूलवारी phúlwárí, a garden attached to a gentleman's house. Bágh is applied to large orchards and mango groves which pay revenue to Government.—B.

Bágar, باگر बागर

A hedge of thorns or twigs.—Hoshangabad.

Ríndhna is used in the same sense in Benares, and Bár in the rest of the North West.

Báhá, باها बाहा

A watercourse; generally an artificial one, but in Dehli it is applied to a natural one; and Kahál and Khálá which generally signify natural, are there applied to artificial watercourses.

Báhná, باهنا बाहना

To plough. The word is in common use, but is not apparently mentioned in any dictionary, except Gilchrist's.

Báhan, باهن बाहन

Fallow land, from Bahna باهنا to plough.

Báhara, باهره बाहरा

The man who stands at the well to upset the water from the Charas, *q.v.*—Dehli.

Báj, باج बाज

A tax; a toll. Originally, tribute taken by one king from another. The "Burhán-i Kátí'" and the "Haft Kulzam" say—

مال باشد که بادشاهان بزرگ از بادشاهان زیردست گیرند

The word is also frequently written باژ. See Altamghá, Part III.

Bájra, باجره बाजरा

Bájrí, باجري बाजरी

(*Panicum spicatum*, Roxb.) (*Holcus spicatus*, Linn.) Bájrá is everywhere cultivated in these Provinces; but very sparingly to the East of Allahabad. The Bájrí is a smaller species of millet than the Bájrá, and ripens a month before it. Village Zamíndárs also comprehend by the term Bájrí, the stalk of the Bájra, used as fodder.—See Jour. A.S. Bengal, 1852, p. 158.

Bákrí, باكري बाकरी

A cow advanced about five months in pregnancy. A small buffalo is sometimes called a Bákrí.

Bákhar, باكهر बाखर

A house; an enclosure. Dwellings contained within an enclosure.

In Dehli the word is applied to cattle sheds.

In Bundelkhand, Saugor, and Malwa, it is an agricultural implement, a sort of bullock hoe, usually employed instead of the plough in the preparation of the black soil of those provinces. It has an iron scythe, in the room of a share, about twenty inches broad and five deep, fixed to the centre of a beam of wood between four and five feet long and six inches broad. This scythe enters about eight inches into the ground, effectually eradicating weeds and grass, and the beam pulverising the earth as it is turned up. The land intended for the Kharíf, or rainy season crop, is once turned by this instrument before the seed is scattered. It is then ploughed to cover the seed, and protect it against the birds. The Rabí land is turned up two or three times with the Bákhar during the rains, and sown with the drill plough about eight inches deep.

Bákand, باكند बाकंद

The proportion of two-fifths of the crop, which is sometimes paid as rent by cultivators to Zamíndárs. It is also known as Pachdo, Pachdoli, *i.e.* do (two) out of panch (five).

Bál, بال बाल

An ear of corn.

Bálá, بالا बाला

A grub which eats the young plants of wheat or barley when they are about six inches high.—Benares.

Bálákhánah, بالاخانه बालाखाना

An upper story; a "balcony," of which word Bálákhánah is the origin.

Bándh, باندھ बांध

An embankment.—See Bandhan.

Bání, باني बानी

Besides the meanings given ordinarily in the dictionaries it is the name of a yellow earth with which potters sometimes ornament their vessels. In parts of Rohilkhand it is called Kapas.

Bángá, بانگا बांगा

Raw cotton; not confined to one species, as mentioned in the Glossary.

Bánjh, بانجھ बांझ

Barren. From the Sanskrit वन्ध्या. It is sometimes used as an abbreviation of the word Banjar, which owns the same root.

Bánk, بانک बांक

A bend in a river. From the Sanskrit root वृज to be curved.

Bánsá, بانسا बांसा

From بانس Báns, a bamboo; the channel through which the

seed descends in a drilling machine. In Dehli it is generally known by the name of Orna. In the North-West the Bansa is generally fixed to the ordinary plough. The month in which the seed is cast is called Daurá or Nálá in the East, and Waira in the West.—See Haltadí.

In Benares the entire drilling machine is called Tár. It is a separate instrument, and not attached to the ordinary plough.

Báns, بانس बांस

A bamboo. It has not, as far as I am aware, been noticed in any work that the bamboo seldom flowers in Bengal till just before its death. At least, so say the natives, and my own experience confirms the supposition. The flowering of the bamboo is said to bring ill-luck to the owner of it.—B.

Bánsarí, بانسري बांसरी

A weed found in parts of the Doáb near the Jumna, which is very injurious, choking the crops, and most difficult to eradicate from arable land.

Báuní, باوني बाउनी

Seed time, also the act of sowing.—Rohilkhand and Doáb; called Baug in Benares and Behár, and Berá in Dehli.

Báolí, باولي बाओली

In upper India a large well where the water lies deep, and steps and galleries underground are made to give access to it.—E. *add.*

Báḳlá, باقلا बाकला

A bean; pot-herbs; the kidney bean (*Phaseolus vulgaris*). From the Arabic بقل. From which root is also derived the familiar word Bakkál بقال, the Arabic name of a Banya, or grain seller; but, originally, a person who sells pot-herbs and beans; a greengrocer.

Báṛ, باڑ बाड़

A fence; a hedge; a margin. Also Beṛha.

Bár, بار बार

Bára, بارہ बारा

Perquisite of the Ahír in milk; generally the milk of every eighth day.—Rohilkhand.

Bára are also the little fibrous roots of trees, which are favorable to transplanting.—E. *add.*

Báráhí, باراهي बाराही

Land, according to the dictionary in the "Tuḥfatu'l Hind."

Bárbardárí, باربرداري बारबरदारी

Carriage hire. From the Persian بار bár, a load, and برداري bardárí, conveyance.

Báṛí, باڑي बाड़ी

A plot for sugarcane or other garden produce; an enclosed piece of ground; a kitchen garden; also cotton. From the Hindí باڑ or بار an enclosure.

Báṛhí, باڑهي बाढ़ी

Interest in kind, paid upon seed grain. From بڑھنا baṛhná, to increase, to rise, to advance.

Bárik, بارك बारिक

Rain; according to the Dictionary in the "Tuḥfatu'l Hind."

Báriz, بارز बारिज

A term in arithmetic. The page of an account book is divided into two equal parts called Zillah; each Zillah is divided into two Rakans. The right hand Zillah is called the Hasho. The first right hand quarter (some say half) of the left Zillah is appropriated to the Bariz, and the remaining portion is called the Iráda. The Bariz contains the sum finally brought to account, after the necessary deductions have been made from the gross amount in the Iráda and Hasho, *q.v.*, also see Printed Glossary, *s.v.*

Básmatí, باسمتي **बासमती**

A fragrant kind of rice and millet. From Hindí **बास** scent. —See Dhan and Jawár.

Bátin, باتن **बातिन**

A tract of land in Etawah, lying between the river Jumna and the Ghar (which see).

Báwag, باوگ **बावग**

Seed time.—Eastern Oudh.—See Baoni.

The act of sowing.—B.

Bechirágh, بےچراغ **बेचिराग़**

Without a vestige: (a village) ruined beyond hope. It means, literally, without a light; بي privative, and چراغ a light.

Bíár, بيار **बीआर**

Seed bed; also air, wind. In the former sense the word is usually spelt with an ژ.

In Dehli, the evening is called Biyár.

In Saugor, it signifies waste land fit for cultivation.

In the Lower Doáb, it is used in the same sense as Pattí is elsewhere; that is, as a sub-division of a village.

Bíás, بياس **बिआस**

Land cultivated, to be sown in the following year; field under preparation for rice cultivation. The word is chiefly used in Rohilkhand.

Bíḍá, بيڈا बीडा

Mounds.—E. Oudh. The word is probably a corruption of بيہڑ uneven, rugged ground.

Bíhaṛ, بيہڑ बीहड़

Sterile land; uneven or cragged land; waste land; land full of ravines.

Bíjmár, بيجمار बीजमार

Failure of germination. From بيج seed, and مارنا to strike, to kill.—See Abij.

Bíjar, بيجر बीजर

A description of soil in which the cereal grains are generally grown.—Lower Doáb.

Bímá, بيما बीमा

Insurance. The word is also written بيمان.

Bínd, بيند बीन्द

A reed; a rush.

Bínḍa, بينڈه बींडा

A kind of rope made of grass or of the fibres of the Arhar plant. The word appears to be derived from بينڈھنا to plait, to braid. Hence بينڈي the hair plaited behind.

Bír, بير बीर

Pasturage. The word is in general use, but is most common in Dehli and the Saugor territory.

Bíṛá, بيڑا बीड़ा

A parcel made up of betel leaves and other ingredients, called Pan sopárí, which comprises betel leaves, areca or betelnut, catechu, quick-lime, aniseed, coriander seed, cardamums and cloves.—Ḳánún-i Islam.

Bírbání, بيرباني बीरबानी

A common expression in the North West, particularly among the Játs, applied to designate a man's own wife. The word बीर víra signifies in Sanskrit a warrior; a man. Bání is derived from the Sanskrit वनिता vanitá, a woman.

Biṭ, بيٹ बीट

A Dehli word.—See explanation under Ang.

Begár, بيگار बेगार

Begárí, بيگاري बेगारी

A person forced to work and carry burdens. Under the former regime, he got no pay. Now, though he gets pay, yet if he is ordered to work by any public official, he is still generally called Begár.

In Shakespear's and Smyth's dictionaries these words are represented as Hindí, but they are Persian also, and are entered in all the best Persian Lexicons.

کار فرمودن بے مُزد بود يعني کار بفرمايند و أُجرت ندهند

And the "Haft Kulzam" adds that the word is spelt either Begar or Bekar.

Behnaur, بيہنور बेहनौर

Behan, بيہن बेहन

Nursery for rice plants.—E. Oudh and Benares.—Panír is more commonly used in the North West, and Jáyí in Bundelkhand. Píad in Dehli is used as a nursery, not only of rice, but of any other plant.

Behrah, بيہرہ बेहरा

Grass kept for pasturage.—Rohilkhand.

The word is probably a corruption of Bír, *q.v.*

Bejhará, بيجهڑا बिझड़ा

A mixed crop, generally of gram and barley.

Bekas, بيکس बेकस

A kind of grass growing in low ground, which resembles the Dúb, but its leaves and stem are larger. It is good fodder for horned cattle, but is reckoned injurious to horses. It grows throughout the North West Provinces.

Beb, بيب बेब

Bábar, بابر बाबर

A grass from which a twine is made, which is much used for native beds. Bábar is also much used for thatching.

Bel, بيل बेल

Bel is the name applied to a spot in which the receiving pans are placed when sugar is manufactured. In most places the pans amount to three, Karáh, Chásní, and Phúlhá, the first being the biggest, and Chásní, which occupies a place between the other two, the smallest. In Dehli, Bojh sometimes takes the place of the Karáh and Karáhí of the Chásní; the Phúlhá being frequently omitted, especially of late years.

Bel is also the name of the thorny quince (*Œgle Marmelos*) and the single Arabian jasmine (*Jasminum Sambac*). Also a creeper, a tendril, a pole for directing a boat, a spade, or hoe.

Belbúṭá, بيلبوٹا बेलबूटा

A bush. From Bel a tendril, and Búṭá, a flower.

Belchak, بيلچک बेलचक

Belchá, بيلچا बेलचा

A small hoe, or spade. Diminutives of Bel.

Belkí, بيلکي बेलकी

A cattle grazier.—Baitúl.

Belak, بیلک बेलक

A small mattock.—See Bel, Belchak.

Bent, بینٹ बेंट

The handle of an axe, hoe, and similar implements. Bent is the correct word; but it is generally pronounced Bítá in Rohilkhand, and Bintá in Dehli.

Byohár, بیوهار ब्योहार

Money lending, or traffic of any kind; a calling; a trade.

In Jabalpúr, the name is applied to a Kanúngo. The Sadr Byohár, besides his salary, holds large rent-free estates. From Sansk. व्यवहार.

Bera, بیر बेर

The lotus of the ancients. J. A. S. B. 1847, p. 235.—See Jharberí.

Beràna, بیرانہ बेराना

A grove of Ber trees. The Ber is the *Zizyphus jujuba*.—See Jharberí.

Birár Pánḍía, برار پانڈیا बिरार पांड़ीया

In Baitúl and the Deccan, is the Kanúngo of the North West Provinces.

Berḥá, بیڑها बेढ़ा

A paling. From Berḥná, to enclose with a fence, to surround. See next article.

Berḥná, بیڑهنا बेढ़ना

Besides the meaning above given, the word signifies in the Doáb, Bundelkhand, and Rohilkhand, "to drive off cattle by force." In this sense it is used generally in Hindústan, but Khedke lejáná is the equivalent term in the Dehli territory.

Beshí, بيشي बेशी

Increase; surplus: From the Persian بيش more.

Besan, بيسن बेसन

The flour of pulse; especially of Chaná (gram), or the chick pea, used for washing with.

Beṭh, بيٹھ बेठ

Sandy unproductive soil.—Rohilkhand.

Bhánkarí, بهانكري भांकरी

A jungle shrub found in great abundance in the Dehli territory. It differs in no respect from the Gokrú, *q.v.* It is used as a specific in certain complaints, and to attract purchasers its vulgar name is transformed by the druggists into Hasd Singhárá.

Bhát, بهات भात

Advances to ploughmen without interest.—Benares and Eastern Oudh.

Bhantá is used in this sense in Rohilkhand.

Bhát is also the name of a soil to the north of the Ganges that retains its humidity for a long time, and contains a large quantity of nitre. It is a peculiar soil, and is not found West of the Gandak.

In the Lower Doáb and Bundelkhand, Bhát means uneven ground.—See Bhatúa.

Bhíṭ, بهيٹ भीट

An elevation of earth made near a tank for the purpose of planting Pan; mounds of a tank; the vestige of an old house.

Bhelí, بهيلي भेली

A lump of coarse sugar; generally consisting of four or five seers.

Bhis, بهس भिस

The edible root of the Lotus. The correct word is भसींर Bhasínr, but it is provincially corrupted into Bhisendá, Bhis, and Basend.

Bhoí, بهوئي भोई

Used in the neighbourhood of the Narmadá (Nerbudda), to signify a "bearer." The same word is used in the Peninsula, and corrupted by Europeans into "boy." Hence the exclamation of "boy," so commonly used at Madras, is not, as has been supposed, a pure English, but a corruption of Bhoí.

Bhoí is also, to the South of the Nerbudda, applied to designate the head of a Gond village.

Bhúmiyá, بهوميا भूमिया

Landlord; a proprietor of the soil; descendant of the founder of the village. It is derived from भूमि land. In Ajmer it is the title of a village watchman who has land assigned him for maintenance. Tod. i. 497.

Bhúmiyáwat, بهومياوت भूमियावत

A general plundering, or more correctly a fight between neighbouring Zamíndárs about landed property.—Saugor.

Bhúṇḍiá, بهونڈيا भूंडिया

One who cultivates with a borrowed plough or hand instrument.—Central Doáb.

Bhúnhará, بهونهرا भूंहरा

A subterraneous dwelling; according to the Dictionary of Khan Arzu.

Bhúṛ, بهوڑ भूड़

A sandy soil. The word is frequently pronounced Bhúḍa. It is in Sahāranpúr the same as the tract called Bhábar in Rohilkhand.

Bhuṛarí, بهڑري भुड़री

A term applied to the corn which remains in the ear after being trodden out.—Rohilkhand and Delhi.

The corresponding word in Benares and the Lower Doáb is Linduri, and in the Upper and Lower Doáb, Dobrí, Pakurí, and Chittí.

These words are applied to the Rabi' grains chiefly, as wheat, barley, etc. To Jawár, Múng, etc. Chanchari, Gúri, Kosí, Karahí and Thanthí are more commonly applied.

Bhus, بهس भुस

Bhúsá, بهوسه भूसा

The husk of corn; chaff. The English gipsies use Pus in the same sense. (Trans. R.A.S. vol. ii., p. 543).

Bhusaurí, بهسوري भुसौरी

Bhusaulá, بهسولا भुसौला

Bhusehrá, بهسيهرا भुसेहरा

The place in a dwelling house for keeping straw. These terms are in general use; but Obrá اوبرا is also so applied in Dehli.

Bhusrá, بهسرا भुसरा

An inferior kind of wheat, *i.e.* one which yields too great a proportion of bran (भूसा).—Saugor.

Bhuṭṭá, بهٹا भुट्टा

The corn-cob or ear of Indian corn; any large bunch.

Bhor, بهور भोर

Dawn of day.

Bhadá, بهڈا भडा

A kind of grass which grows in poor soil, attaining the height of a little more than a foot. It makes excellent fodder.

Bhadbhadáná, بهدبهدانا भद्भदाना

Used in the Upper Doáb in the same sense as Bhadáhar (which see). It also means the shaking of fruit from a tree. Shakespear does not give this application of the term in his Dictionary; but bhadbhad and bhadbhadáhat, are said in it to denote the sound which is made by the fall of fruits.

Bhadwár, بهدوار भद्वार

Land prepared for sugar cane; land ploughed during the Kharíf, and allowed to lie fallow till cotton is sown; land ploughed from Asárh to Bhadon for the Rabí sowings. The name is derived from Bhadon, apparently because the entire rain of that month is allowed to saturate the field when ploughed. It is called Bhadwár Paṛál, from Paṛná, to lie fallow, in parts of Rohilkhand and the Doáb.

Bhadaí, بهدئي भदई

The produce of the month Bhadon. [Especially applied in Behar to the early rice crop. See Aghani. It is also pronounced Bhadoí भदोई بهدوي].

Bhang, بهنگ भंग

Bháng, بهانگ भांग

In Persian Bang. An intoxicating drink made from the leaves of the *Cannabis sativa.* The plant from which it is made has female flowers; the male being the Gánja plant, which is also applied to the purpose of intoxication, and is usually inhaled from a pipe. It is commonly considered that there is no difference between the plants which produce Bhang and Gánja, but natives generally recognise the distinction of the male and female plant noted above.

O'Shaughnessy says that Bang, or Sidhí, or Sabzi, consists

of the large leaves and capsules without the stalks, but makes no allusion to Bhang being produced from a plant different from that which produces Gánja.

The best Bhang of the N.W. Provinces comes from Bahráich and its neighbourhood, and from Dandwári in Kanauj; the best Gánja, from Rajsháhí, in Bengal. Bhang is also known by the name of Bijaya (See Gánja).

Bhangela, بهنگيله भंगेला

A sack or pannier made from the fibres of the Bhang plant. It is not so coarse or strong as the Gon.

Bhangra, بهنگره भंगरा

A small creeping herb with minute flowers which grows in a wet soil (*Verbesina prostrata*). There are said to be two species, the white and the black. The white is very common, and is much used in medicinal preparations; the black is unknown, but is much sought after by alchymists, and is reputed by native practitioners to be a panacea.

Bhare, بهرے भरे

A grass which grows in the jungles to the height of about nine feet, and is used for thatches and tatties. Its canes are known by the name of Núnre.

Bharná, بهرنا भर्ना

To give property in re-payment of a debt, literally, "to fill up."

Bharauná, بهرونا भरौना

A load of wood.—Gharáibu'l Lughát.

Bhaṭṭiyá, بهٹيه भटिया

The poorest kind of land in the Saugor territory and Bundle-khand. It is of a reddish colour, and has Kankar and other stones mixed up with it. It is very shallow in depth, and generally exhausted at the end of the third year, after which it requires a fallow of four years to restore it. Only Kodo and Kutkí, and the poorest sort of corn can be raised on this kind of land. It is more generally called Bhattí and Bhatua in Bundelkhand.—See "Spry's Mod. India," II. 276.

Bhaṭkaṭaiyá, بهتكتيا भटकटईया

(*Solanum Jacquini*). There are two kinds of this herb according to the "Talíf-i Sharíf;" the white is usually called the Katáí, and the large and red kind the Barehta. The flower is called Gulkhár *i.e.* "rose-thorn." It may be doubted if this statement is quite correct. There are generally reckoned to be four kinds of Kaṭaiya, of which the Bhaṭkaṭaiyá, frequently miscalled the camel's thorn, is one, and the common people, who see these weeds growing wild, do not acknowledge that there are two kinds of Bhaṭkaṭaiyá. The only Bhaṭkaṭaiyá which they know is much used in veterinary practice, particularly in diseases which affect horned cattle. It is also devoutly believed that if the roots of the Bhaṭkaṭaiyá, are shown to a man bitten by a snake, he immediately recovers.—(See Jawasa).

The other three kinds of Kataiya are the following.

Bang Kataiya. This resembles a common thistle, and is not applied to any useful purpose. It is known also by the name of Satyánásí, and found in all parts of the country.

Gol Kataiya. This is not so erect as the others, but spreads more over the surface of the ground. It has purple flowers and produces a round berry. It is frequently used in native prescriptions.

Kataiya proper. This is the largest of the four, and is more frequently found in jungles than near the abode of man. It is a prickly shrub, growing to the height of ten or twelve feet, and does not at all resemble the other Kataiyas.

Bhaṭolar, بهٹولر भटोलर

Lands allotted to Bhats or Bards.

Bhaṭulá, بهٹلہ भटुला

The name given to bread made from the grain of Arhar, Chaná and Múng. It is called also Gánkar. It is notorious for its hardness, and is therefore seldom eaten by those who can afford to grow or purchase the better grains.

Bhaṭulá is said to have been the cause of the elevation of the Bhadauriás, and the story, absurd as it may appear, is commonly believed in the neighbourhood of Bhadáwar, and is not denied by the Bhadauriás themselves. One of the Bhadauriá chiefs, Gopal Singh, went to pay his respects to the Emperor Muhammad Shah. The chief had very large eyes, so much so, as to attract the attention of the Emperor, who asked him how he obtained them. The chief, who was a wit, replied that in his district nothing but Arhar was grown, and that from the constant practice of straining at swallowing Bhaṭulá, his eyes had nearly started out of his head. The Emperor was pleased at his readiness, and bestowed on him other Parganahs on which he could produce the finer grains.—See Bhadauriá.

Bhaṭṭhí, بهٹهي भट्ठी

A liquor shop; a distillery.

Bhaṭṭhídár, بهٹهيدار भट्ठीदार

A person who manufactures and sells spirituous liquors.

Bhawan, بهون भवन

A house; a temple; a fort.

Bhaiyábánṭ, بهيابانٹ भैयाबांट

See Bhaíbanṭ and Bhaiyáchára.

Bihaṇd, بهنڈ बिहंड

Land cut up by a torrent; according to the Gharáíbu'l-lughát.

Bikrí, بكري बिक्री

Sale. From Bikná بكنا to be sold.

Bilahbandí, بله‌بندي बिलहबनदी

The Glossary is correct under Bílabandy; but in the North West, the word is most usually applied to arrangements made for securing the revenue.

Billí-loṭan, بلي‌لوٹن बिल्लीलोटन

Valerian. The name is derived from its reputed effect upon cats, who are said to be so delighted with its fragrance, as to roll about in their ecstasies. From billí بلي a cat, and loṭná لوٹنا to wallow; to roll.

Bilaungí, بلونگي बिलौंगी

A species of grass.

Binaulá, بنوله बिनौला

Cotton seed. It is much used as fodder for cattle, and when steeped in oil makes a capital lamp.

Binauriyá, بنوريه बिनौरिया

The name of a herb which grows about a foot and a half high in fields which have been sown with Kharíf crops. It bears several little flowers of a purple colour, and is given as fodder to horned cattle.

Birhána, برهانه बिरहाना

Lands in which culinary herbs are produced.—Rohilkhand.

Birinjphúl, برنجپهول बिरिंजफूल

A species of rice.—See Dhan.

Birkah, برکه बिर्का

A pond; a small well.

Birrá, بِرّا बिर्रा

Gram and barley sown in the same field. Bejara and Bejar are the more usual terms.

In Dehli it is applied to Chaná, or gram, injured by wet.

It is also the name of a ceremony connected with the building of a house.—E. Oudh.

Birwá, بروا बिरवा

A tree. In Eastern Oudh it is the name given to the labourer employed upon the Daurí or Berí, *q.v.*

Birwáhí, برواهي बिरवाही

An orchard. From Birwa بروا a plant; a tree.

Bisátí, بساتي बिसाती

A pedlar. From the Hindí Bisát بسات means; capital; stock. The Arabic Bizá'at بضاعت has also the same signification. "Pars opum," says Golius, "quæ impenditur in mercaturam, lucroque exponitur." Bisátí, etc., is sometimes spelt with an Arabic ط but incorrectly; though, as Bisát بساط means a carpet spread out, there may appear to be some reason in calling بساطي a pedlar; as in that mode Bisátís usually dispose of their goods at country fairs.

Bishnprítdár, بشن پریتدار बिष्णप्रीतदार

Grantees of Brahmin caste to whom land has been assigned in the name of Bishn or Vishnu, from religious and charitable motives by Zamíndárs.—Benares.—E. Oudh.

Bisht, بشت बिष्ट

A provincial term in Kamáon for a kind of Talúkdár, whose office is in the gift of Government.

Biskhapra, بسكهپره बिसखपरा

The name of a grass which is used in medicine (*Trianthema pentandra*). It spreads over the ground, and forms a circle of nearly a yard in diameter.

Bisahrú, بسهرو बिसहरू

A purchaser. From Bisahná بسهنا to buy.

Biṭhak, بٿهك बिठक

Ant hills.—Eastern Oudh and Benares. Literally, a seat or platform, where people meet to converse.*

Bitaurá, بتوره बितौरा

A heap of dried cow dung, called Battaiya in Rohilkhand.

Bitrábandí, بترابندي बित्राबन्दी

The same as Bilahbandí, *q.v.*—Saugor.

Bo, بو बो

Cultivation. It is usually combined with Jot, which signifies the same. Bo is the verbal root of Boná, to sow.

Boárá, بوارا बोआरा

Seed time; sowing. Boáí بواي, Báwag باوگ, and Boní بوني, are also used. From Boná بونا, to sow.

* Also, and perhaps more generally, especially in the second sense it is spelt, बैठक baiṭhak, from बैठना to sit.—B.

Bob, بوب बोब

The sowing of grain by the drill.—Bundelkhand.

The term Jaiyá is so applied in Dehli; and Wair in Rohilkhand and the Doáb.—See Bansa.

Bodá, بودا बोदा

A buffalo.—Saugor.

Bodar, بودر बोदर

A place to stand on for throwing the Daurí or basket by which water is raised to a higher level.—Benares.

Pairá is the corresponding word in Dehli.—See Daurí, Boka, Berí.

Boíbáchh, بويباچه बोइबाछ

Assessment to be realized on cultivation.—Dehli. From بونا to sow and باچه selection, division. See Printed Glossary under Bach.

Bojh, بوجه बोझ

Literally, a load. In agricultural language it comprises about five Dhokas of corn.—See Dabia and Bel.

Bojhbaṭái, بوجه بٹائي बोझबटाई

A mode of division by stocks, or bundles of mowed corn.—Rohilkhand. It is derived from the preceding word.

Boká, بوکه बोका

A basket, pail, or leather bag, for throwing water to a higher elevation: called also Berí and Daurí (which see). This word is not in Shakspeare's Dictionary, but it would appear to be common in India.

Búd, بود बूद

Literally, existing; being; from the Persian بود "was."

In fiscal language Búd is much used in combination with other words, as Hastobúd, Búd-nabúd.—See Hastobúd.

Búk, بوک बूक

Land recovered by the recession of a river.—Rohilkhand.

Búkárá, بوکارا बूकारा

Bears the same meaning, but is applied only when the land is rendered useless, by a deposit of sand.—Rohilkhand.

Bulandí, بلندي बुलन्दी

High land. From Buland, high.

Bun, بن बुन

Unground coffee. Coffee before it is made into kahwa قہوہ.

Búnga, بونگہ बूंगा

A stack of Bhús, or straw. It is frequently pronounced Bonga.

Búnṭ, بونٹ बूंट

A green unripe gram (*Cicer arietinum*).—See Chaná.
Also used for gram in general.

Burída, بریدہ बुरीदा

Fields cut by stealth by a cultivator. From the Persian burídan بریدن to cut down.—Rohilkhand.

Burrí, بُرّي बुर्री

Sowing, by dropping seed from the hand into the furrow; instead of sowing broadcast, or with the drill. The words Gurrí, Gullí, Sí, are also so applied.

Bora, بورہ बोरा

A sack for holding rice.

Boro, بورو बोरो

Marsh rice. The "Fasl," which is added to the word in the Printed Glossary, means the harvest of this rice.

Bauchhár, بوچهار बौछार

Wind and driving rain.

Baulí, بولي बौली

Synonymous with a Khas settlement, according to section 12, Reg. IX. of 1805. The word may be presumed to be meant for Bhaolí. In Behar it is equivalent to Batáí, *q.v.*

Boáí, بوائي बोआई

Sowing. Boní, Bawera and Boara have the same meaning.—See Boara.

Babúl, ببول बबूल

Babúr, ببور बबूर

The name of a tree. Called also Kíkar (*Acacia Arabica*, Roxb.)—See Printed Glossary under Bavalla. The wood is much used in making agricultural implements, such as ploughs, sugar mills, etc., and in the construction of carts. The Babúl produces also a valuable gum, and its bark, being a powerful astringent, is used in tanning by Chamárs.

Bádámí, بادامي बादामी

A species of rice. (See further under Dhan.)

Badbácha, بدباچه बद्बाचा

A false or fraudulent Bach or division.—Dehli

Badí, بدي बदी

The dark half of the month; from full to new moon.

Badhiyá, بڈّھیا बढिया

A disease affecting Jawár, Bájra, sugar cane, and Indian corn, which prevents the head from shooting.

Bagár, بگار बगार

Pasture ground.—Bundelkhand.

Applied generally as synonymous with Banjar.

Bagarí, بگري बगरी

A species of rice cultivated chiefly in the province of Benares. —See Dhan.

Bahera, بہیرہ बहेरा

The Belleric Myrobalan (*Terminalia bellerica*, Roxb.)

Bajídár, بجیدار बजीदार

An agricultural servant in Rohilkhand who takes corn as a recompense for his labour, in distinction to a Mihdar who receives money. The latter is derived from محنت labour, and might therefore apply equally to both.

Bajhwat, بجھوٹ बझवट

Stalk of cereals, without the ear.—Eastern Oudh and Gorakhpúr.

Bakárá, بکارا बकारा

Intelligence forwarded by word of mouth. From Bak باک speech.

Bakel, بکیل बकेल

Twine made from the root of the Dhak tree. The word is chiefly used in the Eastern Provinces, not in the North-West.

Bakhá, بکھا बखा

Grass kept for pasturage.—Rohilkhand.

Bakhár, بکھار बखार
Bakhárí, بکھاري बखारी

A granary or store house.—Khán Arzú spells it بخار.

Bakhar, بکھر बखर

A kind of plough or bullock hoe in use in Bundelkhand, Saugor and Malwa. Its use has been fully described under Bákhar, but the more correct and usual pronunciation is Bakhar.

Bakolí, بکولي बकोली

Name of a green caterpillar destructive to rice crops.

Baláhar, بلاهر बलाहर

A low caste servant; a village guide or messenger. The word is not generally in use to the East of Allahabad. In the "Gharáíbu'l Loghát" it is spelt بلادهر Baládhar. The word is probably derived from bulana بلانا to call; to summons; just as another village menial, the Dauṛáha, is derived from dauṛna دوڑنا to run.

Balbhog, بلبهوگ बलभोग

Taking possession by force of another's right. The word is derived from the Sanskrit Bal बल force, and Bhog भोग possession; wealth; enjoyment.

Bald, بلد बलद

Bullocks; horned cattle. The word is not in the Dictionaries, though Baldiya بلديا is given as a cow-herd, a bullock driver.

Baldeo, بلديو बलदेव

A cow-herd. From the preceding word.

Baluá, بلوا बलुआ

Sandy. The word is used chiefly in Benares.—See Doras.

Balsundar, بلسندر बलसुन्दर

The name of a kind of soil in Azimgaṛh. The origin of all these words is bálú بالو sand.

Bamíṭhá, بميٹها बमीठा

A term applied to ant hills in the Lower Doáb. Bámbhí بانبهي which is the correct word, is used in the North West, and Bithak in Eastern Oudh. Also a snake-hole. Probably derived from मर्मी a stinging insect, and स्थानं a place.

Bamhní, بمهني बम्हनी

Light red soil.—Eastern Oudh.

Banbhánṭa, بن بهانٹه बनभांटा

The wild egg plant (*Solanum melongena*).

Banchari, بن چري बनचरी

A high jungle grass, the leaves of which are much like the Jawar. Wild elephants are very fond of this grass, which is known also by the name of Baro.

Bandá, بندا बन्दा

A grain magazine above ground.—Saugor.

Bandhán, بندهان बनधान

A pension.

Bandhán, بندهان बनधान

Bandhíá, بندهيا बंधीया

Raised earthen embankments for flooding lands. Bándh from bándhná باندهنا to bind, is in more general use.—See Bandhwás.

Bandhán, بندهان बंधान

Bandhúr, بندهور बंधूर

Purchase of grain in advance of the harvest.—Saugor.

Bandhwás, بندهواس बनधवाश

Land embanked all round, or in such manner as to retain the water. It is also generally applied to level ground; uneven ground being called Tagar, and when surrounded by embankments Tagar Bandhia.—Jabalpúr.

Bandlí, بندلي बनद्ली

A species of Rohilkhand rice. Called also Raímunia and Tilokchandan.—See Dhan.

Bandrí, بندري बनद्री

A grass which is found in fields of rice and Kodo. It grows to the height of about two feet, and has an ear, but produces no grain. It is used as fodder for cattle.

Bandtál, بندتال बनद्ताल

Damming a water course for the purpose of irrigation.

Bangá, بنگا बंगा

Is the name given to the white kind of Sarson (*Sinapis dichotoma*, Roxb.) It is also applied locally to well-water, slightly brackish.—Central Doáb.

Bangká, بنگکا बंगका

An aquatic beetle which eats rice plants. It is said to manufacture something like a boat from leaves, and to paddle itself along from plant to plant. It is harmless when the water is let out from the field. It is also called Katua.—Benares.

Bangkí, بنگکي बंगकी

A species of rice cultivated in Benares.—See Dhan.

Bangkaṭaiyá, بنگکٹیا बंगकटइया

See Jawasa and Bhatkataiya.

Bangaunṭhá, بن‌گونٹھا बनगौंठा

Cowdung found in the forests.—See Bankanda.

Bangaliyá, بنگلیا बंगलिया

Literally, Bengali. A species of rice cultivated in the Eastern part of these provinces.—See Dhan.

Banínhár, بنّیہار बन्नीहार

The word is used to signify a ploughman, or labourer, whose services are paid in Banní, or in kind.—Benares.

Banjin, بنجن बंजिन

Land close by the village.

Also the name of a weed about three feet high, which springs up with Kharíf crops. It is much sought after by Fakírs who practice Alchemy.

Bankhará, بنکھرا बनखरा

Lands on which cotton has grown during the past season.—Central Doáb.

The word is derived from ban, cotton, which though very commonly used in this sense, is not in the dictionaries. It is not improbable that it is so applied, because a field of cotton bears resemblance to a ban बन or forest. Baraundha is more commonly used in the same sense as Bankhara, in Rohilkhand and the Upper Doáb; and Múḍí (perhaps from مونڈنا to cut, to shave) in Dehli.

Kapseta is also very generally used for a field of cut cotton; from the Sanskrit karpas कर्पास, the cotton plant, or undressed cotton.

Bankaṇḍá, بن کنڈا बनकनडा

Cowdung found in a jungle or forest, or dried for fuel. From Ban بن a forest, and Kaṇḍa کنڈا cowdung. Bangautha is also used in this sense. Arní Kandá is likewise applied to this useful article of Hindu economy; from the Sanskrit आरण्य a forest. In Dehli this is corrupted into Rana, and coupled with گوسا Gosa, *i.e.* a cake of cowdung. The familiar words U'pla and Gobar are applied to that which is collected at home.

Bankar, بنکر बनकर

Spontaneous produce of jungle or forest land, such as gums, brushwood, honey, etc.* It is generally supposed that the person who possesses the right of collecting Bankar, or any tax or cess in lieu of it, holds necessarily a Zamíndárí title in the ground which produces it. But this is an erroneous impression. The Sudder Dewáni Adaulat have ruled that the sale of Bankar does not convey Zamíndárí right. One case is reported in which A. purchased, at a public sale, a portion of a Zamíndárí.—B. purchased another portion, besides the bankar of the whole estate. The Court ruled that the purchase made by B. conveyed to him a right over all the forest timber of the entire estate, though growing on the portion purchased by A. It was declared however that the latter from his right in the soil was permitted to clear away the trees, and to cultivate it; the proceeds of the timber felled appertaining to B.—(See "Reports," Vol. II., p. 105.)

It will be seen also at Section 9, Reg. I. of 1804, that the British Government consider Bankar as a thing altogether distinct from Zamíndárí.

Bankas, بنکس बनकस

A grass used in making ropes.

* See J. A. S. B. for 1845, p. 543.—E. *add.*

Bankaṭí, بنكتي बनकटी

The right obtained by clearing jungle, and bringing it into cultivation.—Benares.

Banní, بني बन्नी

A portion of grain given to a labourer as remuneration for his services.—Benares.

Bansá, بنسا बनसा

A grass which grows in fields of rice and dál. It is given as fodder for cattle.

Bansí, بنسي बनसी

A kind of wheat with blackish ears.—Hoshangábad.

Bantariá, بنتريا बन्तरिया

A class of wood rangers in some of the northern Parganahs of Gorakhpúr, holding about 20,000 acres granted by the native government in lieu of police services. As the services are no longer performed, the lands have been resumed, and settled at very easy rates with the occupant Bantariás.

Baṛ, بڙ बड़

The Banian tree; the large Bengal or Indian fig tree (*Ficus Indica*). It is commonly also known as the Bargat बरगत.

Baráhí, براهي बराही

A small species of sugar cane.—Saugor, Lower Doáb, and Bundelkhand.

Barár, برار बरार

Tod says (Annals of Raj. Vol. I. p. 143). "Barrar is an

indefinite term for taxation, and is connected with the thing taxed, as Halbarrar, plough-tax."

An apportionment of Bhyachara Kists (or instalments of rent) according to the agreement of the village community. Generally, any division; bearing much the same meaning as Báchh.

The word, though common in the Doáb and Western India, is not found in Hindí dictionaries.

Barban, بربن बर्बन

A North wind according to Khan Arzú.—See Dándwára.

Bardí, بردي बर्दी

Light stony soil. Also Bardár.—Saugor.

Barehṭá, بريهتا बरेहटा

Land of the third quality; also a plot of ground on which sugar cane has been lately grown.—Saugor. See Bhatkataiya.

Barej, بريج बरेज

Barejá, بريجا बरेजा

A betel or pán garden.

Bargan, برگن बरगन

Partition; a share.—Hoshangabad.

Barhá, برها बरहा

A channel for the passage of water from a well to a field, or from one field to another. To the eastward it may be considered the smallest size of watercourse; the size in the ascending scale is indicated by the terms Barhá, Nalkí, Nalí, Narwá and Gúl. But in the West, Barhá is by no means a small water course. The word is probably derived from Baṛhna بڑھنا to increase, though the usual mode of spelling it is against that etymology.

A field in which cows are fed; a rope, or string; especially one by which a harrow is drawn, or one that is thrown over a cart to keep the load from falling or getting injured.

In parts of Central and Upper Doáb, Barhá is the term applied to the land of a township which is farthest from the homestead. Bárá is the nearest to the village; Manjha between both.

Baṛhiyá, بڑهيا बढ़िया

The name of a sugar millstone, extracted from the Chanar quarries.

Barhotarí, بڑهوتري बढ़ोतरी

See Barhí.

Baṛkuiyán, بڑكويان बड़कुइआं

A Kachha well, *i.e.* one without a cylinder of masonry.—E. Oudh.

Baro, برو बरो

The name of a high jungle grass.—See Bancharí.

Baronkhá, برونكها . बरोंखा

A kind of sugar cane with long thin joints.

Baraundhá, بروندها बरौंधा

Cotton land.—Rohilkhand.

Barroh, بروه बरोंह

A name given to the uplands in the Parganah of Jánibrast, *i.e.* the right bank of the Jumna, Zillah Etowah.

Barsáná, برسانا बर्साना

To winnow the grain; literally, to cause to rain.

Bartush, برتش बरतुश

Land sown with sugar cane, after a rice crop.—Rohilkhand.

Barat, برت बरत

A disease which affects rice crops.

A leathern girth, or large cable; especially one used for drawing water by a púr, or large well bag.

In the Dehli territory, Barat, or Barit, is also used to signify the Government Jama, or a portion of it.—See Bharit.

Basíkat, بسيكت बशीकत

Inhabited. From Basna بسنا to dwell.

Basít, بسيت बशीत

The head manager in a village; the same as Mahetya or Mukaddam.—Central Doáb.

Basenḍ, بسينڈ बिसेंड

An edible root which is found in jhíls or marshes.

In Rohilkhand the word signifies a Khákrob, or sweeper.

Basgit, بسگت बसगित

Homestead; site of a village residence. From بسنا to dwell. The word is pure Hindí, but is more used in Eastern Hindustan than in Western.

Basúlí, بسولي बसूली

A small instrument for cutting. The diminutive of Basúla, an adze.

Bastah, بستہ बस्ता

A cloth in which papers are bound up; a bundle of papers. From the Persian بستن to bind.

Baswárí, بسواري बसवारी

Basaur, بسور बसौर

A bamboo garden. From बांश a bamboo.

Baṭ, بت बट

A partition; division. From بتنا to be divided.

Baṭáí, بتائي बटाई

Is derived from the word preceding, and signifies the same as the Metayer system of Europe; but it includes not only the literal Metayer, *i.e.* "à moitié fruit," but the "tier franc," or any share into which the crops may be divided. In poor lands a batáí of one-sixth only is not unfrequently the extent of the Zamíndár's demand.

Batáí navásiya is applied to a division which gives nine shares to one party, and seven to another.—Benares.—See Hariáṅw.

Baṭenth, بتينتهه बटेंथ

Baṭania, بتنيا बटनिया

Proprietor, or holder of a share.—Central Doáb.—See above, under Baṭ and Baṭáí.

Baṭes, بتيس बटेस

A passage; a pathway. Baṭía بتيا is in more general use in the same sense. Both are from the Sanskrit Báṭ बाट a road, a highway.

Baṭhán, بتهان बठान

Pasture ground. From بيٹهنا to sit, to settle, or more probably from बल्द a bullock, and स्थान or ठान a place. Eastern Oudh. —See Baisak; which is also similarly derived. *Abathán* is more usually applied to the little shed erected by cowherds in the jungles to sleep in at night, the cattle being all collected round it. It is also called अरार or अड़ाड़, *q.v.*

Bathuá, بتهوا बथुआ

A herb which springs up with Rabi' crops, and in the neighbourhood of water. It is sometimes cooked as a pot-herb by the poorer classes (*Chenopodium album*).

Bathiyá, بتهيا बथिया

See Bitaura.

Batúrí, بتوري बतूरी

A name given in Benares to Chaní, or the small kind of Chana, *q.v.*

Baṭolan, بٹولن बटोलन

Baṭoran, بٹورن बटोरन

Gathering or collecting grain in one place at the time of harvest. From بٹورنا baṭorná, to gather up.

Batar, بتر बतर

Land in a state fit for the plough.—Saugor. In the Panjab I have heard watar वतर used to signify the rain which falls in January, and by softening the soil enables the young wheat to sprout and grow.—B.

Baṭwár, بٹوار बटवार

A custom or police officer stationed on a road.

A tax gatherer, who collects taxes in kind.

Bawáda, بوادہ बवादा

A herb something like the Turmeric. It springs up in the rains, and it is sometimes sown, as it is considered a specific in rheumatism.

Baib, بيب बैब

Afar off—at a distance.—Bundelkhand.

Baijilá, بيجلا बैजिला

A species of black pulse.—E. Oudh.

Baikhaṭ, بيکهٹ बैखट

Sale.—Eastern Oudh and Benares.

Baisak, بيسک बैसक

A spot in a jungle to which cattle are sent out to graze.—Dehli. It is elsewhere called Kharak (a cowshed) and Batháṇ.—*q.v.* The word is also applied, generally, to old and worn out animals.

Chánda, چاندہ चांदा

A common station of the revenue survey.

Chák, چاک चाक

A wheel. Especially applied amongst cultivators to the pulley over which the lao, or well-rope passes; called Bhon in Dehli, Chalí and Charkhí in Rohilkhand, Garrí and Garílí in Benares and Bundelkhand. But these four last terms are only applied if the wheel is formed out of one block of wood.

Chák means also a mill; rings of earth for forming a well; a vessel in which sugar is manufactured, after being transferred from the Chásní or Karahí.—See Bel.

Chánṭí, چانٹي चांटी

Cesses levied from artizans and others. From Chánṭná چانٹنا to squeeze, to press.

Cháunrí, چاونري चौंरी

A police station; usually the kotwal's.—Saugor.

Cháp, چاپ चाप

The refuse of the Jharberí after the Pála is beaten from it. Dehli and Upper Doáb.—See Jharberí.

Chápṛe, چاپڑے चापड़े

Cakes of cow-dung. They are also known by the names of Gobar, U'pla, Gosa, Doja, Theprí and Chot.

Chára, چارہ चारा

Truss; sheaf; grass; food.

Chásní, چاسني चासनी

A pan in which the juice of the sugar cane is boiled. It is much the same as the Karáhí, except that it is somewhat larger. From the Chásní it is transferred into the Chák, *q.v.*

It is probably a corruption of the Persian چاشني flavour, syrup.

Cháwal, چاول चावल

Rice undressed, but cleared of the husk.

Chíbhar, چيبهر चीभर

Land which remains long moist.—Saugor.

Chík, چيک चीक

Chíkar, چيکر. चीकर

Mud; slime. The name of Chík is consequently given to the turf or rushes on which the water pot of the Dhenklí is made to rest, when it is brought to the top of the well. Párchha and Chilwáí are likewise so applied.

Chíkaṭ, چيکٹ चीकट

Chikṭí, چکٹي चिकटी

Clayey soil.—Saugor.

Chíta, چیته चीता

The name of a creeping herb. It is used in medicine as a cure for leprosy (*Plumbago Zeylonica*).

Chihra, چہرہ चिहरा

A descriptive roll of a servant or fugitive. Literally, a face.

Chíná, چینا चीना

Canary seed (*Panicum Miliaceum*) (*Panicum pilosum*, Roxb.)

It is sown and reaped in the hot season, after nearly all the rabi' crops have been cut. It requires much irrigation, and is a precarious crop ; hence the saying :

चीना जी का लेना
चैादह पानी देना
ब्यार चले तो न लेना न देना

"Take of master Chíná,
Give him fourteen waterings,
Let the wind blow, and you'll have nought to give or take ;"

i.e. You may irrigate your Chíná as much as you like, but a blast will destroy it, and you get nothing for your pains.

Chench, چینچ चेंच

A herb which springs up in uncultivated places during the rainy season. Its fruit is frequently called Jonk, from its resemblance to a leech.

Chhaí, چهئي छई

A pad, to prevent laden bullocks from being galled.

Chháj, چهاج छाज

A basket used in winnowing grain.

Chhákná چهاکنا छाकना

To clean the water of a well.

Chháp, چهاپ छाप

A stamp; generally the Potdar, or cashier's, stamp.

In Dehli and the Upper Doáb it is the name applied to a small bundle or heap of thorns about a foot high. When larger, it is called Khewa کهیوا *q.v.**

Chhápá, چهاپا छापा

The village seal used to impress grain with.—See Chank and Thapa.

It also means the heap of refuse corn and chaff which is formed in winnowing. In a heap of cleaned corn there is about four per cent Chhápá. Also, a small heap of grain appropriated to purposes of charity.

Chhápá is likewise in some places the name given to the basket used for throwing water out of a pond, for the purpose of irrigation.—See Berí, Boka, and Daurí.

Chhár, چهار छार

A bank of a river; hence Chharchittí, a permit, or pass, over a river.

Chhedá, چهیدا छेदा

A destructive little animal similar to the weevil (*Calandria granaria*). From Chhed چهید a hole. It is also the name of the disease which the corn sustains when affected by the ravages of this animal.

Chhída, چهیدا छीदा

Thin, not close—according to Shakespear's Dictionary, "said of a person or animal whose legs are much separated." But it is also applied to corn fields, or plantations, in opposition to Ghaná گهنا or Ghinká گهنکا close, thick.

* See J.A.S. Bombay, No. III., p. 119.—E. *add.*

Chhímí, چهيمي छीमी

A pod; a legume.

Chhínká, چهينكا छींका

An ox muzzle.—Dehli; called Múkha, Mushka, and Jalí in Rohilkhand and the Doáb, Khonta in Benares, and Muska in Bundelkhand. Also a net for hanging pots, etc.—(See Jab.)

Chhínṭa, چهينٹا छींटा

From chhínṭná چهينٹنا to sprinkle; a field in which peas and linseed have been sown by broad-casting, while the rice crops are standing on the ground. When the rice is cut, these crops are left to grow, and harvested in the beginning of Chayt. In Dehli, the term Chhánta is applied to throwing more seed amongst a growing rice crop.

The same word is employed in Gorakhpúr to signify lands in which seed has been scattered after a single ploughing; more particularly at the extremities of villages, with a view to secure possession.

Chhíyúl, چهيول छीयूल

A jungle tree; called also Dhak, *q.v.*

Chheoná, چهيونا छेवना

To extract juice from a tar tree. Literally, "to slice," as the bark is sliced off and a pot hung underneath to catch the sap as it exudes.—B.

Chhikáí, چهكائي छिकाई

Bears the same meaning in Rohilkhand as Farighkhatána, *q.v.* The word is perhaps derived from Chhinkwáná چهنكوانا to cancel.

Chhilká, چهلكا छिलका

Bark; rind.

Chhiṭuá, چهٿوا छिटुआ

Sowing broad-cast. From Chhínṭná چهينٿنا to sprinkle.—Benares.

The usual words in the Doáb, Rohilkhand, and Dehli, are Paberí, or Pabar phenk dena, or Jel karna. In Bundelkhand it is called Chhíntab, from the same root Chhínṭná.

Chhitrí, چهتري छितरी

Said in Shakespear's Dictionary to be "a small basket without lid or handle," but it is more generally understood to be a broken basket, or Daliya ; one nearly ineffective from being worn out.

Chholá, چهولا छोला

Gram—Saugor and Bundelkhand. Also the title of the man who cuts the standing sugar cane. He strips off the leaves, and lops off the head, which he receives as his perquisite, besides about ten canes per diem during the time he is employed. The name is derived from chholna چهولنا to pare, to scrape.

Chholní, چهولني छोलनी

A scraper.

Chhaur, چهور छौर

A large stack of Juwar or Bajra collected for fodder, comprising several smaller stacks called Syí. In years of plenty this is added to, till the village stock amounts to several hundreds of maunds.—Dehli.

In some districts, as in Rohilkhand, this is known by the name of Garrí ; elsewhere by the name of Kundar and Kharaí. —See Garrí.

Chhadám, چهدام छदाम

Literally, six dams ; equal to two damrís. The proper

amount is six and a quarter dams, but by abbreviation it is called Chhadám.—See Damrí, Adhela, and Ganda.

Chhahkur, چهکر छकुर

Division of crops where the Zamíndár gets only one-sixth.—E. Oudh.

Chhakṛá, چهکڑا छकड़ा

A carriage. It is built on the principle of a bailí, has no sides like the Garí, but carries burdens on a sort of platform. It is much used for the conveyance of cotton, to which its construction is well adapted. The names of some of its component parts are Nasaurí, Goriá, Tuláwa, Akarí, Koṛha, Phar, Shagún, Ank, Típh, Dántuá, Chaukhará and Bichuá, the uses of which it is needless to particularise.—See Garí.

Chhaṭáo, چهٹاو छटाव

Clearing rice from the husk.

Chhatrí, چهتري छत्री

A small ornamented pavilion, generally built over a place of interment, or a cenotaph in honor of a Hindú chief. Literally, "an umbrella."

Chihel, چهيل चिहेल

Wet oozy land. From chihlá چہلا mud.

Chikhar, چکهر चिखर

The husk of Chaná, *q.v.*

Chikharwáí, چکهرواﺋﻲ चिखरवाई

Wages for weeding.—E. Oudh; called generally Niraí and Naulaí elsewhere.

Chiknáwat, چکناوٹ चिकनावट

A clayey soil. From Chikná چکنا greasy; oily.

Chillá, چله चिल्ला

A holy place where fakírs abide: so called from the initiatory abstinence of forty days (in Persian چهله chahilá) which they undergo.

Chilwáí, چلوائي चिलवाई

See an explanation of its meaning under Chík.

Chimbur, چمبر चिंबुर

An inferior kind of grass which grows in the Bhattí territory. It is perhaps the same as the Chaprúda of Hariana.

Chin, چن चिन

A kind of sugar-cane.—Upper Doáb and Rohilkhand.—See Ikh.

Chirchirá, چرچره चिर्चिरा

Name of a medicinal plant (*Achyranthes aspera*). Its ashes also are used in washing linen. It is also called Chíchara, Chitirra, and Satjíra. In Sanskrit it is known by the name of Apámárg अपामार्ग. There is a white and a red kind. The former, if it is carried about the person, is firmly believed to render one invulnerable, particularly against scorpions, and the application of it to the part affected is as immediate and certain a remedy as was the application of basil according to the classical writers.

Chirchitta, چرچٿه चिरचिट्टा

The name of a grass which somewhat resembles young Bajra. It produces an ear like that of the Kangní کنگنی (*Panicum Italicum*), and its grain is about the size of a barley corn. This plant also is said in native herbals to have secret virtue. If any one will eat a chatták of its grain he will not feel the pressure of hunger for twenty-one days. As the experiment is easily made, and it is not a common practice to eat Chirchiṭṭa, we may presume it is somewhat nauseous.

Chiṭṭhá, چتّها चिट्ठा

A rough note; servants' pay; a memorandum.

Chiwáná, چوانا चिवाना

A place for cremation; called also Chihaí and Chihaní. These three are derived from Ksháí, ashes. Marghaṭ, Bhoídagdha and Smasan, or Samsan (in Benares) are also employed to signify the same.

Choyá, چويا चोइया

A hole dug in the dry bed of a river to get water. Also a name commonly applied to rivulets.

Chohá, چوها चोहा

A small well. Both these words are derived from Chúná چونا to leak, to be filtered.

Choká, چوکا चोका

Rice.—Saugor.

Chonḍá, چونڈا चोंडा

Kachha wells where the water is near the surface.—E. Oudh.

Chúá, چوا चूआ

Chúá, Battú, or Marsa forms one of the chief Kharíf products of the hills. The flowers are of a fine red color. It is supposed to be the *Amaranthus oleraceus*.

Chúá is also the siliqua, seed vessel, or pod of a pulse.

Chugáí, چگائي चुगाई

Pasturage. From Chugná چگنا to peck; to graze.

Chonchí, چونچي चोंची

A tiny creeper which grows round the Piyází plant and ripens its seeds at the same time with it. The Piyází seeds are eaten by the poorer classes, and during the famine at Ambala in 1861 cases occurred of persons being poisoned by eating Piyází bread in which Chonchí had become mixed. I was not able to learn the botanical name of either plant. Piyází grows spontaneously in fallow lands in April and May.—B.

Chullí, چلي चुल्ली

The supports which are placed below stacks of straw or stores of grain; called by English farmers staddles. In some places the ground is merely cleaned and elevated, and no supports are raised; it is then called Gháí.

Chullú, چلو चुल्लू

The palm of the hand contracted for the purpose of holding water. Sometimes incorrectly pronouned Challú.—See Ajaulí and Chungal.

Chún, چون चून

Chúní, چوني चूनी

Flour; pulse coarsely ground.

Chungal, چنگل चुंगल

A handful of any thing dry; as Chullú is of any thing liquid. Khonch is used in the same sense. In Rohilkhand, Lap, or Laf, is as much as two hands joined can hold; but in Benares, Dehli, and the Doab, it means only one handful.—See Ajaulí, Chullú.

Chúntrú, چونترو चूंत्रू

Head man of a district in Dehra Dún.

Chopná, چوپنا चोपना

To throw water from a Daurí, *q.v.*—U'lchab dena is the equivalent term in Bundelkhand.

Choṭ, چوٹ चोट

An ingenious way adopted by shepherds and husbandmen of folding a blanket or sheet into a covering for the head and shoulders, making it nearly impervious to the rain. It is somewhat similar to the mode by which a Scotchman converts a plaid into a sleeved great coat. It also signifies the tying the end of a blanket in a knot, and so placing it over the head, which in some places is called Ghúnghí; but that word is generally otherwise applied.—See Ghúnghí.

Chau, چو चौ

A ploughshare.—See Hal and Halas.

Chaukhá, چوکھا चौखा

A station where four boundaries meet.—See Chaugadda.

Chaukaṛá, چوکڑا चौकड़ा

Division of a crop, in which the cultivator gives only one-fourth; called also by the name of Chaukúṛ.

Chaulá, چولا चौला

A kind of pulse commonly cultivated in Hindústan (*Dolichos sinensis*). It is also called Rawás and Ramás; but it is best known throughout the country under its Persian name of لوبیا *lobiyá*.

Chauláí, چولائي चौलाई

The name of a weed which shoots up during the rainy season, particularly in old buildings (*Amaranthus polygamus*). It is also sometimes sown and eaten as a pot-herb. There are two kinds of Chauláí, red and green. The one is called Gandar, and the other Marsaí.

Chaunṛá, چونڑا चौंडा

A subterranean apartment for grain.

Chauntálí, چونتالي चौंताली

Cotton pods, in which the fibre is equal to one-fourth of the whole produce. Tihálí, in which the fibre is one-third. Pachdúlí (*i.e.* two out of five) when it amounts to about 16 seers in the maund.

Chaupál, چوپال चौपाल

Chaupár, چوپار चौपार

A small shed in which the village community meet; generally built by the head man of the village, and used by him in former days as a kind of Kachahrí or office.

Chaur, چور चौर

A large open space in the forest.—Rohilkhand.

A large tract of low land.—Eastern Oudh.

Achaur is one of those long low strips of semi-marshy land, formerly beds of small streams so common in Northern Bihár. They are generally appropriated for the purpose of growing rice and indigo.—B.

Chauráha, چوراها चौराहा

The junction of four villages, or roads.—See Chaugadda.

Chaursí, چورسي चौरसी

A granary above ground.—Rohilkhand.

Chaus, چوس चौस

Land four times tilled.—Rohilkhand.

Chausinghá, چوسنگها चौसिंघा

A raised mound indicating where the boundaries of four villages meet.—See Chaugadda.

Chauthiyá, چَوتهيا चौथिया

A measure in general use for grain and about equal to a seer of wheat. Chaukarí is a quarter, and Adhelí is a half Chauthiyá. Five Chauthiyás are equal to a Kuro, or Paserí, and twenty Kuros to one Khanrí. These words are equally used in superficial measures. Thus an area which would require five Paserí of seed to sow it, is about equal to a Bígha (which in Hoshangabad is a little more than a statute acre, being 4,900 square yards), and was rated at about a Rupee of Revenue. A Khanrí would be about equal to four Rupees, and a Mání to twice that amount.—Saugor.—See Bísí and Jaríb.

Chautrá چوترا चौतरा

A Court; corrupted perhaps from Chabútra.

Chah, چه चह

A platform; a pier-head.

Chahlí, چهلي चहली

The wheel on which the rope revolves at the top of a well. —See Chák.

Chahorná, چهورنا चहोरना

To transplant.—Rohilkhand. Elsewhere it signifies to stick

up, to fix. The word Rompna is also frequently used to signify transplanting. In Dehli and the Upper Doáb, Chahorná, though rarely used, is preserved in the word Chahora, which signifies rice dibbled in a field, after being sown in a nursery.

Chahal, چہل चहल

A strong soil, ranking between Rauslí and Dákara, or Dánkra.—Dehli.

Chakká چکا चक्का

The weight (generally of clay) used to press down the small arm of the Dhenkla. The usual meaning is a wheel or circle, and the word may be therefore applied thus, as the Chakká is almost always of a circular form.

Chakkat, چکت चक्कत

The loss of a whole plot of ground by diluvion; the contrary of Ritkat.

Chakwanḍ, چکونڈ चकवनड

A common weed, of which there are generally reckoned to be four kinds, though they bear but little resemblance to one another.—Chakwanḍ, Chakauṅdí or Kasaundí, Gulálí, Batoka. The Chakwanḍ, which grows from about eight inches to two feet high, and bears a long legume, is very common in Mango groves, and in fields grown with Kharíf crops. It is used by the poor people as a potherb.

Chaltí, چلتی चलती

Cultivated lands.—Dehli.

Chambal, چمبل चमबल

A log of wood with grooves, fixed on banks of canals. It is used in drawing water for the purposes of irrigation.

Chaná, چنا चना

Gram. *Cicer arietinum.* The origin of this word has been much disputed, but is, I believe, a corruption of the Portuguese *grama,* meaning *grain* in general.

There are generally reckoned to be three kinds of this widely-used legume:—1. Pílá (also called Rakswá, Chaptáí, and Kasárí in the Eastern part of these provinces); 2. Pachmil, which is a mixture of Pílá and Kassá; 3. Kassá, the superior kind.

There is also a small kind of Chaná, called Chaní and Batúrí, and Chaná itself is frequently to the Eastward called Rehla and Lona. But in general Lona is the name of the oxalic and acetic acid which forms on the leaf of the Chaná. It is used in this country in alchemical processes, and in the preparation of nitric and muriatic acid. Cloths are spread over the plants of the Chaná, and being well moistened by the deposition of dew, they readily absorb the acidulous salt, which the plants secrete abundantly on the surface of their leaves and shoots (Royle, "Antiquity of Hindu Med." p. 42). The presence of this acid is found to injure the feet occasionally when people walk in Chaná fields, and a local tradition has hence arisen that Sítá, when she was going to bathe in the Manwa river, is said to have cursed the plant, and directed that it should not be grown between that stream and the Gogra, and consequently no Chaná is now cultivated between those two rivers.

In the Western part of this Presidency there is a Kabulí Chaná sometimes grown. It differs from the Desí, or country Chaná in having a white flower and smaller leaf. It is also grown in the extreme East, and in Bengal, to the North of the Ganges. It is there considered a fit offering for the gods, probably on account of its rarity.

This useful grain is highly valued in India, and its praises have been sung by the poets. The following doggrel lines, which are attributed to the celebrated minister Bírbal, are greatly esteemed by the natives:—

सब देवों में महादेव बड़े सब अन्न में चकरबत चना
जाकी लमबी सी डार गुलाबसा फूल खूंटत खांटत होत घना
कहैं बीरबल सुनो साह अकबर नून औ मिर्च से अजब बना

Which may be thus literally translated,

"Among all gods, Mahadev is greatest; among all cereals, channá is king:
Whose stalk is longish, its flowers rose-coloured, the more it is picked the thicker it grows.
Quoth Bírbal, listen, Sháh Akbar, with salt and pepper it is wonderfully good."

The favorite way, however, of cooking grain is to parch it. It is then called Chabená, and is generally carried in the corner of the scarf to eat on a journey. By far the most common use of grain is as food for horses, for which purpose it is unrivalled.—B.

Chanchar, چانچر चंनचर

Land left untilled for one, two, or three years.

Chandá, چندا चन्दा

Subscription; assessment.

Chandelí, چنديلي चंदेली

A very fine species of cotton fabric, which is of so costly a description as to be used only in native courts. It is made from Berar, or Umrávatí, cotton, and every care is taken in its manipulation. The weavers work in a dark subterranean room, of which the walls are kept purposely damp to prevent the dust from flying about. The chief care is bestowed on the preparation of the thread, which, when of very fine quality, sells for its weight in silver. It is strange that women are allowed to take no part in any of the processes. From a correspondence published in Vol. X. of the "Journ. As. Soc. of Bengal," it would appear that the Chandelís are made solely from Narma cotton; but this is a mistake, for Umrávatí cotton is alone used, and the Narma, or Narma-ban, instead of being confined to Malwa, is cultivated in small quantities all over Hindustan, and its produce is in great request for the manufacture of the best kind of Brahmanical thread. It is a bushy plant, grows to the height of about seven feet, and lasts about six years.

Chandelís derive their name from the town of Chanderí, on the left bank of the Betwa, in Sindhia's territory.—(See Chandel.)

Chandeyá, چنديا चंदेया

Deep places.—Eastern Oudh.

Chaní, چني चनी

A small species of Chaná; called Batúrí in Benares.

Chaneṭh, چنیٹھ चनेठ

Drugs for cattle.

Changel, چنگیل चंगेल

A herb which springs out of old Kheras, or ruined buildings. It has a round leaf, and its seed, which is used as a medicine, is known generally by the name of Khabají. Also a round basket of straw.

Chanwán, چنوان चनवान

Name of a small species of millet.—Eastern Oudh.

Chaprí, چپري चपरी

A puddle. Also the name of a small pulse somewhat resembling Chaná.

Charí, چري चरी

Unripe Jawár, cut as fodder for cattle. It is always sown

much thicker than the Jawár which is intended for the threshing floor.

Charí is also the name given in the Lower Doáb to small portions of land held rent-free by cultivators: derived either from its chiefly producing fodder, or by a corruption from Sír.—See Chhír.

Charkhí, چرخي चरखी

The pulley by which water is raised from a well by two water-pots tied to the ends of a rope and raised alternately. Literally, a spinning wheel. It is generally made of pieces of bamboo lashed together in the form of a cylinder.—See Chák.

Charní, چرني चरनी

A feeding trough.

Charas, چرس चरस

The exudation of hemp flowers. It is collected in Nepal, and elsewhere also it is said, by persons running through a field of Ganja with leathern aprons to which the exudation adheres. In these provinces the Charas of Bokhara is most admired, and fetches double the price of the country product. Bahadúrgarh in the Dehli Territory appears the grand depôt for the Charas of the Western and Northern States.

Also, the large leathern bucket, or bag, used for filling water from wells; derived from چرسا leather. In some parts of the country it is called Púr and Moṭh. All parts of the apparatus of a well are differently called at different places. Thus, the upright posts over the well's mouth are in one place, Fílpáya (elephant leg), in another Thuní. The beam which they support is in one place called Bharsahá, in another Patao and Bharet. The rope is in one place called Bart, in another Lao. The reservoir into which the water is poured is in some places called Pareha, in others Chabacha, and so on.—See Arhaṭ, Bahoro, Chák, Chaktí, Charkhí, and Gararí.

Charwáhí, چرواهي चरवाही

Wages of a charwáha, grazier or herdsman, in grain. From Charná چرنا to feed, to graze.

Chaṭrí, چٹري चटरी

The name of a herb which springs up with the rabi' grains. It is used as fodder for cattle, and the poorer class of cultivators eat the seeds of it mixed up with barley.

Chail, چيل चैल

Land twice tilled.—Rohilkhand.

Chain, چين चैन

Cultivated land.

Chaití, چيتي चैती

The harvest of the month Chayt (March-April). In Bundelkhand it is applied generally to the Rabi', or spring harvest.

Dáb, ڈاب डाब

The name of a grass, better known by the name of Kús or Kúsha. *(Poa cynosurides,* Kæn:) It is generally applied only to the first shoots of the Kús grass, and is called Dabsa in Rohilkhand. The extreme acuteness of its points is proverbial amongst Hindus. The intellects of a clever man are said to be as sharp as the point of a Dáb, or Kús, leaf (Sir W. Jones' Works, Vol. V. p. 79). Dáb is not in much request as fodder for cattle, but, when soaked, it makes very good twine, and is occasionally used in thatching houses. These are, however, profane uses: for the grass is especially holy, and is in great demand in almost all the votive offerings and religious ceremonies of the Hindus. It is considered very desirable that a man should die upon a bed of Dáb; and it is consequently the duty of attendant relations to spread the grass on the floor, and after covering it with a cloth, to lay the dying man upon it, in order that he may emit his last breath in that hallowed position.

Dábí, دابي दावी
 See Dabiya.

Ḍábak, ڈابک डाबक
 Fresh well water.—Dabká is used in the same sense.

Ḍábar, ڈابر डाबर
 Low ground where water settles; a small tank; a vessel for washing in.

Ḍákará, ڈاکرا डाकरा
 Is the name of the best, or second best, quality of soil in the Upper Doáb or Dehli. It is sometimes pronounced Dhákar and Dankra.

The soil called Rauslí in many places ranks above Dákará.

Dál, دال दाल
 "A pulse, *Phaseolus radiatus*, Linn., *Phaseolus aureus*, Roxb., green gram, or rayed kidney bean."—Ḳánún-i Islam.

In the North Western Provinces it is applied only to the split pea of Múng, Arhar, Urd, and a few other pulses (from *dalná* دلنا to grind coarsely); and there appears reason to apprehend error in the passage quoted from the "Ḳánún-i Islam." The Printed Glossary also says of Dol that it is a sort of pea.—See Dalia.

Ḍál, ڈال डाल
 A bough. In Dehli and the Upper Doáb it is applied to the basket used for the purpose of raising water by artificial means from a canal. From *ḍálná* ڈالنا to throw, to fling. It is made sometimes of leather, but generally of Múnj or of Jhao. Ḍál

irrigation is used where the course of the canal is much below the general level of the country, and is, in consequence of the labour attending it, more expensive than irrigation by Tor, which consists in merely breaking down the field ridge, and allowing the water to pass through it.

Dal, دل दल

Wild rice.

Dámcha, دامچه दामचा

The platform on which a person is posted to protect crops.—Dehli. Jaunda and Tand are also used in this sense in Dehli; and the latter in Rohilkhand also; in the Doáb, Mattúla (from *maṭṭí*, earth), and Menra and Maiṅra* (from its position on the border of the field); and in Saugor, Marwa, for the same reason. Machán and Mácha are in common use elsewhere, and even within the limits of the local words above-mentioned.

Ḍámar, ڈامر डामर

Resin—more especially, in commerce, the resin of the Sál tree (*Shorea robusta*): also called Dhumná and Dhúná.

Ḍanḍ, ڈانڈ डांड

High ground, opposed to Ḍábar; sterile Bhúr land; elevated land of Domat soil; also a fine; a land-mark; a stick. The word is spelt with either an initial ड or द.

Dáng, دانگ दांग

A hill or precipice; the summit of a mountain, as Lál-dáng. In Dehli, and generally in Upper India, the word is used to signify the high bank of a river. It is provincially corrupted into Dháng and Dhayang.—E.

Dángrá दांगडा is common in Nepalese for a hill.—B.

* *Meiṛ, Menḍ,* میںڈ signifies a limit.

Ḍángar, ڈانگر डांगर

Superannuated horned cattle. It is applied also as a term of abuse to a fool. But Ḍángar, in Dehli, is not confined to old cattle; for it is there applied generally to horned cattle, exclusive of buffaloes.

Dántí, دانتي दांती

A sickle. From *dant*, a tooth.

Ḍánṭh, ڈانٹھ डांठ

Refuse of harvest floors, especially applied to Kharíf products; and so is synonymous with Jhora, *q.v.* It is also called Daṭuá and Ḍanthlá.—See Ḍanthlá.

Dánwán, دانوان दांवान

Burning stubble, or a conflagration in a forest. This word is provincially corrupted into *damar* and *do*, and is derived from the Sanskrit दावानल, a conflagration in a forest.—"Yates' Nalodaya," p. 353.

Dánwarí, دانوري दांवरी

See Daurí.

Dáo, داو दाव

A hatchet with a hooked point; a sickle. Among the Singphos and other savages of the north-eastern frontier it is the name of a heavy knife about two feet in length like the Nepalese kukarí.—B.

Dárú, دارو दारू

Spirituous liquor.

Dás, داس दास

This name, which literally means slave, is borne chiefly by men of the Baniá caste, by Bairágí Fakírs, and by Kayaths and

Brahmins. It is usually coupled with the name of some deity, as Shib Dás, Náráyan Dás, etc., etc., to imply subjection to some special tutelary God. It is a mistake to suppose that it is the name of a particular family, as was asserted by a celebrated statesman, who when inveighing against the treatment of some Dás of Lucknow, stated him to be a member of "the Doss family, one of the most distinguished in India."

In the time of Akbar we find it was not uncommon for Rajputs also to bear the name of Dás. Thus we read of Raja Bhagwan Dás, the Kachhwáha, who was the father-in-law of Jahángír, and grandfather of Sultán Khusrú, and who is stigmatized as the first who sullied Rajput blood by a connexion with the Imperial family of Dehli. The name is now seldom given to Rajputs, except to illegitimate children.—E.

By Europeans in India this word is often written and pronounced "Doss," and in that shape it appeared in the earlier editions of this work. The last (or perhaps I should say the last but one) generation of Anglo-Indians always pronounced the long *á* (आ or آ) like *aw* or *o*, this error was originated by that able but eccentric scholar, Dr. Gilchrist, who taught that the sound of *á* was the same as that of the English *a* in *ball*, *wall*, *water*, etc. Hence his pupils persisted in speaking and writing حاضري breakfast, as *hauzree*, پاني water, as *pawnee*, *nabáb* (the Hindi corruption of نواب *nawwáb*) as *nabob* and the like. The fact however is that the long *á* in all Indian languages is sounded like the English *a* in *far*, *father*, *past*, etc. In Persian the long *á* is sounded as in *water*, *war*, etc., and the Persians are said to dislike to hear Indians talk their language because of their pronunciation of the *á*, which they consider effeminate. Thus, a Persian would say نام شما چه باشد *nawmi shumaw chih bawshad*, while an Indian would say n*áh*mi shum*áh* chih b*áh*-shad. The name Dás is in Behar indicative of the possessor's holding the office of village patwárí. It is one of the recognized appellations of the Káyaths, who are all called so-and-so Lál, Parshád, or Dás; also, though less frequently, Singh.—B.

Dásá, داسا दासा

A reaping hook. Also dáṅsá दांसा.

Dháḍá, دھاڈا धाड़ा

Water falling from above; a waterfall.—Rohilkhand. The word is perhaps a corruption of Dhárá, a flowing stream.

In Saugor, Bhadbhada is used in this sense; but its general application is somewhat different.—See Bhadbhadána.

Díyáṛá, دیاڑا दियाड़ा

Díára, or Dáwara, or Díará, signifies an island formed in the bed of a river.—Eastern Oudh and Benares.—E.

It is a Hindi diminutive of Sanskrit द्वीप an island, and means a large sandbank formed by a river, which, after being in existence for a couple of seasons, frequently becomes sufficiently consolidated to be cultivable, but is always liable to be carried away again by a change in the course of the river. Some of these diárás or díaras, as they are also called, are very large and old. The Rámpúr díará in the Ganges near Maldah for instance is forty miles long and two or three broad, and is as firm as the high land on the banks of the river.—B.

Ḍíh, ڈیہہ डीह

Used in the Benares Province and the Lower Doáb to signify the site of a deserted village. The Persian Deh being used for an inhabited one.

Ḍíhá, ڈیہا डीहा

A small mound; same as the above.

Dihúla, دھولہ दिहला

See Dhan.

Dahnímí, دہنیمي दहनीमी

Five per cent.—Dehli. The literal meaning is half of ten.

Ḍehrí, ڈیہري डेहरी

A marshy soil.—See Dahr.

Dihindah, دہندہ दिहन्दह

A Persian word signifying one that is willing to pay or give; a good payer.

Dahyek, دہیک दिहयक

An allowance of 10 per cent., which used to be given to the Amil as his profit, and for the charges of Mofassil management. See Sec. 6, Reg. II. A.D. 1795. In the Printed Glossary it is called Dahyck.

Ḍel, ڈیل डेल

Land ploughed and ready for Rabi' crops.—Bundelkhand. Land prepared for cotton after having been cropped with Gram. —Saugor.

Ḍeulá, ڈیولا डेवला

Mounds; high ground.—Eastern Oudh.

Dháman, دہامن धामन

A grass, of a good quality, which is found in the Bhaṭṭí territory.

Dhán, دہان धान

The rice plant. Very many kinds are grown in these provinces. The best known in the North-West and Rohilkhand are Basmattí, Hansraj, Raímunia (called also Bandlí and Tilokchandan), Kamaura, Motíchúr, Píla, Súnkhar, Jabdí, Súngkharcha, Sohágmattí. These are all of superior quality. The inferior are Anjana, Chakua, Badámí, Dalganjna, Anandí, Kaldhanna, Seodhí, Sáthí, and Seodha.

In Saugor the most common kinds are Maltí, Síamjírú, Nunga, Láyachí, Dilbagsa, Antarbed, Tilsein, Batrú, Seinkhir, Deodhan, Khurában, and Jhanásar.

In the central part of these provinces we find the names chiefly of Deokala, Dúdhí, Sáthí, Bákí, Raímunia, Batásí, Naurangí, Dúnkharcha, Lumbha, Motíchúr, Kála, Hansraj, and Basmattí.

Those cultivated to the Eastward and in Benares are, for the most part, Bagarí, Dehúla, Dúdha, Mutmurí, Selha, Nanhya, Raníkajar, Ríngan, Naindosh, Basmattí, Jiria, Kalíjír, Nainsukh, Khattar, Birinjphúl, Bangalia, Bangkí, Súmbha, Selhí, Motísirrí, Rát, Raibhog, Motíjhúl, Naurangí, Kharrar, Samundar-phen, Hansraj. Of these the best kinds are Naindosh, Basmattí, Hansraj, Nainsukh, and Birinjphúl. Basmattí and Hansraj appear to be the only kinds which are known generally by the same name. The varieties are still greater in Behar and Bengal.

It appears from Abu'l Fazl that the most noted varieties of his time were the Sukhdás of Bharaich, the Dojírah of Gwalior, and Khanjan of Rájaurí.—E.

In Bengal and Behar, where rice is the staple crop, the people say there are two hundred distinct kinds, but, as usual with these exaggerated sub-divisions, they are seldom able to name them all. Many of the names are as purely fanciful as those given by English gardeners to their apples and pears. The better sorts are classed under one head as Arwá, and are the only sorts eaten by Europeans and the upper class of natives. The inferior second sorts are Joshándar avyal, Joshándar doyam, and Lál.—B.

Dhána, دهانه धाना

The Gond portion of a village, which is always separate from the rest. Also applied generally to Marza, Nagla, and Púrwa in the North-West.—Saugor.

Dháp, دهاپ धाप

One-fourth of a koss.—See Dhapiá. Also applied to a Ghat, or passage; a large expanse of low ground.

Ḍhár, ڈهار ढार

A heap of corn.—Benares. It is called more correctly Dher in the North-West.

Dhár, دهار धार

A hollow tree inserted in the mouth of wells in the Tarái, to keep them from falling in.—Rohilkhand.

Dhár or Dhára is also used in the sense given under Dhala and Dharbachh: it is frequently pronounced Dharua.—These words may either be derived from Dhala, as above-mentioned, or from *dharná* دهرنا, to place down, to impose. The word is entered in the Printed Glossary under Dara.

Dhárdharná, دهاردهرنا धारधरना

See Dhariyana.

Ḍhí, ڈهي ढी

A high bank of a river.—Saugor.

Ḍhíhá, ڈهيها ढीहा

Rising ground; mounds. Díha is similarly used.

Ḍhínkhar, ڈهينكهر ढींखर

Is the name applied to the bundle of thorns tied together and drawn by bullocks over corn for the purpose of beating out the grain. It is also used as a harrow for eradicating grass and weeds from ploughed land.—Dehli and Upper Doáb.

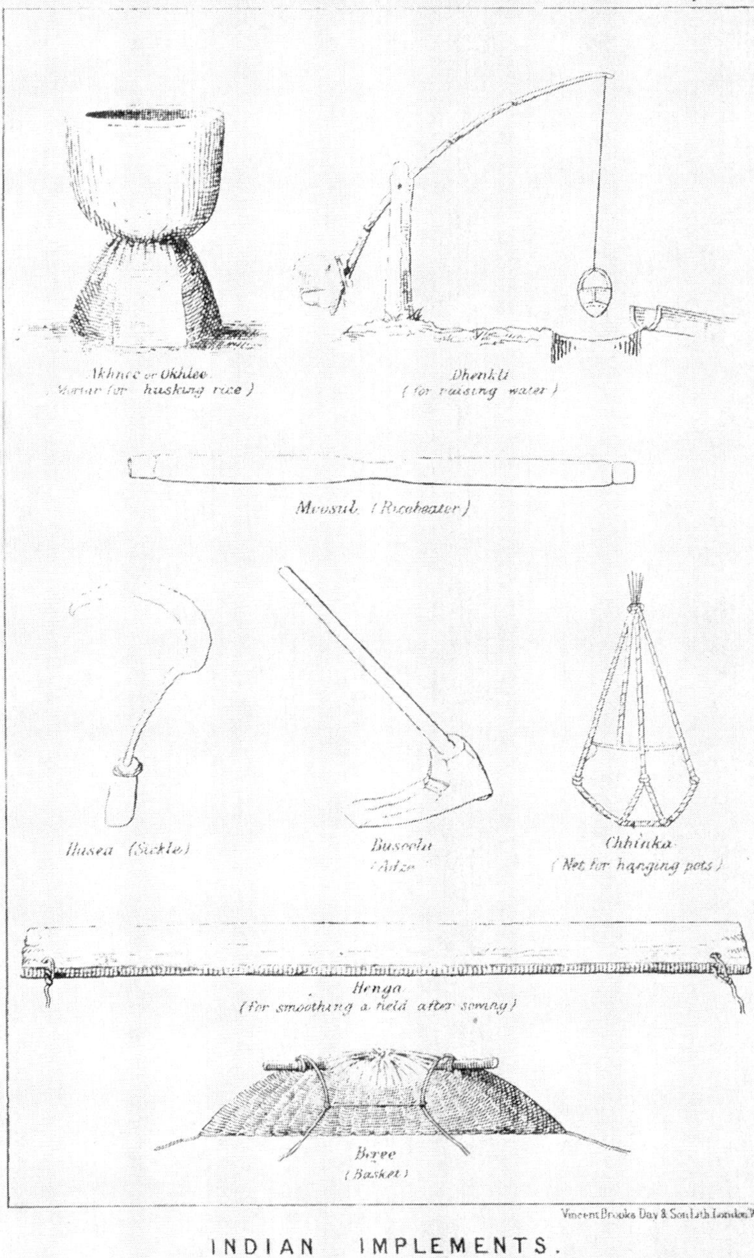

Vincent Brooks Day & Son Lith. London W.

INDIAN IMPLEMENTS.

Ḍhelá, ڈهيلا ढेला

A clod of earth.

Dhen, دهين धेन

A milch cow.

Ḍhenka, ڈهينكه ढेंका

Ḍhenkí, ڈهينكي ढेंकी

An instrument for pounding rice, tobacco, etc. It is worked like the Dhenklí, and is similarly derived; corrupted by Europeans into "donkey."

Ḍhenklí, ڈهينكلي ढेंकली

A machine for raising water, consisting of a horizontal lever with a weight at one end and a bucket at the other. The name is provincially corrupted into Dhúklí, Dhiklí, and in Gorakhpúr into Dheokal. The word appears to be derived from ḍhalkáná ڈهلكانا to roll, to overturn. The posts which act as the fulcra are called Thúnia; the rope, Bart; and the bucket Karwala.

Ḍhenṛí, ڈهينڑي ढेंड़ी

Has the same meaning as Dhondh.—See Dhondh.

Ḍherí, ڈهيري ढेरी

A heap.

In the Upper Doáb it is used to signify a sharer, principally in landed property.

Dhingá, دهنگا धिंगा

See Jelí.

Dhoka, دهوكه धोका

See Daria.

Ḍhoka, ڈهوكه ढोका

Small stones of an inferior quality, extracted from the Chanár quarries. In Regulation XXII. 1795, the names of several other stones are mentioned, such as Chauká, Húrsá, Solí, Jántá, for grinding; and for building, Dápá, Chapetá, A'bhot, Bujautí, Patera, Pattea, Khúnth, Khamha.

Dhoṇḍá, دهونڈا धोंडा
Dhoṇḍí, دهونڈي धोंडी

A grass which grows in rice fields, and sometimes chokes the plant. It produces an ear, and the seed is frequently used by cultivators for making bread. In some places, as in the Bareilly district, it is called Bat; and in Eastern Oudh, Dhauní. It appears to derive its name from Dhán, rice; if we may be allowed to judge from the following familiar couplet, in which both words occur—

बोए थे धान होगया धोंडा।
क्या खाएगा लौंडी लौंडा॥

"We sowed rice, it has come up dhoṇḍá;
What will the family (*lit.* the male and female slaves) eat?"

Ḍhoṇḍh, ڈهونڈه ढोंढ

A capsule, or seed vessel; especially of the poppy, cotton, or gram.—See also Ḍhúṇḍí.

Dhúí, دهوي धूई

Soaked pulse.

Ḍhúṇḍí, ڈهونڈي ढूंडी

The pod of gram *(Cicer arietinum)*.—Benares. The correct word is Dhendí, or Dhenrí, *q.v.* It is also in Benares and many other places called Thonthí. It is known by the local name of Ghittrí in Rohilkhand, Tát in Dehli, Dhaurí in Bundelkhand, and Ḍhúṇḍh, and Ghentí in some places. When it is somewhat unripe, it is called Patpar, Chatká, Ghegará, and

Satpar, in different parts of these Provinces. – See Ḍhonḍh and Ghegara.

Dhus, دھس धुस

A sloping elevation of ground; and hence applied to the glacis of a fort; sterile sandy eminences. It is also the name of a soil in some parts of the Lower Doáb and Benares.—See Dhúh.

Ḍhorá, ڈھورہ ढोरा

Ḍhorá, or Ḍhola, is the name of an insect very destructive to stored gram.

It is also applied to the mound of earth raised by the side of a ditch.

Dhaul, دھول धौल

Dhaur, دھور धौर

A kind of sugar cane.—Rohilkhand, Upper Doáb, and Dehli.

Ḍhaḍḍá, دھڈّا ढडा

Ḍhaḍḍí, دھڈّي ढडी

A term applied to low ground.—Rohilkhand.

Ḍhanḍhoí, ڈھنڈھوي ढंढोई

The scum of the sugar cane juice, of which half goes to the Jhokia, and half to the Jhímar.—Dehli. It is called also Mallí. The corresponding word in Rohilkhand, Benares, and Bundelkhand is Mailia; in the Doáb, Patoí, and Lado.

Dhaniá, دھنیا धनिया

Coriander seed (*Coriandrum sativum*, Linn.).

Dhankar, دھنکر धंकर

A stiff soil producing rice (Dhan), which can only be ploughed and sown in the event of sufficient rain falling.

Also a field which has been cropped with rice during the previous season.

Dhanthiyá, دهنتهيا धंथिया

This also signifies a field on which rice has been cut.—Rohilkhand.

Dhapiá, دهپيا धपिया

A short koss. From Sanskrit धाव going or running; from which also is derived Dháp, a fourth of a koss, or that distance which a man is supposed to be able to run without stopping to take breath.

Dharáwaṭ, دهراوٹ धरावट

Land ascertained and apportioned by estimate; not measured. —Benares.—See Regulation LI. 1795.

Dhariyáná, دهريانا धरियाना

To separate the good from bad grain; to winnow. The word is used throughout the North-Western Provinces, but the process is usually called Dhárdharna in Dehli, Suretna in Rohilkhand, and Usána in Bundelkhand; but this latter, as well as Barsana, is also general in the North-Western Provinces.

Dharingá, دهرنگا धरिंगा

A kind of rice.—Rohilkhand.

Dharohar, دهروهر धरोहर

Deposit. From Dharná, to place.

Dhartí, دهرتي धरती

Land; the earth.

Dhaṛakhá, دهڑکها धड़खा

Dhaṛallá, دهڑلا धड़ला

A scarecrow.—See Bijhgah, Dhokha, and Dhúha.

Dhasán, دهسان धसान
Dhasan, دهسن धसन
Dhasáo, دهساو धसाव
Dhasam, دهسم धसम

A swamp; a quagmire. From Dhasná, to sink into, to enter.

Dig, دگ दिग

Dig, or Dik, is one of the regions of the earth, of which there are reckoned to be ten. They are frequently called by the names of their supposed regents; as Isan for North-East, Nairit for South-West, Agni for South-East, Báyu for North-West, etc. These regions are more usually considered to be eight, but there are in reality ten, by adding Ananta and Brahma, the regents of the nadir and zenith. "Decem mundi partes pro omnes mundi partes, quarum octo quæ sunt hyperbolice decem dicuntur."—Lassen, "Anthologia Sanskritica," p. 234. See also Johnson's Selections from the "Mahabharat," p. 91; Lassen's "Gita Govinda," p. 84, and Bopp's "Nalus," p. 198.

Dighí, دگهي दिघी

A large oblong tank. Corrupted by the English into Diggy.

Dil, دل दिल

A small eminence; the site of an old village.—Benares. Called in other parts of the North-West, Dhíha, Pútha, Tíla, Theh, and Thera.

Docha, دوچه दोचा

Docha or Dohcha is the second reservoir to which water is raised by the Berí and Daurí for the purposes of irrigation. The third is called Tehcha, and the fourth Chauncha. These words are used chiefly to the Westward. To the East other terms prevail.—See Daurí.

Dofaslí, دوفصلي दोफसली

Lands producing two crops a year. It is also known as Dohar, Dosaí, Dosahí, and Juthelí.

Dabehrí, دبيهري दबेहरी

Is the name given to a light kind of plough in the Western parts of Oudh and Rohilkhand. In Eastern Oudh it assumes a masculine form, Dabehra, and is there applied to a large ploughshare.

Ḍabrá, ڐبره डबरा

A marsh; a puddle; a small pond.

A small field, applied synonymously with Tapra.—E. Or rather a plot of land, whether consisting of one or more fields.—B.—Upper Doáb.

Ḍabrí, ڐبري डबरी

Division of profit amongst the village community according to their respective shares.—Upper Doáb.

Dach, دچ दच

Homestead.—Eastern Oudh.

Dadrí, دَدْري ददरी

Unripe corn, chiefly barley, which is cut from time to time, and brought home to be eaten, instead of being taken to the threshing ground. The word is in general use, but Alo, Arwan, Awásí, Kawal, and Kawarí, are also terms in local use.

Daftarí, دفتري दफतरी

A man employed in the vernacular offices of the Civil officials in India in preparing and taking care of articles of stationery, and in ruling or binding sheets of paper for official purposes.

Ḍagar, ڈگر डगर

A path. Also डहर ḍahar. The word is derived from Dag, a pace, a step; now rarely used, but we find it in the familiar couplet describing the fertility of Malwa, which is given in the article Gambhír.

Dahenḍí, دهینڈی दहेंडी

A vessel for holding dahi, or curds, *i.e.* the solid part of the milk separated from the liquid. Dohní is the name of the vessel which holds dúdh, or fresh milk.

Dahiyá, دهیا दहिया

A field; land near a village.—Benares and Saugor. The name perhaps is more generally spelt with a cerebral or lingual *ḍ* or ड.

Dahmardá, دهمردا दहमर्दा

A cart smaller than a Gárí and Chhakrá, and larger than a Rehlú.—Rohilkhand. The name is derived from its capacity to carry ten men. It is also called a Dobardá or Dobaldá, the origin of which is different, being derived from a word signifying two bullocks.

Dahr, دهر दहर

Dahrí, دهري दहरी

Stiff clay soil (in low ground). It is usually applied to a marsh or any inundated land in Dehli.

Dahal, دهل दहल

Sometimes used as the equivalent of Daldal, for a quicksand or quagmire. From Dahalná دهلنا to tremble, to shake. In an extract from a History written in Jahángír's time, and ascribed to Ferishta,—(the author seems wrongly quoted)—it is stated that the name of the Imperial city of Dehli (correctly Dillí,

Díhlí, or Dhillí) is derived from this word—the ground on which it was built being so loose and infirm (dahal) that tent-pins could not be fixed in it.

و دهلي از شهرهاي قديم و جديد است و در شهور سن سبع و ثلثمائه اوديت راجپوت از طايفه تؤران در هندوستان قلعه اندرپت بنا كرده چون جاك او بسيار نرم بود ميخ بدشواري درانجا استوار ميگرديد آن شهررا دهلي موسوم كرد

"And Dihli is one of the cities which are both ancient and modern, and in one of the months of the year 307 (Hijri = A.D. 919) Udit the Rajput of the Tuar clan built the fort of Indarpat in Hindústán, and as the earth there was very soft so that they could with difficulty fix a tent-peg in it he called the city Dihli."

The same origin is ascribed to the word in the Nuzhatu'l Ḳulúb.

Histories usually ascribe a different orign to the name, saying that the city was founded by Raja Delú. Common tradition differs from these accounts. It is universally believed that the name is derived (ढीला or ढिल्ला loose) from the sacrilegious attempt of the Tomar (Tuar) to see whether the iron pillar had really, as was supposed, penetrated the head of Sahesnag.

किल्ली तो ढिल्ली भई तूमर भयो मत हीन
पहिले दिहली तूमर पीछे चौहानु
और पीछे मोगल पठानु

"The pillar became loose (dhillí), the Túmar was foolish :
First in Dehli was the Túmar, then the Chauhán,
And afterwards Mughal and Pathán."

Colonel Tod says the name of Dehli was not given to the Imperial city before the eighth century.—Trans. R. A. S. Vol. III. p. 150. See also Quart. Or. Mag. No. XVI. p. 133.*—E.

* See also J. A. S. B. 1866, vol. XXXV. Part I. p. 199, for a long and carefully elaborated topographical description of the city of Dehli by C. J. Campbell.—B.

General Cunningham fixes conjecturally the original foundation of Dilli in 57 B.C., but says that after a few years it was deserted for 792 years by the kings, though probably not by the people. In 736 it was rebuilt by Anang Pal or Biláu Deo (see Tomar in Part I.). As to the origin of the name the safest course is to acquiesce in the opinion that it has been lost in the lapse of ages. In 57 B.C. the Hindi word ḍhillí certainly was not in existence as far as we know, and the corrupted modern spelling Dihli or Dehli seems to point to a different source. The General's article is too long to quote here; it may be found in J. A. S. B. Vol. XXXIII. for 1864, Appendix.—B.

Ḍahaṛ, ڈھر डहर

Applied in Benares, Oudh, Lower Doáb, and Bundelkhand to a road; elsewhere, Dagar or Dagra is used.—See Dagar.

Daldal, دلدل दलदल

A quagmire.

Daliyá, دليا दलिया

Any sort of split pulse, ground finer than dal—in which the seed is understood to be split only into two pieces.

Dalganjaná, دلگنجنا दलगनजना

A kind of rice.—See Dhán.

Dalhárá, دلهارا दलहारा

A grain seller. From dal, split pulse.

Damká, دمکا दमका

A hillock.—Eastern Oudh.

Damrí, دمري दमड़ी

In the Dehli territory, the term is applied to the sub-divisions of a village. Thus in Gopálpúr of Rohtak, there are 150

Damrís, each Damrí being equivalent to twenty-five kachcha bíghas. But Damrí is commonly known as a nominal coin, equal to $3\frac{1}{8}$ or $3\frac{1}{4}$ Dáms; or between two and three Gandas—so that a Damrí varies from 8 to 12 Cowrís, according to the good will and pleasure of unscrupulous Banyas.

It may be useful to subjoin from the "Díwán Pasand" a table showing the value of Damrís and Dáms:

1 Damrí	....	$3\frac{1}{4}$ Dáms.	
2 ,,	....	$6\frac{1}{4}$,,	...... 1 Chhadám.
3 ,,	....	$9\frac{1}{4}$,,	
4 ,,	....	$12\frac{1}{2}$,,	...... 1 Adhela.
5 ,,	....	15 ,,	
6 ,,	....	$18\frac{3}{4}$,,	...... $\frac{3}{4}$ Paisa.
7 ,,	....	22 ,,	
8 ,,	....	25 ,,	...... 1 ,,
9 ,,	....	28 ,,	
10 ,,	....	$31\frac{1}{4}$,,	...... $1\frac{1}{4}$,,
11 ,,	....	$34\frac{1}{4}$,,	
12 ,,	....	$37\frac{1}{4}$,,	...... $1\frac{1}{2}$,,
13 ,,	....	40 ,,	
14 ,,	....	44 ,,	...... $1\frac{3}{4}$,,
15 ,,	....	47 ,,	
16 ,,	....	50 ,,	...... 1 Taka.

The table is given with some slight variations in the "Zubdatu'l Ḳawánín," but in neither are the smaller fractional amounts given with correctness.—See Chhadám, Ganda.

Damaí, دمئي दमई

Amount of assessment. The word is derived from the Dám of account, which was formerly used in revenue accounts.—Central Doáb.

Ḍanḍá, ڈنڈا डंडा

A collector of market dues, in which sense Ḍanḍia also is

used; the beam of a pair of scales; the step of a ladder; a staff.

Ḍanḍí, ڈنڈي डंडी

A handle; a weighman; the beam of a pair of scales.

Ḍanḍwára, ڈنڈواره डंडवारा

A south wind. Khán Arzú says it is sometimes, but improperly, considered to come from the opposite quarter—and that the real name of the North wind is Barban.

Daránti, درانتي दरांती

A sickle.—See Dantí.

Ḍangwára, ڈنگواره डंगवारा

Reciprocal assistance in tillage.—Dehli and Northern Doáb. —See Angwára, Harí, and Jíta.

Dantáolí, دنتاولي दन्तावली

A harrow, or rake. From Dant, a tooth.

Ḍanthlá, ڈنتهلا डंथला

The bare stalks of Bajra, Jowar, and Indian corn; apparently from Dant, a tooth; but it must be confessed the word is usually spelt with the hard or cerebral *ḍ*, and Ḍanthal is so spelt on the high authority of Professor Shakespear, which, if correct, would militate against this etymology. They are also called Khúnthí, Khúntla, Dúnd, Danthal, Thúnt, Khutel, and Khobari. These names are in use in different places. In some, they represent the crop with the heads of corn cut off the stalks; in others they represent the roots which remain in the ground after the crop has been cut.—See Datoí and Danth.

Ḍanthal, ڈنتھل डंथल

This word bears the same meaning; and is also applied to the roots of Chana, remaining in the ground after the crop is cut.

Dares, دریس दरेस

A road-margin; any line very straight. It is derived from the drill-word "Dress," which has been introduced by our retired Sepoys into their native villages.

Darkhál, درکھال दरखाल

A cattle enclosure.—Benares.

Daṛar, دڑر दड़र

A water-fall, or impetuous flood; corrupted apparently from daṛeṛá دڑیڑا hard rain.

Dasotara, دسوترہ दसोत्रा

Ten per cent. From das دس ten.

Dastí, دستي दस्ती

A present given to native officials at the Dasehra. From the Persian دست a hand.—E.

Also the small portable kalamdán or inkstand which the native amlá use.—B.

Datoí, دتوئي दतोई

Land which has been lately cropped with Makha (Indian corn or maize), Bajra or Jawar.—Dehli or Upper Doáb.

There is much the same difficulty about spelling this word, as in spelling Danthal. Professor Shakespear, whose authority is not to be slighted, gives डठा as a stalk, which would make Datoí to be more accurately represented by डठोई or डटोई. Gilchrist also spells it डठा.

Datatra, دترہ दतरा

A large rake used for gathering high grass together into a cocklet. Kilwaí is a smaller implement of the same kind.—Rohilkhand.

Ḍorí, ڈوري डोरी

A chain, or line, with which lands are measured.—See Ḍaurí.

Doras, دورس दोरस

Literally, two flavours; used in the Eastern districts; as Domat in the North-West, to signify a mixture of two soils, Mattíár and Baluá, clay and sand; and, like Domat, is in some places, as in Azimgaṛh, considered the best quality; in others, as in Gorakhpúr, the second quality of soil, except in Tilpúr and the forest Parganahs, in which the Mattíár is considered too adhesive.

Dosáhí, دوساهي दोसाही

Dosáhí, or Dosáí, signifies lands yielding two crops a year.—See Dofaslí.

Dosarí, دوسري दोसरी

The ploughing of land twice; the land itself when ploughed twice. When ploughed three times it is called Tesarí; when four, Chaurasí.—Dehli.—See Dor and Jael.

Ḍaulá, ڈولا डौला

A boundary.

Daungṛá, دونگڑا दौंगड़ा

A heavy shower. The author of the "Araish-i Mahfil," in his preliminary chapter on the praises of Hindústan, speaks of the Asáṛh kí Daungṛí دونگڑي, Sawan kí Jharíán جهڑيان, and Bhádon kí Daṛeṛí دڑيڑي.

Daur, دور दौर

The slings attached to a basket for irrigation. The more usual terms are Jutá and Jotí.

Dauṛáhá, دوڑاها दौड़ाहा

A village messenger.—See Daláhar.

Daurí, دوري दौरी

The rope which binds the bullocks together when threshing. This is the general name, but there are many others in local use, as Gandâwar, Dâmrí, Garâwar, Dánwarí, Pakhar, and Jor. The stake to which the bullocks are tied is called Mend (limit); and hence Mendhya, the inner bullock. The outer or off bullock is called Pat in Benares, Pagharia in Rohilkhand, and Pankararí in Dehli. Daurí, which is spelt both with the Hindí and Persian Dal, appears to be derived from Dor, a string, a rope; whence Dorea, lace. In the gipsy language, Dorí, which means a riband, is perhaps the same word.*

Daurí is also used to the Eastward in the same sense as Puroha, Berí, Chhápa, Boka, Dúgla, or Leharí, to signify a sling basket used in irrigation, and is generally made of split bamboo. It means also the act of throwing the basket, as Daurí lagá, "irrigation by Daurí has commenced."

The lowest reservoir from which the water is raised is variously styled Nyaní, Gonra, Nandhú or Nadhao. It is raised from that to the Pachú, and from that again to the Thauka. The raised bank between the Nandhú and Pachú is called Odí; and the place where the throwers stand on each side of the Nandhú is called Paidha.

* Doriyá, a dog-keeper, is also similarly derived, because he is presumed to lead dogs with a string. Dorí dalna also is to prolong the stitch of a quilt, or dress; and hence is applied, metaphorically, to the lengthened note of the bird called Chittí, the female of the Amaduvade, or Avaduvat (*Fringilla Amandava*), *i.e.* the Fringilla of of Ahmedabad in the Dekkan, for so the word has been corrupted by the Naturalists.

Dabbiyá, دبیا दब्बिया

A box; also written Ḍibbiyá. A term applied to about ten handfuls (Muttha) of Kharíf produce. Lehna is the word used in the same sense with respect to Rabí produce. About four Muttha make a Lehna; about four Lehna, a Dabbiyá; about five Dabbiyá, a Bojh; and about a hundred Bojh make a Pahí. Five Dabbiyá of Kharíf produce amount to a Dhoka, and about ten Dhoka make a Bojh, or load, and an aggregation of several Bojh make a Kundar. The application of all these words varies very much in different districts, and even in different Parganahs. The text represents the words used chiefly in the Eastern portion of these Provinces.

Doháo, دوهاو दोहाव

The Zamíndár's perquisite of milk from Ryot's cows.

Dohur, دوهر दोड़र

A sandy sub-soil.—Central Doáb.

Dohra, دوهره दोहरा

See Koluh.

Dohar, دوهر दोहर

The old bed of a river.—Eastern Oudh. Johar is elsewhere used in the same sense.

Dohar is likewise applied to land which bears two crops in a year.—Central Doáb.

Dojíra, دوجیره दोजीरा

A kind of rice.—See Dhan.

Dokhí, دوکهي दोखी

A raised mound indicating the junction of two boundaries.—Dehli.

Ḍol, ڈول डोल

Applied locally to signify the richest black soil.—Baitúl.

Ḍol is generally used to denote a bucket for drawing water. From the Persian دلو.

Doláwa, دولاوه दोलावा

A well having two Laos, or well-buckets and ropes. Dopaira is also used in this sense.

Ḍolchí, ڈولچي डोलची

A small bucket.—See above under Ḍol.

Domaṭ, دومٹ दोमट

A mixture of two Mattís or soils, clay and sand, Mattíár and Bhúr. Like Doras, in some places, it is considered the first quality, in others, the second quality of soil. In Agra, Farrukhabad, and parts of Bareily, it is considered the best, but it is more usual, as in Badáon, to rate it as second quality.

Ḍongí, ڈونگي डोंगी

A small boat. From which our dingy is derived, according to some, but there exists also a form डेंगी which is more likely of the two to have originated the word.

Dúb, دوب दूब

Name of a grass (*Agrostis linearis*, Kœn. *Cynodon Dactylon*, Royle). "Its flowers in the perfect state are among the loveliest objects in the vegetable world, and appear through a lens like minute rubies and emeralds in constant motion from the least breath of air. It is the sweetest and most nutritious pasture for cattle, and its usefulness added to its beauty, induced the Hindús in the earliest ages to believe it was the mansion of a benevolent nymph."—(Sir W. Jones' Works, Vol. V. p. 78).

There are generally considered to be three kinds of Dúb. The best, which throws out the creeper-like stem,* is called Paundá. This is essentially the same as the fiorin grass of English farmers. The second, which is smaller, grows on hard ground, and is called Khútya. The third is called the white Dúb from its peculiar colour, and is used by native practitioners as a medicine in fevers. This is called by Wilson ("Sanskrit Dict." p. 279) Gandálí. In Dehli it is frequently called Dhaurí. In Saugor the Khútya is known under the name of Chhattú. Where the division into three kinds is not known, the recognized varieties are Ghur-dúb and Ban-dúbia; the first being derived from Ghora, a horse, as it is excellent pasture grass; the second from Ban, a forest, or jungle, as it is a coarser kind.

The nutritive qualities of Dúb have caused it to be a great favorite with the natives of India, and frequent allusions are made to it by the poets. Its tenacity whenever it once fixes its roots has caused it to be used in a common simile when the attachment of Zamíndárs to their native soil is spoken of.

Nának Shah also, in exhorting himself to humility, uses the following simile respecting the modest charms of this herb, alluding to the fact that it remains green even in the hot weather.

नानक नन्हा हो रहो जैसा नन्ही दूब
और घास जल जाएंगे दूब ख़ूब की ख़ूब

"Nának, be humble like the humble dúb,
Other grasses are burnt up, dúb remains fresh and fresh."

Ḍúbáí, ڈوبائي डूबाई

A term sometimes applied to a bribe, given whether the donor gain or lose his cause; in distinction to Taraí, in which the

* From this peculiarity of creeping along the ground this grass derives its name, from डूबना to be pressed down. It would be more correct, perhaps, to write it डूब, but Hindi spelling is very capricious.—B.

bribe is returned if the suit is lost. The words are used in the Doáb and Rohilkhand, and their existence indicates a degree of refinement in the art of bribery, which perhaps no other language can parallel. The origin of the terms is in the one case, dúbná ڈوبنا to sink, to be immerged; and, in the other, tarná ترنا to pass over safely, to be ferried.

Ḍubsí, ڈبسي डुबसी

Inundated land, or land liable to be flooded. From ḍúbná ڈوبنا to sink, to be immerged.

Dúdhá, دودها दूधा

A species of rice.—See Dhan.

Ḍuḍká, ڈڈکا डुडका

Is the name of one of the many diseases to which the rice plant is subject. There are various others, as Bagulí, Katrí, Purwaí, Kansí, etc.

Dúgla, دوگله दूगला

A sling-basket of large size, round and deep, used for the purposes of irrigation.—See Berí, Boka, Daurí.

Durkhí, دُرکهي दुर्खी

An insect whose ravages are very destructive to indigo, when the plant is young.

Dor, دور दोर

Land ploughed twice. When ploughed three times, it is called Tíar; when four, Chawar, the *ar* in these words being from हर a plough; thus dor = do-har; tíar = tin-har; chawar = chau (for chár) har, etc.—Central and Lower Doáb.—See Dosarí and Jael.

Dúmá, دوما दूमा

Is the name of the leather case in which tea is imported from Tibet into Gaṛhwál and Kamáon. It contains about three seers, and bears a price of six or seven rupees. About one hundred Dúmás are imported annually into Kamáon, which is consumed chiefly by the Bhotiyás of the passes, and seventy Dúmás into Gaṛhwál, of which a portion finds its way to Hardwár and Najíbabad.

Dún, دون दून

A valley. The word does not appear in Shakespear's Dictionary, but is locally applied in the Sewalik Hills under the Himalaya, in this signification: as Patlí Dún, Dehra Dún. The word may perhaps be formed by elision from the Sanskrit द्रोणी "the union of two mountains, the valley or chasm between them" (Sanskrit Dict., p. 431); and hence Dronakas, "the people of vallies (Vishnu Purana, p. 196).

Ḍúnḍá, ڈونڈا डूंडा

A bullock with only one horn. The word is in general use; but in parts of Dehli it is applied to a bullock with two horns, and Túnda to a bullock which has only one. This word also means the broken stump of a tree.

Dundká, دندکا दुन्दका

See Kolhú.

Ḍúngá, ڈونگا डूंगा

Deep; an excavation, such as that of a trough; a canoe.

Fález, فالیز फालेज़

A field of melons.

Farás, فراس फरास

(Tamaris farás.) The Farás occur in the drier parts of the Doáb, and in the neighbourhood of Dehli; where it is called Asal or Atal, because in Arabia the galls which are formed on the tree are called Samrat-u'l Asal. Chhotí Maí is the Hindústání name of these galls. Very little use is made of the tree, except occasionally in building, when nothing better can be procured.—See Jhao.

In the Doáb it does not appear to grow to the East of the Arind river.

Farrásh, فراش फरास

From the Arabic فرش a carpet; a person who spreads carpets; a sweeper. The term is correctly explained in the Glossary under Ferash, Firashe, and Farash. In ancient times his duty appears to have been that of a Khalásí, or tent-pitcher, and the latter term was applied chiefly to sailors.

تنڈیل بزرگ خلاصیان ملاح را بزبان دریا ورزان خلاصي و حاوره گویند
(A'ín-i-Akbarí.)

"Ṭinḍel (our modern word tindal = the boatswain of a native crew) the head of the Khalamis (vulgo clashies) in the language of the sea-going folk; also called Háwarah."

Firárí, فراري फिरारी

Absconding; a person who has absconded. From the Persian فرار firár, flight. The word is more usually pronounced Farárí in India.

Fota, فوطه फोता

A bag; collections made from the tenantry in general; treasure; revenue.

Gáchhí, گاچھی गाछी

A pad put over the back of a beast of burden; called also Gaddí, Gathí, Bakhrá, Palán, Líwá, Padád, Chhaí, and by several other names, which are merely local, and even then not applicable to every beast. For instance, where the pad of the ass is Líwá, that of the bullock is Chhaí-Bakhrá; and so on.

Gád, گاد गाद

The sediment of dirty water.

Gádar, گادر गादर

Gádar, or, more correctly, Gaddar and Gadra, signifies half-ripe fruit or corn.—See Bhadahar.

Gáḍar, گاڈر गाडर

Sheep.—See Gaḍariyá in Part I.

Gáhná, گاهنا गाहना

To tread out corn.—See Daen.

Gáhan, گاهن गाहन

A harrow with teeth for eradicating grass from ploughed land. The Maira, which it resembles in form has no teeth. The implement is little known to the East of Farrukhabad.

Gájá, گاجا गाजा

The first rice sowing in the districts at the foot of the hills. The sowing is in Baisakh (April-May), the cutting in Bhadon (August-September). The word is, perhaps, derived from Gajána, to ferment, to rot, which aptly expresses the condition of this early crop. The second sowing is called Bhijoa; it occurs in Jeth, the cutting takes place in Kuár. The third is called Rassauta, or Rutiya, seasonable, because it takes place in the most natural *rut* (vulg. for *rit*, season). The sowing is in Asaṛh (June-July), or Sáwan (July-August), and the harvest in Kátik (October-November), or Aghan (November-December).

Gájar, گاجر गाजर

A carrot.

Gál, گال गाल

A sort of tobacco.

Gála, گاله गाला

A pod of cotton, or, more usually, a ball of carded cotton, which is known also by the name of Goḍhá گوڈھا.

Gám, گام गाम

A village: more usually Gánw.

Gánḍá, گانڈا गानडा

Sugar-cane—See Agaund, Ikh, and Ganna.

Gánḍal, گانڈل गांडल

Gánḍar, گانڈر गांडर

(Andropogon muricatum). Thatching grass. Gánḍal grows in land subject to inundation; and its root yields the Khaskhas, or scented grass, so much used for taṭṭis or screens against doorways in the hot weather in India. The produce of this grass has of late years much diminished, owing to the great extension of cultivation in those parts where it used formerly to grow spontaneously. Gánḍal is the common name of the grass, but it is known by the name of Pánhí in Dehli.

Gánja, گانجه गांजा

Gánja, or Gánjha, is a plant from which an intoxicating drug of the same name is procured, which is used as a liquor in the Upper Provinces, and smoked like tobacco in Bengal. That which is procured from Balúgarrah in Bengal is of high repute. It is divided into Chapta and Golí,* of which the first is chiefly in demand in Hindustan.

Gánja is largely cultivated in the hills of Sirmúr and Gaṛhwál and the plant grows wild under the hills from Sehâranpúr to Tirhut, and on the banks of the Ganges; but it appears to be not the same as the smoking Gánja of Bengal, as it is declared to have none of the gum-resin qualities peculiar to the latter. O'Shaughnessy describes Gánja to be the dried hemp plant which has flowered, and from which the resin has not been removed. This resin in certain seasons exudes, and concretes on the leaves, stems, and flowers, and is called Charas, and separately taxed and sold.

Buchanan, in his statistical account of Dinajpúr, says that the hemp when young is called Gánja; and Siddhi when the flowers have fully expanded. Authorities, however, seem little agreed respecting the exact difference between Gánja, Siddhi, and Bhang; nor are they more agreed respecting the difference between the Gánja of the Upper and Lower Provinces, and the identity of the *Cannabis Sativa* and *Indica*.

It was only this year that some Gánja procured at Seharanpúr was sent for examination to the superintendent at Rajshahí, who thus comments upon it.

"The specimens sent bear more the character of the hemp plant grown for Sanni, than of the Gánja plant. The *Cannabis Indica*, or Gánja plant, is diœcious, annual, about six or seven feet high; the stem is erect, six or eight inches in circum-

* The three kinds of Gánja, or rather three qualities or methods of preparation, now known in Bengal are *gol*, or "round," which is the natural plant dried in its natural shape; *chiptá*, or "flat," which is the plant pressed flat for convenience of packing; and *roṛá*, or "dust," which is the broken flowers and stalks and refuse generally, and is less valuable than the other kinds.—B.

ference, and branched; leaves alternate or opposite, on long weak petioles, digitate, scabrous, with linear lanceolate, sharply serrated leaflets, tapering into a long smooth entire point. Males lax and drooping; branches leafless at base. Females erect, simple, and leafy at the base. Small jattís, the size of a walnut, form on the branches, of an absorbing nature, containing resinous narcotic juice, which is the part of the plant used. Each plant will yield from 20 to 26 branches, weighing, when dry, from two to two-and-a-half seers.

"The natives prepare the drug in a very rude manner, the branches are cut off when the resinous jattís are ripe, and left to dry for a few days; they are then spread on mats, and the jattís are compressed with the toes. By this means a great portion of the narcotic resin is lost on the mats, and by adhesion to the toes. The sticks being retained is also very objectionable when the drug has to be sent to a great distance; for out of 1000 maunds prepared in the customary way, not more than thirty maunds of the drug can be obtained, the remainder being useless sticks."

It is evident, therefore, that in his opinion the Gánja of Bengal is of superior quality to that of the Upper Provinces, from which intoxicating Bhang only can be extracted, and that the *Cannabis Sativa* is not the same as the *Cannabis Indica*; yet Roxburgh, Wildenow, O'Shaughnessy, and several other authorities declare that Gánja is the *Cannabis Sativa*; and the former, on comparing plants raised from European hemp-seed with the Gánja plant, could not discover the slightest difference between them.—Asiatic Researches, Vol. XI. p. 161.—See Bhang and Charas.

Gánjar, گانجر गांजर

A kind of grass. It is known also by the name Ganjerua, and is considered very difficult to eradicate when it has once taken root.

Gánkar, گانکر गांकर

An inferior kind of bread made of Arhar and other hard grains. It is also, more generally, applied to any bread not baked on an iron plate (the primitive "gribble" of Ireland)—made, in short, in a hurry, and covered with embers till it is considered baked enough to eat. It is also known by the name of Gákar, Girdí, Angákar, Bhaura and Battí.—See Bhatula.

Gánṭá, گانٹا गांटा

Gánṭh, گانٹھ गांठ

Gánṭh is literally a knot, and is applied by agriculturists to the refuse of straw, consisting of the knotted parts of the stalk and ear-ends, which are known to English farmers under the name of "colder." This is formed into a heap, and put aside on the threshing ground. As an illustration of the difference which prevails in the agricultural terms of different parts of these Provinces, it may be interesting to give the names of the various heaps which are at different times raised on the threshing ground, during the process of winnowing the corn. The names which are given as synonymous with Gánṭh, do not all represent the same thing. The words beginning with S signify generally the "colder" after it has been re-winnowed; and some of the other names applied only to Kharíf, or only to Rabbí produce, specially; the same word being rarely used for both.—See Bhurarí.—E.*

* Káli Rai says, "The small heaps put aside for bhúmí ganesh (or the offerings to gods and penates) are called *ujarí* and *syáwaṛh* स्यावढ़; grain left on the threshing floor after removing the bulk of the crop is called *meṛ* मेड़, and *thápá* थापा, and the grain which falls to the ground with the chaff in winnowing is called *ghúnḍar* घूंडर and is the perquisite of the Chamárs. It is also called *gaṭharwá* गठवा. Gleanings of fields which any one may carry off are called सिला *silá*.—E. *add.*

TABLE OF DIALECTIC VARIETIES.

Dehli.	Rohilkhand.	Upper Doáb.	Central Doáb.	Lower Doáb.	E. Oudh, or Gorakhpúr.	Benares.	Bundelkhand.	Saugor.	How composed.
Sillí ...... Dhar	Gurhao Sillí ...	Sillí ... Neora .. Dhar ...	Dehí ...	Kalha .. Guráńw	Kunáo ... Aokán ...	Gurańw ... Ukańw ...	Thúa	Udeyí...	Grain and straw, or winnowed corn unheaped.
Rás, or Tár..	Rás.........	Rás.........	Rás.........	Rás.........	Rás	Rás............	Rás	Rás.........	Heaped grain.
Bhús	Osa	Osa...... Bhus ...	Sillí ...	Sillí ... Bhusaur	Sillí ...... Bhusaur ...	Sillí	Bhusaul	Bhusaura ..	Heaped straw.
Dondlí ... Gantha ... Bhularí ...	Gánth .. Gántá .. Sánta...	Gántha Gánteh	Gathurí Sathurí	Gánta .. Guthrí.. Jangra .	Khúntí ... Gethara ...	Ganth ... Ganteh ...	Gúthrí ... Súthrí ...	Gathua . Sathua .	Refuse straw, or colder.

Gowárí, گواري गोवारी

A dwelling house; a family; a cow-house.—Dehli.

Gabrauṭá, گبروٿا गबरौटा

A large beetle found in old cowdung and dung-hills. It is called also Gabrauṛa and Gobaraunda (*Scarabæus stercorarius*, Linn.). From गोबर cowdung.

Gaḍ, گڈ गड़

A boundary mark.—Dehli.

Gaddí, گدي गद्दी

A throne, or cushion.—See Gachí.

A sheaf of corn. Perhaps this would be spelt more correctly with a Hindí ड ḍ.

Gaddhrí, گدهري गद्धरी

The unripe pod of the Gram plant, or *Cicer arietinum.*—Dehli.—See Dhúndhí and Gaddar.

Gaddar, گدّر गद्दर

Gadrá, گدرا गद्रा

Unripe corn, or fruit.

Gadíchaṭ, گديچٿ गदीचट

A grass generally found growing with Dúb, which it re-resembles, except in being about three times larger. It is much used as fodder.

Gadgol, گدگول गद्गोल

Muddy water.

Gahái, گهائي गहाई

The custom of treading sheaves of corn by bullocks, with the view of separating the corn from the ears and stalks. From the verb Gáhná, *q.v.*—See also Dáín.

Gahná, گهنا गहना

Anything in pledge; the original meaning is jewels, ornaments.

Gajjar, گجر गज्जर

Swampy ground.

Galiyá, گليا गलिया

Galiyá (sometimes, but incorrectly, pronounced Gariyár) is the name given to a bullock which lies down in the midst of its work; generally from its neck (गला) being galled—hence the derivation.

Galtáṛ, گلتاڑ गलताड

The name given to the inner pegs of a yoke. The word appears to be derived from गला Galá, a neck, and आड़ Aṛ, a protection.* Gáta, Shamal, and Pachaí are used in the same sense.—See Hal.

Galtans, گلتنس गलतन्स

Dying without issue. From انس right, lot, inheritance, and گلنا to melt, to be dissolved.

Gambhír, گنبهير गंभीर

A Sanskrit word signifying deep. It is generally applied to soil which is of a rich quality, and attains a more than usual

* I should prefer to write it with र, and derive it from galá, the neck, and तार a thread or string, as its use is to fasten the string which goes under the neck of the ox. The derivation in the text does not account for the त.—B.

depth before the subsoil is reached. This quality is ascribed to the fertile soil of Málwá.

देस मालवा गैहिर गंभीर
डग डग रोटी पग पग नीर

"The land of Málwá is deep and rich;'
At every step bread, on every path water."

The two words Gaihar (for गहिरा) and Gambhír in the foregoing couplet are in fact the same; the former being the modified or Prakrit form of the latter. See Wilson's Introduction to "Specimens of the Hindu Theatre," and "Sanskrit Dictionary," p. 283.

Gandá, گنڈا गंडा

This word is given under Gandál, in the Printed Glossary. Like the Dám, the Ganḍa of account and the Ganḍa of practice do not coincide. Ganḍás of account are but little used in the North-Western Provinces, except in Benares and the Dehra Dún, and, in consequence of its former subjection to Oudh, the Nazarána accounts of Rohilkhand are frequently drawn out in Ganḍas. This Ganḍa is the twentieth part of an Anna. The Ganḍá known to the common people is not of stable amount, sometimes four, and sometimes five, and sometimes even six, go to a packa Damrí, or Chhadám, according to the pleasure of the money dealers, or the state of the market. Notwithstanding this variable amount, as a Ganḍa is equivalent to four Kaurís, "to count by Ganḍas" signifies to count by fours, or by the quaternary scale, to which the natives are very partial,—in the same way as to count by gáhís or panjas, is to count by fives, or by the quinary scale.

As four Kaurís make one Ganḍá, so do twenty Ganḍas make one Pan, and sixteen Pans make one Kaháwan. But there are grades of monetary value even below that of Kauṛí; for the Hindús seem as fond of dealing with these infinitesimal quantities, as they are with the higher numbers, as exemplified in the article Kaṛoṛ. Thus 3 Krant, or 4 Kak, or 5 Bat, or 9 Dant, or 27 Jau, or 32 Dár, or 80 Til, or 800 Sano are each equivalent to one Kaurí. These are not in practical use in the N.W. Provinces, but are entered in several account books, and many of them appear to be employed in the bazaar transactions of Kattack and parts of Bengal.—See "Rushton's Gazetteer," 1841, Vol. I. p. 182.

The Kauṛi or cowry shell, the *Cypræa moneta*, has been subject to strange diminution of value, in consequence of the facilities of commerce, by which their worth has been depressed below that of the precious metals. In 1740, a Rupee exchanged for 2,400 Kauṛís; in 1756, for 2,560 Kauṛís; and at this time as many as 6,500 Kaurís may be obtained for the Rupee.

Kauṛí in Persian is translated by Khar-mohra, literally, a jackass's or mule's shell; because mules are ornamented in that country with trappings of shells, as a Gosain's bullock is in this country. In Arabic it is known by *wada* ودع, which Ibn Batuta says is carried in large quantities from the Maldive Islands to Bengal, where it is used as coin; and therefore there can be no doubt that the *Cypræa moneta* is meant. The Kámús adds تعلق لدفع العين—that it is suspended from the neck to avert the evil eye, as it is in India to this day,* provided the shell is split or broken.—E.

These minute amounts are of great and constantly occurring use in calculating the shares of proprietors in the enormous Zamíndárís in Behar and Bengal under the perpetual settlement. Each estate, however large, being considered for purposes of partition as one rupee, a person whose share is only two or three kránts may have an interest in the estate equal to several thousand acres, and worth many lakhs of rupees.—B.

* Ganḍá is also the name applied to the knotted string which is suspended round a child's neck for the same purpose; but not, apparently, because it has any connection with the Kauṛí amulet.

Ganda-biroza, گندہبروزہ गन्दाबिरोजा

Olibamum, male frankincense, the produce of the *Boswellia thurifera.* The same name is also given to the produce of the Chír *(Pinus longifolia).*—(O'Shaughnessy's Dispensatory, pp. 283 and 612).

Gaṇḍásí, گنڈاسي गंडासी

Gaṛásí, گڑاسي गडासी

An instrument for cutting sugar-cane, Jawár stalks, or thorny bushes. Also, in Dehli, an assessment on the number of Gaṇḍásís, a tax which used to be levied in former days.—E.

The gaṇḍásá of Benares and Behar is a formidable weapon, like a battle-axe, capable of inflicting in the hands of a stalwart Rajput peasant severe wounds, as is demonstrated by the cases of wounding which so frequently come before the criminal courts. In Shahábád the village chokidars are often armed with it.—B.

Gaṇḍerí, گنڈيري गंडेरी

Gaṛerí, گڑيري गडेरी

Pieces of sugar-cane.

Gandhel, گندھيل गंधेल

The sweet smelling grass known as Gandhel (from Gandh, perfume), is most probably the same as Gandbbel, which Royle ("Ant. Hind. Med." p. 143) says is the *Andropogon calamus aromaticus;* from the leaves, culms, and roots of which a fragrant essential oil is distilled.

Gaṇḍarwálá, گنڈروالا गंडरवाला

See Kolhú. Gareran, Gandrára, and Gandhra are also used in a similar sense.

Gandailá, گنديلا गंदैला

Gandailá, or Gandhiyá, is the name of a grub destructive to Chaná and Arhar.—Eastern Oudh. It is usually called Gíndar elsewhere, *q.v.*

Gangálá, گنگالا गंगाला

Lands subject to inundations of the Ganges.—Rohilkhand.

Gangbarámad, گنگ‌برآمد गंगबरामद

Gangbarár, گنگ‌برار गंगबरार

Alluvial land recovered from a river, especially the Ganges. —See Daryábarár.

Gang shikast, گنگ‌شکست गंगसीकस्त

Encroachment of the Ganges, or of any other river, by diluvion.—See Dariyáburd.

Ganj, گنج गंज

A granary; a market, and especially one of grain. It is used chiefly as an affix to proper names; as Islám-gange, Hardoa-gange, Captain-gange.

Ganjelí, گنجيلي गंजेली

The same as Bhangela, *q.v.*

Gankaṭá, گنکٹا गनकटा

Is the title of the man employed to cut the sugar-cane into lengths of about six inches for feeding the mill.

Ganná, گنا गन्ना

Sugar-cane. There are various kinds cultivated in these Provinces. The principal in Rohilkhand are Dhaul (white),

Neülí, Katára, Lakrí, Paunda, Chin, Manga; in Benares, Manga, Paunda, Baraukha, Reora, Khusyar, Sarautí, Katạra, Rakra, and Khiwáhí.

The most noted of the Doáb are Saretha, Dhaul, Paunda, Chin, Kathorí, Dhúmar, Baraukha, Káláganda, Kinára, Karba, Matna; in Dehli, Súrtha, Kálásúrtha, Paunda, Bhúrasúrtha, Lálrí, Gharari, Kinára, Dhaul, and Bejhar. Many of these names are identical; but the kind called Paunda seems to be the only one generally known. It is eaten raw, not manufactured.

The amount of acres under sugar-cane cultivation throughout the North-Western Provinces, in the year of survey, is shewn below:

Dehli Division	5,307	Acres.
Rohilkhand Division	168,277	„
Mírat Division	105,861	„
Agra Division	47,090	„
Allahábád Division	33,410	„
Benares Division	317,535	„
Saugor Division	12,919	„
Total Acres	690,399	

Ganel, گنیل गनेल

A species of long grass, which is used for thatching, and grows on the banks of the Chambal. The word is a corruption of Gandal, *q.v.*

Ganí (gunny), گني गनी

The name given to the coarse bags made from the fibres of the Pát (*Corchorus capsularis*). It is derived from Ganiya, a name which Rumphius gave to the Pát from some native source.

Ganaurí, گنوري गनौरी

A bulrush.—Eastern Oudh.

Ganṭhá, گنٹھا गंठा

A fractional part of a Jaríb.—See Gaṭṭha.

Gaṛá, گڑا गडा

A large sheaf; except in the Dehli territory, where it is usually considered to be a small one. The word is in use chiefly to the westward.

Gaṛá baṭáí, گڑابٹائی गडाबटाई

Division of produce without threshing, by stacking the sheaves in proportionate shares.—Rohilkhand.

Grám, گرام ग्राम

A village; more usually Gáṅw.

Gaṛáo, گڑاو गडाव

An instrument used for cutting Jawár stalks, etc., for fodder.—Central and Lower Doáb. It is called Gaḍásí in Rohilkhand, and Ganḍásá and Ganḍásí elsewhere.

Garárí, گراری गरारी

The block over which the well-rope traverses.—Benares, Bundelkhand, and Lower Doáb. Garílí, Garrí, and Girrá are also similarly used.—See Chák.

Garḍauṅrá, گرڈونڑا गरडौंरा

A small pit.—Baitúl.

Gaṛeran, گڑیرن गडेरन

See Kolchú and Gandarwála.

Gargawá, گرگوا गर्गवा

A grass which grows in low ground during the rainy season.

When it gets into rice-fields it checks the growth of the plant, and is very injurious. Buffaloes are fond of the grass, but other horned cattle do not like it.

Gáucharáí, گاوچرائي गौचराई

Grazing; a grazing tax. From Gau, a cow, and Charána, to graze. It is known also as Kahcharáí. From Kah, grass.

Gáolí, گاولي गावली

A cowherd.

Gáṛí, گاڑي गाड़ी

Gáṛí, or Gáḍí, is a cart, and the man who drives it is called a Gáṛíwán, given in the Printed Glossary as Gaḍíwan The following are the names of the different parts of the North-Western Gáṛí:—Harsa is the long wood extending on either side, from the front to the back; the transverse pieces are called Pattí; those extending beyond the wheels are called Takání. Bánk, or Painjaní is the wood that joins the two Takánís; and Chakol the pin by which the wheel is attached to the Bánk; Sújah, the pins which attach the Bánk to the Takánís; Bánkara and Gaz, two pieces of wood in the front of the Gáṛí, where it narrows to a point; Phannah and Untara are parts that project beyond the yoke; Kharruá, the upright posts that support the covering or awning; Dandelí, something like a drag; Nah, the nave; Putthí, the quadrant of a wheel. The native wheelwrights make their wheels in four parts, each with a double spoke, which are afterwards joined together. Each of these parts is a Putthí.

Gáṛah, گاڑه गाड़ह

Low lands on which water does not lie long.—Upper Doáb. It is, perhaps, a corruption of *gáṛha*, deep.

Gáṭá, گاٹا गाटा

The yoking of bullocks together for the purpose of treading out grain.—Dehli.

Gáṭá is also applied in Dehli to a Brahman, or Banya, that forms an illicit connexion with a woman.

Gáṭá is also used, generally, in the N.W. Provinces to signify a plot; a piece of land; a division of a village; a field.

Gehúṅ, گیہوں गेहूं

Wheat. There are several names of wheats in different parts of the country, but they all, according to native opinion, resolve themselves into the two families of red and white; the former is known by the names of Lál, Laliyá, Kathiyá, Bansiyá, Samariya, Rattiyá, Jaláliyá, Pisiyá, etc. The latter by the names of U'jur, Situa, Dhaula, Pílí, Dáúd Khání, etc. The beardless wheat (Múṅṛiyá, from मूंड़िया Múṅṛiyá, to shave), is also both red and white, and in seed, flavour, and price, does not differ from the bearded kind. In opposition to Múṅriyá, Tikúrárí, or Túndiyá, is used to represent the bearded kind. The beardless wheat appears to be much more common in the Eastern than the Western parts of these provinces.

The following table shews the number of acres under wheat cultivation in the N.W. Provinces, during the year of Survey:

Dehli Division	225,084	Acres.
Rohilkhand Division	883,009	,,
Mírat Division	890,309	,,
Agra Division	472,364	,,
Allahábád Division	423,901	,,
Benares Division	535,642	,,
Saugor Division	953,687	,,
Total Acres	4,383,996	

Gháná, گهانا घाना

Ghání, گهاني घानी

A sugar-cane press.

Ghár, گهار घार

Clay soil in low situations, where rain-water lies for a time. Land worn away by running water is said *ghár ho jána.*

A sub-division of Mattiyár. Also, a long strip of land* in Etawa, lying for the most part between the Jumna and the high road to Agra. In Sekandra of Kaunpúr it is called Khár.

All these words are probably mere corruptions of Gahra, a cavity. The former is spelt with a common, and the latter with a hard or cerebral *r*, and Ghár itself is also spelt indifferently with either letter. The word bears a close resemblance to, and is possibly a corruption of, the Arabic Ghár غار a cavity, a hollow.

Ghárí, گهاري घारी

Cattle sheds.—Eastern Oudh.

A valley, or ravine.—See Ghár.—Rohilkhand.

Ghenṭí, گهينٹي घेंटी

The unripe pod of gram, arhar, and other pulses.—See Dhúndí (correctly Dhendí, Ghegará, and Thonthí).

Ghonghí, گهونگهي घोंघी

Ghonghí, or Ghoghí, signifies the tying the end of a blanket in a knot, and so placing it on the head as a protection against

* On the opposite side of the river there are other strips of land called Ghár, as Kachhwáha-ghár, Tauhar-ghár, and one in Sehάranpúr (see Gújar); but whether it is applied to the oblong shape of the land, or to the worn surface of the soil in the neighbourhood of rivers, on the banks of which those Ghárs occur, it is not easy to say.

rain. It also signifies the enveloping oneself entirely in a sheet or blanket, so that, when one sits down, no part of the body, except, perhaps, the head, is discernible. It is also applied as Chot, *q.v.* The application of these words varies in different provinces.—See Khúrhú.

Ghúí, گهوئي घूई

The name of a herb which grows during the rains on high ground.

Ghun, گهن घुन

A weevil, destructive to wood and grain; hence, Ghuna, weevil-eaten. The term appears generic as well as specific, for it is applied to the Bhábí, Dholá, Pápá, Páthá, Khaprá, Kírí, Pitárí, Sursarí, and various other insects destructive to stored grain. Indeed Ghun is in many places not known as a grain-weevil, but, that it is nevertheless properly so applied, the common proverb teaches us,

गेहूं के साथ घुन पिस गया

"The weevil has been ground with the wheat;" applied to any indiscriminate calamity which involves equally both high and low.—See Journal of Agricultural and Horticultural Society of Bengal, Vol. III. Part 2, p. 89.

Ghundí, گهنڈي घुंडी

The name of a herb which grows in rice fields after the crop is cut. Camels are very partial to this herb; and it is used as a specific in various diseases by the country quacks.

Ghungchí, گهنگچي घुंगची

A small red and black seed (*Abrus precatorius*). It is known also by the name of Rattí, Chhontilí, Chirmithí, and Surkha; and as it is the primary unit of Indian weights, it is important to establish its exact value. From a series of experiments detailed in the thirteenth number of the "Mírat Magazine," it appears that the average weight of 267 seeds amounted to 1·93487 grains. Prinsep, in his "Useful Tables," gives the weight of the Masha (8 Rattís) at 15½ grains, which, divided by 8, affords 1·9375 for the weight of the Rattí. As these results were obtained independently, we shall be quite safe if we assume the Ghungchí, or Rattí, as equivalent to 1·933 grains.

Ghúngí, گهونگي घूंगी

An insect destructive to crops of certain kinds of cereals.—See Gindar.

Ghúr, گهور घूर

The name given to the soil of the sandy ridge to the East of Muzaffarnagar. Also pronounced घुड or घुढ़.

Ghurat, گهرت घुरत

Cattle pens.—Eastern Oudh.

Ghusránd, گهسراند घुसरांद

A kind of creeping grass with a yellow flower. It bears a bitter fruit resembling the Kakorí. It is used as a condiment for horses, but it is considered poisonous to men.

Ghoṭí, گهوٹي घोटी

Land which has been under a rice crop.—Bundelkhand, Lower Doáb, and Benares. Dhankar is used in the North West. The word is probably derived from ghoṭná گهوٹنا to shave.

Ghalla, غله घल्ला

Grain. The word is Arabic, but in common use.

Ghangol, گهنگول घंगोल

The name of the water lily which produces the celebrated Nílúfar flower. It produces a greenish fruit about the size of an orange, and the seeds of it are eaten by the poorer classes.

Ghaná, گهنا घना

From ghaná گهنا dense, close; a sporting preserve; the same as ramná or shikárgáh.

Ghaṛá, گهڑا घडा

An earthen water pot.

Gharkí, غرقي गरकी

Overflowed; inundated. From the Arabic غرق ghark, drowning.

Gharaṛ, گهرڑ घरड

The dry Moth plant, cut and given as fodder to cattle.—Dehli.—It is in some parts pronounced Kurar.

Ghaṭṭí, گهٹي गट्टी

Loss; decrease; deficiency.

Ghai, گهئي घै

A platform of earth, artificially raised and levelled and smoothed, on which stacks of corn are placed; when staddles or supports are used they are called Chullí, *q.v.*

Ginḍurí, گنڈري गिंडुरी

A pad of grass to support an earthen pot.—See Jurá.

Gindar, گندر गिन्दर

An insect which is very destructive to growing Gram and Arhar. Júí, Jurái, and Ghúngí are similarly applied, but chiefly in Bundelkhand, Benares, and the Lower Doáb.

Gintí, گنتي गिनती

From *ginna*, to count, signifies number; reckoning; the first day of the month; a muster; of which word Gilchrist observes that "it is much used in India for a *sample*, but why I know not, except from *mister*, a rule." The truth is, that *muster* in its Anglo-Indian sense is derived from the Portuguese *amostra*, a sample, a word which, as well as our *muster* in its ordinary sense, is derived from the Latin *monstrare*, to show.

Giráni, گراني गिरानी

Dearness of provision; scarcity.

Girjí, گرجي गिर्जी

A sort of grass which grows about a yard high, and is found in certain parts of Hánsí, particularly in that part known as "Skinner's Bir." The names of other grasses found there are gaṇḍá, or "scented;" sarwálá, or "head-bearing;" kheoṅ, bur, ganthíl, or "knotty;" palwá, or "large-straw;" and roish.—E. *add.*

Giro, گرو गिरो

Giro, or more correctly girau, is a pledge, a pawn.

Girwí, گروي गिरवी

Anything pledged or pawned.

Girwí is also, in Persian, an insect mischievous to standing corn. This is the same, no doubt, as the Genrúí of the Hindús which is a disease of the *cerealia*, in which the plant dries up and assumes a reddish colour. The word is derived from Genrú, a kind of red earth or ochre, and is in common use, but Ratá is the term used in the Doáb, Benares, and Rohilkhand, and Ratwaí, Rorí, and Ratua in Dehli. From *rat*, or *rata*, which is the origin of, and bears the same meaning as, *red*.—See Halda.

It is a popular delusion entertained in some parts of the country that the neigbourhood of Alsí, or linseed, is necessary to generate this disease; but in most parts of the N. W. Provinces the opinion is now repudiated. Nevertheless, as the disease first attacks Alsí, and the ova floats in the air, the precaution is perhaps wise of eradicating it, as farmers do the barberry-bush at home, which in many parts is supposed to be a great generator of rust.

The real nature of the disease has hitherto, as in the case of similar diseases in Europe, eluded the search of enquirers, whether practical or scientific; but an interesting account of its ravages has been given by Colonel Sleeman.

"It is at first of a light beautiful orange colour, and found chiefly upon the Alsí (linseed), which it does not seem much to injure; but about the end of February the fungi ripen, and shed their seeds rapidly, and they are taken up by the wind and carried over the corn fields. I have sometimes seen the air tinted of an orange colour for many days by the quantity of these seeds which it has contained, and that without the wheat crops suffering at all when any but an easterly wind has prevailed: but when the air is so charged with this farina, let but an easterly wind blow for twenty-four hours, and all the wheat crops under its influence are destroyed. Nothing can save them! The stalks and leaves become first of an orange colour, from the light colour of the farina which adheres to them; but this changes to deep brown. All that part of the stalk that is exposed seems as if it had been pricked with needles and had exuded blood from every puncture, and the grain in the ear withers in proportion to the number of fungi that intercept and feed upon its sap; but the parts of the stalk that are covered by the leaves remain entirely uninjured, and when the leaves are drawn off from them, they form a beautiful contrast to the others, which have been exposed to the depredations of these parasitic plants.

"It is worthy of remark that hardly anything suffered from the attacks of these fungi but the wheat. The Alsí, upon which it always first made its appearance, suffered something, certainly, but not much, though the stems and leaves were covered with them. The gram (*Cicer arietinum*) suffered still less; indeed, the grain in this plant often remained uninjured, while the stems and leaves were covered with the fungi, in the midst of fields of wheat that were entirely destroyed by ravages of the same kind. None of the other pulses were injured, though situated in the same manner in the midst of the fields of wheat that were destroyed. I have seen rich fields of uninterrupted wheat cultivation for twenty miles by ten, in the valley of the Narbadda, so entirely destroyed by this disease, that the people would not go to the trouble of gathering one field in four.

"The great festival of the Holi, the saturnalia of India, terminates on the last day of Phagoon, or 16th of March. On that day the Holi is burned; and on that day the ravages of the monster (for monster they will have it to be) are supposed to cease. Any field that has remained untouched up to that time is considered to be quite secure from the moment the Holi has been committed to the flames. What gave rise to the notion I have never been able to discover; but such is the general belief. I suppose the silicious epidermis must then have become too hard, and the póres in the stem too much closed up to admit of the further depredation of the fungi."—Rambles and Recollections, Vol. I., pp. 250-262. See also Spry's Modern India, Vol. II., p. 282.

Girwínámah, گروي نامه गिरवीनामा

A deed of mortgage.

Goál, گوال गोआल

Unclaimed land.—Dehli.—See Gyal.

Gurhaur, گرهور गुरहौर

Stacks of cowdung.—Eastern Oudh.

Gurab, گرب गुरब

Deep weeding, in which the ground is broken and pulverized. It is the opposite of Niráí, which applies only to superficial weeding. The word is derived from a rustic word, Gurabná, to dig—a common verb, but not in Shakespear's Dictionary, in which we rarely have occasion to notice any omission.

It is also the name given to the process of ploughing through a field of Bájrá or Jawári when the plant is about a foot high. The operation requires some nicety to prevent the young plants sustaining injury. Gurab, as applied to this process, is in general use, especially in the Upper Doáb and Rohilkhand; but Bidáhná and Chhantá dená are more common in Dehli and the Central Doáb, and Dadahrná in the Lower Doáb.

Guṛarí, گڑری गुडरी

See Júra.

Gophaná, گوپهنا गोफना

A sling used by persons stationed on a Dámcha, *q.v.*

From गौ a cow, and फना or फन्दा a sling, as it is used to keep the cattle from eating the crops.—B.

Gorá, گورا गोरा

Applied to men, it means fair-complexioned; but when applied to horned cattle, it signifies red.

Goṛait, گوڑیت गोडैत

A village watchman; an intelligencer. The meaning is correctly given under Gúṛáit and Goráyát in the Printed Glossary.

Goṛhá, گوڑھا गोढ़ा

The homestead ; fields near the village.—See Goeṇd.

Gorú, گورو गोरू

A cow ; cattle in general.

Gorasí, گورسي गोरसी

A milk-pail. From, *goras*, cow-juice, *i.e.* milk.—See Jhákarí.

Got, گوت गोत

In common parlance Got has the same meaning as the more classical Gotra of the Glossary. Properly, those only are Gots (v. Colebrooke, Trans. R.A.S. Vol. I. p. 237), which bear the name of some Rishi progenitor, as Sándilya, Bharadwáj, Bashisht (Vasishtha), Kasyapa ; but it has become the custom to call all sub-divisions of tribes Gots, and, according to the Ṇirnaya Sindhu, there are no less than ten thousand. The early genealogies of the Rajputs frequently exhibit them as abandoning their martial habits, and establishing religious sects, or Gotras. Thus, Reh was the fourth son of Purúravas of the Lunar Race, "from him in the fifteenth generation was Hárita, who with his eight brothers took to the office of religion, and established the Kausika Gotra, a tribe of Brahmans."—See Colebrooke's Miscellaneous Essays, Vol. I. p. 115 ; Journ. R.A.S. Vol. III. pp. 354, 356 ; Sansk. Dic. p. 298 ; and Vishnu Purana, p. 405.

Gothán, گوتهان गोथान

Place of assembling the cattle of a village. From the Sansk. गोस्थानं.—Saugor.

Gauchaná, گوچنا गौचना

Gauchaná, or Gochaní, is a field of wheat and Chaná (gram) sown together. The practice of sowing culmiferous and leguminous plants together has been much ridiculed, and has been brought forward as a proof of the ignorance of Indian agriculturists. Mill emphatically declares it (Hist. of India, Vol. II. p. 26) to be "the most irrational practice that ever found existence in the agriculture of any nation." But, notwithstanding this denunciation, which is too much in accordance with the usual spirit of his comments on everything Indian, the real fact is that the practice is highly advantageous to the land, as well as to the crop. Dew readily forms on the leaves of the Chaná, or gram, which would not form on the wheat; and in seasons of drought the practice is very often the means of preserving both crops. It may be carried, perhaps, to too great an excess in Madras, but the same charge cannot be made against the agriculturists of these provinces. As for its being irrational, it is a practice encouraged by the first agriculturists of Europe. Nothing is more common than to sow clover with barley, flax, oats, and Lent-corn; and with the same object which has established Gauchaná in native agriculture as a highly rational and beneficial system (Von Thaër, "Principes Raisonnés d'Agric. Vol. IV. § 1304).—See Gojáí.

Gauhání, گوهاني गौहानी

Lands situated close round a village; the village itself; fields on which cattle graze. Gauhání is also a general term for the entire lands of a village.—E.

This word is probably substituted for **गांवहनी** *gáṅwhani,* which is rather difficult to pronounce, and is derived from the Sanskrit **ग्रामिनी** (sc. **भूमि**), of or belonging to a village.—B.

Godhaṛ, گوڈهڑ गोढड

Is the name given to the weeds and grasses which are collected from a ploughed field by the Dhínkhar.—Dehli.

It is known to the eastward by the name of Khedhí کهيڈهي, Guṛhal گڈهل, Akan آکن, and Ghúr گهور.

Goḍarí, گوڈري गोडरी

See Júra.

Goín, گوين गोईं

A pair of plough oxen; sometimes called Dogáwa. Gorá is more used in Dehli.

Goenḍ, گوينڈ गोएंड़

Goenḍ, or Gwenḍá, signifies a suburb; vicinage; fields near a village; homestead.

Goháí, گوهاي गोहाई

The treading out grain by bullocks. From Gahna, *q.v.*—Rohilkhand. More correctly spelt *gaháí.*

Gohárí, گوهاري गोहारी

Rich, highly-cultivated land; derived, perhaps, from its capacity of growing Gohuṅ, the provincial pronunciation of गेंहूं *geṅhun,* wheat.—Saugor.

Gojá, گوجا गोजा

In Behar an ox-goad; also a bamboo staff—B.

Gojhá گوجها गोझा

A species of thorny grass which springs up during the rains. It is used medicinally, and Chamars eat it as potherb.

Gojará, گوجره गोजरा

Barley and Chaná sown together. It is known also by the name of Bejhará and Jauchaní.—See Gojaí and Gauchaní.

Gojaí, گوجئي गोजई

Wheat and barley sown together in the same field. Adhgawán, Gojí, and Gojarí are used in the same sense. This mixed crop is scarcely known in Saugor, Dehli, Lower Doáb, and Benares, but it is very common in the Upper and Central Doáb, Rohilkhand, Gorakhpúr, and Bánda.

Gokhrú, گوکھرو गोखरू

The name of a herb which springs up on Bhúr land; called also Hathíchinghar, Kanthphil, and Bhankarí. It produces a small fruit, covered with several prickles. In famine, the poorer classes of Hariáná feed on the pounded seed of this plant. It somewhat resembles Chaná, or the chick pea, and is known by botanists under the name of *Tribulus lanuginosus* (Roxb.). There is a large kind called the Gokhrú dakhiní, of which the fruit is of a triangular shape, and has prickles at the angles; hence the name is given to the iron crowsfeet thrown on the ground to check an advance of cavalry.

Gol, گول गोल

A party from another village sojourning with their cattle for pasture.—Dehli.

Gond, گوند गोंद

The name of a rush which grows in marshy ground, and is much used in making mats and baskets.

Goṅrá, گونڑا गोंरा

This is the name given in the Central and Lower Doáb to the reservoir from which water is raised by the Leharí, or Berí, to the reservoir above it, which is called Parchha, Odh, and Ulaha.

Sometimes Goṅrá is applied only to the straw or reeds which are placed to protect the side of the upper reservoir.—See Doarí, Docha, and Ríkh.

Gudṛí, گدڑي गुदड़ी

A daily market.

Gúl, گول गूल

A channel cut to convey water to a field.

A road; a path.—Saugor.

An unripe bunch of Indian corn; when ripe it is called Kukrí.—Dehli.

Gulál, گلال गुलाल

A farinaceous powder which Hindús throw on each other's clothes during the Holi. It is generally the meal of barley, rice, or Singhara, dyed with Bakkam wood.

Gulkhár, گلخار गुलखार

See Bhatkataiya.

Gulphunaná, گل پھنا गुलफुनना

The name of a herb which grows in fields sown with Kharíf grains. It somewhat resembles the Gúma.

Gulú, گلو गुलू

The pod of the Mahwá tree (*Bassia latifolia*). It yields a very useful oil, and is sometimes eaten by the poorer classes; but it contains no intoxicating qualities, like the blossom of that valuable tree, from which a spirit is produced by distillation, which is much used in Benares and Bahár in spite of its sickly smell. The word appears to be a corruption of Gilaunda, which is said in Shakespear's Dictionary to be "the blossom after it has fallen off;" but this application of the word is not known in these Provinces. The blossom is called Mahwa, like the tree, and the pod only is called Gilaunda, or Gulenda.

Gúlar, گولر गूलर

Cotton pods which have not yet burst.—Rohilkhand.—See Dhúndá and Ghegara.

Gúma, گومہ गूमा

A medicinal herb which grows on high ground during the rains, and in fields grown with Kharíf crops (*Pharnaceum mollugo*). It produces several small flowers, the beauty of which is much admired by natives.

फल पर फूल फूल पर पाती
तिस पर जुगनू सब रंग राती

"On fruit flower, on flower leaf,
On that a firefly all coloured red,"

Is a distich applied by some poet to the regular order in which the flowers of the Gúmá alternate with the leaves, as well as to the appearance of the flowers which are said to resemble fire flies.

There are two species of Gúmá, one grows to the height of about two feet, the other seldom exceeds a foot.

Gúnṭh, گونٹھ गूंठ

Land assigned rent-free for religious purposes; the endowment of a temple.—Kamaon and Gaṛhwál. This word is sometimes, but incorrectly, pronounced Ghúnt.

Guṛ, گڑ गुड़

Molasses. The gipsy name for sugar is Gúrlo and Gadlo (Trans. R.A.S., Vol. II., p. 553). This is no doubt derived from our Gur.

Guráo, گراو गुराव

A stook, or collection of sheaves.—Rohilkhand. A similar

word, but with the addition of a penultimate nasal *n*, is used in the Lower Doáb and Benares, to signify a heap of mixed chaff and corn.—See Ganteh.

Gurbháí, گربهائي गुरभाई

Fellow disciple. From गुरु Guru, a spiritual teacher, and भाई brother. The priests and teachers of the Sikh religion generally take the title Bháí.—B.

Gurdá, گردا गुर्दा

See Kolhú.

Gaṛhí, گڑهي गढ़ी

A village fortification of mud, flanked with towers. Under the former government there was scarcely a village without its Gaṛhí. Under our strong administration it is scarcely known except by name.

Gaṛhaí, گڑهئي गढ़ई

A small pond.

Garrí, گري गर्री

A hay-stack; a rick; a stack of thatching grass; more correctly, Kharhí.

A small mound raised between heaps of corn and bhúsa on the threshing floor.—Lower Doáb.

A large stack of wheat or barley, containing two or more senká, which generally comprises several thraves of corn, the produce of one field.—Dehli and Upper Doáb.

A large stack of Kharíf produce.—Rohilkhand.

Kundṛá کنڈڑا is in general use elsewhere in the same sense, and also within the limits in which Garrí obtains, but in the latter case is always larger than a Garrí.—See Chhaur, Dabiya, Garáhí, Jhúha, Pahí, and Sántrí.

Gashtí, گشتي गश्ती

Presents to a revenue officer on his tour. From the Persian گشت gasht, rounds.

Gaṭhí, گٹهي गठी

See Gachí.

Gaṭhaund, گٹهوند गठौन्द

A deposit, or trust bound up in a bag (gaṭhrí).

Gaṭhrí, گٹهري गठरी

Literally, a bag; and hence applied to money brought in payment of revenue in a bag.—Benares.

Gaṭhwánsí, گٹهوانسي गठवांसी

The twentieth part of a Gatha.

Gaṭhiyá, گٹهيا गठिया

A pannier; a sack; a bundle.

Gayárí, گياري गयारी

See above under Gyal.

Gairá, گيرا गैरा

A sheaf of corn.

Hálí, هالي हाली

A man employed for the duties of ploughing—from هل a plough. In the Glossary, Halís are said to be agrestic slaves; it would have been more proper to say, labourers.—See Harwaha.

Hápar, هاپر हापर

A nursery for sugar-cane.

Hár lená, هاڑ لینا हाड लेना

To examine the correctness of a pair of scales.—Dehli and Doáb. Tár lena is used in Rohilkhand. Sádh lena to the Eastward.

Háta, حاطه हाता

Premises; an enclosure; a compound in Anglo-Indian language. It is a corruption of the Arabic Ihata.

Háthíchak, هاتهي چک हाथीचक

Is the name of a grass which grows about a foot high, and is given as fodder to cattle. It is also, by an easy conversion, the name given by gardeners to the prickly, and to the Jerusalem (*girasole*) artichoke.

Híṭhá, هیٹها हीठा

A person appointed to take care of the standing crops.—See Ahíta.

Hengá, هینگا हेंगा

A harrow. This word, as well as Sohága, Mai, Mainra, and Siráwan, is in general use; but the implement is known locally by various other names, as Patoí, Pahtan, Patela, Patrí, and Dandela. The part to which the ropes, or thongs, are attached is called Marwah. The cylindrical harrow, or roller, is called Rarí in Rohílkhand; Bilna and Belan in the Lower Doáb and Benares; and Gherí, Girarí, and Kolhú in Dehli and the Upper Doáb. The harrow made of two parallel timbers joined together, is called Mainra Sohága in Dehli and the Doáb, and Sohal in Rohilkhand. Gáhan is the name of a forked harrow.—See Gáhan.

Hirankhurí, هرن کهري हिरनखुरी

The name of a creeping herb which grows in the rainy season.

Its leaves resemble an antelope's hoof, and hence it derives its name—Hiran, an antelope, and Khurí, a cloven hoof.

Hulhul, هلهل हुलहुल

Hurhura, هرهره हुरहुरा

A small herb which springs up in the rainy season, and is used as a culinary vegetable, The commonest kind has a white flower, and produces a long pod, like that of the Múng, and is used as a medicine in fevers (*Gyandropsis pentaphylla*, formerly *Cleome pentaphylla*, or *viscosa*). There are said to be four kinds —white, red, purple and yellow. The three latter are much sought after by alchymists.

Hunḍh, هنڈه हुंढ

See Jíta.

Haulí, هولي हौली

A liquor shop. The word is common, except in Saugor and Dehli.

Hadbast, حدبست हदबस्त

This word also signifies the demarcation of boundaries, preparatory to survey.

Hakárná, هکارنا हकारना

To drive oxen. A corruption of Hánkna, to drive.

Hal, هل हल

Har, هر हर

A plough,—if an instrument may be dignified by that name which has neither coulter to cut the soil nor mould-board* to

* But when anything like a mould-board is required, the people have sufficient ingenuity to frame one. The only occasion which calls for such an expedient is when

turn it over. Nevertheless, simple as the Hal is, and wretched in construction, it is admirably adapted to our light Indian soil, and does its duty well under the able agriculturists of our provinces. Of the operations of this simple plough, Dr. Tennant, who has led the van in the abuse of everything Indian, observes ("Indian Recreations," Vol. II. p. 78), "Only a few scratches are perceptible here and there, more resembling the digging of a mole than the work of a plough;" yet this prejudiced and superficial observer remarks in another place that the average produce of the Province of Allahabad is fifty-six bushels* of wheat to the English acre: as if these "scratches and diggings of a mole" could by any possibility produce *double the average* of the scientific cultivators of England. He had forgotten also to remark that the drill, which has only within the last century been introduced into English field husbandry, and has even yet

sugar-cane is sown. Large and deep furrows are then required, and various means are resorted to, to make the plough accomplish the purpose. In Dehli and the Upper Doáb it is usual to bind canes on the part into which the sole is fixed. Generally not more than two ploughs are used when planting sugar, but in the Doáb as many as four sometimes follow one another, on two of which are fixed mould-boards of the name of Roh and Pákhí, the former being stronger and smaller than the latter. The Roh is made of one piece of wood, the Pákhí of two.

* The yield of wheat would certainly not be so great now, whatever it might have been in the Doctor's days. It may be as well to make this reservation, with reference to the very common remark, that land in Upper India does not yield now so much as it did in former days. Where this is really the result of observation, the causes are obvious—the greater infrequency of fallows—the little manure that is given being diffused over more fields than formerly—the decrease in the fall of the periodical rains, owing to the immense mass of forest and jungle which has been cleared away—and the fields being less cultivated than formerly, when ploughs and hands could only be employed upon a limited number of fields. These are all to be traced to the operation of a more remote cause—the entire security afforded by the British Government. The number of hands, ploughs, and bullocks has not increased in proportion to the increase of cultivation.

It should never be forgotten that the decrease in the fertility of the soil is an old and popular complaint, and arises chiefly from the universal tendency to depreciate the present and exalt the past.

in the northern counties to combat many native prejudices, has been in use in India from time immemorial. If he had only reflected on this single fact (leaving out of consideration the universal practice of rotation and complete expulsion of corn-weeds), he would have saved the poor Hindus from much of the reproach which has been so lavishly heaped upon them by Mill and his other blind followers.

The principal parts of an Indian plough are—हरस Haras, the beam; हथीली Hathílí, हथा Hathá, चिरिया Chiriyá, or मुथिया Muthiyá, the handle or stilt; पन्हारी Panhárí or परौथा Parauthá, the sole, which is generally at the end shod with an iron share, called फाला Phálá, चौ Chau, or कूसा Kúsá. The Hal, or नांगल Nángal, is the body of the plough, the main piece into which the Panhárí and Haras are joined; but these terms, besides being exclusively applied to a particular part of the plough, are used to signify the entire plough. The ओग Og is a peg, or wedge, which fixes the Haras firmly into the Hal; a second is sometimes added which is called गंधेली Gandhelí; the पचेला Pachelá, पछीला Pachhílá, or फन्ना Phanná, is a wedge which fixes the Panhárí to the Hal. The खूरा Khúrá, बर्नेल Barnel, or नर्हेल Narhel, is an indented, or notched, part at the end of the beam, corresponding to the copse, or cathead, to which the yoke is attached by a leathern thong, called a नदह Nadah. In some parts the beam is not notched, but drilled with holes, into which pieces of wood are inserted. The yoke consists of the जूआ Júá, or upper piece, and the तर्माची Tarmáchí, or lower piece. The सैल Sail is the outer pin, and Gata the inner pin which join the Tarmáchí and the Júá, and which are on each side of the bullock's neck when it is yoked. These are the names usually applied to the parts of a plough in the Doáb and North-West; but in Benares and the Eastward the names are somewhat different. There, the चन्दौली Chandaulí answers to the Chiriyá, पाथ or पाठ Path to the Og, नरेली Narelí to the Pachelá. Har is the part on which the share is fixed. There

Vol. II. p. 342.

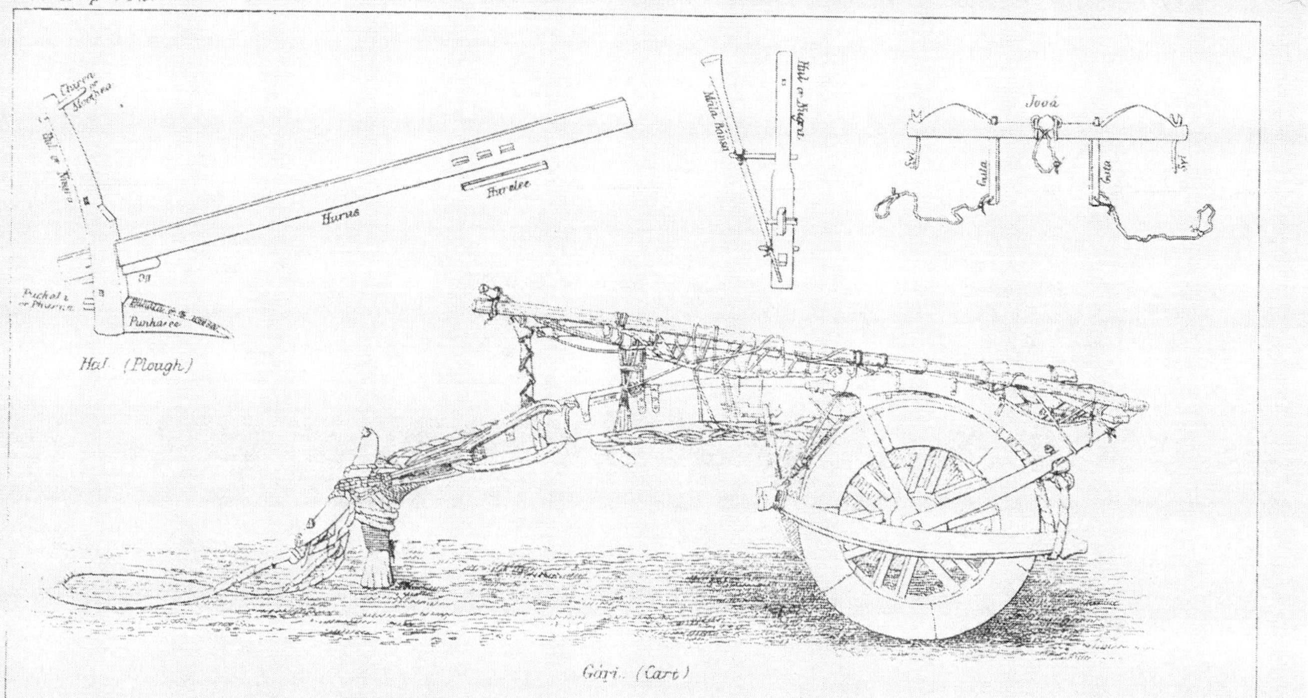

Vincent Brooks Day & Son Lith. London W.C.

THE INDIAN PLOUGH AND CART.

are knots also, called Mahádewa, on the yoke of the Benares plough; and some other differences not worth mentioning.

Besides the common Hal of the country, there are others used in some places which vary but little in their structure from it. There is, for instance, the Nagar plough, which is used in Bundelkhand for planting sugar-cane. It is very heavy, requires six, seven, or eight bullocks to draw it, and enters very deep into the ground. The cane is put into a hole of the wooden part of the plough, through which it is passed and deposited in the earth, to as great a depth as the share can attain. The American cotton planters were much pleased with this plough, and preferred this manner of sowing sugar-cane to any they could adopt with the American plough. There is also the बाखर Bákhar, used to take off the crust when the soil is hide-bound, and by skimming the surface clears the soil from grass, weeds, and stubble.—See Bákhar. There are also the Kudhiya, the Kadh, the Kathú, the Kusiyar, the Pachranga, etc., which need no particular description.—See the illustration.

Haldá, هلدا हलदा

Hardá, هردا हरदा

A disease of the Cerealia, in which the plant withers, and assumes a yellow tinge. The word is derived from Haldí, turmeric. This kind of mildew differs but little from the Girwí, *q.v.*, except in attacking the plants in an earlier stage of their growth.

Haliyák, هلياك हलियाक

Wages of ploughmen.—Dehli and Upper Doáb.

Haltaḍḍí, هلتڈي हलतड्डी

A drill plough.—See Bánsá.

Halas, هلس हलस

Hanas, هنس हनस

Haras, هرس हरस

The beam of a plough. Shakespear says wrongly Harís is the tail of a plough. Dr. Carey gives Is as the beam of the Dinagepúr plough.—Asiatic Researches, vol. x., p. 25.—E.

It is probably from हर and ईश ísh, 'lord or ruler,' as it is the principal part of the plough.—B.

Hanḍá, هنڈا हंडा

A grass which is found on the banks of tanks and marshes. It produces a little red flower, but is not applied to any useful purpose.

Hansráj, هنسراج हंसराज

Literally, "goose-king," *i.e.* Brahma to whom it is sacred. A herb which springs up on brick walls during the rains. It is used medicinally.—Rohilkhand. It is known by the name of Pareshawáshan in the Doáb. It is also the name of a kind of rice.—See Dhán.

Haráí, هرائي हराई

The portion of land in a field which is included within one circuit of a plough. To commence another circuit is styled Haráí phándná, "to knot the plough-circle."

Harghasíṭ, هرگهسيٹ हरघसीट

All the cultivated land of a village is so called. From har, a plough, and ghasíṭna, to draw.—Lower Doáb.

Harhá, هرها हरहा

Unbroken and vicious cattle; plough bullocks.—Dehli and

Doáb. Besides these local meanings, it is generally applied to stray oxen.

Harjins, هرجنس हरजिनस

Grain of sorts. From har, every, and jins, species.

Harkára, هركاره हरकारा

A messenger. From har, every, and kár, business. The usual occupation of an Harkára at present is by no means in accordance with the derivation.

M. Garcin de Tassy, in a note to p. 219 of his "Kámrúp," observes on this word—"À la lettre factoton. Ce nom désigne un des trente-sept domestiques! que les Indiens, et les Europeans, ont a leur service." *

Harkaṭ, هركٹ हरकट

Cutting rice while it is green and unripe.—Rohilkhand. From hara, green, and kaṭna, to cut.

Haraurí, هروري हरौरी

The occupation of ploughing, or place where ploughing is going on. Haraurí par jao signifies, "go and put your hand to the plough."

Also, an advance of about two rupees in money, and two maunds in corn, given to a ploughman when first engaged.—Benares.

Sondhár is the term applied in the North-West.

* In spite of the implied sneer in the text the learned French author is right both as to the literal meaning of the word, the original occupation of the officer, and the number of servants usually maintained by both Europeans and wealthy natives. In fact, to this day the indigo planters keep a servant called harkára whose business is precisely that of a factotum. He has to be constantly perambulating the land under indigo cultivation, and keep the ryots up to their work besides making himself useful in a vast variety of ways. The Hindu ryot of Behar and E. Oudh, however, corrupts the word into *halkára*, as though from *hal*, a plough, because one of the harkara's duties is to see that the lands are properly ploughed.—B.

Harsingár, هرسنگار हरसिंगार

The weeping Nyctanthes (*Nyctanthes arbor tristis*). It is a small forest tree growing to the height of about twelve feet. Harsingár yields a deliciously fragrant blossom, from which a yellow dye is prepared, which was borne on our tariff as an excisable article till the late revision of the Customs law. Harsingár is also much used in medicine by native practitioners, and is occasionally cultivated in gardens.

Harsot, هرسوت हरसोत

Harsot, or Harsotiya, signifies ploughing a furrow; the first ploughing of the season.—See Halaeta.

Affording assistance in ploughing.—See Angwara, Dangwara, and Jíta.

The term is also used to signify the bringing the plough home across the back of a bullock, or with the share inverted, after the conclusion of the day's work:

> Videre fessos *vomerem inversum* boves
> Collo trahentes languido.
>
> —*Hor. Epod. II.* 63.

These terms are used in Dehli; and, in the last meaning, in Brij also.

Harsajjá, هرسجا हरसज्जा

Literally, a sharer in a plough; reciprocal assistance afforded in ploughing fields.—Bundelkhand. From har, a plough, and sajja, partnership.—See Angwara, Dangwara, and Jíta.

Haraṭ, هرٹ हरट

A Persian wheel for drawing water from a well. The word is a corruption of Arhaṭ, *q.v.* Eight bullocks employed at a Haraṭ are capable of irrigating an acre of ground during the day.

Harwáhá, هرواها हरवाहा

A ploughman. The word is most commonly used in the East. Hálí is more usual in the West.

Hariyá, هريا हरिया

A ploughman; a worshipper; a devotee. The double meaning attached to this word is very elegantly conveyed in the following couplet.

हरिया हर से हेत कर ज्यों किसान की रीत
दाम घनेरा रिन घना तबहूं खेत से प्रीत

"Love Hara, o worshipper, after the fashion of the peasant,
The rent is heavy, his debts are many, still he loves his field."

The two first words signify "Ploughman and Plough," as well as "Worshipper and Hara (Siva);" which gives the poet the opportunity of conveying the moral, that no vicissitudes of fortune should affect a man's love for labor and devotion.

Hasiyá, هسيا हसिया

A reaping hook. Hansiya is also correct.

Hattá, هتا हत्ता

A large wooden shovel or spoon, about five feet long, used for throwing water into fields from aqueducts.—E. Oudh.

Íkh, ايکهه ईख

Sugar-cane; a field of sugar-cane.—Ganná.

Íkh is used in Western Hindustan, úkh in Eastern. In the Panjab the name is कुमाध kumádh.—B.

Ekfardí, يکفردي एकफर्दी

Land producing only one crop annually; opposed to Jútiyári and Dofarda. It is also known by the name of Ekfaslí, Fard, and Fardháí.

Ekfaslí, يكفصلي एकफसली

Land yielding but one crop annually.

Íṇḍhuá, ايڈّهوا ईंढुआ

A pad placed on the top of the head to support a water-jar.—See Júra.

Induri, انڈّري इंडुरी

A pad for supporting a round-bottomed jar.—See Júra.

Iráda, اراده इरादा

A term in arithmetic.—See under Bariz.

Isband, اسبند इसबन्द

The name of a herb which springs up on the banks of tanks during the rainy season. It produces a round thorny fruit, of which the seed is much used in exorcism and other superstitious practices.

Ismwár, اسموار इसमवार

Literally, nominal. From ism, a name; entry in statements according to the order of individuals' names.

Istiklál, استقلال इस्तिकलाल

Confirmation; perpetuity; fixedness.

Istikrár, استقرار इस्तिकरार

Confirmation. These three last words are tenth infinitives of Arabic roots.

Itsiṭ, ائسٹ इटसिट

A root like osier-twigs, or like Chiretá, used in the Chaj Doáb, in the Panjab, together with other drugs, to procure abortion.—B.

Izáfa, اضافه इज़ाफा

Increase. These three words are also derived from the Arabic.

Jáb, جاب जाब

Jábí, جابي जाबी

An ox-muzzle. Jálí, Múnhchhínka, and Múncha are also used, as well as the words mentioned under Chhínka.

Jáíl, جايل जाईल

A term used in the Western parts of Rohilkhand to signify twice-ploughed land. When ploughed three times, it is called Tase; when four times, Chaus; when five times, Pachbásí; and so on. In the Northern Parganahs of Bareilly, the corresponding terms are Dobar, Tábar, Chonwar, Pacháwar; and the first ploughing is called Eksirí.—See Dor and Dosárí.

Jákhan, جاکهن जाखन

The wooden foundation of the brick-work of a well. It is generally made of the green wood of the Gullaṛ tree (*Ficus glomerata*), because it is said to be less liable to rot than any other kind. The wood of the Pípal (*Ficus religiosa*) is also in request on the same account, but it is considered inferior to Gullaṛ. This foundation is also known by the name of Newar and Nímchak. Sweetmeats are generally distributed, and sometimes a drum is beaten, on the occasion of its being adjusted and fixed. The word is perhaps derived from Jakarna, to tighten, to pinion; as great care and time are necessarily taken in binding the separate parts (gandwála) together, so that they may form a compact cylinder for the support of a heavy superstructure of masonry.—See Jamuwat.

Jálí, جالي जाली

An ox-muzzle; a net bag for weighing Bhus (chaff).—See Chhínka and Jab.

Jánt, جانت जांत

A wooden trough for raising water.

Jántá, جانتا जांता

A species of hand mill-stone; a stone mill for grinding.

Jáṭh, جاٹھ जाठ

The name of the post fixed in a tank to denote that its water has been dedicated to the deity, or has been married to a grove. Also the revolving beam or axis of a sugar-mill.—See Kolhú.

Játrá, جاترا जात्रा

A religious festival or fair.

Jíra, جيرا जीरा

Cumin seed.

Jítápatr, جيتاپتر जीतापत्र

A favorable decision.—Benares.

Jihát, جهات जिहात

Plural of Arabic جهت jihat, a cause, an object. Duties on manufactures. They were reduced by Akbar from 10 to 5 per cent., but were imposed during the decline of the monarchy at a much heavier rate by every petty ruler in his own principality.

Jel, جيل जेल

The chain of buckets on a Persian wheel.—See Arhaṭ.

Jelí, جيلي जेली

Jelí is a kind of pitchfork, or rake, for collecting and adjusting the ears of corn on the threshing-ground. It is also known to the Eastward by the names of Pancha and Panchángurá, from its having five (panch) prongs. Dhinka, or Dhínka, is a smaller kind of Jelí, which is used by a man in a sitting posture, and differs from a Jelí in having curved prongs.

جيلي در رساله چوبي دوشاخه كه خوشه‌هاي كوفته كه در خرمن باشد بدان برداشته برهوا اندازند تا غله از كاه جدا شود سكو بسين مهمله مكسور و كاف مفتوح ليكن در جهانگيري سكو چوبي كه آنرا سه شاخه و چهار شاخه سازند سه شاخه را سكو و چهار شاخه را چهار شاخه خوانند و آنرا اشنه و نواشه و چكك نيز كويند و بتازي مدري و بهندي دنبالي گويند و صاحب جهانگيري سكو بفتح اول گفته اما اول اقوي و هندي متعارف گواليار كه افصح السنه هنديست پنچانگرا ببا و جيم هردو فارسي و نون غنه بعد الف و كاف فارسي و راي مهمله بالف كشيده

(Gharáíbu'l Lughát.)

I translate only so much of the above as refers to the matter in hand: "Jelị is a piece of wood with two prongs, with which they toss into the air the ears of corn on the threshing floor after threshing them, to separate the chaff from the grain. Also called Sikau, but in the Jahangírí Sikau is restricted to a three-pronged fork; one with four prongs is called a 'Chahár-shákhah.' It is also called in Hindí dambálí, and at Gwalior Panchángurá."—B.

Jeonár, جيونار जेवनार

Is sometimes used in the sense of Jaunal, *q.v.*

Jenṭá, جينٹا जेंटा

A thick rope used for tying mould round the roots of trees when transplanting them.—E. *add.*

Jeoṛí, جيوڑي जेवड़ी

Bears the same meaning as Jaríb, *q.v.* A cord, a rope.

Jhábar, جهابر झाबर

Low land on which water lies, and which produces rice, or a grass called Tín. Sometimes, when the water dries up quickly, Rabbí crops are also sown in it.—See Jhab Bhomí in the Printed Glossary.

Jhad, جهاد झाद

Land on which Dhák, Híns, and other jungly bushes grow.—Upper Doáb.

Jháḍá, جهاڈا झाडा

Lands which remain under water during the rains. A swamp.—See Jhábar.

Jhákaṛí, جهاکڑي झाकड़ी

A milk-pail. From the Jhákarí, or Dohní, the milk is transferred into other vessels—the Kadhauní, the Jamauní, the Biloní, according to the particular process it has to undergo, till it reaches the ultimate stage of Ghí.

Jhám, جهام झाम

A large instrument in the shape of a hoe, or Phaurá, used for excavating earth in well-sinking. The use of it is peculiar to this country, and it is very ingeniously applied. The mode of its application has been fully detailed in the Asiatic Society's Journal.

Jhángí, جهانگي झांगी

Bramble and brushwood.—Eastern Oudh.

Jháú, جهاؤ झाऊ

(*Tamarix dioica*). A common shrub in the Upper Provinces, growing in marshy or inundated ground. It is much used for thatching, hedging, and burning. Galls are produced on it, called Ṣamratu't turfa, or Baṛí-máí.—See Faras.

Jhárí, جهاري झारी

A pitcher with a long neck.—See Ghara.

Jháṛí, جهاڑي झाडी

Jungle; small bushes.

Jháwar, جهاور झावर

Flat or low land flooded by the rains.—See Jhábar.

Jhíl, جهيل झील

A shallow lake or morass, called in Bengal बील bíl.

Jhirí, جهري झिरी

Withered wheat; blight. The word is perhaps derived from Jhurna, to fade.

Jhojhurú, جهوجهرو झोझुरू

A grass to which camels are very partial, and which is occasionally given as fodder to horned cattle. It grows to the height of about two feet, and is known also by the name jangalí níl, or wild indigo.

Jhokand, جهوكند झोकन्द

Is the place at which the Jhonkayá stands.—See Kolhú and Jhonkayá.

Jhola, جهوله झोला

A cold wind which affects wheat by drying up the ears.—Upper Doáb and Dehli.

Jhonkayá, جهونكيا झोंकिया

The man who keeps up the fire when sugar is boiling. The word is sometimes pronounced Jhúkwa and Jhokya,—but incorrectly, for it is derived from Jhonkna, to supply fuel to an oven.

Jhúhá, جهوها झूहा

Jhúha is in Rohilkhand what Chaur is in Dehli. A large stack of Jawar or Bajra. A Jhúhá generally contains from ten to twenty Bojh, or loads.

Jhúlí, جهولي झूली

A cloth, or sheet, made into a fan for winnowing grain, when there is no wind.—Dehli. The word is derived from Jhúlna, to swing, or perhaps from Jhalna, to fan. The corresponding term in Bundelkhand is Sarwa. In Rohilkhand and Upper Doáb, Partwaí. In Benares, Páthí and Parauta; and in the Lower and Central Doáb, Parauta, Partowa, and Partí.

Jhúngá, جهونگا झूंगा

Bramble; brushwood. The word is sometimes pronounced Jhángí.

Jhúngá signifies also a bullock whose horns project forward. There are many similar words significant of peculiarities in the shape of horns.—मैना mainá is a bullock the tips of whose horns join in the centre. A superstition prevails against their use in draft or agriculture, and they are consequently always bestowed upon Brahmans.—Morá is a bullock whose horns grow backwards.—Múndrá, one whose horns are stunted and ill-developed.—Mundá, one whose horns are broken.—Phulsapel (literally one who shoves against a doorway), one whose horns project to the right and left.—Kainchá, one whose horns are one up and the other down. In some places, this is called Sarg-pátálí, *i.e.* heaven-and-hellwards.—See Dúnda.

Jhúnṭhar, جهونٹهر झूंठर

Fields yielding double crops. It is sometimes pronounced jhúṭhan and juṭhiyáil. Júṭhiyan and júṭhelí are also used in a similar sense.—See Júṭiyan.

Jhúpá, جهوپا झूपा

A pile of mangoes or other fruit.—Lower Doáb.

Jhúṛná, جهوڑنا झूडना

To shake fruit from the tree. Jhuṛna, with a short vowel, is to fall as fruit from a tree.

Jhorá, جهورا झोरा

The haulm or stalks of leguminous plants, such as Múng and Moth, used as fodder.

Jhauwá, جهوا झौवा

A large open basket; so called because it is made from the twigs of the Jhaú, *q.v.*

Jhabrá, جهبرا झबरा

Jhabrá, or Jhabbúa, is an epithet applied to the ears of animals when they are covered with long hair. From jhabba, a tassel. One of the bucolic maxims respecting the choice of horned cattle says in approval of this point,

कार कक्षौटा झबरे कान
इन्हें छांडि न लीजिये आन

"Hairy ears
Buy these, do not let them go."

Jhajharká, جهجهرکا झझर्का

Early dawn before it is easy to distinguish objects.—Gharáibu'l

Lughát. The word is spelt jhajhalka in the Tuhfatu'l Lughát-i Hindí. Neither word is in Shakespear's Dictionary.

Jhakorá, جهكورا झकोरा

A shower.

Jhalár, جهلار झलार

A thicket; brushwood.

Jhamáka, جهماكه झमाका

A heavy shower.

Jhamjham, جهم جهم झमझम

Heavy continued rain. The term Jhamájham is similarly used.

Jhamarjhamar, جهمرجهمر झमरझमर

A light rain; raining drop by drop.

Jhanḍá, جهنڈا झंडा

Jhanḍí, جهنڈي झंडी

A flag staff; a flag used by surveyors as a mark by which to direct their observations.

Jhanjiá, جهنجيا . झंजिया

A subdivision of the Mar soil.—Lower Doáb.

Jhankhaṛá, جهنكهڑا झंखडा

Jhankhaṛá, sometimes pronounced Jhankara, signifies a leafless tree,—the contrary of Jhanḍúlá جهنڈولا which is applied to a tree with thick foliage.

Jhaṛ, جهاڑ झड

Heavy rain; hence jhará-jhar, heavily, rapidly; and jharí, continued rain, wet weather.

Jhaṛberí, جهڑبیری झड़बेरी

From jhar, or jhár, a bramble, and ber the name of a tree, which appears to be the same as the sidar of Africa and Arabia, the *Zizyphus napeca* of modern botanists, and the *Rhamnus spina christi* of Linnæus, and probably identical with the tree which yielded the famous fruit of the Lotophagi (Herod. IV. p. 177).

The Jhaṛberí seldom exceeds two feet in height, but the Ber is a large tree which sometimes grows to the height of between twenty and thirty feet. The Jhaṛberí is often called the Pála shrub, and is used for many useful purposes. In appearance it is no better than a prickly bush, the fruit, however, which resembles a small plum, affords food to the destitute in famine, and is collected for that purpose by the women and children. It is either mixed with milk and water, or eaten in its natural state with bread, if procurable, and if not, by itself. The leaves are threshed and collected for fodder for the cattle; the briars and thorns form barriers for the fields, and cattle sheds, and, when no longer required, are used as fuel. During the year of famine (for it seems to grow equally luxuriant in a drought) the people to the West of the Jumna fed their cattle, and paid a large proportion of their revenue, from its sale. Indeed, in villages where the crop entirely failed, the only collections were from this source. In such cases the people retained one-half for consumption, and disposed of the remainder. Pála leaves, in an average year, sell from six to twelve maunds the rupee. The Jharberí produces also very good gallnuts.

Jharuá, جهروا झरवा

The name of a nutritious grass of which the grain is something like that of Shámákh (*Panicum frumentaceum*), of which it is reckoned to be a wild species. It springs up during the rains. The grain is eaten by Hindús on fast days, and Chamárs commonly make it into bread. The stalks are cut up and given to cattle, or applied to the purpose of improving the quality and quantity of milk. It is known also by the name of Sáwan and Sawaín, because it ripens in the month Sáwan.

Jhaṛotá, جهڑوتا झडोता

The close of a season.—See Jhúrna.

Jins, جنس जिन्स

Grain; commodities; products.

Jinwár, جنوار जिनवार

See Janwar, which is the most usual pronunciation.

Jiriá, جريا जिरिया

The name of a rice cultivated in Benares.—See Dhan.

Jog, جوگ जोग

The name of the person upon whom a draft or bill of exchange is drawn.

Johaṛ, جوهڑ जोहड

The name given to a large pond or lake.—Dehli.—See Ahar.

It is also applied in the Central Doáb to any inundated land, and is there pronounced Jhor.

In Shakespear's Dictionary, Júhar is said to signify "Pits filled with water at the bottom of mountains."

Jokhái, جوکهائي जोखाई

Weighment; the weighman's perquisite. From jokhná, to weigh.

Júá, جوا जूवा

The yoke of a cart or plough.

The word is preserved in many of the Indo-European languages.—See Garí, Hal, and Halas.

Júí, جوئي जूई

An insect destructive to certain crops.—See Gindar.

Jugálná, جگالنا जुगालना

To chew the cud.

Júná, جونا जूना

Júṛá, جوڑا जूडा

A rope of twisted grass, or twine, made to support a round-bottomed jar. It is called also Indurí, Endhua, Chakwa, Gurarí, Ginduri and Godarí. The original meaning of Jura is the knot into which Hindús tie their hair at the back of the head.

Júṛemárí, جوڑيماري जूडेमारी

Literally, brought under the yoke. The term is generally used to signify land actually in possession, in distinction to that which a man is entitled to by virtue of descent from a common ancestor.

Jutá, جتا जुता

Is the name given to the rope connecting the leherí, or irrigating basket, with the killí, or handle. From jotna, to yoke.

Jútiyán, جوتيان जूतियां

Land which bears two harvests during the year,—opposed to

ekfarda, which bears only one.—Benares. The word is derived from jotna, to cultivate.

Júthálí, جوتهالي जूथाली

Júthálí bears the same meaning as Jútiyán above.

Jorí, جوڑي जोडी

A pond smaller than a Pokhur.—Dehli.—See Ahar.

Jot, جوت जोत

Cultivation; tillage; tenure of a cultivator. It is also sometimes used to signify the rent paid by a cultivator.

Jotá, جوتا जोता

Jotár, جوتار जोतार

Jotiyá, جوتيا जोतिया

Jotan, جوتن जोतन

A cultivator of land.—See above under Jot.

Jau, جو जौ

Barley,—but not exclusively such as is raised by artificial irrigation, as stated in the Printed Glossary.

The Jau, or barley-corn, is in India, as in many other countries, the primary unit of measures of length. The Asiatics, however, in that fondness for minute quantities which prevails with them, assume a certain number (6 or 8) of hairs of a horse's tail or mane, as equivalent to a Jau. Between Europe and Asia, there is also this difference in the use of the Jau as the basis of measures of length, that in the former it is more usual, though not universal, to take the length of the grain; in the latter, the breadth:—thus, in England, three barley-corns placed end to end make an inch, and in India, eight barley-corns' breadths make a finger. The former is more likely to be correct as an invariable standard than the latter.

The following table shews the quantity of barley in cultivation in the Upper Provinces during the year of survey.

Dehli Division	90,053	Acres.
Rohilkhand Division	182,476	,,
Mírat Division	153,050	,,
Agra Division	359,811	,,
Allahabad Division	430,633	,,
Benares Division	1,301,887	,,
Saugor Division	854	,,
Total Acres.........	2,518,754	

Jauchaní, جوچني जौचनी

A mixed crop of barley and chaná.—See Gojara.

Jaunál, جونال जौनाल

Land cultivated alternately by Rabí and Kharíf sowings. Land in continual cultivation.—Rohilkhand and Doab.

In Dehli and Oudh it is applied generally to land which has been cropped during the past season with wheat and barley, which in the Upper Doab is called Binar, and in some places, Narua. In Benares the same word, or rather Jaunar, means a field in which barley is sown without having borne a previous Kharíf crop. In Bundelkhand it means land on which any Rabí crops have grown.—See Jaunar in the Printed Glossary.

It is probable that the meanings ascribed to this word are derived from different sources. When it is applied to Rabí land alone, we may perhaps look for its root in Jau, barley. Where it means land under constant cultivation, we may perhaps look for its root in Jun, time. Thus, in many places land exhausted by over-cropping is styled Juní.—E.

The root of these words is probably to be found in the now little used Hindi word जेवना to eat.—B.

Jaunchí, جونچي जौंची

A kind of smut in barley and wheat, in which the ears produce no corn.

Juár, جوار जुवार

A species of millet.—See Jawar.

Jaunṛa, جونڑا जौंडा

Payment of village servants in kind. The word appears to be a corruption of Jiora, *q.v.*—Eastern Oudh.

Jabdí, جبدي जबद्दी

A species of rice cultivated in Rohilkhand.—See Dhan.

Jaḍhan, جڈھن जढन

Jaṛhan, جڑھن जढ़न

A large species of rice, cropped at the close of the rainy season.

Jagní, جگني जगनी

A small grain from which oil is extracted. It appears to be the same as the Ramtilli of the Gonds.—Saugor.

Jajmán,ججمان जजमान

A person from whom Brahmans, or menials, such as barbers, washermen and sweepers, have an hereditary right to claim certain perquisites, on occasion of any ceremonies or services which they are called upon to perform.

Jal, جل जल

A jungle shrub which grows in Bhaṭṭí territory.

Jala, جله जला

A lake. From jal, water.

Jaláliyá, جلاليا जलालिया

A fine species of wheat with reddish ears.—Saugor.

Jalása, جلاسه जलासा

A pool of water; a tank.

Jalkar, جلکر जलकर

The produce and piscary of rivers, jhíls, tanks, etc.; also, the revenue assessed thereon.—See Jelkora and Jalkar in the Printed Glossary.

Jalm, جلم जलम

Birth; birthright. Used to denote proprietary right, especially in the soil.—Saugor. The word is a corruption of Janam, birth.

Jalním, جلنيم जलनीम

A bitter herb which grows on the banks of tanks. It is used medicinally as a cure for the itch, and has a purgative quality. It has obtained its name from its springing up only in the vicinity of water.

Jal pípal, جل پيپل जल पीपल

A herb somewhat resembling the pepper plant. It is called also Aspabúta in the Taraí Parganahs. In the Talíf-i Sharíf it is called Jalpílbaka.

Jamúwaṭ, جموٹ जमूवट

The foundation of a well. From jamna, to join, to adhere. Hence the word is applied to the festive ceremony on the occasion of completing the foundation of a well.—Benares. In the Dehli territory this ceremony is called Naichak and Nímchak, which are names applied also to the foundation of the well. Newar (from नेव foundation) is the most usual word elsewhere.—See Jakhan.

Jamowá, جموا जमोवा

Indigo planted before the rains, and irrigated by artificial means.—Central Doáb.

Jamowá is also the name of a tree.

Jamaiya, جمیا जमैया

The name of a grass in Dehli.

Jandrá, جندرا जंद्रा

Shakespear says, Jandrá means a pitchfork; but in the Upper Provinces it is most usually applied to a kind of rake used during irrigation for dividing a field into small beds. It is used by two men—one holds the handle, and the other holds a string attached to the forks of the rake in a direction opposite to the handle. It is an inconvenient method of employing two men to do the work of one. The name Jandrá is used chiefly to the Westward. Elsewhere, the same implement is known by the name of Mánjho and Karha, and solid wood more sensibly supplies the place of the forks of the rake.

Janewá, جنیوا जनेवा

A kind of fragrant grass which grows in fields which have been cultivated with Kharíf crops. Its flower is like that of the Doáb, but its stem is erect, and grows to about the height of a foot and a half.

Jangrá, جنگرا जंगरा

The haulm of Kharíf produce.—Lower Doáb.

Jantrí, جنتري जन्तरी

An almanac, or register. It originally meant a perforated piece of metal through which wire is drawn, and may have subsequently been applied to an almanac on account of its having many open compartments, or ruled divisions.—E.

I should be inclined to think that the two meanings have no connection with each other; the wire-drawer's metal is merely a diminutive from the Sanskrit यन्त्र yantra, meaning a tool or instrument of any sort; and the almanac was so called because it contained the record of astronomical observations made with yantras or instruments, such as the wonderful stone and brass circles, etc., still to be seen in the Man mandil at Benares.—B.

Jaríbkash, جريب‌كش जरीबकश

Surveyor; measurer. Literally, a drawer of the measuring chain.

Jurímána, جريمانه जुरीमाना

From جُرم jurm, a crime; fine, penalty; given as Jerumana in the Printed Glossary.

Jaṛíṭá, جڑيٹا जड़ीटा

Brushwood; brambles. The word is used provincially, and is perhaps a corruption of the Hindí Jhúṛ झूड़, which signifies the same.

Jarela, جريله जरेला

The name of a rice cultivated in Rohilkhand.

Jargá, جرگا जरगा

The name of a grass given as fodder to cattle, especially to horses. It grows generally on high ground.

Jaṛwí, جڑوي जड़वी

The name given to the small shoots of the rice plant, when it first springs from the ground.

Jaṛwaṭ, جڑوٹ जड़वट

The trunk of a tree.

Jatar, جتر जतर

Cultivated land.—Upper Doáb.

Jawálí, جوالي जवाली

Jawála, or Jawálí, signifies gram mixed with barley as food for cattle. Also, a small mixture of barley with wheat.

Jawár, جوار जवार

A species of millet which grows from a height of eight to twelve feet on a reedy stem *(Holchus sorghum)*. It is known also by the names of Jondhrí, and in some places, of Jaundí. There are generally reckoned to be four kinds of Jawár. The red kind, or Joginia Jawár, is large, bears a lower price than the other qualities, and its stalk is not good fodder for cattle. The Baunia (from Bauna, a dwarf) is small, very white, grows straighter than the other kinds, and its stalk is also considered an inferior fodder. The third and best is the Píria or Sáer. Its head bends more than the rest, its stalk is much approved as fodder, and, as the grain grows more compactly, it ripens later than the other kinds. The fourth and rarest is the Básmatí, which is a very fragrant kind, but scarcely repays the expense of cultivation.

These may be considered the kinds most ordinarily known in the Doáb; but there are several others known elsewhere, as the Alápúrí like the Joginia, Dúleria or Domunhí, Jaterya, Khowa, Charka, Bidara, Lukú, Gutwa, Málatí, Chúneha, Baksí, Magha, Gapuráí, Bhadelí or Kúárú, Dugdí, Kumaria, Latúghar and

Bánda; the specific differences of which it is needless to mention.

Jawára, جوارہ जवारा

As much land as can be ploughed by a pair of bullocks. If a man says he has two Jawáras, he may be considered to have cultivation sufficient for the employment of two ploughs. A Jawárí of the Central Doáb, in which province the word is chiefly used, could not at the most be considered as more than eight acres.

In Dehli, Jawára is used to signify the area ploughed in half a day, which is the same as the Chhakwár of the Doáb. A Sanjhlo (literally, till the evening) signifies that which is ploughed during the whole day, and comprises two Jawáras, equivalent to the Aratram, Arrura, Earing, and Avera of our law books.

The words Jawárí and Jawára are derived from Júa, a yoke, it being as much land as one yoke of bullocks can plough.

Another meaning of the word Jawára is a yoke, or pair of bullocks, especially when employed at a well.

Jawára is likewise the name of the barley which is forced in earthen pots by the Brahmans for presentation at the Dasehra, or by women, for presentation to their brothers or fathers on the same festival.—See Jaí.

Jawára also signifies, in some parts of these provinces, the small shoots of rice, which germinate when steeped in water. In Shakespear's Dictionary it is said to mean "large maize." I never heard of this application of the term.

Jawása, جواسہ जवासा

Jawása, under the name of Javassa, is described in the Printed Glossary to be "a slender thorny shrub, which assumes its most lively verdure in the heights of the warmest and driest weather, and languishes and fades under the influence of rain."

It is the prickly-stem Hedysarum (H. Alhagi), a thorny bush on which camels browse; hence, says Khan Arzú, in his Dictionary, it is also called Unt-katára. But Khan Arzú appears to be wrong in saying the Jawása is the same as Unt-katára. The peasantry look upon these as entirely different plants, and in appearance they do not in the least resemble each other. The real Unt-katára, or Katela, is something like a thistle (*Echinops echinatus*, Roxb.), and has a yellow flower. It is called in different parts of the country by different names, such as Ghamoí, and Bang-kateya, and Satyanásí. The Bhat-kateya and Gol-kateya are of the same family.—See Kateya. But, though the Jawása is not called Unt-katára, it certainly is a camel's thorn, and being therefore classed under the name of Ushtar-khar, Khan Arzú might easily have been misled. The name of Alhagi is derived from the root *haj*, which denotes in Arabic its connection with a place of pilgrimage. One of the species, the Alhagi Maurorum (which is said by some to be the Jawása itself) is celebrated for its production of the manna of the desert.

Jawása is áonsidered a good medicine in bilious disorders, but is chiefly known to Europeans as a substitute for Khaskhas in Tattís. In ancient times Jawása appears to have been eaten by bullocks as well as camels: for we find those animals represented in the Mrichchhakaṭi as chewing Jawása. If they were able to accomplish this, their palates must have altered considerably; unless, as perhaps was the case, the prickly herb was chopped up into little bits, and given as fodder in that state.

Jawáz, جواز जवाज

A Persian word signifying a wooden mortar; a sugar-mill; an oil-mill.

Jazar, جزر जजर

A term in arithmetic signifying *duplation*, or doubling a number, which, like *mediation* or halving, is considered in

Oriental works to be a separate operation from ordinary multiplication, or division, and is so entered in European books on arithmetic of the sixteenth century.

Jaichí, جايچي जैची

A weed which springs up with Rabí crops.—See Jaití.

Jaí, جئي जई

Oats. The name has been only lately introduced into the N.W.P., as the grain was not known before the acquisition of this country by the British. It may perhaps have been so called from its being considered a small kind of barley; thus, from jau, jauí, jaí; as from chana, chaní; and urd, urdí. The word, however, is not new, though the application of it is; for the small shoots of barley (especially cultivated by Brahmans for the purpose, in anticipation of the season) which are carried about in the turbans of Hindús during Dasehra, are in many places known by the name of Jai, or Jaí,* either because of the smallness of the barley, or in commemoration of the Jai, or triumph of Rama over Ravana, the demon-lord of Lanka.

It is worthy of remark that in Benares, Bundelkhand, and the Lower Doab, oats are called Ramjau, *i.e.* the barley of Rama. As the Hindus already had an Indarjau (*Echites antidysenterica*), Ramjau was not altogether an unnatural combination to represent a new grain which bore a resemblance to barley. Ramjau, therefore, being the name which the natives

* This is likewise the name given to the first sprouts of germinating rice (see Jawára) when the seeds are steeped in water previous to sowing. There is also a small species of barley well known in Rohilkhand as Jai, or Jaí, as is shown by the following couplet, in which its easy and rapid growth is remarked :—

कोठी चढ़े पुकारे जई
षिचरी षाकर क्यौं ना बई

"The Jaí halloos out from the house tops, 'Why not sow me after eating Khecharí?'" (*i.e.* Makar Sakrant) which implies that its growth is very quick.

chose first to give this grain, it is not altogether improbable that we may derive our Jaí from the ceremony above alluded to, rather than from its being considered a small species of barley. The very name of Ramjau would instantly suggest Jai—both being words intimately connected with the festival of the Dasehra.

Jaití, جيتي जैती

Jaití, Jauchí, or Jaichí, is the name of an *Euphorbia* in the Western part of these Provinces, which springs up with the Rabí crops, and yields an excellent oil. The plant is about two feet high and three in circumference, and the seed yields about one-fifth of its weight in oil. In a paper presented in May, 1843, to the Horticultural Society of Calcutta, it is stated as an extraordinary thing that the seed will not come up on the ground on which it was last shed, if that land has in rotation been under a Kharíf crop. But there appears nothing wonderful in this (even if the statement is true to the fullest extent, which perhaps it is not), because land under a Kharíf crop is always most thoroughly weeded, and the Jaití seed would not be allowed to remain in it. If the land remain uncultivated during the Kharíf, a few Jaití plants would come up, but not of course so many as would appear had the land been ploughed and prepared for a Rabí crop. In these respects it obeys some of the conditions of Matauna.—(See Kodo.) The previous ploughing for the Rabí has such an effect upon Jaití, that it will spring up the third year after it is shed, even if the land has been under an intermediate Kharíf crop. It is not therefore necessary to suppose that it has any natural affinity with the Rabí grains; the mere ploughing, and exposure of the soil to the genial influence of the atmosphere, are sufficient to account for its germination.

Jaití does not appear likely to repay the trouble of cultivation, notwithstanding the expectation held out in the paper above-mentioned.

Kachhwara, کچھوارہ कछवारा

Any portion of ground cultivated by Kachhís. The Province of Katchh derives its name from the same source. (See Vishnu Purana, p. 190). In the Upper Provinces the term Kachhwara, or, more usually, Kachar, is applied to alluvial formations under the banks of a river, and the term has been said to be derived from Kach, a corner; on account of Kachars forming chiefly in the re-entrant angles of a river's bank: but this does not seem so probable as the derivation above given, as the land is well adapted for garden produce, and therefore cultivated, or fit to be cultivated, by Kachhís. Or the word may come from Kachha, new, fresh.

Kamla, کملا कमला

A caterpillar, so called from its woolly coat.—See below.

Kamal, کمل कमल

A blanket; a coarse woollen garment worn universally by the peasantry of the Upper Provinces.

The best Kamals in these Provinces are made in Alwar and in the neighbourhood of Mírápúr in Mírat. The Sánslá Kamal of the latter place sometimes sells as high as twenty-five rupees. It is made of the wool of lambkins, shorn about three days after their birth. The Sánsla is from six to eight yards long and about two broad. The ordinary Kamal sells for from twelve annas up to two rupees.

Karia, قریہ करिया

A village. From the Arabic قرا assembling together, concourse. The word is not frequently used now, but we have it preserved in Kariat Mittú, Kariat Síkhar, Kariat Dost, and Kariat Mendhú, the names of Parganahs in the Province of Benares.

Kás, کاس कास

Saccharum spontaneum. A grass which is found in every part of the Upper Provinces. Its existence is generally considered to be indicative of extreme poverty of soil, but this is not always the case. It particularly affects soils which have been allowed to remain long untilled, and as its roots strike deep, it is very difficult to eradicate.

In the Saugor territory it is said to grow in great abundance on lands which have been exhausted by over-cropping; it is also said that when the weed rots and disappears, it denotes that the soil has gained heart again, and is fit for cultivation; that it is stronger in proportion as the lands are richer; and that the strongest disappears in fourteen years.

Kás, however, is not altogether useless; it is sometimes applied as a thatch; is in much demand for twine; and elephants, horses and horned cattle do not object to it as fodder.

The grass grows from three to fifteen feet high, and it flowers in great profusion after the rains. The base of the flowers is surrounded with a bright silvery fleece, which whitens the neighbouring fields so much as frequently to resemble a fall of snow. It is hence frequently called in aid by the Hindú poets:

> "Like Siva's ashen whiteness, autumn bears
> The budding grass, and like the foul hide wears
> The dun clouds," etc.
>
> —*Mudrá Rákshasa*, p. 196.

The word is more generally pronounced Káṅs, with a nasal *n* as the penultimate letter; but it is correctly Kás, as in Kásgange. The familiar couplet, in which the hunger and avarice of Brahmans are sportively alluded to, shows the correct pronunciation as well as the season of its flowering—

आया कनागत फूले कास
बामहन बैठे चूलहे पास

"The Kanágat* has come; the Kás flowers,
Bámhans (low Brahmans) are sitting round the fireplace."†

* Festival of deceased ancestors; also called Shraddh, performed in Asin (Kuár).

† *i.e.* To get their doles of food, usual on such occasions.

Káshtkár, كاشتكار काश्तकार

A cultivator. This is a Persian word; the Hindí Kisán is in more general use.

Karíl, كريل करील

Capparis aphylla. The caper bush. It grows to the height of from ten to fifteen feet, and its evergreen branches, or twigs, which are leafless, produce a red flower, from which proceeds the well-known fruit called Ṭenṭ, which is eaten as a pickle by the poorer classes.

The Karíl grows chiefly in the North-West, and its being found in great quantities in the neighbourhood of Birj, has given rise to the following trite couplet, in which the taste of Raghonath is impugned for not giving the best article to the place of his own mortal abode.

कहा कहैं रघुनाथ की गई सतलो नांह
काबुल में मेवा करी टेंट बिर्ज की मांह

"Folks say Raghunáth's capriciousness has not left him,
He has given fruit to Kábul, and (only) Ṭenṭ to Brij (his former house)."

When the fruit is large, it is called Tenta, when small, Tentí.

Kodo, كودو कोदो

A small grain, sown early during the rainy season (*Paspalum frumentaceum*, Kœn.). The season for sowing it is indicated in the following lines :—

पुख पुनर्बस बोइये धान
असलेखा कोदो परमान
मघा मसीना दीजिये पेल
फिर दीजिये परहल में ठेल

"In Pukh and Punarbas sow rice;
In Aslekha Kodo is directed."

The first word in each of the three first lines is the name of a lunar asterism, which points to the proper time of sowing various kinds of grain.

It is a very curious fact, but one which does not admit of doubt, that this grain is frequently found to have inebriating properties, when made into bread. Such Kodo is known by the name of Matauna (from Matt मत्त drunk, intoxicated); but in appearance it resembles Kodo in every respect. It is sown as ordinary Kodo, and comes up as Matauna, but only in those fields on which Kodo has been previously grown, and only, perhaps, in one instance out of ten even in such cases. If wheat or barley is grown, it will not come up, nor will it ever spring up on newly broken soil. It is therefore a necessary condition of the produce of Matauna, that Kodo was sown the preceding year. The effects of the mania are fortunately not very injurious, and death never supervenes. The intoxication which it causes is generally that of a cheerful kind, lasts for two or three days, produces no convulsion or ulcers, and inflicts no permanent injury on the constitution. In these respects it differs from Raphania, which is caused by eating rye affected by ergot.

These curious properties of Kodo have invested it with a degree of mystery in the eyes of the natives, and some classes even worship it as a god. Thus, the Kákan Rajputs of Gházípúr are said to pay worship to this divinity. They never cultivate or eat Kodo; and the reason assigned is that, while under the influence of Matauna, they were set upon by some of the neighbouring tribes, and thus lost the greater part of their once extensive possessions.

This intoxicating effect of Kodo is by no means imaginary, as many may be induced to suppose. Independent of its notoriety in these provinces, it has been witnessed in distant parts of the country by medical officers who have borne testimony to the fact. Dr. Irvine, in his statistical account of Gwalior, mentions it, and Dr. Francis Buchanan has seen its effects in Behar and and Bhagalpúr. He states that the natives, as they do in these provinces, attribute the narcotic quality of the grain in certain fields to its being infected by a large poisonous serpent, called Dhemna; and he is disposed to ascribe the lameness called Maghya lang to the common practice of sleeping on Kodo straw, which may, perhaps, emit narcotic exhalations.

Kisári *(athyrus sativus)* is another grain which is found to have injurious properties. A curious instance of a general paralysis caused by it is given in Colonel Sleeman's "Rambles and Recollections," Vol. I. p. 134.

Kolhú, کولهو कोलह

A sugar mill. To illustrate the difference of language in different Provinces of this Presidences, the names of the component parts of the mill are given below in the language of Benares and Rohilkhand. In Dehli and the Doáb other variations occur, but they are few. The Lower Doáb inclines more to the Benares dialect—Dehli and the Upper Doáb to that of Rohilkhand. Bundelkhand has a mixture of both. For instance, there Kattrí is the horizontal, and Jath the upright beam.

ROHILKHAND.	BENARES.	EXPLANATION.
Pát	Kattrí ...	The horizontal beam to which the bullocks are attached.
Láth and Játh	Pat	The upright beam which moves in the mill.
Malkham	Khúnta ...	The upright post which is parallel to the last.
Chirya	Dhenka ...	The wood by which the two preceding are joined to one another.
Orí	Orí	The basket on the horizontal beam, from which the mill is fed.
Nárí	Narí	The leather thong by which the horizontal beam is connected with the yoke.
Paith...........	Ghagra ...	The circle in which the bullocks move.
Saya	Saika	The cup in which the expressed juice is transferred into the boiler.
Jhokand	Jhokand...	The place from which the fuel is supplied to the fire under the boiler.
Dhúndra	Dhúndka..	The outlet for the smoke.
Dhor............	Dohra ...	The spoon for taking the juice out of the boiler.
Chandwa	Gurda......	The scrape to prevent the sugar resting at the bottom of the boiler.
Ota	Nesur	The raised blocks on which the cane is cut.
Gandarwala ..	Gareran ...	The receptacle for the sugar-cane before it is cut.

This simple mill has, like the native plough, been much ridiculed for the rudeness of its construction; but it is, nevertheless, a very efficient instrument, gaining in power what it loses in rapidity of execution. Every particle of the cane is subjected to three crushings in the Kolhú. In the European triple-roller wheel it is subjected to only one. Native Zamíndárs repay us with their contempt for our process, by pointing to the juice in the refuse cane, which the European roller has been unable to express.—E.

These words are by no means the only set of words in use; in fact, every province and every district has its own long list for every small component part of every implement in use. It is not surprising, therefore, that no really complete dictionary of this exuberently copious language has ever yet been written.—B.

Kora, كورا कोरा

Is the mercantile name of plain silk cloth dyed. Bandanna is the same article dyed. The word is derived from كورا Korá, new, raw, fresh.

This article of Indian manufacture has lately been depreciated in the English market, in consequence of the dishonesty of the native workmen, who prepare goods of inferior quality and weight, and conceal the deficiency by a composition of rice-paste and sugar. It is said that a sound Korá ought to weigh from thirty to thirty-two Sikkas, faithfully woven throughout with 1700 threads. The deteriorated Korá has only 1400 threads, and weighs from twenty-six to twenty-nine Sikkas, brought up to the proper standard by the above-named composition, which may be easily detected by washing.

Kaulá, كولا कौला

Kauliyá, كوليا कौलिया

Derived from كولي Kaulí, an embrace or armful, and hence

applied to bundles of sheaves of corn given as perquisites to reapers and village servants. The word more generally used in Benares is Kakhíalí. From Kánkh کانکه an armpit.

Kerauny, كراني करानी

An English clerk in a public office, generally of mixed European and native descent. The origin of the name has been disputed, and is, it is believed, utterly unknown. It may probably be a corruption of some Portuguese* word, or it may be a mispronunciation of Karana, by which the Kayeth (Kayastha), or writing tribe, is designated in Bengal; and as most native writers in public offices are of the Karana caste, it is not unlikely that, by merely extending its signification, the same word might have been used to designate English† writers. The word from being utterly harmless in its application, has begun of late years to be considered decidedly dyslogistic (to use an expressive word coined by Bentham) and is consequently

* It is strange that Abúl Fazl, in detailing the officers of a ship's company, say the ship's steward was called Kerani.

كراني نبكچي خرچ كشتي و آب همه مردم رساند

This might imply a Portuguese origin, as many nautical terms are derived from that language.

† Should this really be the origin of the word, it is worthy of observation that Kayeths themselves at one time were called by a title, which was originally peculiar to foreign writers. In a treatise on Revenue Accounts by Raj Rúp, who calls himself a pupil of Raja Todar Mal, but who in reality wrote in, or after, Aurangzeb's reign, he says that, since those who in Iran followed the occupation of writing, were called Khwaja, it came to be considered an attributive word, and was in course of time appropriated to Hindú writers.

و ازانجا که در ایران نویسنده را خواجه خوانند همین سبب این لفظ
و صفي دانسته نویسندگان هنودرا نیز خواجه گویند

There is no reason to suppose that in India Kayeths are now ever called Khwaja, though that word is in common use for other classes. In other Muhammedan countries, however, the term is still applied to writers and teachers.

avoided by all officials of good feeling, for fear of giving offence.—E.

The derivation of this word still baffles enquirers. The simplest and most obvious derivation is from the Hindi काम करानेवाला Kám Karánewálá, which is equivalent to the English "overseer;" as this class of East Indians has generally been employed in the higher grades of the subordinate executive service, this name would be very appropriate and applicable to them, and is moreover very similar to the Bombay term Kárkan.—B.

Katían,

In the Printed Glossary, should be Khateoní, Khatauní, or Khátábandí, words signifying the posting of several items together, after abstracting them from the Khasra. From کھاتا Khátá, an account book. The meaning is correctly entered in the Glossary.

INDEX.

C.

D.

H.

I.

K.

L.

R.

S.

STEPHEN AUSTIN, PRINTER, HERTFORD.

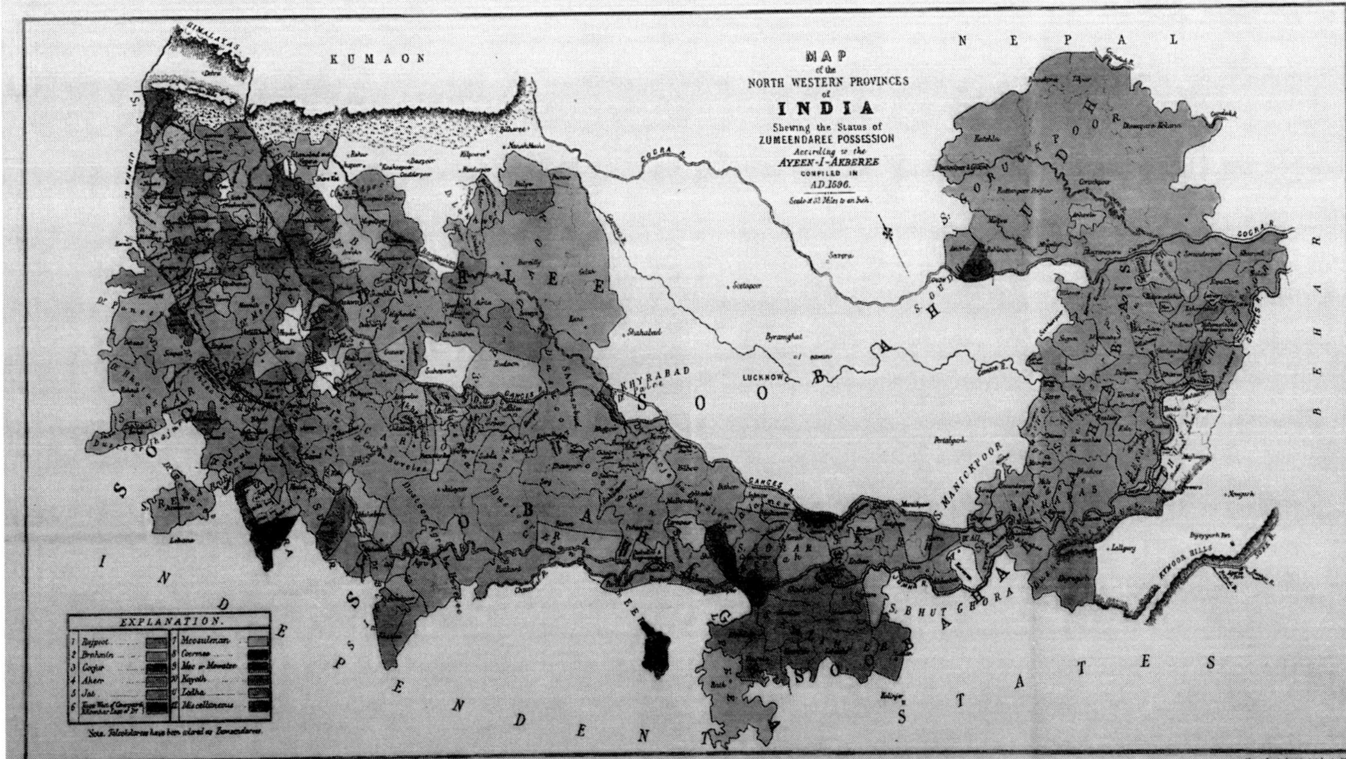
MAP
of the
NORTH WESTERN PROVINCES
of
INDIA
Shewing the Status of
ZUMEENDAREE POSSESSION
According to the
AYEEN-I-AKBEREE
COMPILED IN
A.D. 1596.
NEPAL
KUMAON
HIMALAYAS
SOOBA
LUCKNOW
KHYRABAD
MANICKPOOR
S. BHUTGHORA
KYMOOR HILLS
GANGES R.
GOGRA R.
JUMNA R.
BEHAR
INDEPENDENT STATES
EXPLANATION.
1 Rajpoot
2 Brahmin
3 Goojur
4 Aheer
5 Jat
7 Moosulman
8 Coormee
9 Meo or Mewatee
10 Kayeth
11 Lodha
12 Miscellaneous
Note. Talookdars have been sated as Zumeendarees.

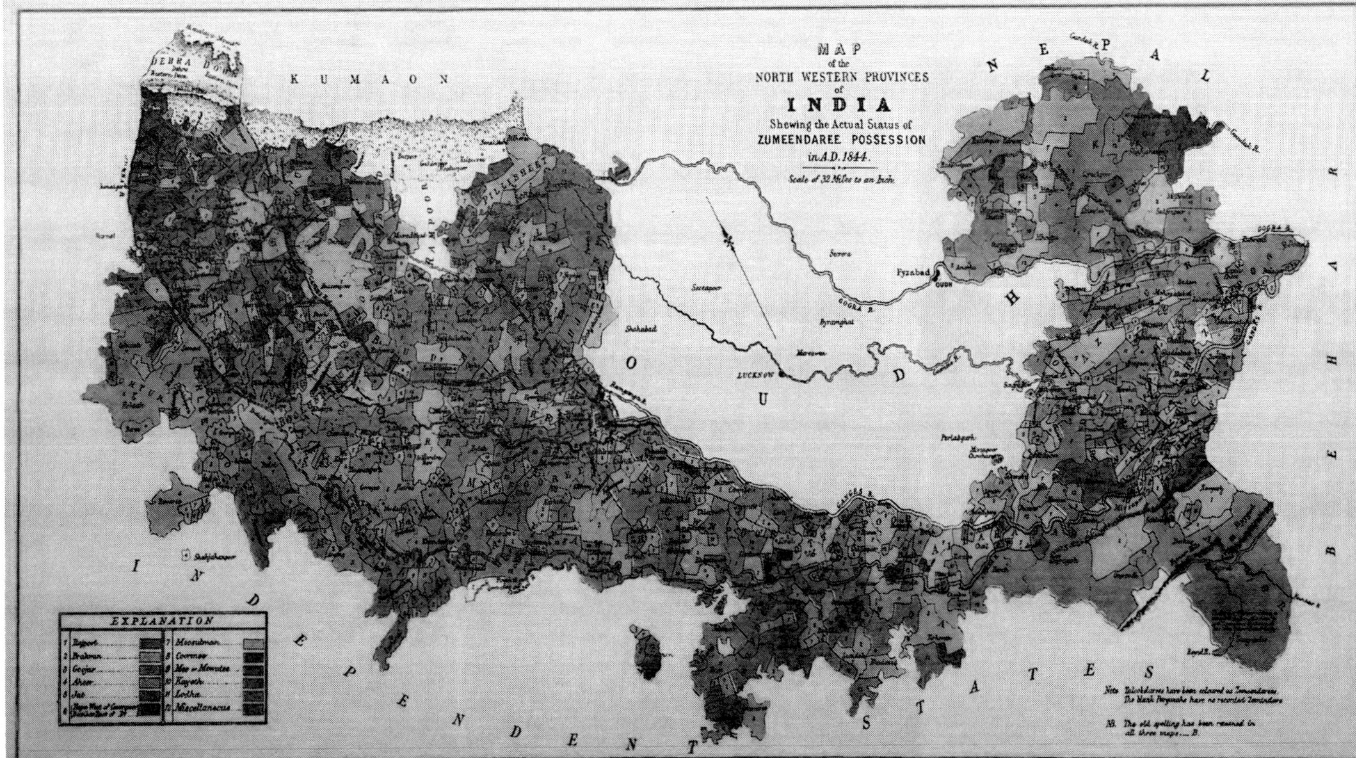
MAP
of the
NORTH WESTERN PROVINCES
of
INDIA
Shewing the Actual Status of
ZUMEENDAREE POSSESSION
in A.D. 1844.
Scale of 32 Miles to an Inch
KUMAON
NEPAL
BEHAR
OUDH
INDEPENDENT STATES
DEHRA DOON
RAMPOOR
PILLIBHEET
Lucknow
Fyzabad
Gogra R.
Ganges R.
EXPLANATION
1 Rajpoot
2 Brahmun
3 Goojur
4 Aheer
5 Jat
7 Moosulman
8 Coormee
9 Mee or Mewatee
10 Kayeth
11 Lodha
12 Miscellaneous
Note. Talookdarees have been coloured as Zumeendarees.
The blank Pergunahs have no recorded Zemindars
NB. The old spelling has been retained in all three maps.... B.

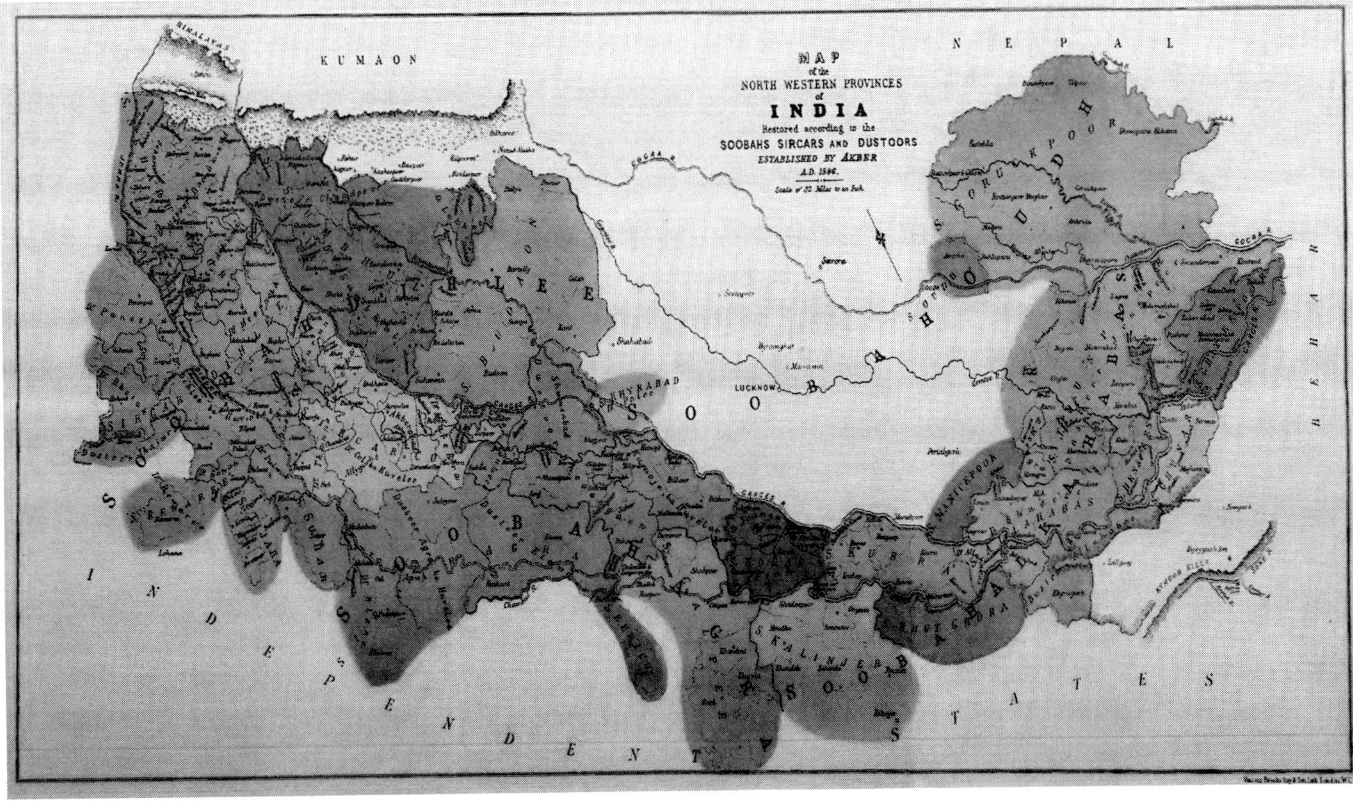
MAP
of the
NORTH WESTERN PROVINCES
of
INDIA
Restored according to the
SOOBAHS SIRCARS AND DUSTOORS
ESTABLISHED BY AKBER
A.D. 1596.
Scale of 32 Miles to an Inch.
KUMAON
NEPAL
HIMALAYAS
LUCKNOW
SOOBAH OUDH
COGRA R.
GANGES R.
INDEPENDENT STATES
BEHAR